Dimensions of China's Foreign Relations

edited by
Chün-tu Hsüeh

The Praeger Special Studies program—utilizing the most modern and efficient book production techniques and a selective worldwide distribution network—makes available to the academic, government, and business communities significant, timely research in U.S. and international economic, social, and political development.

Dimensions of China's Foreign Relations

PRAEGER SPECIAL STUDIES IN INTERNATIONAL POLITICS AND GOVERNMENT

Praeger Publishers New York Washington London

Library of Congress Cataloging in Publication Data
Main entry under title:

Dimensions of China's foreign relations.

(Praeger special studies in international politics
and government)
Includes bibliographical references and index.
1. China—Foreign relations—1949-   —Addresses,
essays, lectures.   I. Hsüeh, Chün-tu, 1922-
DS777.55.D53   327.51   76-24354
ISBN 0-275-56780-X

PRAEGER PUBLISHERS
111 Fourth Avenue, New York, N.Y. 10003, U.S.A.

Published in the United States of America in 1977
by Praeger Publishers, Inc.

© 1977 by Praeger Publishers, Inc.

Printed in the United States of America

TO THOSE ASIAN-AMERICANS WHO HAVE STRUGGLED

FOR GENERATIONS IN THE UNITED STATES

The foreign relations of the People's Republic of China may be studied within a framework of three worlds: the first world of the two superpowers; the third world of underdeveloped nations in Asia, Africa, and Latin America; and the second world juxtaposed between the two made up of the developed capitalist countries and developing socialist countries. The PRC's foreign relations may also be analyzed in a conceptual framework of perception, interaction, and the making of foreign policy, or from the viewpoint of policy process. They may be observed in three dimensions: state-to-state, party-to-party, and people-to-people relations; or explained in terms of ideology, nationalism, national interest, the theory of contradictions, and revolutionary strategy such as the united front. The chapters contained in this volume cover some of these aspects.

The bipolar world no longer exists, but Steven Levine's chapter illuminates Soviet-American global competition over China in a polarizing international environment partly as a result of the reemergence of Russia as an Asian power after World War II. He approaches his subjects through a study of the multiple levels of competition within a complex, quadrilateral relationship in China involving the United States, the USSR, the Chinese Nationalist government, and the Chinese Communists. Such a comparative approach helps to explain the predispositions for the constraints against great power intervention in postwar China and to elucidate the strategies of the internal antagonists in terms of their dependence upon external support. The article represents a contribution toward understanding the emergence of the Cold War in East Asia and the linkage between the East Asian and international political systems in the immediate postwar period. It provides a better perspective of the current triangular relations of the three countries.

The chapter by Robert North and myself is a study of how a changing environment has affected Peking's perception of Soviet-American relations, how changing perceptions have affected basic policy and interaction patterns among all three countries, and how the change of policy has in turn altered China's views of Soviet-American relations. King Chen's chapter focuses on one aspect of China's response to the United States: U.S. actions in post-1969 Indochina.

Japan belongs to the "Second World." As pointed out by A. M. Halpern, normalization and the change of Peking's views of Moscow have brought about several changes in Sino-Japanese relations.

Peking has deemphasized "people's diplomacy," and has opened communications through governmental channels. It no longer charges the threat of Japanese militarism revival and has dropped its opposition to the U.S.-Japan mutual security treaty. Sino-Japanese relations are conducted by Peking in the context of the PRC's relations with the superpowers. Meanwhile, Japan is painfully caught in the middle between China and the Soviet Union, each attempting to prevent Japan from drawing closer to the other.

Both the PRC and the Democratic People's Republic of Korea are socialist countries belonging to the Third World. My chapter on Korea is an attempt to analyze China's policy from a framework of several basic factors, interaction variables, and Korea's response to a changing international environment. Other regions of the Third World are discussed in separate chapters by Robert Worden and Yitzhak Shichor. Worden's findings on Latin America have conformed with Peking's behavior in Southeast Asia and other parts of the world since the mid-1970s, that is, a shift of emphasis from supporting people's wars and liberation movements to developing state-to-state relations with the countries with which Peking has established diplomatic relations. The shift reflected changing domestic and international environments, as well as China's increasingly active participation in the international system. Shichor's study sheds new light not only on Peking's policy toward the Palestinians in the context of China's relations with the superpowers and the Middle Eastern countries but also provides a better understanding of the PRC's attitude toward liberation movements and people's wars.

The last two chapters of the book deal with a unique dimension of China's foreign relations and policy process, respectively. Shao-chuan Leng's chapter, which focuses on the ethnic Chinese in Southeast Asia, concerns itself not only with the PRC's perception and exercise of the right of protecting its nationals abroad under international law but also with its capacity to coordinate and reconcile its interest in the overseas Chinese and its broad foreign policy objectives. The chapter begins with an examination of Chinese efforts to resolve the dual nationality issue, followed by a study of Peking's responses to the various forms of mistreatment of the Chinese abroad. The PRC's policy of encouraging the overseas Chinese to integrate with the local population is believed to serve China's national interests as well as the genuine interest of the Chinese abroad.

Foreign relations are often viewed in terms of the motivations of states or individual leaders as actors, but the real intermediaries in international relations in most cases are foreign affairs bureaucracies. The role played by a Chinese embassy is not substantially different from embassies of other countries. These institutions are stability conscious. Their normal task, to broaden and deepen

vii

relations between states, evolves its own kind of professional ethic. When the norm is challenged by extraordinary events in the home government, the stress on the foreign diplomat is likely to be great. How diplomats, Chinese diplomats included, behave under such conditions has an intrinsic interest typical of all crisis studies. The behavior of diplomatic organizations under stress deepens our insight into the normal roles played by such institutions in the policy process. Roger Dial's chapter, which is a case study of Sino-Nepalese relations during the Cultural Revolution, is designed to illustrate policy process in China's foreign relations.

Any collection of original essays has inherent weaknesses. In his introductory chapter, however, Davis Bobrow presents an overview of the themes and lends some perspective to the diverse aspects of China's foreign policy and foreign relations explored in the chapters of this book. His introduction also suggests directions toward which the study of Chinese foreign policy can be oriented.

It will be apparent to the reader that the contributors to this volume do not necessarily agree with each other's interpretations of the facts and events under discussion, and needless to say, the authors alone are solely responsible for their own writings. It should also be noted that the book was not designed to cover all areas of China's foreign relations. Some of the topics were selected partly because they have not received adequate attention from scholars. For instance, much has been written on the great power triangle of China, the Soviet Union, and the United States, but little has been said about Peking's perceptions of Soviet-American relations.

The book brings into focus various studies that reflect bi- and multilateral patterns of interaction between China and other states in the international system, the conceptual framework under which the Peking leaders conduct foreign affairs, and how relationships have changed over time. Although during periods of isolation Peking was violently against the international status quo, and its leaders are still pleased to point out repeatedly the "great disorder under heaven," this does not mean that Peking has ever intended to use aggressive wars to implement its foreign policy. Contrary to many observers in the past, I have always been of the opinion that the U.S. perception of Peking's threat in the 1950s and 1960s was a misconception, and that it is important for Peking to have peace in order to carry out its socialist construction. There was no indication after Chairman Mao's death in September 1976 that China's "revolutionary line and policies in foreign affairs" would be changed in the foreseeable future.

ACKNOWLEDGMENTS

Thanks to many friends and colleagues, this project has finally come to fruition. First of all, I wish to thank the contributors for their cooperation and interest in the project. My thanks also go to the following institutions that supported my projects in recent years.

The California Arms Control and Foreign Policy Seminar, which was funded by the Ford Foundation, sponsored my study of Peking's perceptions of Sino-American relations. A grant from the Joint Committee on Contemporary China of the American Council of Learned Societies and the Social Science Research Council enabled me to journey to Hong Kong during my sabbatical leave in the spring of 1972. The Asia Foundation sponsored my short trip to Seoul in June 1972 that gave me an opportunity to meet some Korean scholars and helped me to gain a better perspective of the secret negotiations between two Korean governments. A summer research grant awarded by the General Research Board of the Graduate School of the University of Maryland in 1973 is also gratefully acknowledged.

I would like to take this opportunity to acknowledge belatedly a sense of gratitude to Professor John K. Fairbank of Harvard University. It has been more than a quarter of a century since I left China for Singapore to study at Raffles College in 1946 and came to the United States as a graduate student at Columbia in 1949. But it was through the "Harvard connection" that I was able to start my academic career at Stanford, which proved to be crucial to my subsequent profession in this country.

Finally, I wish to thank Fifi Huang, Leticia Cheung, Rona Samman, Jean A. Sproull, Barbara Amberg, and Susan Finn for typing part of the manuscript. My wife, Huang Te-hua, has continuously given encouragement to my endeavors.

CONTENTS

LIST OF ABBREVIATIONS

CARIBCOM	Caribbean Community
CARIFTRA	Caribbean Free Trade Agency
CCP	Chinese Communist Party
CPSU	Communist Party of the Soviet Union
DPRK	Democratic People's Republic of Korea
DSP	Democratic Socialist Party
FALN	Fuerzas Armadas de Liberacion Nacional (Venezuela) (Armed Forces of National Liberation)
FAR	Fuerzas Armadas Rebeldes (Guatemala) (Armed Rebel Movement)
FBIS	Foreign Broadcast Information Service
ICRC	International Committee of the Red Cross
JETRO	Japan External Trade Recovery Organization
JITPA	Japan International Trade Promotion Association
JSP	Japanese Socialist Party
KCNA	Korean Central News Agency
KMT	Kuomintang (Nationalist Party)
KWP	Korean Workers' Party
LDP	Liberal-Democratic Party (Japan)
MIR	(Movimiento de Izquierda Revolucionaria (Movement of the Revolutionary Left)
NCNA	New China News Agency
NPC	National People's Congress

OCAC	Overseas Chinese Affairs Commission
OPANAL	Organization for the Prohibition of Nuclear Weapons in Latin America
OPEC	Organization of Petroleum Exporting Countries
PKI	Indonesian Communist Party
PLA	People's Liberation Army
PLO	Palestine Liberation Organization
PRC	People's Republic of China
ROK	Republic of Korea
SALT	Strategic Arms Limitation Talks
SEATO	Southeast Asia Treaty Organization
SWNCC	State, War, Navy Coordinating Committee
UNCURK	U.N. Commission for the Unification and Rehabilitation of Korea

Dimensions of China's Foreign Relations

ACTIVITY, PURPOSE, AND PERFORMANCE
Davis B. Bobrow

THE PROBLEMS OF FOREIGN RELATIONS ANALYSIS

Those who devote themselves to the analysis of another country, as for example, China in this volume, have both the pleasure
and the weakness of developing the same sorts of involvements as
ethnographers do with "their tribes." One wants others to believe
in the intrinsic fascination of tribal behavior, to recognize that it is
special--and best of all unique--in some sense, to recognize the essential human legitimacy of the tribal lifeways and to admire them
as problem-solving measures. The ethnographer can become a self-
appointed ambassador or interpreter of the tribe to the larger world
and thus acquire some stake or vested interest in the accomplish-
ments of and importance attached to the tribe. Many will recall discussions between Western experts on the Soviet Union and those on
China in the early 1960s that resembled those between fans of opposing sports teams.

To complicate matters further, the leaders of the tribe have a
clear interest in manipulating the conclusions of the ethnographer.
The fact of observation may well alter the behavior of the observed
system. The Chinese elite is well aware of the Talmudic dissections
made of their visible actions, which are largely verbal. In social observation there are a number of steps and arguments to lessen the
misleading effects of manipulative behavior by the observed individuals and groups. As the reader explores treatments of Chinese foreign relations, he may wish to keep them in mind.

One step is to seek nonreactive measures, that is, observables
in which there is little likelihood that the party of interest was aware
of the observer. Another is to establish patterns of behavior across
time and issues in the belief that even the most manipulative subject

of analysis will only invest so much effort in deception and masking behavior. A third is to devote special analytic attention to contrasting instances where there is relatively objective evidence of the presence or absence of behaviors of special interest and to examine less reliable or more ambiguous sources to see if they discriminate the cases.

These steps all involve particular technical actions on the part of the foreign relations ethnographer, as well illustrated in A. M. Halpern's chapter, and may well be made very difficult by the lack of information or its inaccessibility for secrecy or other reasons. Nevertheless, the researcher can still posit what information and tests would be required to have confidence in conclusions and thus suggest to the reader the degree of uncertainty in the absence of those tests and data.

There are also some pertinent arguments. The most persuasive, and that most threatening to the analyst of the foreign relations of another country, is that the other really treats foreign relations as a residual policy area secondary to the pursuit of internal goals. Statements supposedly indicative of important foreign policy aims and stratagems may simply be gambits in bureaucratic life (as Roger Dial elegantly illustrates in his chapter in this volume), or counters in major domestic power struggles (as Soviet China policy largely was in the Stalin-Trotsky power struggles), or purposeful attempts to secure resources for major collective domestic goals (such as fertilizer technology for increased agricultural production). For the analyst and the readers of the work of the analyst, there always is a fundamental alternative to foreign relations attributions of purpose-- the domestic or internal affairs alternative. And this alternative needs to be examined for plausibility on a case-by-case basis. Perhaps the most modest version of the internal affairs alternative treats foreign relations as constrained by the allocation of minimal resources. If, as the argument goes, internal affairs in essence limit foreign relations to verbal acts, then they have already accounted for most of the important variance in foreign relations.

Another argument is that a government under observation cannot afford to distort substantially the observables it produces. And the primary observables in this case are a small fraction of Chinese mass media (print and broadcast) and official Party and government statements. Other sorts of information--on economics and military matters in particular--have not been generally available to the Western academic community. Two points need to be made. First, those unavailable data are high-cost items to distort. Second, the other large set of generally unavailable data (limited circulation media) is also costly to distort. While these observations do not mean that it is costless to the Chinese to distort the open media that Western

students of Chinese foreign relations rely on most heavily, it does
mean that it is relatively inexpensive for the Chinese to provide only
a small part of "the story" in open media, a part open to numerous
alternative interpretations in the absence of the other data sets.
Halpern's chapter nicely shows how analyses can adapt to such im-
perfect data.

The absence of other data sets--those mentioned, as well as
internal foreign policy and decision-making and confidential international communications to and from leaders of governments and move-
ments--poses obvious difficulties for description, explanation, and
prediction of Chinese foreign relations activities, purposes, and performance. And these limitations are still substantially present even
when the analyst limits him- or herself to the perspectives of perception and signaling. After all, political rhetoric in most places at
most times abounds in statements intended to affect audiences as well
as to convey the genuine views of the source. And in the world of
modern intelligence technology (and for China increasingly that of
traditional diplomacy), open media that are inherently not focused on
particular foreign relations audiences as a matter of course pose
special interpretive problems. Who are the Chinese signaling with a
particular article or the inclusion or omission of a particular phrase?

The preceding comments do not imply that the study of Chinese
foreign relations is a hopeless task; rather, that if pursued through
the developed tradition of textual analysis, it often resembles detec-
tive work in the absence of a known crime and is plagued by the
plausibility of alternative explanations. And the thoughtful reader
of analyses of China's foreign relations needs to be acutely aware
of the problems and limitations noted. Later in this introductory
chapter, it will be appropriate to suggest an orientation to the study
of China's foreign relations that may make us less vulnerable to
some of these difficulties, but that deprives us of many of the plea-
sures and rewards of the foreign relations ethnographer.

A FOREIGN RELATIONS MATRIX

It may be helpful to try to place the chapters in this volume
in the context of the study of foreign relations of nation-states in
general and of China in particular. Foreign relations, like the
proverbial elephant, can be discussed from numerous perspectives.
A brief discussion may raise questions to be asked of the essays
in this book. Most generally, we can conceive of the field as a
matrix of the form:

		Foreign Relations Substance		
		Activity	Purpose	Performance
	Description	1	2	3
Results of Analysis	Explanation	4	5	6
	Prediction	7	8	9

General questions can be associated with each of the numbered cells: (1) What are the Chinese doing or have they done? (2) What are or have been their foreign relations goals? (3) With what degree of success have they achieved or are achieving those goals? (4) Why are they engaging in or have engaged in those activities? (5) Why have they pursued or are currently pursuing those goals? (6) Why have they achieved or are now achieving particular degrees of success? (7) What activities will they engage in? (8) What goals will they seek to achieve? (9) How well will they do? Obviously, the answers to many of the questions are not limited to the traditional domain of foreign affairs instrumentalities and rationales nor to the attributes of China itself. And it is equally obvious that no single piece of analysis can attempt to answer even one of the questions for all aspects of Chinese foreign relations.

Accordingly, it is necessary to focus on some part of Chinese foreign relations. Analysts in the general field of foreign policy and international relations have tended to cut the pie in a number of different ways. Some have sorted in terms of major actors; others, in terms of issues; still others, in terms of process attributes. Whatever their choice, they still must decide upon the time period they will examine. How do the subsequent contributions relate to these distinctions?

With regard to major actors, different authors focus on China's relations with the superpowers (see the chapters by Levine, Hsüeh and North, and Chen); with peripheral states and their governments and movements (see the chapters by Chen, Halpern, and Hsüeh); with the Third World and national liberation movements, real or ostensible (see the chapters by Shichor and Worden); and overseas Chinese (see the chapter by Leng). With regard to issues, there is some discussion of trade (see the chapters by Halpern, Hsüeh and North, and Worden), arms control and disarmament (see the chapters by Hsüeh and North and Worden), economic aid (see the chapter by Hsüeh and North), and environmental and natural resource issues (see the chapters by Halpern and Worden). As for process themes, various authors explore complexity (Levine), realism and flexibility (Hsüeh and North, Chen, Hsüeh, Leng, Shichor, and Worden), and coordination (Dial).

This book primarily deals with relations with particular actors rather than with issues or process attributes. To return to the matrix, one consequence is to exclude many possible foreign relations goals and performances from consideration. The focus on relations with particular actors external to the People's Republic lessens attention to internal determinants of Chinese foreign relations activity and purposes (questions 4 and 5), limits the set of performance criteria applicable to Chinese foreign relations to those that tend to be divisible in terms of relations with particular governments and movements (questions 3, 6, and 9), and limits attention to those that are less easily related to particular external actors. Yet the latter include a number of crucial matters (economic self-sufficiency, deterrent posture). And, unavoidably, important actors receive relatively little attention, for example, Chinese relations with foreign private sector firms, public enterprises, and trading organizations.

There are, of course, positive arguments to be made for the actor orientation. Perhaps the most familiar is that foreign relations is essentially a matter of transactions between organized groups with a territorial focus, that it is geographic rather than functional. Issue consequences are arrived at through the behavior of groups, and thus the actor focus should receive priority. A supporting argument is that the sets of memories, including precedents that foreign policy elites draw on, are largely organized in terms of actors, for example, the historic relationships with Korea or with Western economic entrepreneurs.

Whether these rationales compensate adequately for the handicaps of the actor-centered approach is for the reader to judge. However, again it is stated that the reader needs to be fully aware of the emphases that are automatically downplayed with the actor approach. Perhaps the single most important point involves the reasons or preferred outcomes that lead national leadership (which is not equivalent to foreign relations cadre) to care about foreign relations. Most bluntly, relations with particular other actors are means, not ends. In foreign affairs, there are most of the time multiple sets of means that offer some promise of achieving any given collective outcome, for example, peace. It is the choice of means and the intensity of preferences that lead to variation in behavior. When the preferred outcomes are largely domestic, the focus on foreign actors can obscure the driving forces in foreign relations. Also, it tends to direct attention solely to foreign affairs specialists rather than to the other groups within nation-states that affect what governments do and intend toward each other and the capabilities they acquire.

The consequences of inattention to process attributes are equally significant. Particularly if one views foreign relations as interactive, process attributes are central to predictions of response, to

interpretation of stimuli, and to attempts at policy influence. How
long will it take the Chinese to respond to X? How do they learn
about external matters? What messages will they consider as bind-
ing? Which of their signals are clearly indicative of changes in policy? While these matters are touched on in some chapters (for example, Chen's attempt to develop a hierarchy of signal sources),
they clearly provide little in the way of a basic framework for the
treatment of Chinese foreign policy decision making.

To return once again to the matrix, the essays in this volume
are devoted primarily to the first two rows (description and explanation) rather than to the third of prediction. Some of the historic
bases for prediction are provided with regard to Chinese relations
with particular countries and with respect to changes in behavior
over time as policies have proved successful as well as disappointing.

One may well describe the main thrust of the essays as charac-
terization of aspects of Chinese foreign relations and a review of
their origins and evolution. A variety of the familiar questions are
raised and often reformulated in more fruitful terms, for example,
the desanctification of "ideology" in the essay by Hsüeh and North.
Once again, one is impressed by the ability of Chinese history to
yield precedent and of Maoist doctrine to provide rationale. Also
once again, there remains the nagging feeling that precedents and
rationales can be found in those well-stocked vaults for almost any
conceivable Chinese foreign policy action or inaction. It is difficult
to see how after-the-fact analysis, at least in the absence of rather
precisely formulated alternative hypotheses, can ever pin down the
importance of these sources of foreign relations perspectives and
expectations.

As a final reference to the matrix, the performance questions
merit a little more discussion. There is by no means consensus or
clarity on what analysts mean by foreign relations performance, let
alone on how to measure it or on the degree of success that indicates
superior accomplishment. Yet surely at some point performance is
exactly what we do want to know about a nation's foreign relations.
And historic treatments should at least be able to give some assessment of it after the returns are in. For any given regime, an assessment of performance requires us to establish to our satisfaction what
the regime was or is trying to accomplish, what resources and costs
it is willing to bear for some return, and over what time period it is
calculating costs and benefits. To the extent that we recognize diversity within a regime, we may need to establish these desiderata for
a number of groups or individuals. These issues are indeed complex,
given that we must necessarily deal with the conjectural questions of
what might have happened had the regime in question behaved differently. Also, any attempt to work this ground must take into consideration the numerous goals a regime may be pursuing simultaneously.

QUERIES FOR THE CHAPTERS

The chapters that follow tend not to deal with the performance issue in the sorts of terms spelled out here. Germane discussion is pretty much confined to the question of goals. The time period, or discount rate, issue would seem to benefit particularly from the research tools and concepts used, but it is not explored, nor is the matter of expenditures of scarce resources. Here are some questions readers may wish to raise about the information in the following chapters:

What would have been different if the Chinese leadership had pursued a different policy than that attributed to them? For example, would the United States and the USSR have gone to war over Manchuria after World War II or the Kuomintang remained in power (question of Levine)?

How would the nuclear stockpiles and acquisition programs of the world be different if China had not (a) acquired a nuclear capability, (b) rejected the test-ban and nonproliferation treaties and (c) called for regional nuclear-free zones? Would Chinese security vis-a-vis the USSR be better or worse? (question of Hsüeh and North)

If China had behaved differently would the United States have concluded its involvement in the Vietnamese conflict differently? Would Sino-Vietnamese-Soviet relations be very different? (question of Chen)

If China had not supported liberation wars as policy in Latin America, how would China's relations with Latin American governments have been different? (question of Worden)

Would China's relations with Arab states and Palestinian organizations be much different if China had provided different verbal treatment of the latter? (question of Shichor)

Even in situations where the ostensible purpose of Chinese policy was not realized, the costs of failure can easily be misestimated. What else would have been done with the resources? What side benefits were achieved? For example, even though the world has not been swamped with revolutions along Chinese lines, did verbal support for them lead others to treat China as a major international force and help persuade China's own population that China was such a force?

Barring the very difficult tasks that a complex performance assessment poses, it does seem important to look at behaviors that seem sufficiently anomalous in terms of conventional wisdom to cast doubt on accepted performance notions. For example, one popular notion can be summarized as "words are cheap and China has few other resources." Substantial economic aid, especially to Africa, seems to pose problems for that notion, especially since African recipients are not in the traditional periphery emphasized in other familiar explorations of Chinese foreign relations.

Some of the outlines of a portrait of future Chinese policy are clearly presented later, especially in the chapters by Halpern, Hsüeh and North, and Worden. They clearly involve more active use of certain instruments and currencies of international leverage than has been made previously. Especially important areas include technology transfer, government-to-government diplomacy, and depletable natural resources such as oil. There is little reason to assume that the primary reasons for a change from almost complete reliance on public media exhortation to such tools of foreign relations reflect some change in ideology or preferred outcomes. These tools simply are increasingly available, and the leverage provided by being the voice for revolutionary militancy has declined with the rise of more militant regimes (especially on a regional basis). And once we accept that Chinese domestic and foreign policy are not separate, and that factional conflicts make use of foreign policy arenas, we will not expect a stable policy. The Chinese will use minimal resources to buy latitude and time, as they have done since 1949.

If this is to be done while maintaining a drive for self-sufficiency and the mobilization of human capital, several general courses of action seem required. These include a finite second-strike deterrent posture; selective mutually beneficial transactions for specific purposes with numerous other nations and movements; a contribution to the maintenance of serious international distractions for the Soviet Union and the United States that do not go so far as to provoke military retaliation, yet prevent them from concentrating their national power against China; creation of the belief among the superpowers that China can indeed "heat up" and "cool off" such distractions; and regional policies of conciliation and splitting to minimize the need for a high degree of military readiness and massive investments in conventional forces.

If we are to relate these courses of action to the rhetoric of public statements, it will remain important to be aware of what those statements are trying to do. First, they seek to cultivate the image of China as the Rome of the Third and Fourth Worlds in order to improve bargaining power with its members and nonmembers. Second, they seek to create awareness of external threat conducive to substantial military expenditures for the People's Liberation Army (PLA) and continued forgoing of domestic consumption. Third, they seek to generate support for the view that expenditures for the PLA are high enough and the policy of autonomy is viable. Fourth, they seek to establish that the source remains true to the ideals of the revolution in order to avoid internal attack and also because those are the "ideals" of the system no matter how discrepant they may be from less public foreign policy actions. The mix of purposes varies, but all are being served almost daily.

2

SOVIET-AMERICAN RIVALRY
IN MANCHURIA AND
THE COLD WAR
Steven I. Levine

A key interlocking triangle in the complex geometry of international relations in East Asia and the Pacific is that of China, the
United States, and the Soviet Union. (At times, Taiwan gives this
triangle a suspiciously quadrilateral shape.) For most of the Cold
War years, communications and exchange between the American and
Chinese components of this triangle were so minimal as to be almost
nonexistent. For the first ten years of the People's Republic, China
seemed to be welded firmly to the Soviet bloc and for the next ten
years, it seemed to be an independent antagonist of both the United
States and the Soviet Union. Not until the fortuitous conjunction of
the end of the Cultural Revolution and the beginning of Nixon-Kissinger
diplomacy was the potentiality for Sino-American rapprochement
tested for diverse but overlapping policy motives in Washington and
Peking.

Since then, a complex pattern of competition and cooperation
has emerged among the powers. The odd man out views each of the
bilateral relationships through a prism of doubt and suspicion. Thus
Moscow views Sino-American rapprochement as an anti-Soviet plot,
while Peking sees the tenuous Soviet-American detente as an effort
to divide the world between the superpowers. Informed speculation
in the United States grapples with the consequences for Sino-Soviet
and Sino-American relations of a post-Mao leadership.

Research for this chapter was conducted during the author's
tenure as a Junior Fellow at the Research Institute on Communist Affairs of Columbia University, whose financial support and stimulating
intellectual environment are gratefully acknowledged.

With the decline of the Cold War, the potential for scholarly reconstruction and analysis of the period immediately after World War II has been enhanced.[1] Perhaps not surprisingly, the reemerging features of that period look not too dissimilar to those that are encountered today in the analysis of East Asian international politics, with the significant difference of the vastly enhanced roles of both China and Japan. A reexamination of postwar Sino-Soviet-American politics yields no firm clues to policymakers, but suggests the rich array of competing interests and possible combinations existing then and still surviving in altered forms in the present.

INTRODUCTION

By the end of World War II, the emerging confrontation between the United States and the Soviet Union already promised to become the most important single factor determining the structure of postwar international politics not only in Europe but in East Asia as well. Although the United States easily was able to rebuff sporadic Soviet attempts to share in the occupation of Japan, throughout most of the critical first postwar year, Soviet-American competition for power and influence in China became a major factor affecting its internal political struggles. International and domestic conflicts were linked in a complex pattern in the Chinese arena.

The concept of "intervention" developed in international relations theory provides us with a convenient way of approaching our problem.* Wide-scale external intervention--of the Soviets in Manchuria and the Americans in North China--was a vital aspect of the postwar period in China. Factors in both the international and domestic environments contributed to external intervention and ensured that the internal Chinese political struggle would become enmeshed in the larger issues of world politics.

The main systemic factor creating a predisposition for external intervention in the Chinese civil war was the altered structure of the international system after World War II. As the prewar pattern of multiple-state competition and an unstable balance of power yielded in the postwar period to a loose bipolar system dominated by the United States and the Soviet Union, the impetus to intervention increased.[3] Each of the two dominant powers in such a system must act against a possible defection from within its own alliances, for

---

*The most precise, and therefore restrictive, definition of intervention is that of James Rosenau, who points to two features: the convention-breaking character of intervention and its authority-oriented nature.[2]

this might engender a fatal weakening of its bloc. A further impetus
to intervention is the desire to forestall a hitherto nonaligned state
caught in the grip of internal changes from joining the rival camp.
So intervention may serve a prophylactic function. Also, a dominant
state may act to increase the strength of its bloc by taking advantage
of internal change in a state to induce it to switch sides or abandon
its previous neutrality.[4]

In the period of our concern, these theoretical characteristics
were as yet only partially manifest because the actual structure of
the new postwar international system was still being established and
the marks of transition were to be seen everywhere. The disintegration of the wartime Grand Alliance was a gradual process. Within
the democracies, it was partly slowed by groups that pressed for
policies of accommodation and bargaining rather than confrontation
in dealing with the Soviets.[5] Even as the Cold War consensus was
taking shape in Washington in the latter half of 1945, the Truman Administration continued to test the possibilities of partial accommodation with the Russians.

In Moscow, a similar mood of ambivalence prevailed as Stalin,
on the one hand, reasserted the orthodox Leninist doctrine of the in-
evitability of war and, at almost the same time, talked about the possibilities of peaceful coexistence and the prospects for parliamentary
paths to socialism.[6] This ambivalent mood in Moscow and Washington was essentially evanescent, however, the fading image of a dissolved partnership. In the concrete actions that established the
framework of the postwar international order, the fear of conflict
rather than the possibility of cooperation was the touchstone of decision.

No less important in inducing intervention were pressures
from within China. Here the question was not whether intervention
would occur, but rather what form it would take and whom it would
benefit.

During internal wars it is common for one or more of the antagonists to make explicit bids for foreign intervention in order to
tilt the balance of forces in its favor and, if possible, to achieve a
breakthrough in a stalemated conflict. Normally it is the weaker
party that has a stronger incentive for inviting intervention in order
to compensate for its inability to mobilize internal resources.[7] The
outcome of the intervention, of course, may not always accord with
expectations. Particularly in a struggle where the mantle of nationalist legitimacy is an important contested value, the side that invites
and is dependent upon external intervention may find its policy counterproductive.*

---

*Howard Wriggins raises the important related point that a
regime that becomes dependent upon external military assistance

Through American and Soviet intervention in postwar China, both the Nationalists and the Communists saw opportunities for advancing their own goals. Each side tried to manipulate the two foreign powers whose competition for influence enhanced the competitive bargaining position of each of the Chinese parties to the point where they could bid for concessions as well as beg for favors.[9] Their attempted manipulations were part of an even more complicated process in which the Soviets and the Americans, likewise, were trying to affect the behavior of the Chinese antagonists to serve their own ends. This multilevel pattern of complex competition is the framework of our analysis.

SOVIET POLICY: BETTING ON ALL THE HORSES

What were Soviet aims in China at the end of the war? Emerging from the conflict as one of the two major world powers, the USSR expanded the range of its interests and demanded certain traditional great power prerogatives. However, without abandoning the ideological tenet that the fundamental contradictions between the capitalist and Soviet systems must eventually be resolved by history in favor of the forces whose leadership he embodied, Stalin, in the 1945-46 period subsequent to the enormous wartime gains in East and East-Central Europe, was ready for a period of consolidation. The basic reason for this stance was the hollowness of Soviet power in the aftermath of war.[10] Moreover, Soviet military power was primarily land-based, which acted to constrict severely the sphere in which Soviet interests could effectively be asserted.[11]

This fact had important foreign policy implications, one of which suggested a prudent approach to the question of supporting foreign revolutions. Only in East and East-Central Europe, where Soviet arms helped enforce a transformation from above, was Stalin a revolutionary. Elsewhere he was not prepared to hazard the inherent high risk of supporting foreign revolutions in a period of superior Western strength. Thus Stalin opted for a kind of rough and ready coexistence, a recognition of the new balance of forces although without a commitment to maintain that balance indefinitely.

---

may jeopardize its long-term survival because "Not needing to be responsive to its critics in the short run in order to survive it may postpone correcting evils so long that these form the base for clandestinely organized political movements which then overthrow the regime."[8]

Stalin was eager to delineate spheres of influence within which the great powers might exercise their dominion in relative isolation from each other.[12] Within his sphere Stalin sought a free hand to implement policies that might range from overt support of local Communists to collaboration with conservative politicians who recognized the imperative of deferring to the Soviet colossus.

Stalin's prudence did not imply any weakening of control over the international Communist movement. Rather, in return for a free hand in his sphere of influence, Stalin was ready to counsel and command his foreign followers to respect the bounds of legality and to engage in peaceful political struggle. This was the orthodoxy of the immediate postwar period. Stalin had no compunctions about sacrificing the interests of local Communists (if they interpreted their interests differently than he did) or even in allowing their destruction, as in Greece in 1944-45.[13] This is not to suggest that Stalin was indifferent to the fate of communism in Europe or Asia, but he continued to define the interests of the Communist movement in terms of its subordination and subservience to the USSR and his own power. The seeds of potential Soviet-Chinese Communist conflict were contained in that view, which his successors failed to disavow sufficiently.

Where did China fit into the Soviet sphere of influence conception? In 1945, China's role in the postwar international order was still uncertain. Arbitrarily graduated by the United States into the ranks of the great powers, China, in fact, again lay open to the countervailing pressures of her senior allies. Cognizant of American wartime support of China, during 1945 as Soviet-American tensions mounted, Stalin had to weigh the potential effect of China's adherence to a developing American bloc, which he viewed as his future enemy. What he apparently could not countenance was the implicit American assumption that China fell within an American sphere of influence. Therefore Soviet policy sought to reverse the wartime tendency by formally acknowledging American influence in China in the short run while actually seeking to undermine it as rapidly as possible.

After prolonged hard bargaining, Stalin signed a treaty of friendship and alliance with Nationalist China in August 1945, but it is hardly likely that he harbored any illusions about the long-term community of interests between the USSR and China. In fact, not only in 1945, but even after the Communists triumphed in China, Stalin pursued what might be termed a "weak neighbor policy"--a powerless China would be most amenable to Soviet influence. Although there was little likelihood in 1945 that China itself could soon challenge Soviet interests in Asia, there was a real danger that China might lend itself to the hostile purposes of more potent enemies of the Soviet Union. This fear, too, has a contemporary ring to it.

Primary Soviet interests in Asia were concentrated in the northern border regions of Manchuria and Mongolia. By obtaining Chinese recognition of the satellite regime in Outer Mongolia in the August treaty, Soviet diplomacy secured the perpetuation of a vast buffer zone to protect strategically exposed eastern Siberia. Russia's objective of securing a de facto sphere of influence in Manchuria achieved at least temporary American support in the Yalta agreement. But uncertainty about continued American support reinforced the Soviet desire to consolidate its position in Manchuria and to seek to neutralize the American presence in the rest of China. As the Cold War took shape in the waning months of 1945, the minimal Soviet policy of securing a nonaligned China increasingly clashed with the American goal of cementing a Sino-American relationship as part of America's new world order.

But who were the Soviet's potential enemies in East Asia? Stalin was prescient enough to realize that despite her present weakness, a unified China controlling the industrial strength of Manchuria might one day challenge Soviet positions in Northeast Asia. The post-Stalin leadership of the USSR saw this eventuality come to pass in fewer years than Stalin might have imagined. At the end of the war, the disproportion between Soviet strength and Chinese debility was enormous. Within the means at his disposal, Stalin sought to perpetuate this disproportion for as long as possible.

Even more disturbing than a direct Chinese challenge to Russia was the possibility that Manchuria might become an industrial and strategic base harnessed to an American threat to the Far East. The Kuomintang's apparent pro-American orientation made this plausible, and suggested the dual strategy of securing Soviet military and economic position in Manchuria while trying at the same time to lure away Generalissimo Chiang from his American connection through a combination of threats and promises. In short, this was part of what might be called a Soviet policy of containment designed to check the global expansionism of the United States at key points along the periphery of the Soviet Union.

A final scenario that we have reason to believe Stalin envisaged involved a resurgent Japan. The Soviet leader thought that under American tutelage Japan would quickly recover from defeat and again become a major Asian power.[14] It might again wrest control of Manchuria from a weak China and renew its threat to Soviet security.

However, Stalin undoubtedly had more than a purely defensive interest in Manchuria. Through the Sino-Soviet treaty, the Soviets acquired a privileged position in an area where they at least formally recognized Chinese sovereignty. Control of Port Arthur gave them an important naval base that could supplement fleet headquarters in Vladivostok, secure the Soviet position in North Korea along its western flank, and challenge American naval superiority in the waters off North China. Economically, Russia's preeminent position in Dairen and its joint ownership of the Manchurian trunk rail system were bases from which further attempts to grasp control of the economy in the Northeast could be essayed. Finally, the combination of military and economic advantages in the region would increase Soviet influence in China and improve its ability to maneuver among Chinese political forces. (These elements of policy, one should add, were not necessarily pursued with equal vigor by all the various Soviet political and military organizations with interests in China.)

Confronting the reality of two governments in postwar China, Stalin quite skillfully pursued a two-China policy that inevitably involved a great deal of tacking and maneuvering. [15]*

In accordance with his generally low risk approach to international politics, Stalin chose to deal primarily with Chiang Kai-shek and his government as the more substantial of the two existing Chinas that would likely remain in at least nominal control of China for the foreseeable future. Dubious about the prospects for armed Communist revolution in 1945, Stalin urged the Chinese Communists to enter a coalition with the Nationalists.† This rejected advice anticipated the ideological battle between the Soviets and the Chinese Communists in the 1960s over the question of revolutionary strategy in the Third World.

Stalin's misjudgment of the competing Chinese forces is readily understandable. All the indices by which he was likely to judge pointed to continued Nationalist hegemony. Chiang's vast army was being stiffened with American-trained and -equipped divisions. Control of China's cities with their industry, finance, commerce, foreign trade, skilled workers, and educated elite was his. In addition, Chiang could count on American aid. Against this, Mao's guerrilla armies, rural dominion, and primitive technology bulked small indeed. In other words, Stalin shared a Western concept of power as deriving from the urban, industrialized, and technological--in short, the

------

*While the tension in American foreign policy can often be explained by the complexity of the decision-making process involving multiple inputs in the policy formulation stage, as well as the various means of implementation, such an explanatory model is of doubtful relevance for the late Stalin era. By all accounts, Stalin himself was in sole control of the main lines of foreign policy. The development of Soviet interest in the study of international relations, in part a reflection of increasing complexity in Soviet policy making, is a post-Stalin phenomenon. [16]

†This was of a piece with the instructions given to the West European Communist parties at the same time. [17]

modernized sectors of society. From this perspective (normal for a Marxist), the Kuomintang (KMT), despite its inner weakness, looked strong and the Chinese Communist Party (CCP) seemed weak. Stalin may have thought that at best the Communists could retain control in North China under the nominal jurisdiction of a coalition government in which the Kuomintang would be the senior partner.

By recognizing the Nationalists as the dominant force in China, the Soviets secured recognition of their special interests in Manchuria and Mongolia, and hoped for at least Chinese nonalignment in the impending division of the world into competitive Soviet and American power blocs.

An additional benefit of Stalin's overall posture was its anticipated effect on his relations with the United States. To a certain extent, the proximate goals and methods of Soviet and American policy in China coincided. Soviet recognition of Chiang, the desire to avoid a civil war in China, support for the goal of a coalition government, and willingness to cede to the United States the dominant role in mediating China's political conflict raised hopes in Washington that China would not be a contentious issue in postwar Soviet-American relations. However, like two trains with different destinations running for a time along parallel tracks, the ultimate divergence of Soviet and American policies in China was temporarily obscured. Yet, had Stalin succeeded either in detaching Chiang from his American protector or in his bolder hope of substituting a Soviet for an American presence, the repercussions from the United States might have been enormous. For this reason, a large measure of dissemblance was needed in order to reassure the Americans of the compatibility of Soviet and American purposes.

This policy of reassurance took the form first of reiterating support for Chiang in May and again in December 1945 in talks with top-level American officials. Second, the Russians sought to foster the widespread American illusion that the Chinese Communists were not genuine Marxist-Leninists but rather "margarine Communists," as Patrick J. Hurley was told.[18] The Soviet leaders certainly did not share the illusions of American believers in "so-called Chinese communism," that the moderate program followed by Mao at Yenan was proof of his unorthodoxy, because such reformism was the orthodoxy of the united front period. In a deeper sense, the Chinese were margarine Communists because as independent national leaders they were ultimately untrustworthy in Stalin's paranoid but cannily perceptive view. But this was not a point to be communicated to the Americans.

The policy of reassurance was primarily intended to minimize the extent of American interference in Sino-Soviet relations. In seeking to preserve the exclusively bilateral character of their relationship with the Nationalists, the Soviets acted in the knowledge that in such a relationship the unequal weight in power would greatly facilitate the attainment of their objectives. Chiang himself knew this only too well.

Stalin's decision to deal with the Nationalists did not predetermine the nature of his relationship with the Chinese Communists. Although the basic choice was to strive for Soviet objectives by working through Chiang's government, the continued existence of a strong Communist party afforded Stalin considerable freedom to maneuver. In Manchuria, where the Nationalists became critically dependent upon the degree and quality of cooperation they might obtain from the Soviet occupation authorities, this became extremely important. The existence of the Communist challenge to Nationalist hegemony in Manchuria transformed the character of Soviet-Chinese Nationalist relations and strengthened the Soviet hand. The open or implicit threat to switch Soviet support to the CCP could be a lever for extracting further concessions, particularly in Manchuria. The limiting factor in exploiting this threat, however, was the possibility that the Nationalists might succeed in eliciting an American reaction.

Beyond this was Soviet recognition that the Communists did control a significant portion of Chinese population, territory, and resources and that it would have been imprudent not to have cultivated ties with the CCP. Since northeast China was not only the focus of Soviet interests, but also a region where Communist prospects for achieving power were quite good, there were particularly compelling reasons to strive for good relations there with the CCP.

These various considerations shaped a Soviet China policy that may be characterized in essence as one of extreme flexibility or opportunism.[19] Its most consistent characteristic was the desire to keep all options open and to avoid too close identification with one side or the other. In short, the Soviets engaged in that duality of tactics that was as old as their China policy itself.[20] Support for the revolutionary side is balanced by support for the status quo. Like a rich matron at the racetrack, Stalin bet on all the horses to be sure of a winner.

AMERICA'S CHINA POLICY IN
SOVIET-AMERICAN FOCUS

Until shortly before V-E day, the dominant American view of the postwar world was that a concert of the major powers working through the United Nations would be able to secure peace and deter any would-be aggressors. As apparently intractable problems emerged concerning political arrangements in the occupied and liberated countries of Europe, the mood in Washington changed. The semtimentalized view of Stalin's Russia as a staunch and reliable ally was gradually replaced by a realization that the Soviet Union possessed a concept of European and world security incompatible with the American view and a conviction that Russia was a rival and even a potential enemy of the United States.

Obviously, the strength of this conviction varied. When, on May 19, 1945, Acting Secretary of State Joseph Grew wrote in a private note that, "A future war with Soviet Russia is as certain as anything in the world," he was penning a thought that many in Washington would still have dissented from at the time.[21] More prevalent was the view of such men as Ambassador Averell W. Harriman, General John R. Deane, Admiral William D. Leahy, and Secretary of the Navy James Forrestal that the only way to deal with the Soviets was through hard, no-nonsense tactics using all the diplomatic, military, and economic power one could muster. These were the advisers who surrounded Harry Truman upon his accession to the presidency.[22] In brief, the adversary view of Soviet-American relations that lay at the heart of the Cold War existed from at least the spring of 1945.

The United States asserted its interests in global terms, but, already concentrating on the confrontation with Russia, American leaders viewed Europe as their top foreign policy priority. By comparison, throughout most of the immediate postwar period, China was seen as a secondary arena, although there were moments in which a vital interest was presumed to exist.

For most of the first postwar year, little public or congressional interest was evinced in America's China policy. Events such as the Amerasia affair, Ambassador Hurley's sensational resignation, announcement of the Marshall mission, and the revelation about the Yalta agreement were greeted indifferently even by those who subsequently were loudest in their condemnation of American policy.* Even within the Congress, which was soon to become a battleground over China policy, there was but limited and sporadic interest in the first postwar year. In the autumn of 1945, vocal critics like the left-wing Washington Democrat Hugh Delacey, supported by a handful of others like then Representative Mike Mansfield, condemned the continuing presence of U.S. troops in China and warned of the dangers of involvement in a civil war.[24]

When Hurley resigned and issued a statement blaming the failure of his policy on the opposition or sabotage of the career foreign

---

*For example, the first major effort of Alfred Kohlberg's American China Policy Association, a manifesto charging the Marshall mission was helping the CCP, was issued as late as July 24, 1946.[23]

officers, several congressmen called for an investigation, but the
hearings generated little public response. Even Representative
Walter Judd remained silent and only the "extremists" supported
Hurley's charges.[25] There were as yet no congressional groups or
lobbies interested in constructing a viable political issue out of
Hurley's allegations.[26] In short, this was a period when administration officials were basically free of outside constraints in the
process of determining China policy. *

At the end of the war, it was natural, of course, for public
and congressional interest to shift back to parochial concerns. Even
within the top echelon of the Truman Administration, where foreign
policy continued to be of the highest priority,[28] China was normally
viewed as an area of distinctly secondary concern. In this respect,
Truman was an apt pupil of President Franklin Roosevelt. Toward
the end of the war, Roosevelt tended to view China more as a potential irritant in postwar Soviet-American relations than as an independent issue. Therefore he sought to encourage Sino-Soviet cooperation
as a means of providing Russia with the security it sought and to work
toward a peaceful resolution of the KMT-CCP conflict that threatened
to draw the United States and the USSR into opposing camps of a civil
war.[29] It was hoped that the Yalta agreement on the Far East would
also form the basis for stable relations between Chiang Kai-shek and
Stalin.

After Truman's assumption of the presidency, in large measure
Soviet-American relations continued to be the prism through which
China was viewed. Even then, it was only when anxiety over Soviet
intentions in Manchuria mounted, as in the fall of 1945 and the winter
of 1946, that China became a subject for cabinet-level discussion.
This crisis-generated interest in China may be seen for example in
the diaries of Secretary of the Navy Forrestal, who otherwise paid
no attention to China.[30] Insofar as China policy concerned the traditional pursuit of American commercial interests and even the traditional political goal of fostering the growth of a strong China, it
was a matter left to the State Department's Far Eastern experts. It
was only when China moved across the field of Soviet-American relations that it engaged the attention of the president and his closest
advisers. Even the Marshall mission, which was conceived and dispatched at a time of mounting anxiety over Soviet intentions in Manchuria, fits into this pattern. When Stalin reiterated his support for

---

*Nor did they yet seek to create an inflamed anti-Communist
public opinion that later itself became a severe constraint on policy
making. Richard Freeland shows how the Truman Administration
combined a domestic witchhunt and a baroque anti-Communist rhetoric
to muster support for its foreign policy.[27]

Chiang and U.S. policy in China in December 1945, Washington lost much of its interest in George Marshall's mission until the spring of 1946, when fears were renewed by Soviet actions in the Northeast. Except for the initial policy directive, Truman provided encouragement but no guidance for Marshall, who operated in China with proconsular freedom of action like Douglas MacArthur in Japan, but without the latter's power to shape events.[31] Truman was primarily concerned with "what the Russians were up to" in China.[32]

China's significance as a factor in the Soviet-American relationship was somewhat obscured primarily by the legacy of traditional policy, one element of which was the promotion of a strong and united China friendly to the United States. Toward this end, an American effort to help bring about a peaceful resolution of China's political problems seemed warranted. Moreover, the United States viewed China as an integral strategic link in an Asian and Pacific security system designed to check the reemergence of a Japanese threat. Thus, despite the accumulated evidence of Nationalist weakness, there were strong reasons for continuing American mediation in China.[33] A second traditional element was concern for securing the commercial Open Door; however, very few of the top policy makers were interested in this question. Averell Harriman and Henry Stimson feared that Soviet hegemony in Manchuria might lead to closing the door in an area that had long attracted U.S. commercial and financial interests. They pressed the president to secure a Soviet promise to respect this traditional interpretation of the Open Door, but Truman was only casually concerned and at Potsdam accepted Stalin's calming reassurance at face value.[34]

The real importance of the Open Door, however, was not in the realm of foreign economic policy at all. The American diplomatic documents of the time suggest that for most officials the Open Door was much more an inherited language or a residual framework for talking about China policy than it was an active concern. Even when the issues under discussion related to national security and realpolitik, the language of expression was the old Open Door formula.

In the postwar period, the traditional concern for China's territorial integrity became part of an American strategy of denial motivated not by vague feelings of "friendship" for China but rooted in the developing Soviet-American rivalry. The key region was Manchuria because of its strategic and industrial importance.[35] As American policy shifted from a focus on preventing the renewal of Japanese militarism to a preoccupation with the Soviet threat, the salience of Manchuria increased. Only a unified China that included Manchuria could act as a partial counterweight to the expansionist designs of the USSR in East Asia. If Manchuria were to be detached from China and integrated economically into the USSR, this would have a severe disequilibrating effect on the global balance of power.

The Subcommittee on the Far East of the State, War, Navy Co-ordinating Committee (SWNCC), a key Washington institution, warned ominously in a memorandum of June 1, 1946, that, "without substantial control of Manchurian resources, China may increasingly become an economic and political vacuum into which a powerful and aggressive Russia may inevitably be drawn, regardless of American deterrent action short of war."[36] The SWNCC study stated that:

> In Manchuria especially the U.S.S.R. is expected
> to seek to foster the establishment of an autonomous
> state dominated by the Soviet Union. Such a state
> would be receptive to Soviet requests for economic
> concessions, would eliminate any potential threat
> to Siberia, and might eventually be absorbed into
> the Soviet Union. With or without physical incor-
> poration into the USSR, a Manchuria integrated
> into the Russian economy would prove a grave
> threat to the United States as well as China. The
> resulting self-sufficiency of the USSR in the Far
> East would, taken together with her western in-
> dustries, place under the control of the Soviet
> Union the greatest agglomeration of power in the
> history of the world. China without Manchuria
> would be no effective counterpoise to maintain
> the balance of power in the Far East.[37]

This same memo further asserted that, "No area is a zone of greater potential danger to Soviet-American relation."[38] The thinking articulated so forcefully in this SWNCC memorandum had underlain American China policy from the autumn of 1945 when the Marshall mission was in preparation.[39]

We must, however, qualify this assertion. If the American perception of China's strategic importance had remained at such a high level throughout the postwar period, American acquiescence in the Communist victory in China would have been unthinkable. In fact, the recall of General Marshall in January 1947 signified not only that America lacked the capability to affect the outcome in China but also an admission that American interests there did not warrant a major commitment after all.[40]

In the last half of 1946, a change occurred in the American estimation of China's strategic importance because the ongoing civil war appeared to nullify China's capacity to affect significantly the global balance of power. America's withdrawal from China was facilitated by the dawning realization that the Soviets were not going to intervene further on behalf of the CCP. There came into being, then, a tacit mutual agreement between the two Cold War rivals that China would not, after all, be an arena of conflict between them.

Let us look more closely now at the main contours of American postwar policy in China. Resolution of the major question of how firmly committed the United States should be to the Nationalist government entailed, among other things, an evaluation of the strength of the CCP and its international orientation, the strength and continued viability of the Nationalists, and an estimate of the probable course of Soviet policy. Baldly stated, the two main options for the United States were support for Chiang's government (with or without pressure on it to reform) or, alternatively, a de facto two-China policy (like that of the Soviets) seeking to develop a working relationship with the Chinese Communists despite Chiang's opposition. As is often the case in foreign policy questions, what might have been a great debate on this issue occurred only in fractured form.

As is well known, a number of foreign service officers in China strongly recommended that U.S. policy take into account the rising strength of the CCP, and they predicted, as John Paton Davies put it, that "China's destiny is not Chiang's but theirs."[41] Furthermore, on the basis of soundings from Mao and other Communist leaders, the officers concluded that while the Chinese Communists were not indissolubly wedded to a pro-Soviet orientation, U.S. inaction would likely force the CCP into dependency upon the Russians. Their critical insight, in other words, was that a competitive situation existed in which both the Americans and the Russians could bid for influence in and over the CCP. (This view foreshadowed the present triangular power relationship of 30 years later.) Unlike most other Communist parties, the CCP was not a Bolshevized political force looking submissively to Moscow for leadership and direction. An important corollary was that the United States need no longer pussyfoot in its dealings with Chiang, who had lost the aura of the indispensable man.

Ambassador Hurley decisively rejected this realistic but heretical perspective on China policy and, in March 1945, having gained President Roosevelt's renewed support, angrily engineered the transfer from China of the men he felt were obstructing his policy of supporting the Nationalist government.[42] Thereafter "ideological thinking" replaced political realism.[43] An "orthodox" view of the Chinese Communists as instruments of Russian expansionism triumphed in Washington and every bit of evidence that tended to confirm this was carefully gathered and collated. For example, the final report of the Yenan Observer Group (Dixie Mission) by Colonel Ivan Yeaton concluded that, "Direct positive proof based upon personal observation together with much circumstantial evidence definitely establishes the fact that the Soviet Union is guiding the destinies of one of its strongest satellites, the Chinese Communist party, as it has in the past and

will in the future."[44] This erroneous conclusion was bolstered by
the mechanical transference of knowledge about relations between
the USSR and other Communist parties in Europe. *

An obsession with the threat of a Sovietized China also under-
lay the medium-range goals of U.S. policy in China--the formation
of a unified coalition government and an integrated national army.
General Marshall's pursuit of these aims was based on the hope that
political unification and military integration might be the means by
which the Communist "threat" to China from within and without could
be contained and even dispersed. As Marshall counseled Foreign
Minister Wang Shih-chieh in February 1946, "China must proceed
with her projected unification at the fastest possible pace so as to
eliminate her present vulnerability to Soviet undercover attack,
which exists so long as there remains a separate Communist Government and a separate Communist Army in China."[46]

For reasons that are by no means clear, but may perhaps relate to a deep-seated faith in the capacity of constitutional democracy
to effect a transsubstantiation, Marshall and others believed that
CCP political behavior would be radically altered if it entered into a
coalition government. It is true that over the long run participation
in electoral political systems may greatly modify Communist party
behavior and norms in constitutional democracies, such as those in
Western Europe. But, given the wild improbability of even approximately reproducing in China the conditions that elsewhere lured Communist parties from their Leninist model, the American hope was
misplaced. In this respect, the standard allegation that the thinking
undergirding the Marshall mission was naive is correct. John Carter
Vincent expressed the American hope most succinctly in stating that,
"a reduction in the influence of the Communists might be more readily achieved if the Government 'took them in' (in more senses than
one) on a minority basis rather than try to shoot them all."[47] The
continuing American pressure on Chiang to accept the substance as
well as the form of coalition government was certainly not based upon
any sympathy with the Communists' political objectives, as right-
wing critics subsequently charged.[48] Yet, the Americans who hoped
to hoodwink the Communists were probably deceiving only themselves.

The concrete American program for shoring up a non-Communist government in China focused on supporting the KMT in North and
East China. American efforts to assist the Nationalist recovery of

---

*In fact, Yeaton himself had been brought in by Albert C.
Wedemeyer in 1944 as a Soviet expert to replace Colonel David
Barrett, an old China hand, who allegedly had failed to provide suf-
ficient information about the CCP's ties to Moscow.[45]

Manchuria, however, encountered the stubborn fact of the Red Army occupation. A direct American military role, such as that of the Marines in North China, was precluded so as to avoid possible clashes with Soviet troops. The essence of the American approach, therefore, was to hold the ring for the Nationalists in North China, thus freeing their forces to advance into the Northeast. This aid was crucial, for without it the Nationalists could not expect to recover Manchuria in the face of Chinese Communist hostility and Russian ambivalence. In addition, through limited diplomatic pressure on the Soviets, the Truman Administration hoped to moderate Soviet economic demands in Manchuria, speed the withdrawal of the Red Army, and reduce the threat of Soviet-CCP collusion in the region.

In foreign policy analysis there is always the danger of ascribing greater consistency and internal cohesiveness to a policy than it may actually have had. American policy in postwar China was neither the liberal illusion that American right-wing politicians attacked in the McCarthy period nor was it a thoroughly tough-minded, well-reasoned strategy to maximize American interests vis-a-vis an expansionist Soviet Union in the Far East. The paradoxical reality was that, although the weakness of the Nationalists was recognized, it was also ignored. The Soviet threat to Chinese territorial integrity in Manchuria was greatly feared, yet almost simultaneously minimized. The Chinese Communists were viewed as both disruptive but yet somehow manageable.

The keys for understanding this schizophrenic reality are two. One is the force of inertia that operated powerfully to perpetuate policy lines that bureaucrats were accustomed to from long practice. This "manana" tendency, or "muddling through,"[49] was reinforced by a widely prevalent faith in the capacity of the United States to determine the outcome of historic development in China in such a way that everything would turn out for the best all around.[50]

Men like John Service and John Paton Davies had a realistic understanding of the limits that Chinese political reality imposed on American policy, but once they were transferred this insight disappeared. In this light, General Marshall's experience in China may be viewed as a year of disillusionment in the most literal sense. The realization of American impotence to effect a settlement in China came only after the failure of a far-ranging intervention that had involved military, diplomatic, political, and economic means to shape a China in America's image. But even Marshall's hard-won knowledge failed to inform post-1949 American policy, which again presumed to affect the outcome of Chinese political struggles, including the unfinished civil war.

The termination of Marshall's mission, like its origin, was connected with Soviet-American relations. Soviet failure to pursue

its advantage actively in China allayed American anxieties. Soviet
troops withdrew from Manchuria in May 1946, and the Russians refrained from demanding a role in mediating China's civil war as
Marshall had feared they might. If, to the contrary, the Russians
had intervened actively on the Communist side in 1946, it seems
highly probable that the United States would have increased greatly
its support for Chiang's government rather than stepping back from
the conflict. In any case, the Americans finally arrived at the conclusion that the Soviets had reached earlier: the Chinese conflict
was not amenable to a foreign solution. By its pragmatic tacking
and maneuvering, Russia had managed to keep lines open to both the
CCP and the Nationalists, but the United States had all but dissipated
its chances of constructing a satisfactory working relationship with
the Communists.

THE NATIONALISTS AND MANCHURIA:
RELYING ON OTHERS

In a number of colonial Asian countries, the swiftness of the
Japanese collapse and the precipitate end of the war imperiled the
restoration of the status quo ante bellum, as political initiative
passed to the hands of local nationalists, including Communist-led
resistance groups. In China, the "legitimists," as represented by
the Nationalist government, were similarly disadvantaged. Even
prior to the war, the Nanking government had been little more than
a regional regime whose authority was restricted even within many
of the provinces that it nominally controlled.[51] Once it lost its base
in central South China, its position worsened considerably. Confined to its southwestern refuge, the Nationalist government was, in
effect, a government in exile, although still based on Chinese soil,
facing a task of far greater magnitude than that of most of the European governments in exile.[52]

Yet Chiang Kai-shek's outlook was by no means entirely bleak.
In the provinces touched by the war (for example, Szechwan, Sinkiang,
Yunnan, and Kweichow), warlord power had been undermined and central power extended. Before the war, the generalissimo had faced
myriad internal enemies. Now, like a man consolidating his debts
by taking out a loan from a finance company, Chiang had only one
problem to deal with--the Communists.

The recovery of the key area of Manchuria was part of a larger
problem. In September 1945, much of intramural China remained in
the hands of undefeated enemy troops, while the government's elite
forces were deployed far from East, North, and Northeast China.[53]
By contrast, the Communists were close to the urban centers of

North and East China and within striking distance of Manchuria,
where the situation was complicated, as we have noted, by the presence of the Soviet Red Army. In Manchuria, as in intramural China,
the Nationalists became critically dependent upon external support
to expedite their recovery effort. Here Chiang's legitimist status
conferred a great advantage as it had during the war, enabling his
government to be the sole recipient of foreign aid and support.
After the war, Chiang's basic strategy vis-a-vis the United States
was to appeal to American fears of communism in order to secure
an extended commitment. [54]

A different approach was needed for dealing with Russia, of
course. If Chiang could demonstrate his ability to satisfy Soviet
political and military requirements, particularly in Manchuria, perhaps he need not fear that Stalin would throw his support to Mao.
This was the obverse side of the analogy with Poland, where non-
Communist groups had been obdurate in their rejection of Soviet
territorial demands. Chiang's difficulty lay in trying to satisfy the
Soviets' minimum demands without leaving the door open for their
maximum demands to be pressed upon him. *

Despite the Soviet-American fait accompli of Yalta, the Chinese
raised serious objections to what they rightly considered a serious infringement of their sovereignty, but they received an unsympathetic
response from the Truman Administration. [56] Thereupon, Generalissimo Chiang resorted to a strategy that he employed regularly thereafter. He asked that the United States and Great Britain join in any
Sino-Soviet agreement in order to ensure Soviet compliance. [57]
Chiang's calculation was that in Sino-Soviet bilateral relations,
China, lacking sufficient power, would have nothing to fall back on
in resisting Soviet demands except appeals to Soviet good faith and
moderation. Therefore, Chiang tried constantly to substitute multilateral arrangements for bilateral ones. If he could successfully re-
define Sino-Soviet issues to involve American interests, then Stalin
would be forced to consider an entire new range of factors in his
policy making. Chiang's strategy was an application of the old ploy
of the fox trying to borrow the prestige of the tiger, as the Chinese
saying expressed it. [58] American strength would compensate for
Chinese weakness. [59]

---

*The minimum demands involving the reassertion of Russia's
pre-1905 privileges in Manchuria, including control of Port Arthur,
special rights in Dairen, and joint ownership and operation of the
trunk rail lines in the Northeast, had been conceded already by the
United States at Yalta. Moreover, the Soviets had expressed their
willingness to sign a pact of friendship and alliance with China
against Japan. [55]

In this instance the gambit failed, as Truman refused to be out-
foxed and spurned the generalissimo's request. Subsequently, in the
course of negotiating the Sino-Soviet treaty, Foreign Minister T. V.
Soong repeatedly attempted to involve the United States as a counterweight to the Soviets, who were trying to stretch the Yalta terms.
However, at a critical juncture, Truman turned down Chiang's pleas
and never sanctioned more than a weak intervention in the negotiations on Chiang's behalf.[60] This pointed to a fatal weakness in
Chiang's strategy. The strength of the strategy of multilateraliza-
tion lay in its recognition that because the United States wanted to
check the growth of Soviet power, it could be expected more often
than not to respond to Chinese calls for assistance. But Chiang was
clearly tempting fate. His strategy could succeed only if he could
convince his foreign supporters that their interests coincided with
his own. This was obviously not always the case.

Rather than attempting to develop domestic bases of support,
Chiang's strategy in both domestic and foreign policy was to play the
dangerous game of manipulating foreigners. The drawback of this
approach was particularly indicated in his Russian policy. Stalin
had been willing to deal with Chiang, albeit from a superior position
reflecting the disproportion of power between them. The generalissimo, however, refused to recognize the limits his weakness imposed, a refusal characteristic of his postwar leadership. In some
men, blindness to the imperatives of a harsh reality is a key to great-
ness impelling them to marshal the inner strength and resources to
transcend the present and create their own realities in the future.
(Such blindness, however, requires an interior vision.) In Chiang's
case, the urge to transcend the reality of his weakness too often was
transmuted into an attempt to enlist the aid of foreign protectors who
were ultimately unreliable, not only because their interests differed
from his own but also because their ability to control history was
limited.

Chiang's determination to seek control of Manchuria illustrates
this point. Persistently pursuing his goal in the face of great difficulties, Chiang ultimately dissipated much of his elite military forces,
fatally weakened his position in North China, and accelerated the collapse of his government. In quest of the long-term revolutionary goal
of Chinese reunification, Chiang and the Kuomintang considered that
after the war the prospect of extending Nationalist control over Manchuria had improved because of the weakening of the prewar Manchurian regional elite. Chiang approached the goal of integrating
Manchuria into the Nationalist domain by excluding rigorously the
old Manchurian elite from top-level positions of authority in the

postwar regional administration. These were reserved primarily for members of the political study clique.*

The most important factor propelling the government to recover control of the Northeast was its knowledge that by inaction the region would pass by default to the Communists, and this might well tip the balance in a civil conflict. Given Communist hostility and America's cautious attitude with regard to Manchuria, Nationalist prospects hinged on the attitude of the Russian occupation forces. In the August 1945 treaty, Chiang had won pledges of exclusive Soviet support to his government, as well as recognition of Chinese sovereignty in Manchuria, in return for the concessions in Manchuria and Mongolia.[61] This seemed a fair price, for with Soviet as well as American aid denied to them, the Chinese Communists, unable to penetrate the Northeast, could reasonably be expected to come to terms with the Nationalists.[62] Events soon demonstrated the error of this view.

Communist determination to contest control of Manchuria transformed the nature of the Nationalists' takeover problem, and a much higher level of Soviet cooperation became essential. Given the initial weakness of the Nationalists' position, what they now required of the Russians was a holding operation--maintaining the status quo in Manchuria until Chinese government forces were brought into the region. Unlike the defeated Japanese and the victorious Americans who fulfilled a similar role admirably, the Russians consistently refused to extend the requisite degree of cooperation. In every new evidence of Kuomintang weakness, they saw a further opportunity to angle for their own advantage.

Although looking mainly to the United States for support, Chiang Kai-shek sought to maintain good relations with the Soviets, and, in the face of intraparty opposition, he stressed the importance of Sino-Soviet friendship and hoped to secure Soviet aid for his takeover of

---

*Once the attempt to recover the Northeast had been launched, the factional character of Kuomintang politics helped to lock the government into a fixed course of action. When government policy encountered resistance from the Soviets and the Chinese Communists in the winter of 1945-46, the political study clique leaders in the Northeast (Hsiung Shih-hui, Chang Kia-ngau, and so on) were subjected to a withering fire of criticism from the clique within the Central Executive Committee of the Kuomintang, as well as in the press. Chiang Kai-shek, whose own policies were at issue, was forced to make a personal defense of his representatives in an effort to still the criticism.

Manchuria. But though he asked for much, he offered very little in
return. In response to the Soviet demand for further economic concessions in Manchuria during the winter of 1945-46, Chiang sanctioned negotiations that essentially were an effort to buy time. He
would not purchase Soviet amity by further sacrifices of economic
sovereignty. [63]

Moreover, the generalissimo was rigidly opposed to high-level
political negotiations with the Soviets. In January 1946, and again
during the Manchurian crisis four months later, Chiang rejected
Stalin's proposal for a summit meeting, ostensibly from fear of undermining Sino-American relations.[64] At a time when the CCP was
demanding a regional coalition government in Manchuria, Chiang may
well have feared direct Soviet pressure on him to accept a solution of
the Manchurian crisis on terms requiring a sharing of power with the
CCP. As before, Chiang sedulously avoided the trap of bilateral
"solutions" to Sino-Soviet problems.

In the absence of positive evidence, we may speculate that
Stalin's purpose in twice proposing a meeting with Chiang Kai-shek
was, among other things, to press for his maximum program in
China, a prime aspect of which was to remove American power from
the country in return for Soviet support of Chinese economic development. He had dwelt on this subject in his January 1946 talks with
Chiang Ching-kuo. If there is any truth to this supposition, then
there may well have existed an alternative to the Nationalists' pro-
American orientation throughout this postwar year. By acceding to
Stalin's desire for a neutral China not locked into the developing
American alliance system, Chiang might have purchased Stalin's
favor, at least in the short run. But rather than explore the possibility of a deal with the Soviets, Chiang sought to strengthen the
American commitment to his government. A political settlement of
the Manchurian crisis of spring 1946 might have been possible on the
basis of reorganizing the regional administrative bodies, recognizing
the Communist armies, and sharing power at the regional and pro-
vincial levels. The United States and the USSR would probably have
supported such a settlement. But Chiang apparently preferred to
prolong the crisis in the hope of achieving either a decisive military
victory or a complete polarization of forces and a consequent un-
equivocal American commitment.

In sum, the generalissimo, in pursuit of the chimera of un-
divided power, may have discarded an opportunity for a compromise
solution in the Northeast and Soviet support for an independent neutral China. Ultimately, of course, it probably would have made
little difference whether Chiang chose a pro-American or a pro-
Soviet orientation since neither of his potential benefactors could
control the CCP or compensate for the Nationalists' political and
military weakness.

When the United States and the USSR shared a common intermediate objective, such as establishment of a coalition government,
Chiang was left without recourses. He overestimated his capacity
to play on the great powers' rivalry because he exaggerated China's
importance in the competition. In the final analysis, neither the
Soviets nor the Americans considered China sufficiently vital to risk
conflict through increased intervention. Realizing that their maximum
objectives were unattainable at the level of commitment they were prepared to make, they backed off. Chiang found himself unable to lean
to one side or the other.

THE CHINESE COMMUNISTS:
THE LIMITS OF DEPENDENCE

For the Chinese Communists, external intervention was more
of an obstacle than a solution to the problems they faced in postwar
China. Like the Kuomintang, the CCP also attempted to compete for
foreign support, but this was a secondary part of its political strategy.
The CCP received a limited measure of Russian aid in Manchuria, but
it failed in its efforts to neutralize American support for the Nationalists. Its basic policy of mobilizing internal resources proved to be
much more effective than the Nationalists' strategy of seeking external support.

During the 1930s, the Communists had failed to establish secure
base areas in Manchuria, and by 1940, the Japanese had succeeded in
eradicating their guerrillas and destroying the Communist party organization. [65] Renewed Communist efforts within the region in the
last year of the war had proved unsuccessful as well. Thus, in August 1945, Manchuria was a political vacuum.

Despite impressive wartime gains, particularly in North China,
the postwar balance of military forces apparently was still heavily
weighted against the Communists. A successful government takeover
of all the people, resources, and territory held by the Japanese would
have further disadvantaged the CCP. Thus, for the Communists
merely to hold on to and consolidate their gains would have been to
suffer a loss in the rapidly evolving political situation. This consideration, coupled with their long-term aim of achieving power, dictated an active policy of expansion. Despite this imperative, in writing about the power tasks of the party, Mao Tse-tung shrewdly adopted
a defensive posture, warning that civil war was almost inevitable because Chiang Kai-shek would try "to rob the people" of the fruits of
their wartime resistance. [66]

Despite Cultural Revolution charges, it seems likely that broad
agreement existed within the CCP leadership on the need to test the
option of peaceful political struggle in postwar China. (Undoubtedly,

there were important differences in emphasis among the leadership on tactical issues.) More important even than international pressures was the existence within as well as outside the party of hopes for a peaceful future, which the Communist leadership could have ignored only at great peril. In August 1945, Mao expressed the CCP's readiness to make concessions in the forthcoming negotiations with the government as long as these did not damage "the fundamental interests" of the people, a formula by which Mao meant to retain control of the Communist areas and sufficient troops to defend them. [67] Meanwhile, the Party moved vigorously to expand the territory under its control.

When the Chungking negotiations began, Communist troops were first entering the Northeast. The region still lay outside "the fundamental interests" that Mao swore not to concede, but Manchuria was the prime area of opportunity in Communist postwar strategy. At no point were they ready to concede control of it because of its intrinsic value in both peace and war.

The success of Communist plans for expansion into northeast China hinged partly on the attitude of the Soviet Union. Unfortunately, the relations between the CCP and Moscow during the Yenan period are still rather obscure, and the available sources must be treated with more than the usual scholarly skepticism. It is known that Soviet contact with the Communists was established by radio as early as 1936. [68] Subsequently, channels of communication between Moscow and Yenan were maintained through the presence in northern Shensi of war correspondents who doubled as Soviet agents. [69] According to a recent Soviet source, however, rather than providing these men with up-to-date, accurate information that could be transmitted back to the Soviet government, the Maoist leadership hounded them with security personnel, kept them isolated, and regarded them with extreme suspicion. [70]*

Furthermore, the Soviets charged that in the first days of Barbarossa, they appealed to the CCP to coordinate military activities with the USSR in case Japan opened a second front in Siberia. Although Chu Teh gave assurances of such coordination to the head of the Soviet mission in Yenan, absolutely nothing was done to transform this promise into operational planning. [71] These allegations, if true, cast a new light on this obscure relationship.

---

*Incidentally, this, if true, suggests that the CCP leadership was aware of developments in the international Communist movement, such as the great purges that decimated foreign Communist leaders. Such awareness would certainly have justified a very high degree of suspicion of the motives and activities of Soviet agents.

Whatever the precise character of the Moscow-Yenan link, the CCP clearly hoped to benefit from Soviet entry into the Pacific War based primarily on its expectation that the Russians would collaborate with whatever Chinese forces they encountered in Manchuria. Consequently, they strove to be in a position from which they could achieve maximum advantage from a linkup with the Red Army. Mao's hope of receiving support from the Russians was dealt a rude blow with the signing of the Sino-Soviet treaty of 1945. Many within the CCP were resentful and suspicious of Soviet policy at the leadership level as well as among the rank and file.[72] Nevertheless, CCP leaders still sought to pursue a strategy of securing Soviet aid. Putting a bold face on the situation, an inner-party document dating from this period took note of the overriding importance of Soviet-American relations. The document asserted that, "The signing of the Soviet-Chinese Treaty has eliminated the possibility of conflict between the USSR and the USA on the Chinese question and has made open intervention by the USA on the side of the Kuomintang against the Communist Party of China more difficult; this is very important."[73] Was this anything more than a hope?

During the postwar Soviet-CCP discussions in Moscow, Stalin confirmed his rejection of a revolutionary attempt in China and counseled the CCP to enter a coalition with the Nationalists. However, the Soviets publicly indicated continued support of their Chinese comrades in a _Pravda_ article of August 31, 1945, which reported without comment the contents of the CCP Central Committee's declaration of August 25, which featured democratization and the creation of a coalition government as the essence of the Party's political program.[74] _Pravda_'s publication of this program constituted an indirect endorsement of the CCP's position, and appearing directly after the publication of the Sino-Soviet treaty, served to indicate that the Soviets were not abandoning the CCP. The inference to be drawn was that Soviet support of the Nationalist government in China would depend, in part, on the degree to which Chiang was willing to transform his regime to accommodate the Communist proposals. The August treaty was far from a blanket endorsement of the Nationalists.

Manchuria was the test case of Soviet policy. Following the August treaty, Communist troops continued to enter Manchuria, and Soviet-Chinese Communist contacts increased significantly.[75] As is well known, the Red Army allowed large quantities of Japanese weapons to come into the hands of the CCP, and Soviet authorities stood aside as the Communists engaged in intensive military recruitment and established an increasingly well-articulated network of Party organizations and local government administrations.[76] At the same time, the Russians were interposing a variety of obstacles to the Nationalist attempt at recovering Manchuria. Without in any way minimizing the significance of this Soviet support for the CCP, it must be stressed that Stalin had hardly made an open-ended commitment to the CCP. Soviet officials in Changchun and Chungking continued throughout to negotiate with the Nationalists in the expectation that the Nationalist effort to recover Manchuria might be delayed but could not be indefinitely postponed.

In answering the question of how dependent the CCP was upon Soviet support in Manchuria, we must bear in mind that Communist determination to expand into the region almost certainly antedated any arrangements with the Soviet Union. [77] Thus, the relevant question is what limits the Chinese Communists might have accepted from the Soviets on their activity in Manchuria.

One can hardly suppose that the Communists would have obeyed a Kremlin directive to stay out of Manchuria. Mao's loyalty to the Soviet Union (to the degree that it existed) was based on more than ideology. It arose from the ideologically derived presumption of a certain congruence of interests (though not an identity) between the homeland of communism and the revolutionary Communist movement in China that he headed. If the Communist leaders could accept the pact of August 1945, it was not because they headed a Bolshevized, disciplined, and therefore obedient Communist party, but because they must have calculated that when the chips were down the Soviets would not fail to support them. [78]

The central point about Soviet policy toward the CCP was that, with the possible exception of turning over Japanese weapons, the stance was quite passive. The Communists had not entered Manchuria, after all, in response to a Red Army "invitation." Only an active Soviet policy of keeping them out might have thwarted their determination to turn the Northeast into a revolutionary base, and this would have entailed an improbable Soviet attempt to seal off the land and sea access routes and a willingness to use force against the Communist troops particularly along the lengthy Jehol border. Similarly, only an active Soviet policy could have prevented the Communists from organizing and dominating local governments in Manchuria. As it was, the Russians had only to acquiesce in the CCP's transformation of the local power structures.

In sum, Mao's hopes of benefiting from collaboration with the Soviets in the Northeast were realized within the limits just described. But in the context of overall Communist strategy, Soviet aid to the CCP was of marginal importance.

There was an American arrow in Mao's quiver as well, although he was unable to shoot it very straight or very far. Throughout the war, the Communists had attempted to obtain American military support and supplies. [79] They had favorably impressed a wide array of Americans with the informality and egalitarianism of life in

Yenan, their commitment to the anti-Japanese struggle, and their populist outlook, which was sometimes mistaken for a commitment to democracy. [80] Although Communist contacts with Americans were accompanied by expressions of friendship and interest in the United States, it would be naive to ascribe this to anything other than calculation. (The recent wave of American euphoria over things Chinese in the aftermath of the Nixon visit shows that this is an unpalatable truth.) CCP leaders concluded that the United States as the major world power would inevitably continue to play a vital role in postwar China. *

In January 1945, Mao and Chou En-lai made their extraordinary effort to go to Washington for an "exploratory conference" with President Roosevelt, hoping to circumvent Ambassador Hurley. [82] The Chinese leaders probably hoped for American military support and an opportunity to impress Roosevelt with the CCP's strength and potential role in postwar China. However, the request reached the president only to be rejected. [83] At the time of the Japanese surrender, the CCP again tried to deflect the United States from intervening in China on the Nationalist side, but Chu Teh's message requesting American neutrality was turned down by the American military. [84] With the United States locked into a position of hostility, the CCP turned to the Russians, but a final Communist attempt to elicit American support still lay in the offing.

At the time that the Marshall mission was announced, the Communists responded correctly but without great enthusiasm. Once in China, Marshall entered into the difficult negotiations of the Committee of Three, which culminated in the January 1946 cease-fire. The contrast between his fairness, tact, inventive diplomacy, and ability to grasp quickly the essential issues and Hurley's blustering incomprehension must have produced a great effect on the Communist elite. After presumably intense debate within the Politburo, another remarkable attempt was made to wean the United States away from its attachment to the Kuomintang.

In a meeting with Marshall on January 31, 1946, Chou En-lai conveyed the gratitude of Mao and the CCP Central Committee for Marshall's efforts to secure the cease-fire order. [85] He concluded his remarks to Marshall by hinting in unmistakable terms that Mao would welcome an opportunity to visit the United States. [86] Chou's remarks were reinforced by a letter from Mao to Marshall in which

---

*As Mao told John Service early in 1945, "America does not realize her influence in China and her ability to shape events there. Chiang Kai-shek is dependent upon American help. . . . There is no such thing as America not intervening in China." [81]

the chairman fulsomely thanked the American for his "fair and just attitude in the course of negotiating and regulating the truce agreement" and looked forward to his "impartial help" in the solution of remaining problems.[87]*

Why did the Communist leadership make such an unusual approach to the United States? In Marshall's diplomacy, the Communists must have perceived not merely the attribute of an individual but a new direction in American policy looking toward the construction of a working relationship with the CCP. The possibility that the United States genuinely wanted to act the part of neutral mediator to bring about a coalition government could not be rejected out of hand. Chou's demarche and Mao's letter were signals to the United States that the CCP, for its part, welcomed a continued strong American presence in China as long as it was not designed exclusively to shore up the Nationalist government.

The Communists, aware of the American suspicion that their Party was an instrument of Soviet expansionism that Moscow could manipulate at will, tried to alter the American perception through a series of reassurances. While maintaining their principled commitment to the ultimate goal of socialism, the Communists indicated that for the foreseeable future the CCP hoped not for a Russian but for an American connection. Over the next several months, on repeated occasions, Chou En-lai explicitly dissociated the CCP from Soviet goals and policies in China. This, then, was Mao's new democracy for an American audience.

There is no record in the documents I have examined of an explicit American response to this initiative. Yet it is clear that within a very few weeks the CCP was disabused of the hope that it could achieve a close working relationship with the United States. Here the various reasons can only be listed. First, the CCP was unable to persuade the Americans of their independence of Moscow given the apparent Soviet-CCP collusion in Manchuria in March–April 1946. Second, Marshall's negotiating strategy of separating military from political issues ran counter to that of the CCP. Third, the United States continued to provide aid and support for the Nationalists while carrying on the tripartite negotiations. Communist faith in Marshall's neutrality waned accordingly.† As Chou remarked bitterly in February

---

*It should be noted that Mao's letter said nothing about following the American model or a possible trip to the United States.

† Marshall brought to his mediation effort impressive personal qualifications of the kind that are essential for a successful effort of the type he undertook. He was a prominent figure of high rank who commanded respect both for himself and the power that he represented. Although his direct knowledge of China was slight at first,

1947, Marshall "was partial to Chiang Kai-shek and the Kuomintang except in the first two months of his stay in China."[90]

The basic reason for the failure of U.S.-CCP relations during this period was the underlying difference in their goals. American policy was aimed at minimizing the influence and power of the CCP, while the latter aimed at expansion and, ultimately, national power. In the limited areas where an overlapping of purpose occurred, cooperation was possible to a degree, but the underlying goals were incompatible. Despite desultory Communist participation in the continuing Marshall-Stuart negotiations of 1946, it was not really until June 1946 on the eve of victory that the CCP gave any indications of renewed interest in relations with the United States.[91]

CONCLUSIONS

This chapter has attempted to outline some of the complex interactions in a quadrilateral relationship involving multiple levels of competition. Internally, competition existed between the CCP and the KMT, the two chief rivals for power in postwar China. Internationally, the USSR and the United States were involved in a global competition of which their rivalry in China was a component. There was constant interaction between these two main levels of competition as the four parties strove to improve their competitive positions visa-vis each other.

The intervention of the two great powers in the internal conflict transformed the struggle from one involving national issues into one affecting the basic and conflicting interests of the intervening powers.[92] That the Chinese civil war did not turn into a veiled confrontation

---

he had an impressive capacity to absorb knowledge in usable form and a great degree of skill in framing negotiating issues, articulating proposals, and resolving procedural difficulties. Moreover, whatever his innermost thought may have been, his impartiality impressed the Communists as well as the Nationalists.

The essential character of mediation, however, is a desire to produce a settlement in which the mediator has no personal stake. In other words, where a settlement to a dispute occurs along the spectrum of conflicting aims and values of the two parties, it should not affect the interests of the mediating party. The absence of what Oran Young calls the quality of "independence" was the fatal flaw in the Marshall mediation effort.[88] This point was stated with characteristic clarity by Thomas Hobbes, ". . . no man in any case ought to be received for arbitrator to whom greater profit or honor or pleasure apparently arises out of the victory of one party than of the other. . . ."[89]

between the Soviets and the Americans was due to two basic factors: First, there was a fundamental lack of congruence in the interests of the internal and the external actors. The Soviets and the Americans basically wanted to check each other's influence in China. The Chinese parties, however, were concerned with the internal struggle for power and had an instrumental view of the great power competition. It was possible for the Soviets and the Americans to attain their goals without aligning themselves completely with one or the other of the Chinese parties. In other words, although the two planes of competition intersected, they never coincided. The polarization of internal and external forces that Chiang Kai-shek hoped to effect was never realized in China.

Paradoxically, the character of competition in the postwar bipolar international system also acted to restrain Soviet-American competition in China, although it had helped to engender it originally. Through the Yalta agreement, the Russians had already achieved their minimum desiderata in the Far East and they could, therefore, adopt a low posture in pursuing their secondary goals in China. An active policy of support to the Communists or the application of too great pressure on the Nationalists might have elicited an American response not only in China but in Europe as well where Soviet interests were greater by far. Similarly, the United States concluded that the goals it had set itself in China were not worth an extensive commitment or risk taking given the larger stakes in other areas of Soviet-American competition. Thus, as already suggested, a tacit understanding emerged between the two great powers that China need not and would not be an arena of Soviet-American confrontation. As both rivals stepped back from the competition, there seemed every reason to believe that the Chinese civil conflict would drag on for many years.

Thirty years have passed since the events analyzed here. Mao Tse-tung and Chou En-lai, denied permission to visit Washington in 1945, enjoyed playing host to an American president in 1972. In the aftermath of that visit, it became fashionable to speculate on the might-have-beens of postwar Sino-American relations. [93] Too much of this speculation simplistically omits the harsh context of the postwar international environment that left little room for affirmations of independence or diluted allegiance to the developing Cold War camps by countries like China. It seems unlikely that even if Washington had pursued a more flexible policy in 1945-46, Mao's lean-to-one-side speech of July 1949 would have read much differently. What is certain is that the quadripartite relationship, with its multiple options for alignment, remains a vital part of the contemporary international environment, fostering uncertainty in statesmen and scholars alike.

NOTES

1. On Eastern Europe, see Lynn Etheridge Davis, The Cold War Begins: Soviet-American Conflict over Eastern Europe (Princeton, N.J.: Princeton University Press, 1974).

2. James Rosenau, "Intervention as a Scientific Concept," in The Scientific Study of Foreign Policy (New York: Free Press, 1971), pp. 275-303.

3. Morton A. Kaplan, "Intervention in Internal War: Some Systemic Sources," in International Aspects of Civil Strife, ed. James Rosenau (Princeton, N.J.: Princeton University Press, 1964), pp. 92-121.

4. For other systemic characteristics affecting intervention, see Oran R. Young, "Intervention and International Systems," in International Aspects, op. cit., ed. Rosenau, pp. 180-81.

5. John Lewis Gaddis, The United States and the Origins of the Cold War, 1941-1947 (New York: Columbia University Press, 1972), chap. 7.

6. Myron Rush, ed., The International Situation and Soviet Foreign Policy (Columbus, Ohio: Charles E. Merrill, 1969), pp. 117-23; Joseph Starobin, "Origins of the Cold War," in The Conduct of Soviet Foreign Policy, ed. Fredric Fleron and Erik Hoffman (Chicago: Aldine, 1971), p. 285.

7. George Modelski, "The International Relations of Internal War," in International Aspects, op. cit., ed. Rosenau, pp. 14-44.

8. Howard Wriggins, "Political Outcomes of Foreign Assistance: Influence, Involvement or Intervention," in International Aspects, op. cit., ed. Rosenau, p. 226.

9. Bruce Russett, "Toward a Model of Competitive International Politics," in International Politics and Foreign Policy, ed. James Rosenau (New York: Free Press, 1969), pp. 121-22.

10. Adam Ulam, The Rivals: America and Russia since World War II (New York: Viking Press, 1972), p. 11.

11. The lack of naval forces as a constraint in Soviet foreign policy was suggested by Robert Herrick, "The Cold War and the Soviet Navy" (Paper delivered to Seminar on Communism, Columbia University, March 21, 1973).

12. Ulam, op. cit., p. 35.

13. For an instructive account of the political emasculation of the Communist-led European resistance movements, see Gabriel Kolko, The Politics of War (New York: Random House, 1968), pp. 79-98, 172-93, 435-56.

14. In his conversations with Chiang Ching-kuo in August 1945, Stalin said that Japan would recover its power in five years. Chiang

Ching-kuo, "Wo-ti fu-ch'in fan-kung san-shih nien," Chung-kuo chien-she (November 1957): 5.

15. V. L. Glunin et al., Noveishaia istoriia Kitaia (Moscow, 1965), p. 215.

16. See William Zimmerman, Soviet Perspectives in International Relations, 1956-1967 (Princeton, N.J.: Princeton University Press, 1969).

17. Martin Herz, Beginnings of the Cold War (New York: McGraw-Hill, 1966), pp. 136, 151 n. 66.

18. Foreign Relations of the United States, 1944 (Washington, D.C.: U.S. Government Printing Office), vol. 6, pp. 253-56 (hereafter cited as FR). See also Russell P. Buhite, Patrick J. Hurley and American Foreign Policy (Ithaca, N.Y.: Cornell University Press, 1973), p. 198.

19. Cf. Tang Tsou, America's Failure in China, 1941-1950 (Chicago: 1963).

20. For the genesis and early development of this duality, see Allen S. Whiting, Soviet Policies in China 1917-1924 (New York: Columbia University Press, 1954).

21. Joseph Grew, Turbulent Era (Boston: 1952), vol. 2, pp. 1445-46.

22. Gaddis, op. cit., p. 206.

23. Joseph Keeley, The China Lobby Man: The Story of Alfred Kohlberg (New Rochelle, N.Y.: Arlington House, 1969), p. 236.

24. James Alan Fetzer, "Congress and China, 1941-1950" (Ph.D. dissertation, Michigan State University, 1969), pp. 53-54.

25. Ibid., pp. 57-63; Athan Theoharis, The Yalta Myths: An Issue in U.S. Politics, 1945-1955 (Columbia, Mo.: University of Missouri Press, 1970), p. 38.

26. Earl Latham, The Communist Controversy in Washington (Cambridge, Mass.: Harvard University Press, 1966), p. 265.

27. Richard Freeland, The Truman Doctrine and the Origins of McCarthyism (New York: Alfred A. Knopf, 1972).

28. For a contrary view, see Lisle Rose, After Yalta (New York: Charles Scribner's Sons, 1973).

29. Cf. John Stewart Service, The Amerasia Papers: Some Problems in the History of U.S.-China Relations (Berkeley, Calif.: Center for Chinese Studies, University of California, 1971), pp. 75-135, which emphasizes Ambassador Hurley's departures from Washington's guidelines.

30. Walter Millis, ed., The Forrestal Diaries (New York: Viking Press, 1951).

31. FR, 1946, vol. 9, The Far East: China (Washington, D.C.: 1972), pp. 380, 828-29, 846-47, 1426.

32. Ibid., p. 511.

33. Warren Cohen, America's Response to China: An Interpretive History of Sino-American Relations (New York: John Wiley & Sons, 1971), pp. 173 ff.

34. U.S. Department of State, The Conference of Berlin (Potsdam) (Washington, D.C., 1960), vol. 2, pp. 1225-27, 1241 (hereafter cited as Potsdam Papers).

35. For details of Manchuria's industrial and resource potential, see H. Foster Bain, "Manchuria: A Key Area," Foreign Affairs (October 1946): 106-17.

36. FR, 1946, op. cit., vol. 9, p. 945.

37. Ibid., p. 935.

38. Ibid., p. 941.

39. For a similar though less developed view, see Forrestal's diary entry of November 20, 1945, after the SWNCC discussion on China policy in Millis, ed., op. cit., p. 108.

40. Cohen, op. cit., p. 193.

41. FR, 1944, op. cit., vol. 6, p. 671.

42. Latham, op. cit., pp. 262-63; Service, op. cit., pp. 115-16; Buhite, op. cit., pp. 188-209.

43. For a definition of "ideological thinking," see Morton H. Halperin et al., Bureaucratic Politics and Foreign Policy (Washington, D.C.: Brookings Institution, 1974), pp. 22-23.

44. FR, 1946, op. cit., vol. 9, p. 779. This is a report dated April 15, 1946.

45. Charles F. Romanus and Riley Sunderland, Time Runs Out in CBI (Washington, D.C.: Office of the Chief of Military History, Department of the Army, 1959), p. 584.

46. FR, 1946, op. cit., vol. 9, pp. 427-28.

47. FR, 1946, op. cit., vol. 10, p. 164.

48. Keeley, op. cit., pp. 155, 183.

49. Charles E. Lindblom, "The Science of 'Muddling Through,'" Public Administration Review 19 (1959): 79-88.

50. Jim Peck correctly notes that Tang Tsou's America's Failure in China, op. cit., is shot through with this outlook. See Jim Peck, "America and the Chinese Revolution, 1942-1946: An Interpretation," in American-East Asian Relations: A Survey, ed. Ernest R. May and James C. Thomson, Jr. (Cambridge, Mass.: Harvard University Press, 1972), p. 325.

51. The best study of the Nationalist government during the Nanking decade is Hung-Mao Tien, Government and Politics in Kuomintang China 1927-1937 (Stanford, Calif.: Stanford University Press, 1972). See also Paul K. T. Sih, ed., The Strenuous Decade (New York: St. John's University Press, 1970).

52. James C. Thomson, Jr. , While China Faced West: American Reformers in Nationalist China, 1928-1937 (Cambridge, Mass: 1969), p. 8.

53. See Romanus and Sunderland, op. cit. , p. 382, for the Chinese order of battle as of August 31, 1945. See also Chang Ch'i-yun, K'ang-Jih chan-shih (Taipei, 1966), p. 406.

54. John Paton Davies predicted this as early as 1943: Dragon by the Tail (New York: W. W. Norton, 1972), p. 273.

55. U.S. Department of State, The Conferences of Malta and Yalta (Washington, D.C.: U.S. Government Printing Office, 1955), p. 984.

56. Harry S. Truman, Memoirs (Garden City, N.Y.: Doubleday, 1956), vol. 1, pp. 300-01.

57. Herbert Feis, The China Tangle (Princeton, N.J.: Princeton University Press, 1953), p. 314.

58. Hu chia hu wei.

59. The chief of the Division of Chinese Affairs in the State Department, John Carter Vincent, shared this view. See Potsdam Papers, vol. 2, p. 1242.

60. See Steven I. Levine, "Political Integration in Manchuria, 1945-1949" (Ph.D. dissertation, Harvard University, 1972), chapter 3; FR, 1945, vol. 7, pp. 1227-44, 948-50; Potsdam Papers, pp. 1225-27, 1241.

61. See China White Paper (Stanford, Calif.: Stanford University Press, 1969), pp. 585-87; see also China Handbook 1937-1945 (Stanford, Calif.: Stanford University Press, 1967), pp. 168-69.

62. Feis, op. cit. , pp. 415-16, 397; China White Paper, p.131.

63. Carsun Chang, Third Force in China (New York: Bookman Associate, 1952), pp. 165-66.

64. Chiang Kai-shek, Soviet Russia in China (New York: Farrar, Straus & Giroux, 1957), pp. 147-49; Chiang Ching-kuo, op. cit. , p. 6; Chiang Ching-kuo, Wo-ti fu-ch'in, unpaged.

65. Levine, op. cit. , chap. 2.

66. Mao Tse-tung, "The Situation and Our Policy after the Victory in the War of Resistance against Japan," in Selected Works of Mao Tse-tung (Peking: 1961), vol. 4, pp. 11-22.

67. Tang Tsou, op. cit. , p. 319.

68. Vera Vladimirovna Vishnyakova-Akimova, Two Years in Revolutionary China, 1925-1927 (Cambridge, Mass.: East Asian Research Center, Harvard University, 1971), p. 93.

69. O. Vladimirov and V. Ryazantsev, Stranitsy Politicheskoi Biografii Mao Dze-dung (Moscow: 1969), p. 53; FR, 1946, op. cit. , vol. 9, p. 778.

70. Vladimirov and Ryazantsev, op. cit. , pp. 52-53.

71. Ibid., p. 54; see also S. Sergeichuk, SShA i Kitai 1948-1968 (Moscow: 1969), p. 7.

72. E. Iu. Bogush, Mif ob 'eksporte revoliutsii' i Sovetskaiia vneshniaia politika (Moscow: 1965), p. 99; Cohen, op. cit., p. 182.

73. Bogush, op. cit., p. 108.

74. Pravda, August 31, 1945, p. 4.

75. Feis, op. cit., pp. 377-78; Charles McLane, Soviet Policy and the Chinese Communists, 1931-1946 (New York: Columbia University Press, 1958), p. 216.

76. See Levine, op. cit., chaps. 4 and 5.

77. Gunther Stein, The Challenge of Red China (New York: DaCapo, 1945), pp. 456-57.

78. Cf. Adam Ulam, Expansion and Coexistence (New York: Praeger, 1968), p. 476.

79. James Reardon-Anderson, "Chinese Communist Policy Towards the United States, 1944-1946" (Ph.D. dissertation, Columbia University, 1975).

80. See Kenneth Shewmaker, Americans and Chinese Communists: A Persuading Encounter (Ithaca, N.Y.: Cornell University Press, 1971.

81. FR, 1945, op. cit., p. 277.

82. See Barbara Tuchman, "If Mao Had Gone to Washington," Notes from China (New York: Collier Books, 1972), pp. 77-78, citing documents from the Dixie and Marshall missions.

83. Ibid., pp. 80-111.

84. FR, 1945, op. cit., p. 520.

85. FR, 1946, op. cit., vol. 9, pp. 151-52.

86. Ibid., p. 152.

87. Ibid.

88. Oran R. Young, The Intermediaries: Third Parties in International Crises (Princeton, N.J.: Princeton University Press, 1967), Chap. 3.

89. Thomas Hobbes, Leviathan, Oakeshott edition (Oxford, 1960), p. 102.

90. FR, 1947, vol. 7, The Far East: China, p. 42.

91. U.S., Congress, Senate, Committee on Foreign Relations, The United States and China in 1949-1950, 1973.

92. Karl Deutsch, "External Involvement in Internal War," in Internal War: Problems and Approaches, ed. Harry Eckstein (New York: Free Press, 1964), p. 102. Deutsch speaks of war by proxy, which, however, he fails to establish as conceptually different from an internal war with external involvement.

93. See, for example, Tuchman, op. cit.

PEKING'S PERCEPTIONS OF
SOVIET-AMERICAN RELATIONS
Chün-tu Hsüeh
Robert C. North

INTRODUCTION

During the 1950s and early 1960s, combinations of political, economic, and military power were viewed as critical variables in the foreign relations of the People's Republic of China (PRC); but ideology was widely accepted as the prime motivator of Peking's foreign policies, the overriding determinant of world bipolarity, and China's relations with both the Soviet Union and the United States. The course of events since the 1960s has seriously challenged this view. Changes in relationships among China, the Soviet Union, India, Pakistan, Bangladesh, and other countries suggest that power and related considerations have overridden ideological determinants in a number of critical circumstances.

The purpose of this chapter is to examine against the background of a changing environment some important alterations in how the PRC has tended to perceive U.S.-Soviet relations and how changing perceptions have affected basic interaction patterns among all three countries.

For Marxist-Leninist proponents, whether in Moscow or Peking, the state has been viewed as the instrument of the ruling

This chapter is a revised version of a 1973 preliminary study under the auspices of the California Arms Control and Foreign Policy Seminar, Santa Monica.

class, and its leaders articulate the national interest.* If the ruling class is bourgeois, the state, its values, its purposes, its interests, and its behavior will be shaped accordingly. If, on the other
hand, the ruling class is proletarian, the state will serve as an
instrument of the working class and its behavior will be shaped by
working-class interests.

In line with these fundamental assumptions, the world view of
the Chinese Communist leadership centered originally on the two-
camp theory, which seemed to be consistent with the realities of the
world situation and the policies of the two superpowers in the 1950s.
For practical as well as ideological reasons, Chairman Mao decided
to "lean to one side." The validity of both his perception and policy
was reinforced by the apparent reality of Sino-Soviet solidarity at
the time. Under these circumstances, the imperatives of ideology
seemed to serve realpolitik quite effectively, but once China and the
Soviet Union were in open conflict, how were their disputes to be
accommodated and accounted for within a theory that forced antagonists into one of two carefully defined camps? What, in fact, happened to ideology as world politics moved from bipolarism to
polycentrism?

Clearly, as assumptions behind the two-camp theory were increasingly violated, something had to give. In part, Chinese Communist theoreticians solved the ideological impasse by denouncing
Soviet leaders as revisionists, or even by casting doubt on the proletarian nature of the Russian Revolution itself, just as ideologues
in Moscow dismissed the Chinese Communist revolution as essentially peasant in its character. But then, as ideology and reality
became more and more at odds, the two-camp theory itself was
conveniently shelved in the 1960s, if not completely discarded.
Since then the Chinese Communist have seldom used the term (in the
sense of two blocs) in analyzing international relations.[†] Reacting

---

*According to a Russian view, "Foreign policy is a combina-
tion of the aims and interests pursued and defended by the given
state and its ruling class in its relations with other states, and the
methods and means used by it for the achievement and defense of
these purposes and interests." Furthermore, it is "closely bound
up with character of the social and state system of the states in
question, and it is a direct continuation of domestic policy."[1]

†The Soviet Union continues to uphold the two-camp doctrine.
For a discussion of the revised doctrine of the two camps, see an
article by a Soviet analyst[2] and one by R. Judson Mitchell.[3] According to the Soviet writer, there is no possibility of a "convergence"
between the two social systems. However, the criterion for

to the hostility of the two superpowers toward them, the Chinese
adopted a domestic policy of self-reliance. Influenced by extreme
internal revolutionary fervor during the Cultural Revolution, China
took a hard-line position against "imperialism," "revisionism,"
"reactionaries," and "social imperialists."

In the meantime, U.S. perceptions of monolithic communism
and of Peking's intentions and capabilities had also changed. On
both sides, however, there was a tendency to assimilate the new
perceptions with the old ones, and unconsciously, perhaps, to distort what was seen in such a way as to minimize any conflict with
previous expectations. The "straining toward consistency," a
phenomenon well known to psychologists, persisted. Eventually,
Chinese Communist leaders, perhaps rudely prodded by reality,
became convinced of U.S. sincerity in wanting to end the Vietnam
War and to improve Sino-American relations. These changes in
reality and perception made it possible for President Richard Nixon
to visit Peking in February 1972. In July, Chairman Mao reportedly
told French Foreign Minister Maurice Schumann that the world was
no longer divided into blocs. In April 1974, Peking leaders declared
that the socialist camp was "no longer in existence," and that the
world today actually consisted of three parts, or three worlds, which
were "both interconnected and in contradiction to one another."[4] As
a result of these developments, there have been some corresponding
alterations in Chinese views of U.S.-Soviet relations. Such changes
raise questions about the extent of conflicts between ideology and
national interest.*

---

membership in the socialist camp is adherence to Marxist-Leninist
ideology as interpreted by the CPSU. Third World political systems
that lean in this direction may be provisionally included. All others
are objectively aligned with the capitalist camp. It may be recalled
that the two-camp doctrine of Stalin's day was intimately connected
with the concept of "capitalist encirclement." In 1959, Khrushchev
declared that the capitalist encirclement had come to an end because
of the change in the world balance of power. He introduced the concept of "three camps." The third camp was formed by newly liberated and independent nations after World War II.

*It should be stressed that as a tactical move, it has been per-
missible for Communists to ally with internal bourgeois elements
and compromise with the capitalist states. As Lenin put it, "One
must be able to analyse the situation and the concrete conditions of
each compromise, or of each variety of compromise."[5] In his report to the Tenth National Congress of the Chinese Communist Party
in August 1973, Chou En-lai pointed out that "in both international

In the 1970s, Peking identifies itself with the Third World, with special emphasis against superpowers and their hegemonies. This chapter will examine some pertinent variables and their interaction in order to understand several of the changes that have taken place, or are likely to take place, in China's foreign affairs.

IDEOLOGY AND "REALITY"

A major weakness of ideology as a useful concept for the social sciences stems from the variety of meanings assigned to it.[7] In a broad sense, ideology is the science that deals with the evolution of human ideas. In terms of a more specialized definition, ideologies are "characterized by a high degree of explicitness of formulation over a very wide range of the objects with which they deal," and for their adherents, "there is an authoritative and explicit promulgation." As compared with other patterns of beliefs, they are "relatively highly systematized or integrated around one or a few pre-eminent values, such as salvation, equality or ethnic purity." Consensus and complete individual subservience to the ideology are normally demanded from those who accept it.[8]

According to another definition, ideology consists of "selected or distorted ideas about a social system or a class of social systems when these ideas purport to be factual, and also carry a more or less explicit evaluation of the 'facts.'"[9] A difficulty with such a definition for purposes of disciplined analysis is the problem of subjective bias and the inability of human beings to establish among themselves, beyond any shadow of doubt or controversy, what "true reality" is. By whom are the pertinent ideas perceived as "selected or distorted," and according to whose criteria?

The word "ideology" is often employed disparagingly to characterize an opponent's belief system. As used by Marx and Engels, ideology referred to elaborate beliefs promulgated by the capitalist class in order to justify its favored position in society. Later, the term was frequently used with reference to a set of values determined by irrational or quasirational considerations.[10] In the United States and elsewhere, ideology is used with reference to nazism, fascism, Marxism-Leninism, or the thoughts of Mao Tse-tung.

---

and domestic struggles," one must not forget "necessary struggles" when there is "an alliance with the bourgeoisie," and that one should not forget the "possibility of alliance under given conditions" when "there is a split with the bourgeoisie."[6]

In this chapter the term "ideology" is presumed to mean "a pattern of beliefs and concepts (both factual and normative) which purport to explain complex social phenomena with a view to directing and simplifying sociopolitical choices facing individuals and groups."[11] An ideology might thus refer to any widely shared and socially or legally sanctioned body of assumptions, expectations, or other perceptions, as well as values and imperatives, about the universe, man's role and purpose in it, and man's proper relations with his fellowman. As thus defined, almost any society may be said to possess an ideology, but in some countries, particularly in those inspired and organized by Marxist-Leninist doctrine, the ideology tends to be more highly rationalized and cohesive than in others. It is regularly interpreted, reviewed, and reinterpreted by persons in authority, and adherence to its major imperatives is often enforced by Party or government sanctions.

Any given ideology must be fundamentally dependent upon and shaped by a wide range of human perceptions about the nature of man and the workings of the universe. Without perceptions of the past, the present, and various possible futures, ideology could not exist. Indeed, no human being, beggar or king, has informational contact with his environment at all, or even with himself, except through his nervous system. This is true of leaders and citizenry in any country. In these terms, prevailing assumptions, expectations, values and imperatives--the foundations of any ideology--are dependent upon and shaped by a wide range of perceptions about the nature and workings of human beings and of the larger universe.

What human beings perceive as "reality" appears to be so solid and unmistakable that it is difficult for national leaders and others to recognize the extent to which that "reality" is inferred by them and their advisers and "may not match the reality which future events reveal."[12] Thus, in many ways, national leaders, like all other human beings, construct the reality in which, day by day, they actually operate.[13] There are, as a result, as many subjective realities as there are individual perceivers, although many such constructs may overlap sufficiently to permit broad consensus and collective action.[14]

Human perceptions are notoriously fallible. Indeed, a perception may be viewed as a "choice" or a "guess" about the true nature of whatever is perceived.[15] A person's accuracy of guess or choice may be influenced by idiosyncratic experience, faulty memory, "false" belief based on past experience or indoctrination, fatigue, anxiety, fear, uncertainty, expectation, hope, and a wide range of other considerations. Normally, "The perception that actually occurs is the one that requires the least reorganization of the person's other ideas." But if an environmental change is sufficiently unmistakable and its implications sufficiently overwhelming, a considerable and possibly quite painful reorganization of belief may be difficult to resist. Because of the mediating function of perception, it follows, therefore, that as ideology may affect events, so also events may affect ideology. The two tend to be intensely interactive.[16]

As long as the assumptions, expectations, and other perceptions embodied in a prevailing belief system and acted upon by the national leadership are not critically at variance with reality, that ideology may be expected to exert a strong influence upon policy and behavior. To the extent that conditions and events of the objective environment persistently challenge a prevailing ideology, on the other hand, disturbing tensions and uncertainties are likely to be generated, and if the discrepancies increase in frequency and importance, at least some elements of the belief system will tend to be reinterpreted, modified, or replaced--especially if the implications of the environmental alterations are too pressing to be ignored.[17] Under such circumstances, however, there is likely to be a lag of months or perhaps years between the point where the first discrepancies become evident to the leadership and the time when major ideological reinterpretations, modifications, or replacements are undertaken. During this period, changes in policy and behavior that are considered indispensable may be rationalized as temporary measures or in other ways until such time as the leaders and/or their constituents are psychologically ready for the needed ideological adjustments. Thus, radical changes in the environment, critical alterations in the international configuration of power, for example, can so widen the gap between reality and belief as to render prevailing ideologies obsolete and force policy changes that may run counter to the most fundamental ideological assumptions and tenets.

TWO VIEWS OF THE TWO-CAMP THEORY

The standard theme in Marxist-Leninist doctrine, that the world is divided into two hostile and irreconcilable camps--the socialist camp and the capitalist or imperialist camp--was shared by the Soviet and the Chinese Communists for a long time. Until the end of the 1950s, the Chinese supported the Soviets in opposing the capitalist camp, headed by the United States, and they consistently backed the Soviet Union in its dealings with the other Communist states and parties. The policy of "leaning to one side" declared by Mao Tse-tung in July 1949 and the 1950 Sino-Soviet treaty of military alliance were, in considerable part, the outcome of this Chinese world view, but it may have been derived also from the attitudes and policies of other countries, especially the United States, where many people tended to share the fundamental perception that the world was indeed divided into two camps.

During World War II, however, and even immediately after, views on both sides had been much more flexible. Some American observers recently suggested that if Mao or Chou En-lai had been invited to visit the United States in early 1945, or if John Leighton Stuart, United States ambassador to the Nationalist government, had gone to Peking in June 1949,[18] the People's Republic of China might have leaned somewhat differently, or possibly walked upright between the two sides. Under such circumstances, it would have been difficult to conceive of the Peking regime, whether in a geopolitical context or in terms of economic and military power, as a realistic threat to the United States.

To argue the "if's" of history is often a useless pastime, but is it conceivable that Chinese Communist foreign policy may have been influenced by Washington, above, beyond, or aside from the proclaimed Marxist-Leninist-Maoist ideology? Admittedly, the friendly gestures of the Chinese Communists toward the United States in 1944-45 were made when they were engaged in a power struggle with the Nationalists, and according to Mao himself, Stalin did not begin to trust him until after the outbreak of the Korean War.[19]

It would have been to the advantage of the Chinese Communist leaders if they could have gained contact with or support from the United States during 1944-45 because of "political effects on the Kuomintang."[20] Given the situation of the United States in World War II, one might not have expected Washington to shift its support from a recognized, legitimate, allied government to encompass the Communist movement. Yet the United States did go out of its way to endorse the Communist demand for a coalition government in China --a fact that many liberal critics of U.S. policy seem to have forgotten.[21] One may argue, perhaps, that if President Harry Truman had approved Ambassador Stuart's proposed trip to Peking, relations between the two countries in subsequent years might have been different. Against this background, it is worth speculating on the extent of the influence of the attitude of the United States in May and June 1949 on Mao's policy of "leaning to one side," which he expounded in July.

Even as late as August 22, 1949, the National Security Council accepted the view that Chinese Communist success in surmounting their internal difficulties--overpopulation, undeveloped natural resources, technical backwardness, and social and political lag-- might well lessen rather than intensify their subservience to the Kremlin. Similarly, a Chinese Communist failure to achieve a viable economy might force the Peking government to depend more, rather than less, on the USSR.[22] The National Security Council also conceded that any attempt on the part of the United States "openly" to deny Chinese territory such as Formosa to the Communists would probably react to the benefit of the Communists by rallying all the anti-foreign sentiments to their side."[23]

Four months later, on the other hand, after Communist power had been established on the Chinese mainland, the joint chiefs of staff informed the National Security Council that "a modest, well-directed and closely supervised program of military advice and assistance to the anti-Communist government in Formosa would be in the security interests of the United States."[24] This partial and still somewhat tentative shift in position was an early indicator of what became, with the outbreak of the Korean War, a generally consistent and hostile policy toward the People's Republic and a broad containment policy which, in Asia at least, leaned heavily upon an assumption of Sino-Soviet collaboration.

The fundamental shifts in United States perceptions, assumptions, and policies are documented in the Government Printing Office edition of the (so-called) Pentagon Papers. Essentially, during the early 1950s, policy makers in Washington were apprehensive lest the United States find itself confronted with an alignment of the USSR, Communist China, and a rehabilitated Japan. In the weeks that immediately followed the close of World War II, the USSR, as viewed by the National Security Council, had become an Asian power of the first magnitude "with expanding influence and interests throughout continental Asia and into the Pacific."[25] As perceived from Washington, however, the Soviet Union could not build "a powerful, self-sufficient, war-making complex in Asia without access to and control over Japan."[26]*

With the outbreak of the Korean War in June 1950, U.S. leaders feared that Communist expansion on the Asian mainland, by denying Western-Japanese access to rice, tin, iron ore, rubber, oil, tungsten, fibers, and other vital resources of Asia, would drive Japan into the Soviet-Chinese bloc.† For without such vital raw

---

*Many eminent scholars have been reluctant to accept this explanation of United States policies in Asia, and undoubtedly there were other considerations involved. But these documents from the National Security Council reveal the importance of the interdependency of resources and strategy in the influencing of United States policy.

†In these terms, Indochina was of much greater strategic importance than Korea--and critical to U.S. security interests.[27]

materials and markets, acquired under one guarantee or another, Japan could not maintain a tolerable living standard, let alone thrive and grow. The denial of Soviet--and by extension, Chinese and other Communist countries--access to Southeast Asia and other parts of the Asian mainland thus became an indispensable prerequisite for the successful barring of Soviet influence and control over a potentially revitalized and highly productive Japan.

In this way, the resource requirements of Japan and the strategic interests of the United States (as both were perceived in the National Security Council) became powerful elements in the complex blend of motivations that drove the concerns and activities of the United States deeper and deeper into eastern and Southeast Asia. These considerations also contributed to the American version of the two-camp theory in that the United States required a rationalization and public justification for its Asian policy and activities.*

In its Communist and non-Communist versions of the two-camp theory, each side was thus provided with a persuasive explanation of events as they unfolded in Asia during the 1950s and provided the leadership concerned with convenient rationalizations for their policies and actions. In effect, each bloc acted like the mirror image of the other. On the one hand, China and the United States were at war in Korea, and at times it looked as though U.S. forces might cross the Yalu River to overthrow the new regime on the Chinese mainland. On the other hand, the Peking government had a pressing need for Russian economic and military aid, and there was at least an appearance of Sino-Soviet solidarity. Reciprocating Peking's hostility, the United States denounced the PRC as aggressive and expansionist and as an instrument of the Soviet Union. After the Korean armistice in 1953, Washington continued to deny the legitimacy of the Peking government, maintained an isolation and containment policy against it, and blocked it from taking its seat in the United Nations. As late as 1957, Secretary of State John

---

*This latter consideration does not mean that leaders in Washington merely "invented" an ideology to deceive the public and cover up their concern for strategic, resource, and other critical factors. Nor does it necessarily deny the reality of Soviet ambitions in Asia. Rather, it documents the intense interconnections between ideological and other, more pragmatic factors. Given the world situation, the assumptions, expectations, perceptions, and other elements of the "ideology" came easily to many of the leaders themselves and it seems quite probable that few of them ever fully distinguished in their own minds between the various factors contributing to their motivations.[28]

Foster Dulles still asserted that communism in China was a passing phase.[29] Misinterpretations of the intentions of leaders in Peking and overestimation of China's capability even prompted discussion in the United States of the possibility and desirability of allying with the Soviet Union against the Chinese, a subject with an undertone of racism.[30] Through their stubborn adherence to a set of basic assumptions and to the respective policies that seemed to flow from them, the Cold War partisans on both sides tended to create their own outcomes almost in defiance of underlying "reality."

Just as the United States persisted in denying legitimacy to the Peking government for more than a decade after the Sino-Soviet conflict became publicly manifest, so China clung to the idea of two camps long after it ceased to approximate world realities. Although the Sino-Soviet dispute had its beginnings in Nikita Khrushchev's secret speech denouncing Stalin at the Twentieth Party Congress in February 1956, the two-camp theory was reaffirmed by Mao when he talked to the Chinese students in Moscow in November 1957.[31] As late as spring 1959, Chinese leaders and writers were still discussing international politics in terms of "two worlds."[32] Yet the doctrine of two hostile and irreconcilable camps had already come into question.

The uncertainty stemmed from the interaction of a number of factors. The turning point was Khrushchev's visit to the United States for talks with President Dwight D. Eisenhower in September 1959, which took place shortly after the Soviet government had abrogated unilaterally the 1957 Sino-Soviet agreement on new technology for national defense and refused to provide the Chinese with a sample atomic bomb or technical data concerning its manufacture. The Chinese, perceiving the Soviet action as a gift to the United States, reciprocated by an invitation to the Soviet premier to visit the country.[33]

Under such circumstances, the Chinese may have concluded that the two camps were not really as irreconcilable as had originally been thought. The theory became even more untenable as the Sino-Soviet dispute intensified and the U.S.-Soviet detente further developed in the 1960s. As a theoretical basis for the new situation, the Chinese hurled charges of Soviet revisionism. The argument was that the rise to power of revisionism signals the rise to power of the bourgeoisie and the emergence of common interests between that privileged class and U.S. capitalists.[34]

CHINESE VIEWS OF SOVIET-U.S. RELATIONS

During the 1960s, Chinese views of Soviet-American relations centered on the following themes: collaboration, collusion, alliance,

encirclement of China, superpowers, nuclear plot, struggle for
hegemony, capitulation on the part of the Soviet Union, the superpowers colluding and at the same time contending with each other,
and the Soviet Union as an accomplice of U.S. policies. Some of
these themes were briefly mentioned in the early 1960s when the
Chinese Communist party and the Communist party of the Soviet
Union began to engage in polemics. During the Cultural Revolution
(1966-69), the Chinese elaborated on all of them.

In the celebrated Nine Articles (September 1963-July 1964),
commenting on the Open Letter of the Central Committee of the
Communist Party of the Soviet Union, the Chinese began to attack
explicitly Khrushchev's line of "Soviet-U.S. cooperation for the
settlement of world problems." They criticized Soviet leaders for
being "intoxicated with the idea of the two 'superpowers' establishing
spheres of influence throughout the world." The Soviet leadership
was accused of being "increasingly anxious to strike political bar-
gains" with the United States at the expense of the interests of the
socialist camp and the international communist movement. The
Cuban missile crisis was cited as an outstanding example of the
Soviet "error of capitulationism."

Chinese Communist apprehensions about Soviet-American relations were exacerbated by the escalation of the Vietnam War, by
the increasingly hostile and militant Soviet attitude toward Peking,
and by insecurities, frustrations, and suspicions generated by the
Cultural Revolution.[35] Encirclement and collusion became the
themes most frequently mentioned in the Chinese press and by the
Peking leaders.[36] As viewed from Peking, the United States already
had many military bases around mainland China--in Taiwan, Japan,
South Vietnam, and the SEATO countries, such as Thailand and the
Philippines. Now the United States was seen as shifting the emphasis
of its global strategy step by step from Europe to Asia in order to
complete its "arc of encirclement."[37] At the same time, Soviet
Russia was not only going out of its way to bring about detente in
Europe but was also vigorously encouraging and supporting the resurgence of Japanese militarism.[38]

Since there remained some cracks and breaches in the "cor-
don," Soviet leaders came forward to patch them up, making India,
Mongolia, and other countries the flanks in the encirclement of
China. Vice President Hubert Humphrey's meeting with Alexei
Kosygin in New Delhi in January 1966 was viewed by the Chinese as
a Soviet-U.S.-Indian "united front against China."[39]

Soviet Foreign Minister A. A. Gromyko's visit to Japan in
July 1966 "close on the heels" of Secretary of State Dean Rusk was
seen by Peking as a "new counter-revolutionary 'Holy Alliance'" of

the United States, Japan, and the Soviet Union.* One writer considered that the "Soviet-Japanese collusion" was "the extension of U.S.-Japan collusion, a variation of U.S.-Soviet collaboration, and a product of America's imperialist policy of containment of China."[41] And the Japan-U.S. joint communique after the Sato-Nixon meeting in November 1969 was denounced by Premier Chou En-lai as a "new stage" in the "military collusion" between the United States and Japan.[42]

Soviet activities in Southeast Asia--shipping munitions to Rangoon, increasing Soviet naval strength in the Indian Ocean, supporting the Suharto government in Indonesia, establishing diplomatic relations with Singapore and Malaysia, encouraging the Vietnam peace talks, and bringing about the Indo-Pakistan rapprochement-- were all perceived as part of Moscow's efforts to organize an anti-China ring in collaboration with the United States. The Chinese concluded that the United States no longer regarded the Soviet Union as an enemy, but looked upon it as a friend.[43] The Soviet leadership had ceased to support the world revolution and had become an accomplice of the United States in suppressing peoples' revolutions the world over.†

Closely associated with the development of the cordon, as Peking saw it, was a network of specific Soviet-American collaborative undertakings and collusions. Specific charges within the framework of the collusion theme were often repeated by the Chinese press throughout 1967 and 1968.[47] In regard to Vietnam, Soviet leaders were accused of placing the Vietnam question within the framework of Soviet-American cooperation and of easing the European situation so that the United States could transfer more of its troops to Vietnam.

---

*In the words of the People's Daily Observer, "the Soviet Union is not only going out of its way to bring about a 'detente' in Europe but is also vigorously supporting and encouraging the all-round resurgence of Japanese militarism and its ambitions for overseas expansion in Asia."[40]

†In his speech at the reception given in Peking by the Albanian ambassador to China on November 29, 1966, marking the twenty-second anniversary of Albanian liberation, Premier Chou En-lai accused the Soviet Union of being an accomplice of U.S. imperialism. On more than one occasion, Chou ridiculed the Soviet leadership as "busy running errands" for the United States.[44] A detailed analysis of American global strategy in February 1968 condemned the Soviet's "notorious activities as the No. 1 accomplice of U.S. imperialism."[45] This theme had been stated by Foreign Minister Ch'en Yi in his speech to the Peking masses.[46]

Soviet policy toward North Vietnam was "sham support and real betrayal," plotting and peddling various kinds of "peace talk frauds," and scheming to use so-called "united action" to control North Vietnam and to sow dissension between the Chinese and Vietnamese peoples in order to undermine their military unity. [48]

Soviet leaders were charged with carrying out a "policy of three-fold assistance": to help the United States promote the "peace fraud," escalate the war, and encourage "anti-China madness" in the United States. The Chinese interpreted the Soviet occupation of Czechoslovakia as a "political dirty deal" between the superpowers. According to a Chinese commentary, the occupation of Czechoslovakia was carried out "with tacit U.S. consent" in return for "the tacit consent and support" of America's war in Vietnam. [49]

Chinese views of the United States and the Soviet Union in the Middle East reflected the idea that the two superpowers apparently had agreed to work toward preventing a direct military confrontation, but otherwise they remained in conflict in that area. The various proposals the two countries submitted in 1967-69 to settle Middle East issues were considered by the Chinese as the basis for "collusion and bargaining between imperialism and social imperialism." [50] The Chinese accused the Soviet Union of forcing the Arab countries to seek peace with Israel by giving up territories and stamping out the flames of the Palestinian people's armed struggle, [51] thus directly serving "U.S. imperialism and its tool of aggression, Israel." [52]

Until the Peking government represented China in the United Nations, the world organization was often treated by Peking with scorn. It was frequently considered to be an instrument of the United States, an organ "in the service of old and new colonialism," "a vile place for a few powers to share the spoils," [53] and a "U.S.-Soviet political stock market." [54] The Chinese accused the Soviet representative at the U.N. General Assembly of "attempting to bring the Korean question into the orbit of Soviet-U.S. collaboration for world domination." [55] At one time the Peking leaders even suggested the establishment of a "revolutionary United Nations." [56]

As is well known, one of the main reasons for the Sino-Soviet dispute was the Soviet failure to live up to its commitments to assist China's nuclear development. [57] The late Foreign Minister Ch'en Yi reportedly said that China must have atomic bombs even if the Chinese people do not have pants to wear. Peking viewed the Soviet agreement with the United States on the prevention of nuclear proliferation as a plot to monopolize nuclear weapons and collusion in the conspiracy against China's security. The partial nuclear test ban was denounced as "nuclear blackmail" [58] and a "big fraud," [59] aimed at "tying China's hands." [60] The 1967 draft treaty on the

nonproliferation of nuclear weapons was attacked by Peking as a
"major step" in Soviet-American "collaboration on a worldwide
scale" and "another treacherous crime" committed to contain China's
influence abroad. [61]

China refused to sign the 1968 Nuclear Non-Proliferation
Treaty. In the first public Chinese reaction to the strategic arms
limitation treaties (SALT), signed between the United States and the
Soviet Union during President Nixon's visit to Moscow in May 1972,
Premier Chou En-lai reportedly argued that the treaties actually
marked the beginning of a new stage of the arms race between the
two superpowers. [62]

INTERACTION OF PERCEPTION, REALITY, AND POLICY

To what extent did Chinese views correspond to the realities
of Soviet-American relations in the 1960s? How did Peking leaders
respond to world events as they perceived them? How did their
perception, the real-world situation, and Chinese foreign policy
interact?

It is not necessary to examine each Chinese allegation of
Soviet-U.S. collusion, nor is it possible, in view of the limited information available, to discuss the private beliefs of leaders in
Peking as opposed to their official views, the differing opinions on
crucial issues, or the variance between public statements and those
expressed in secret channels. But public statements provide useful
indicators, however rough, of Chinese official views at any given
time.

An examination of public statements from Peking suggests that
some were rationally calculated to create particular impressions at
home or abroad; some were based on misperceptions, the outcome
of self-isolation; and some were not much more than ideological
rhetoric. But even when careful allowance is made for considerations of this kind, it seems evident that many of the views held by
Chinese leaders were not unfounded. From the perspective of an
observer in Peking, the People's Republic was indeed being en-
circled--by U.S. forces in Japan, Taiwan, Southeast Asia, and
South Asia, and by the USSR along a vast perimeter from Sakhalin
to Western Siberia and to some extent from Afghanistan to the Indian
Ocean and even North Vietnam. And Chinese fears of attack, including a possible Soviet preemptive strike, were not entirely unjustified.

Against the background of the Sino-Soviet controversy, overtures of the USSR toward Japan could only deepen Chinese anxieties.

Japan had always been considered by the Chinese as the core of the U.S. military alliance in Asia and the hub of its ring of encirclement of China. Thus, it was not until Prime Minister Kakuei Tanaka's visit to the People's Republic and the establishment of diplomatic relations between the two countries in September 1972 that Peking changed its attitude toward the Japanese government. Since then, the Chinese press's attacks on Japanese militarism have been conspicuously absent--an illustration of how perceptions of national leaders, reality, and the policies of other countries can interact.

However misconceived the Chinese collusion theory may have appeared from the perspective of Washington or Moscow, there was an element of reality in it, as more recent events have made evident. Both superpowers have been in favor of maintaining the status quo in the world, and each has given up attempting to interfere in the other's sphere of influence. In the Taiwan Straits crisis in 1958 and in the Sino-Indian conflicts in 1959 and 1962, Washington and Moscow had a parallel interest in preventing a deterioration of those conflicts into direct confrontations; at times, they even found themselves on the same side of the barricade, with Peking on the other side. This policy of restraint held through the later 1960s (for example, West Berlin, the Wall, Cuba, Czechoslovakia). Even some Europeans have harbored misgivings similar to those of the Chinese. In his April 1969 press conference, President Nixon mentioned that he had found concern on the part of European countries about the possibility of a "U.S.-Soviet condominium" in which, at the highest level, the two superpowers would make decisions affecting Europe's future. One European statesman used the term "Yalta" in his conversation with the president. [63] And today it appears that on many dimensions of their activities, Soviet-American restraints of the past are providing a basis for new, more explicit cooperation.

During the Cultural Revolution, some of the anxieties and hard-line policies of the Chinese Communists were outcomes of the country's domestic struggle. But three major events that took place at that time undoubtedly reinforced Chinese attitudes: the United States escalation of the Vietnam War, dating from 1965; the Soviet invasion of Czechoslovakia in August 1968; and the Sino-Soviet border clashes of March and August 1969.

Chinese leaders were concerned that the Vietnam War might lead to a military confrontation between China and the United States. A strategic response to such an eventuality was indicated by Premier Chou En-lai. In an interview given to a Pakistani correspondent in April 1966, Chou made it quite clear that China would not take the initiative to provoke a war with the United States. But once war broke out, it would not be contained or limited. [64]

With regard to the role of the USSR in Vietnam, Soviet leaders were virtually compelled to support North Vietnam and oppose the United States for reasons of solidarity with a Communist state and of competition with China.* But apparently they wanted to avoid an open-ended involvement that would endanger basic Soviet-American relations and their global interests. In his press conference on March 4, 1969, President Nixon asserted that the USSR was in a very delicate position, that the Soviet government had been helpful in terms of getting the Paris peace talks started, and that the Russians would like to use what influence they appropriately could to help bring the war to a conclusion.[66]

As to the nuclear issue, it was apparent to the Chinese that the United States and the Soviet Union were engaged in a nuclear arms race while at the same time sharing a common interest in maintaining nuclear superiority. To break the nuclear monopoly of the two superpowers, China assigned a high priority to the production of its own nuclear weapons through self-reliance. Until the Sino-Soviet controversy, Peking had consistently supported Moscow's position on nuclear negotiations. The dispute was intensified when the Soviet Union proceeded to negotiate the partial nuclear test ban treaty with the United States.

Through the development of limited nuclear capability, the Peking government greatly altered its position in the international configuration of power with the result that it no longer felt the need, as it did in the mid-1950s, for the protection of another country's nuclear umbrella.

Peking's policy statements on the subject of nuclear weaponry have undergone no basic changes despite China's successful nuclear development in recent years, partly because the nuclear policy of the superpowers vis-a-vis China has remained essentially the same and partly because China's buildup has not reached the level of full deterrent capability to protect national security. While some of the Chinese proposals--total prohibition of nuclear weapons and the dismantling of nuclear bases on foreign soil--may be considered unrealistic and rhetorical, to date China is the only nuclear power that has declared that it will never, at any time or under any circumstances, be the first to use nuclear bombs.[67]

The word "collusion" suggests an explicit intention that is difficult to identify in the documentation available. In many respects

---

*Harrison E. Salisbury has observed: "I had long been certain that had it not been for the Sino-Soviet confrontation, the Russians would long since have traded off their Vietnam position for large-scale wheat or machinery sales by the United States."[65]

the Soviet-American detente had little to do with China, but undoubtedly the Soviet Union and the United States had parallel interests,
as well as the common interest in keeping China at arm's length.[68]
As viewed from Peking, however, parallel actions of the two superpowers amounted to collusion. Irrespective of either side's intention, U.S.-Soviet collusion--or, at any rate, parallelism--took
shape whenever the vital interests of the two countries demanded it.

Given the perceptions maintained by Chinese leaders of a "new
Holy Alliance" against China, their belief that revolution was the
main trend in the world, and their assumption that all political forces
were undergoing a process of upheaval, division, and reorganization,
their response to this perceived situation took the form of opposing
simultaneously the United States, the Soviet Union, and reactionaries
all over the world.[69] The Peking leadership also actively supported
national liberation movements in Asia, the Middle East, Africa, and
Latin America--the "storm center" and "first intermediate zone"
separating the United States from socialist countries.*

A NEW REALITY

"When the extreme is reached, the reverse will set in." During the early 1970s, this old Chinese saying proved applicable even
to Communist dialectics. Peking's extreme and inflexible policy
could not long be sustained after consolidation of the domestic
struggle and in the midst of other changes that were taking place.
The policy violated the most elementary rules of diplomacy.

After the Sino-American rapprochement and changes in Peking's attitude toward the Vietnam War, the Chinese no longer accused the Soviet Union of being America's accomplice in the war.
In fact, during 1972, Chinese comments on the war hardly mentioned
the Soviet Union. On the other hand, by the end of the 1960s the
United States had abandoned, in part at least, its previous justification of the war in terms of containing Chinese expansion. Instead,
ironically enough, President Nixon's trip to Peking was partially

---

*The concept of the "intermediate zone" was originally applied
to the international scene by Mao in his talk with Anna Louise Strong
in August 1946: "The United States and the Soviet Union are separated by a vast zone which includes many capitalist, colonial and
semi-colonial countries in Europe, Asia and Africa."[70] It was revived in 1964 in the context of an attempt to build the "Third Force"
in world politics, based on anti-imperialism and Gaullism. The
first intermediate zone is the Third World.

rationalized in terms of seeking Peking's support for ending the war. When an agreement was finally signed in January 1973, both Peking and Moscow endorsed it.

For generations classic writers in the field of diplomacy have maintained with considerable consistency that the foreign policies and external activities of any country, but especially those of a great power, are likely to be explained best in terms of the struggle for survival, the maximizing of power, and the defense of national interests.[71] For two decades after World War II, the international configuration of power did not seem to change significantly: the world remained essentially bipolar. Then the entire system underwent rapid alterations in the direction of multipolarity. To some extent this new trend was the result of a decline of United States power, nationalism, and the emergence of many new nations and to some extent it was attributable to the remarkable rise of Japan. But developments inside the People's Republic of China, new needs and problems within the Soviet Union, and outcomes of competitions and conflicts between Peking and Moscow were probably of even greater importance.

Although General Eisenhower had told President-elect John F. Kennedy that any change in China policy by the incoming administration would bring him out of retirement fighting, Washington began to show signs of flexibility toward the People's Republic under the Kennedy Administration.[72] The various friendly, if sporadic, gestures by the United States toward Peking since 1962 are so well known that there is no need to retell them here. Suffice it to say that at first the Chinese were suspicious of the new signals from Washington;[73] but by the end of 1970 they finally were convinced of United States' sincerity in wanting to end the Vietnam War, to avoid taking sides in the Sino-Soviet dispute, and to improve Sino-American relations. Chairman Mao decided to welcome President Nixon to visit China.[74]

The alteration of the world configuration that began in the late 1960s and early 1970s also can be explained in considerable part by such objective factors as the relatively successful integration and domestic growth of China in spite of the "Great Leap Forward" and other setbacks; the Chinese capacity for self-reliance and for considerable self-sufficiency in terms of many basic resources; the increased need within the People's Republic of new equipment, replacement parts, and specialized technologies, especially as time passed after the disruption of Soviet technical assistance programs; the achievement and continuing development of a Chinese nuclear capability; the erosion of United States efforts in Vietnam and elsewhere as a result of fatigue, frustration, and competing domestic requirements; Soviet failures in agriculture and the growing Soviet

need for new, highly refined technologies; and the rapid growth of
Japan in terms of industry, commerce, and specialized, refined
technologies that, along with those of the United States, West Germany, and elsewhere, were in demand by the USSR and increasingly
by China. All of these factors seem to have contributed to an alteration in relative capabilities and power among the countries, the
generation of new demands, and a groping toward new relationships.

For much of the nineteenth century and well into the twentieth,
China had been characterized by a population that was large (relative to readily available resources) and growing; a technology that
lagged in comparison with the West; and vulnerability to economic,
political, and military penetration by Western powers and later by
Japan. In order to rectify these weaknesses, the society somehow
had to accumulate capital, mobilize labor and resources, and develop
new capabilities. During the early 1950s, the Peking government,
with considerable reliance upon Soviet technical assistance, developed a program along these lines that involved tight government
control of production, minimal consumer consumption, and strict
regulation of priorities.

There were serious weaknesses in the Chinese Communist
program, but over the long run it was sufficiently successful, even
after the "Great Leap Forward" and the withdrawal of large-scale
Soviet assistance, to place the People's Republic in the running as a
major world power. Between 1961 and 1970, the percent of change
in the gross national product of the People's Republic was 114.3 (as
compared with 89.5 for the United States, 101.2 for the USSR, and
71.5 for India). The average rate of change over the same years
was 8.8 (as compared with 7.2 for the United States, 8.1 for the
USSR, and 6.2 for India). In economic strength, the People's Republic by 1970 ranked seventh in the world (after the United States,
the USSR, Japan, West Germany, France, and the United Kingdom);
as a military power, it ranked third (after the United States and the
USSR).[75]

The basic assumptions underlying United States attitudes toward China and much of the rest of Asia during the late 1940s and
early 1950s have been touched upon earlier. Once these assumptions
had been made explicit in top echelons of the government, the reason-
ing behind the domino theory and the justification for the expansion
of United States power and influence on the Asian mainland became
difficult to refute. The Sino-Soviet conflict, the rapid growth of a
Western-Oriental Japan, the Chinese Communist achievement of
nuclear weaponry, and the failure of the United States to force a
decisive outcome anywhere on the Asian continent combined to cast
doubt upon the underlying premises, however, and by the late 1960s,
the cost of American involvement was beginning to erode public

support. It was no longer clear what the country's purpose was, and there were growing anxieties about where it might lead.

The Soviet antagonist, meanwhile, was suffering difficulties of its own. The Chinese had largely repudiated Moscow's leadership of the Communist world and were competing for influence over many local movements. And, viewed from Moscow, Chinese progress in the development of nuclear weaponry posed a new threat to the USSR along its eastern borders. The consideration that, in view of the superior military power of the Soviet Union, it is difficult for outsiders to understand this "threat" does not decrease its potency. Perhaps it is akin to the "threat" that Japan felt about a regenerate China in the 1930s and the United States about the PRC for two decades after World War II. Aggressive, stronger powers often feel that they are being threatened while overlooking the fact that they are actually threatening others.

There were further difficulties. Confronted by new failures in the agricultural sector and by a rapidly growing need for highly specialized Western (and Japanese) technologies, the Soviet Union was reaching toward the United States, Japan, West Germany, and elsewhere on the basis of increased trade and technical exchange agreements.

As an outcome of its remarkable postwar recovery and its spectacular economic growth during the late 1950s and early 1960s, Japan has begun to play a pivotal role, being in a position to supply both the USSR and the People's Republic with technology, machinery, and parts in exchange for basic resources. At the same time, however, the dependence of Japan upon raw materials and markets beyond its borders makes the country deeply dependent upon unbroken trade access and favorable exchange in many parts of the world. In this sense, the economic well-being of Japan depends to a large extent upon the skill of the Japanese in maintaining viable relations not only with the United States but also with the USSR and the People's Republic of China--a difficult feat in the best of circumstances.

The infrastructural changes that have come about in relations among the People's Republic, the United States, the USSR, Japan, and other countries are suggested by the sharp change in trade patterns during the 1960s and early 1970s. As late as 1957, Communist countries were receiving 72 percent of China's exports, and their own goods accounted for 66 percent of Chinese imports. These relationships contrasted sharply with the 28 percent of Chinese exports received by non-Communist countries and the 34 percent of Chinese imports accounted for by non-Communist countries. By 1966, these patterns had been sharply reversed, however, and they have continued to be so since. Thus, in 1970, only 25 percent of China's exports were being received by Communist countries, as opposed to 75 percent by non-Communist nations. And a mere 15 percent of China's imports were supplied by Communist countries as contrasted with 85 percent supplied by non-Communist nations.[76]

Amidst these many changes leaders in Peking began to realize that neither their perceptions nor the policy based on them conformed entirely to reality on the world scene. Some major reassessments were required. Presumably, a dramatic change in relations with the United States was not the only option available to the Chinese Communists. Peking might have sought an accommodation with the USSR and the reestablishment of comradely relations. But Mao seems not to have trusted the Soviet leadership. Moreover, in historic, geopolitical, and other terms, the Soviet threat to the People's Republic appeared both more real and more imminent than that of the United States. In addition, a Sino-Soviet rapprochement would not have enabled Peking to solve the Taiwan problem, which remained an important issue in the unification of China. Solution of that problem is dependent upon reaching an understanding with the United States.[77]

The ping-pong diplomacy of April 1971 opened a new trend in Sino-American relations. Many Western commentators have inferred that the Chinese may have viewed the Nixon visit as analogous to the payment of tribute by foreign barbarians to the court of the Middle Kingdom. This comparison amounts to one of those far-fetched and misleading attempts at explanation made by those who tend to account for the China of today almost wholly in terms of the past. Perhaps Mao's meeting with Chiang Kai-shek in Chungking for peace negotiations after World War II is a more appropriate analogy, except that in the case of Nixon's visit it was a president of the United States who made the journey to negotiate. In any case, the Nixon visit to Peking undercut the Chinese charge of Soviet-U.S. collusion in the encirclement of China, and since then, that theme has seldom been mentioned in the Chinese press or in official government statements. Peking kept silent on President Nixon's summit conference in Moscow in May 1972,* and Premier Chou En-lai made only a passing remark about Leonid Brezhnev's visit to the United States in June 1973.[78]

---

*However, on the day of Nixon's departure for the Soviet Union on May 20, 1972, the People's Daily prominently carried an article written by a group of workers condemning the two powers as the "arch-criminals" in modern time. While the commentary made no mention of Nixon's trip, it reiterated the theme that the two superpowers were colluding and at the same time contending with each other for world domination, and that the Third World had formed a united front against the two "paper tigers."

However, the collusion charge made a brief reappearance in November,[79] and again in Chou's report to the Tenth Party Congress in August 1973. Chou's major theme was that the two superpowers were colluding and at the same time contending with each other for world hegemony. However, "contention is absolute and protracted, whereas collusion is relative and temporary."[80] He also introduced for the first time the theme that the Soviet Union was "making a feint to the East while attacking in the West."* Thus the perceived Soviet threat was shifted from China to Europe, which has been considered by the Chinese as the "focus of superpower contention."

A content analysis of the Peking Review for 1974-76 suggests that Peking virtually has abandoned the collusion theme, at least for the time being. However, Chou En-lai's other themes have since been reiterated on numerous occasions. Beginning with the 1974 New Year's Message, Peking has stressed the contending aspect of Soviet-American relations, repeatedly attempted to expose the falsehood and myth of detente, and linked superpowers with hegemony.[82] In the view of the Peking leaders, "detente is a superficial phenomenon," used by the Soviet Union to "hoodwink the people, lull the vigilance of the adversary, divide Western Europe and dominate the world." It lulls the West by creating a false sense of security. However, the "stark reality is not that detente has developed to a new stage, but that the danger of a new world war is mounting." Detente "in words is designed to camouflage intense rivalry for hegemony in deeds," and the fierce contention makes "the outbreak of war hard to avoid."[83] It is significant to note that many Americans have also criticized detente as a one-way street, and that President Ford deemed it necessary, for domestic political purposes, to abandon the use of the term in the spring of 1976.

After the public rapprochement, the first practical convergence of views and policy between the United States and China occurred during the Bangladesh conflict in late 1971. The Chinese considered that the treaty of "peace, friendship and cooperation" concluded between India and the Soviet Union in August 1971 was not only in substance a "treaty of military alliance" and made India's war against Pakistan possible;[84] it also represented another step on the part of the Soviet Union to "expand its sphere of influence so as to contend with another superpower for world hegemony."[85] China thus joined with the United States in lending support to Pakistan, while the

*The theme was reiterated by Teng Hsiao-p'ing in his banquet speech welcoming former British Prime Minister Edward Heath.[81]

Soviet Union supported India. Similar parallel interests between
China and the United States to halt Soviet expansion and influence
have developed in Africa, Southeast Asia, and elsewhere.

Meanwhile, China has to meet the continuing challenge of an
"imperialist" United States and a "social imperialist" Soviet Union.
If the 1960s were characterized by revolutions and peoples' wars,
Peking now perceives an important new trend emerging for the current
historic period: an increasing number of medium-sized and small
countries are joining forces in order to oppose the hegemony and
power politics of the superpowers.[86] This appraisal is the basis of
a policy that has been facilitated by Peking's representation in the
United Nations since the fall of 1971.

For a decade starting in 1956, the People's Republic extended
aid on a fairly sustained basis to less developed non-Communist
countries in Africa, East Asia, South Asia, and the Middle East.
Then, in 1967, this aid began to taper off. Since 1970, China has
again greatly increased its aid programs for Third World countries.[87] Against a background of common experience, sympathy,
and interest, the Chinese appear to have identified themselves genuinely with the peoples of Asia, the Middle East, Africa, and Latin
America. As Foreign Minister Ch'iao Kuan-hua stated in his first
major speech at the U.N. General Assembly in November 1971, China
belongs to the Third World.[88] Peking has stressed repeatedly that
the Chinese people have suffered too much from foreign oppression
for them to want to become a superpower, bullying smaller countries.[89] Chairman Mao reportedly told French Foreign Minister
Maurice Schumann in July 1972 that despite its possession of nuclear
weapons China is not a superpower.[90] That remark may be considered as a revelation of intention as well as a realistic self-assessment
of power.

The Third World comprises over 100 developing countries, in
Asia, Africa, Latin America, and other regions, constituting more
than 70 percent of the world's population.[91] The medium-sized and
small countries, if they all work in concert, may yet tip the scales
of the balance of power. This assertion may seem less extravagant
if placed within the context not only of the energy crisis but also of
predicted scarcities in many other resources critical to the functioning of a highly industrialized society. According to Leninist theses,
colonies and semicolonies have always been the foundation and life-
line of imperialism. In any event, the growth of the ranks of the
Third World has changed the makeup of the United Nations.

When the United Nations was founded in 1945 there were only
51 member states. By the end of 1975, the membership had increased to 144. Of the 93 members that joined the world organization
after its founding, the overwhelming majority achieved independence

after World War II.   Their role in the United Nations has been steadily growing, and they have become a force that cannot be ignored.[92]

Contrary to many observers' misgivings in the past on seating
Peking in the United Nations, the People's Republic has played a
constructive rather than a disruptive role in the world organization.
At the same time, the Chinese delegates have consistently backed
the claims of many Afro-Asian and Latin American countries. They
supported, for example, the draft resolution put forward by Ceylon
and 12 other countries on declaring the Indian Ocean to be a peace
zone.[93] In line with the claims of several Latin American nations,
they also have insisted that those countries should have jurisdiction
over the seas within 200 nautical miles, as opposed to the 12 nautical
miles advocated by the United States and the Soviet Union.[94] It is
expected that China will continue using the United Nations to implement its Third World policy.

Although the People's Republic has adopted a policy of forming
an international united front of small and medium-sized countries
against the two superpowers, Peking's adversarial relationships
with the United States are currently in a somewhat lower level of
conflict than those between China and the Soviet Union, and both are
different now than they were during the antagonisms of the 1960s.
According to Mao, "There are many contradictions in the process of
development of a complex thing, and one of them is necessarily the
principal contradiction whose existence and development determine
or influence the existence and development of the other contradictions."[95] The relationship between China and the Soviet Union
clearly has developed into the principal contradiction, while the
contradiction between China and the United States has become a
secondary one. Hence Peking applies to the United States its domestic revolutionary formula of "uniting and at the same time struggling"
as well as its policy of "isolating and separating enemies." In these
terms, Peking will continue to struggle against the United States in
some areas and on a number of issues, but use that country at the
same time as a counterweight to the Soviet Union.

In order to unite all the forces that can be united, Peking has
sought out also the Second World, the developed capitalist countries
that have been subjected to superpower pressure. China thus has
encouraged Japan to oppose hegemony, especially Soviet hegemony;
supported Western Europe in its assertion of political independence
from the United States; and encouraged Eastern Europe to resist
Soviet domination. As one European scholar put it, there is an objective geopolitical link between China and Europe in that both are
the principal neighbors of an expansionist Soviet Union.[96] Having
reversed its earlier views on the enlarged European Economy Community, Peking now considers that a Common Market of ten countries

may be a serious obstacle to U.S.-Soviet hegemony. There has
been exchange of visits between Chinese and European leaders in
recent years, and in May 1975, Peking decided to accredit a representative to the European Economic Community. Furthermore,
repeatedly Peking has warned the West on the falsehood of the
detente.* As for Eastern Europe, the PRC has always enjoyed a
reservoir of goodwill there despite ideological differences. Peking's
championship of equality among all the socialist countries cannot but
favorably impress many people in that area.

Although there might be conflicting and competing perceptions
of Soviet-American relations held by different groups in the People's
Republic of China, it is extremely difficult to discern reliable factional perceptions in that country. Hence, the prevailing views of
the dominant group as expressed by the government and mass media
at any given time are considered China's perceptions. China has
its own short-term goals and long-range aspirations, but, as stated
earlier, its foreign policy is also partially a response to the Chinese
leaders' views based on the interaction of a number of variables,
including their perceptions, the foreign policies of other countries,
and appraisal of the world situation. As the variables undergo
change, the policy will change accordingly.

NOTES

1. V. I. Lenin, Diplomaticheskii Immunitet (Moscow, 1949),
pp. 4-5, quoted by Vernon V, Aspaturian, "Internal Politics and
Foreign Policy in the Soviet System," in Approaches to Comparative
and International Politics, ed. R. Barry Farrell (Evanston, Ill.:
Northwestern University Press, 1966), p. 213.

2. International Affairs, August 1970.

3. R. Judson Mitchell, "The Revised 'Two-Camps' Doctrine
in Soviet Foreign Policy," Orbis 16, no. 1 (Spring 1972).

4. Teng Hsiao-p'ing, speech at a special session of the U.N.
General Assembly, April 10, 1974; Peking Review, April 12, 1974,
Supplement.

5. Vladimir I. Lenin, Left-Wing Communism: An Infantile
Disorder (New York: International Publishers Co., 1940).

---

*China's perception of the world situation and its foreign pol-
icy have remained the same after the death of Premier Chou En-lai
and the dismissal of Teng Hsiao-p'ing in 1976. See, for example,
Premier Hua Kuo-feng's speech at the banquet welcoming New
Zealand Prime Minister Muldoon.[97]

6. Chou En-lai, Peking Review, September 7, 1973, p. 21.

7. Cf. Edward Shils, "The Concept and Function of Ideology," and Harry M. Johnson, "Ideology and the Social System," both in the International Encyclopedia of the Social Sciences (1968), vol. 7, pp. 66, 76-77.

8. Shils, op. cit., p. 66.

9. Johnson, op. cit., p. 77.

10. Gordon W. Allport, "The Historical Background of Modern Social Psychology," in The Handbook of Social Psychology, ed. Gardner Lindzey and Elliot Aronson, 2nd ed. (Reading, Mass.: Addison-Wesley, 1968), p. 21.

11. Julius Gould, "Ideology," in A Dictionary of the Social Sciences, ed. Julius Gould and William L. Kolb (New York: The Free Press, 1964), pp. 315-17.

12. Joseph de Rivera, The Psychological Dimension of Foreign Policy (Columbus, Ohio: Charles E. Merrill, 1968), p. 21.

13. Ibid.

14. Richard A. Brody, "Cognition and Behavior: A Model of International Relations," in Experience, Structure and Adaptability, ed. O. J. Harvey (New York: Springer, 1966), pp. 334-39.

15. de Rivera, op. cit., p. 20.

16. Ibid., p. 22.

17. See Karl W. Deutsch, The Nerves of Government (New York: The Free Press, 1963), pp. 94-97.

18. For an account of the episode, see Seymour Topping, Journey Between Two Chinas (New York: Harper & Row, 1972), pp. 83-84, 89. See also U.S. Senate, Committee on Foreign Relations, The United States and Communist China in 1949 and 1950 (Washington, D.C.: U.S. Government Printing Office, 1973), pp. 10-17.

19. Mao Tse-tung, speech to the 10th Plenary Session of the Eighth Central Committee, September 24, 1962, "Excerpts from Confidential Speeches, Directives and Letters of Mao Tse-tung," New York Times, March 1, 1970.

20. Mao Tse-tung, remarks to John Service in August 1944, in John S. Service, The Amerasia Papers (Berkeley, Calif.: Center for Chinese Studies, University of California, 1971), p. 171.

21. Cf. Barbara W. Tuchman, "If Mao Had Come to Washington: An Essay in Alternatives," Foreign Affairs, October 1972, pp. 44-64.

22. "Draft Report by the National Security Council on the Position of the United States with Respect to Asia," United States-Vietnam Relations, 1945-1967, Book 8 (Washington, D.C.: U.S. Government Printing Office, 1971), p. 243.

23. Ibid., p. 244.

24. Ibid., p. 245.

25. Ibid., p. 228.

26. Ibid., p. 255.

27. See "National Security Council Staff Study on United States Objectives and Courses of Action with Respect to Communist Aggression in Southeast Asia," ibid., pp. 468-76.

28. See Ole R. Holsti, "Cognitive Dynamics and Images of the Enemy: Dulles and Russia," in Enemies in Politics, ed. David J. Finlay, Ole R. Holsti, and Richard R. Fagen (Chicago: Rand McNally, 1967), pp. 25-96, for an appreciation of some of the implications and complexities of the cognitive dynamics of a national leader. Note references to China on pp. 69n, 74, 75, 81, 83-85.

29. See John Foster Dulles, "Our Policies Toward Communism in China" (Address before the International Convention of Lions International, San Francisco, June 28, 1957) in State Department Bulletin, July 15, 1957, pp. 91, 95; also quoted in Dean Acheson, Power and Diplomacy (New York: Atheneum, 1963), p. 132.

30. Morton A. Kaplan, "Bipolarity in a Revolutionary Age," in The Revolution in World Politics, ed. Morton A. Kaplan (New York: Wiley, Inc., 1962), p. 259.

31. Mao Tse-tung, Mao Chu-hsi tsai Su-lien ti yen-lun [Chairman Mao's Statements in the Soviet Union] (Peking, 1957), pp. 14-15; also quoted in Stuart R. Schram, The Political Thought of Mao Tse-tung, rev. ed. (New York: Praeger, 1969), pp. 407-08.

32. See, for example, an article on economic competition in two worlds, Shih-chieh chih-shih [World Knowledge] (Peking), January 5, 1959, pp. 16-17; see also Chou En-lai, Report on the Work of the Government (Peking: Foreign Languages Press, 1959), pp. 56-72.

33. "Statement by the Spokesman of the Chinese Government," Hung-ch'i [Red Flag], August 15, 1963; Peking Review, August 16, 1963.

34. Red Flag Commentator, "Confessions Concerning the Line of Soviet-U.S. Collaboration Pursued by the New Leaders of the C.P.S.U.," Hung-ch'i [Red Flag], February 11, 1966; English translation in Peking Review, February 18, 1966, p. 10. See also the editorial departments of People's Daily and Red Flag, On Khrushchev's Phoney Communism and Its Historical Lessons for the World: Comment on the Open Letter of the Central Committee of the CPSU (9), July 14, 1964 (Peking: Foreign Languages Press, 1964); and the editorial departments of People's Daily, Red Flag, and Liberation Army Daily, "Leninism or Social-Imperialism?", Peking Review, April 24, 1970, p. 7. For the Chinese view that the CPSU has become an instrument of bourgeois dictatorship in the name of the Party of the entire people, see Peking Review, December 8, 1967, pp. 32-34.

35. For the origin and early development of the Cultural Revolution, see Chün-tu Hsüeh, "The Cultural Revolution and the Leadership Crisis in Communist China," Political Science Quarterly, June 1967, pp. 169-90.

36. For the Chinese perception of American threat and encirclement, see the map showing "American imperialism's military encirclement of China" in the People's Daily, January 29, 1966, reproduced in Arthur Huck, The Security of China (New York: Columbia University Press, 1970), p. 12. The theme of encirclement was often expressed by Peking leaders. See, for example, Premier Chou En-lai's speech at the reception celebrating the twentieth anniversary of the founding of the PRC, Peking Review, October 3, 1969, p. 18.

37. Peking Review, January 29, 1966.

38. "Kremlin's New Tsars Rig up Anti-China Encirclement," Peking Review, April 4, 1969, pp. 25-27.

39. Peking Review, February 18, 1966, p. 10.

40. Peking Review, August 5, 1966, p. 18.

41. Shih-chieh chih-shih, February 25, 1966, pp. 5-8.

42. Chou En-lai, speech at the banquet given by Premier Kim Il Sung at Pyongyang, April 5, 1970; Peking Review, April 10, 1970, p. 13.

43. The Observer, "Confession of Worldwide U.S.-Soviet Collusion on a Big Scale," People's Daily, October 16, 1966; Peking Review, October 21, 1966, pp. 20-21.

44. See People's Daily, November 30, 1966; English translation in Peking Review, December 2, 1966; also People's Daily, June 22, 1967; for a slightly different wording, see Peking Review, June 20, 1967.

45. New China News Agency, February 29, 1968.

46. People's Daily, July 11, 1966; reprinted in Shih-shih ts'ung-shu (Current Event Series), no. 6 (Hong Kong: San-lien, 1966), pp. 24-25.

47. For example, see Peking Review, August 25, 1967, pp. 19-20; July 5, 1968, p. 33; and July 19, 1968, p. 29.

48. Peking Review, January 7, 1966; June 13, 1966; June 23, 1966; July 8, 1966, p. 22. In the month between September 24 and October 24, 1966, the People's Daily published two editorials and three articles signed by "The Observer," condemning U.S.-Soviet collusion on the Vietnam War in and out of the United Nations. In addition, it published four New China News Agency dispatches and reprinted one article each from Albania and Australia dealing with the same theme. For a collection of these articles, see Shih-shih ts'ung-shu, no. 16 (Hong Kong: San-lien, 1966).

49. Peking Review, August 30, 1968, pp. 19-20; also "Communique of the Enlarged 12th Plenary Session of the CPC Eighth

Central Committee," adopted on October 31, 1968, Peking Review, Supplement, November 1, 1968.

50. Peking Review, May 30, 1969, pp. 20-21.

51. Ibid., Peking Review, May 23, 1969, p. 30.

52. Peking Review, July 19, 1968, p. 29.

53. People's Daily, January 6, 1965; quoted in, the editor, "Blueprint for a House Divided," Current Scene 3, no. 27 (September 17, 1965).

54. Shih-chieh chih-shih, December 10, 1965, pp. 5-8.

55. Peking Review, January 1, 1967.

56. Chou En-lai, remarks, People's Daily, January 24, 1965.

57. Spokesman of the Chinese Government, statement, August 15, 1963, Peking Review, August 16, 1963.

58. Editorial, People's Daily, July 19, 1963; English translation in Peking Review, July 26, 1963; see also The Observer, "Why the Tripartite Treaty Does Only Harm and Brings No Benefits," People's Daily, August 10, 1963; Peking Review, August 16, 1963.

59. Red Flag, August 1, 1963; Peking Review, August 2, 1963.

60. Editorial, People's Daily, August 3, 1963; see also Peking Review, August 9, 1963.

61. People's Daily, September 3, 1967; Peking Review, September 8, 1967, p. 34.

62. Washington Post, July 18, 1972.

63. "A Report on Our Foreign Relations," Department of State Publication, no. 8445, March 1969, p. 4.

64. Peking Review, May 13, 1966, p. 5. Ch'en Yi had also made a similar remark at a press conference in the fall of 1965, Peking Review, October 8, 1965.

65. Harrison E. Salisbury, To Peking and Beyond (New York: Quadrangle, 1973), p. 226.

66. "A Report on Our Foreign Relations," op. cit., pp. 13-15.

67. For Peking's policy statements on nuclear weapons, see the following issues of Peking Review: July 26, 1963, pp. 47-48; August 2, 1963, pp. 7-8; Special Supplement, October 28, 1966; and December 3, 1971, pp. 14-16. China has consistently adhered to the stand declared on the above occasions, with a possible exception that China has not proposed an Asian-Pacific nuclear-free zone since the end of 1964 (the proposal was made in August 1960). See William J. Cunningham, Arms Controls in Northeast Asia (Washington, D.C.: Senior Seminar in Foreign Policy, Department of State, May 1972), p. 15.

68. Michael Tatu, The Great Power Triangle (Paris: Atlantic Institute, 1970), reprinted in U.S. Senate, Subcommittee on National Security and International Operations, Committee on Government Operations, International Negotiation (Washington, D.C.: U.S. Government Printing Office, 1971), pp. 211-12.

69. This "three-anti" policy was written down in the Chinese Communist party's constitution adopted in April 1969. See also the joint editorial of the People's Daily, Red Flag, and the Liberation Army Daily, August 1, 1969; Peking Review, August 6, 1969, p. 6. It was reiterated in the Party's constitution adopted in August 1973.

70. Mao Tse-tung, Selected Works (Peking: Foreign Languages Press, 1961), vol. 2, p. 99.

71. Cf. Stanley Hoffman, "International Systems and International Law," in Power, Action and Interaction, ed. George H. Quester (Boston: Little, Brown, 1971), p. 371; Hans J. Morgenthau, "Another 'Great Debate': The National Interest," ibid., p. 56; Arnold Wolfers, "The Pole of Power and the Pole of Indifference," ibid., pp. 149-50; Glenn H. Snyder, "Balance of Power in the Missile Age," ibid., p. 461; and Inis L. Claude, Jr., "International Law and Organization," in American National Security: A Study in Theory and Policy, ed. Morton Berkowitz and P. G. Bock (New York: The Free Press, 1965), p. 290.

72. James C. Thomson, Jr., "On the Making of U.S. China Policy, 1961-9," China Quarterly, no. 50 (April/June 1972): 221.

73. "The Chinese," remarked the People's Daily editorial of April 6, 1966, "are not taken in." Peking Review, April 8, 1966, p. 7.

74. Edgar Snow, The Long Revolution (New York: Random House, 1972), p. 172.

75. U.S., Arms Control and Disarmament Agency, World Military Expenditures, 1971 (Washington, D.C.: U.S. Government Printing Office, 1972), pp. 22-23, 50. For an elaborate and different assessment of national power, see Ray S. Cline, World Power Assessment: A Calculus of Strategic Drift (Washington, D.C.: Center for Strategic and International Studies, Georgetown University, 1975).

76. Audrey Donmithorne, "China as a Trading Nation," Current Scene, February 7, 1972, pp. 1-4.

77. Cf. Aldo Beckman et al., The China Trip--Now What (Chicago: University of Chicago Center for Policy Study, 1972), p. 12.

78. Peking Review, September 7, 1973, p. 23.

79. Yeh Chien-ying, speech, Peking Review, November 10, 1972, p. 3; and Li Teh-sheng, speech, Peking Review, November 17, 1972, p. 3.

80. Chou En-lai, "Report to the Tenth National Congress of the Communist Party of China," Peking Review, September 7, 1973, p. 22. The theme was reiterated by Teng Hsiao-p'ing in his address to a special session of the U.N. General Assembly, April 10, 1974. Peking Review, April 12, 1974, Supplement. The first major comment on the contending-colluding subject in the 1970s appeared in the Peking Review of March 20, 1970 on the occasion of U.S.-Soviet

agreement on cultural exchange, which began in 1958 and renewed negotiation every other year. The theme subsequently has been reiterated on many occasions. The origin of the superpower theme may be traced to Liao Ch'eng-chih's remarks on December 1961, Peking Review, December 22, 1961, pp. 12-14. See also an article written by the editorial departments of People's Daily and Red Flag, March 31, 1964; and The Proletarian Revolution and Khrushchev's Revisionism (Peking: Foreign Languages Press, 1964).

81. Teng Hsiao-p'ing, speech, Peking Review, May 31, 1974, p. 8.

82. For example, speeches by Foreign Minister Ch'iao Kuan-hua, chairman of the PRC delegation to the U.N. General Assembly session, October 2, 1974, Peking Review, October 11, 1974, pp. 9-10; September 26, 1975, Peking Review, October 3, 1975, p. 10. Peking's view on detente was dramatically presented (and widely noted by the mass media in the United States) by Foreign Minister Ch'iao Kuan-hua in his banquet toast, welcoming Secretary of State Kissinger who came to Peking in October 1975 for the preparation of President Ford's impending visit (Peking Review, October 24, 1975, p. 8), and by Vice Premier Teng Hsiao-p'ing in his banquet toast to President Ford in December (Peking Review, December 8, 1975, p. 8). For an earlier view of detente, see Peking Review, October 3, 1973, pp. 12-13. See also "Third World Struggle Against Hegemony," Peking Review, September 21, 1973, pp. 13-15.

83. Peking Review, January 18, 1974, pp. 7-11; February 15, 1974, pp. 16-18; March 29, 1974, p. 7; October 25, 1974, p. 8; January 17, 1975, pp. 6-8.

84. Chinese Government, statement, December 16, 1971, Peking Review, December 17, 1971. On this point, see M. R. Masani, "Is India a Soviet Ally?" Asian Affairs, January 1974, pp. 121-35, especially 125-26. The former Indian ambassador to Brazil concluded that the Indo-Soviet Treaty was a "treaty of alliance."

85. Huang Hua, permanent representative of the People's Republic of China on the U.N. Security Council, statement, at an urgent meeting of December 5, 1971, Peking Review, December 10, 1971, p. 9. For a similar remark by Ch'iao Kuan-hua, see Peking Review, December 17, 1971, p. 12; also January 28, 1972, pp. 14-15.

86. Peking Review, January 6, 1972, p. 9; see also "Medium-Sized and Small Nations United to Oppose Two Superpowers' Hegemony," Peking Review, January 28, 1972, p. 14.

87. For a study of economic aid of the Soviet Union, China, and East Europe, see "Communists Fall to Third in Economic Aid to Developing Nations," International Policy Report (Washington, D.C., April 1976), vol. 2, no. 1. During 1970-71, China extended

nearly $1.2 billion in economic aid to the developing countries--total commitments amounting to almost 55 percent of all such extensions of aid by the Peking government since 1956. Leo Tansky, "China's Foreign Aid: The Record," Current Scene 10, no. 9 (September 1972): 2.

88. Peking Review, November 19, 1971, p. 8.

89. Chinese Government, statement, October 29, 1971, on the United Nations resolution seating the Peking government in the U.N. Similar statements have been made on a number of occasions, for example, the 1971 New Year's Day joint editorial of the People's Daily, Red Flag, and Liberation Army Daily and remarks made by Chou En-lai to a Canadian delegation, July 28, 1971. See also Teng Hsiao-p'ing, speech, at a special session of the U.N. General Assembly, April 10, 1974, Peking Review, April 12, 1974, p. 5.

90. Washington Post, July 12, 1972.

91. Peking Review, April 12, 1974, p. 8. See also "Rise of Third World and Decline of Hegemonism," Peking Review, January 10, 1975, pp. 6-8.

92. Jen Ku-ping, "The Third World: Great Motive Force in Advancing World History," Peking Review, November 1, 1974, p. 6.

93. Peking Review, December 17, 1971, p. 19.

94. For China's stand at the U.N., see Peking Review, March 31, 1972, p. 17.

95. Mao Tse-tung, Selected Works (Peking: Foreign Languages Press, 1965), vol. 1, p. 331.

96. Alain Bouc, "Peking Now Wants a United Europe," European Community, no. 154 (March 1972): 85; New China News Agency, June 29, 1971; Vladmir Reisky de Dubnic, "Europe and the New U.S. Policy Toward China," Orbis 16, no. 1 (Spring 1972): 87.

97. Hua Kuo-feng, speech at banquet welcoming New Zealand Prime Minister Muldoon, Peking Review, May 7, 1976, p. 11.

4

CHINA'S RESPONSE TO THE UNITED STATES: FROM VIETNAM TO RAPPROCHEMENT
King C. Chen

INTRODUCTION

During the first three years (1969-71) of the Nixon Administration, the Vietnam War still remained as one of the obstacles to a Sino-American thaw. China had long regarded American involvement in Vietnam as part of its containment policy against China, and the continuation of the war meant, therefore, the continuation of the containment. From 1972 to 1975, the Vietnam situation developed from a peace pact to a complete Communist victory; meanwhile, China and the United States reached a rapprochement. Observers of China wondered: Did China see the war as a threat to its security? What persuaded China to disentangle Sino-American relations from the Vietnam issue, and how did it do it? And what are the implications of the development of Sino-American rapprochement? While answers to these questions vary, one consensus seems to have been reached: The development of the rapprochement already has begun to show a more complicated impact on the international situation than expected.

This chapter attempts to explore these questions through a study of the Sino-American interaction during this period,* with the

---

*The interaction model in international relations as advanced by several scholars in the field is generally applicable to the diplomatic interaction between China and the United States during 1969-75.[1]

Research for this chapter was conducted during the author's tenure as a Senior Fellow at the Research Institute on Communist Affairs of Columbia University, whose financial support is gratefully acknowledged.

rationale that the issue can be explained better by a China-centered
approach. Four basic factors serve as elements for explanation.
For simplicity, the four elements will be introduced first, then a
discussion of U.S. policy and China's response to it, and finally
some analyses will be presented.

FOUR ELEMENTS FOR EXPLANATION

The four elements for explanation are China's national interests, the theory of contradictions, Chinese nationalism, and Mao's
strategy of weakness against strength. To be sure, they are not
elements announced by the Chinese government; they exist as we in-
terpret the Chinese behavior. They sometimes reinforce one another
on some issues and sometimes compete for supremacy on others.
None of these four, however, dominates the issues. Nevertheless,
they constitute an analytic unit for the study of the complex situation.

Chinese National Interests

Regardless of the nature of a Communist state, China often
observes the conventional concept of national interests as a guiding
principle in conducting its foreign policies, including its relations
with the United States, Vietnam, and the Soviet Union. Generally,
China undoubtedly is interested in the maintenance of national security, the achievement of unification, the ending of all foreign intervention, the development of national economy, the promotion of power
and prestige, and the establishment of an Asian as well as world leadership. Specifically in Indochina, China is concerned about the security of North Vietnam, interested in seeing an end to Western intervention there, enthusiastic in the success of the revolution in the peninsula, and intends to establish its leading position in the area. As in
Korea, China's interests there are important and real.

Yet, China's interests in Vietnam are interrelated with its interests in Asia. To pursue a leading position in Asia, China must
demonstrate its strength and magnanimity to other Asian nations.
It also has to compete with Western powers for supremacy in the
area.[2] Since 1950, China and the United States have had at least
three confrontations with or without military conflict: Korea, the
Taiwan Straits, and Vietnam. In all these confrontations, one overriding guideline to Peking's consideration of reactions was national
interests: how to safeguard China's security from American military
actions and how to remove American military protection from Taiwan.
Such a guideline continues to direct China's response to the U.S.-

Vietnam policy as well as its reaction to the U.S. search for rapprochement.

The Theory of Contradiction

Like the Soviets, the Chinese leaders apply Communist ideology to shape their world outlook, formulate their policy, and justify their international actions. As they stated in 1950, their policy is founded on the "scientific principle" of Marx, Engels, Lenin, and Stalin and on the "scientific knowledge" of the laws of social development. They are able to clothe in ideological terms virtually every issue. And one of the most fundamental and important theories is the principle of contradiction, as laid down by Mao Tse-tung: "Contradiction is universal and absolute," Mao says. "It is present in the process of development of all things and permeates every process from beginning to end. . . . This is a universal truth for all times and all countries, which admits of no exception."[3] In the international field, it is a key to China's interpretation of various issues and problems, and it helps us to see more meaningfully China's subtle behaviors.

A few examples will suffice to support this point. In 1949, Mao Tse-tung asserted that the world was polarized into two opposing sides (camps), imperialist and socialist, and that Communist China leaned toward the socialist side.[4] In 1964, Peking presented its long conceived "intermediate zone" theory, recognizing the Third World, Western Europe, Oceania, and Canada as a vast region existing politically and geographically between the two camps.[5] In 1969, Peking theorized that the world situation was characterized by four major contradictions: between the oppressed nations, on the one hand, and imperialist and social-imperialist countries, on the other; between the proletariat and the bourgeoisie in the capitalist and revisionist countries; between imperialist and social-imperialist countries and among the imperialist countries; and between socialist countries, on the one hand, and imperialist and social-imperialist nations, on the other.[6] In April 1974, Peking divided the world into "three worlds."

China applied the theory of contradiction to the Vietnam War and Sino-American relations. One hard evidence is the secret Kunming Documents,[7] which say, for instance, that "the signing of the Vietnam armistice agreement dealt a blow to Soviet revisionism and aggravated the contradictions between the United States and the Soviet Union." And Peking's invitation to Nixon to visit China, according to the same documents, was "to exploit contradictions" between the United States and its "lackeys"; by the same token, it was to exploit Japan's international contradictions. It is clear, therefore, that Peking has made full use of the contradiction theory in its response to the United States.

Chinese Nationalism

In the past century, almost every significant Chinese political movement has been inspired by a fierce nationalistic (antiforeign, anticolonialist, and antiimperialist) sentiment, with a determination to wipe out the humiliation of past foreign encroachments and a desire to remake China into a unified and strong world power. Such sentiment and determination can be seen clearly through numerous political events, from the reform movement of 1898 to the Sino-Soviet armed conflict on the Ussuri River in 1969. It has become a deep-rooted and strong factor in Chinese foreign policy.

Succinctly, Chinese nationalistic policy aims at the ending of foreign interference, the maintenance of complete independence and freedom, and the restoration of China's traditional position and prestige in Asia as well as in the rest of the world. Sometimes these nationalistic objectives and national interests overlap; sometimes they stand out separately. On several occasions, the Chinese leaders quite successfully have utilized nationalist-oriented policies to rally people's support and to achieve international prestige. The impacts are often more dynamic than those created by ideology. The border conflict with the Soviet Union on the Ussuri River is a case in point.[8] On the issue of ending the American involvement in Vietnam, Peking sees eye to eye with Hanoi. Yet, on the restoration of China's traditional position in Asia, Hanoi differs from Peking.

Mao's Strategy

Because of the lack of data, it is difficult to apply the decision-making approach to Mao's policy-making process;[9] more difficult to probe is the psychological factor.[10] But, as a good strategist, Mao often broods in silence and prepares new games to deal with the enemy. From several Chinese Communist crises in the past, Mao's strategy of the weak against the strong generally can be described to have three characteristics. The first is his ability to establish cooperation or alliance, the second is his insistence on concentration of strike at one direction, and the third is his flexible practice of the tactic of "alliance and struggle."

When a crisis or new situation arises, Mao's first response is caution and restraint. He also displays great patience to avoid unnecessary confrontation with the enemy in order to preserve his weak force. When he sees opportunity for strikes, he decides to attack at only one target (direct) with a concentrated and far superior force.[11] This tactic has brought him many victories since 1928. If, however, the enemy is too formidable, Mao will then appeal to outside forces for an alliance or cooperation. These outside forces may be his friends, his former enemies, or even his "less evil" enemies. But they, for a variety of reasons, may not wholeheartedly or constantly cooperate with Mao. When they are cooperative, Mao is allied with them; when they are noncooperative, Mao struggles against them. [12]

A few examples from the past can explain these characteristics. In his first days in the Chingkang Mountains, Mao skillfully adopted a policy of caution, accommodation (with local armed units), and one-direction attacks against his enemy--the government. [13] During the Sian incident, he deliberated and debated repeatedly with his comrades on how to handle the kidnapped Chiang Kai-shek. He was very cautious. He feared that if Chiang were released, the latter might resort to a military retaliation against the Chinese Communists rather than join in a united front against Japan. But the united front policy finally prevailed. During the Sino-Japanese War (1937-45), the CCP, under his leadership, used the alliance and struggle tactic against the Kuomintang. After the armed conflict on the Ussuri, Mao employed his cooperation strategy with the "less evil" United States against the "more evil" Soviet Union. It must be made clear that such a strategy is not an international united front. Mao must have realized that such rapprochement would help to end the Vietnam War and relax international tensions. But with the threat to China's security shifting from the South to the North, rapprochement with the United States became necessary. As to the issue of dealing with the new co-operators, Mao can still exercise his tactic of "alliance and struggle." Consequently, it is clear that these characteristics of Mao's strategy have been, and will be, operating in a complex and subtle way in conducting his external and internal policies.

One may say that these four elements can also be used to explain Soviet policy toward the United States, and, therefore, what is the distinctive value of applying them to China? One reason is the continuity of the sense of history. Any national-conscious Chinese over the age of 40 finds it hard to brush away completely the bitterness imposed on China by big powers in the past century, and Peking leaders in their 60s to 80s are no exception. As Chou En-lai told James Reston of the New York Times in 1971, he could never forget Japan's military invasion of China in the past. [14] Also unforgettable are the aggressive acts of czarist Russia. Such nationalistic sentiment obviously is different from that of the Soviet Union or the United States. It often plays a special role in policy making.

Thus, these elements contain common as well as specific characters for this study of China's response to the United States. They may not be simultaneously applicable to every situation, but to rule out any of them is to misread China's behavior. Before a discussion

of China's response, President Richard Nixon's Vietnam policy is
examined briefly.

NIXON'S VIETNAM POLICY AND RAPPROCHEMENT

Thirteen months before he was elected president in November
1968, Richard Nixon had viewed the restoration of domestic tranquil-
ity as the first priority in national politics and the handling of Asian
affairs as the second.[15] However, since the domestic disorder was
largely caused by the Vietnam War, a gradual removal of the cause
would help restore domestic order. A new Vietnam policy, therefore, should be directed to defuse the war so as to ensure tranquiliz-
ing domestic uproar. The Nixon doctrine, which was announced in
July 1969, was developed under such circumstances.

As already well known, the doctrine clearly indicated a large
reduction of American military role in Asia generally and in Vietnam specifically.[16] In Asia, President Nixon hoped that Japan, by
playing a constructive role, would fill the gap that might be created
by the reduction of American engagement. On Vietnam, he repeatedly stated his departure from past policy. In his 1971 report to Congress on U.S. foreign policy, for instance, he said, "Clearly, we
could not have continued the inherited policy on Vietnam. Just as
clearly, the way in which we set about to resolve this problem has a
major impact on our credibility abroad and our cohesion at home."[17]
He ruled out a military solution because of the nature of the conflict,
the costs of such a solution, the risks of a wider war, and the sentiment of many Americans. He emphasized a settlement through negotiations and a Vietnamization program to shift American responsibilities to the South Vietnamese.[18]

For a negotiated solution, Nixon made his first formal proposal
on May 14, 1969. Subsequently, proposals and counterproposals
were made at numerous open and secret sessions of the Paris peace
talks. To increase the chances for reaching a settlement, Nixon
made an unprecedented surprise move to seek an accommodation
with the People's Republic of China and the Soviet Union. Apparently, he was convinced that rapprochement with China and detente with
Russia, North Vietnam's biggest allies, would help dampen the Communist morale and achieve a peace settlement.

For the reduction of American military role, Nixon also made
a suggestion in the same proposal for a mutual withdrawal of all
foreign troops from South Vietnam. Although the Communist reactions were negative, while conferring with South Vietnamese President Nguyen Van Thieu on Midway Islands on June 8 of the same
year, he announced that the United States would unilaterally withdraw

25,000 troops by the end of August. This was the first official announcement of troop withdrawal. The American ground force was reduced progressively from 543,400 to 24,200 by the end of 1972, and war casualties were also reduced from an average of 181 per week in 1969 to about 6 in 1972.[19] Meanwhile, the South Vietnamese fighting responsibilities and death tolls increased.

Another main aspect of Vietnamization was the modernization of the South Vietnamese forces, the first phase of which was to improve the equipment and organization under American supervision. It included bringing the force strength to 1.1 million men, creating several new units, and developing logistical capabilities.[20] The second phase emphasized qualitative improvements in leadership and morale.

In withdrawing, however, the United States found that the Communists continued to strengthen their strategic positions and to increase their war supplies. To protect his withdrawal plan, Nixon escalated the air war.[21] He also launched a Cambodia incursion, helped a Laos operation, and bombed and blockaded North Vietnam. Finally, improvement of relations with China and the Soviet Union helped to achieve the Vietnam cease-fire accords in January 1973, which, ironically, paved the way for the final Communist victory in 1975.

CHINA'S RESPONSE

A discussion of China's response to the United States from 1969 to 1975 will center around the aforesaid stormy events. Although a detailed account here of China's reaction to the United States in Vietnam prior to 1969 is beyond the scope of the study, for the sake of continuity an outline is necessary.

In January 1965, one month before the escalation of the air war in North Vietnam, Mao Tse-tung told Edgar Snow that the United States would not expand the war to the North and that China would not go to war with the United States unless attacked first by Americans.[22] The bombing in the North had certainly surprised the Peking leaders. As China watchers asserted, the Chinese leadership held a series of strategic debates on three key issues: how to respond to the U.S. war challenge, how to reply to the Soviet call for a "united action," and how to keep North Vietnam in the fight.[23] By early November of the same year, Mao emerged as the victor from the debates, defeating the hawks, who asserted more military involvement in Vietnam, and the Chinese "revisionists," who intended to cooperate with the Soviets. Peking, therefore, repeatedly made known that China would not take the initiative to provoke a war with the United

States.[24] It formally announced its refusal to support the Soviet "united action" proposal,[25] and strongly persuaded the Vietnamese to fight their people's war. *

China's decision on how to respond to the United States in Vietnam was reflected by its actions there. Peking avoided a direct military confrontation with the United States, but sent a squadron of MIG-15 and MIG-17 jets to Hanoi, constructed new jet airfields in Yunnan and Kwangsi for Hanoi's air sanctuaries, dispatched some 50,000 engineer soldiers to repair damaged roads and bridges caused by U.S. air raids, and increased military and economic aid.[27] Meanwhile, China insisted on its "no-peace-talk" policy with the United States. As the war continued, China saw significant advantages in the fight: it served to "freeze Soviet-American relations" as Brezhnev had complained, presented a model for wars of national liberation in the Third World, aroused anti-U.S. sentiment in China and around the world, and promoted the antiwar movement and other internal difficulties in the United States. China, therefore, disapproved of any peace talk proposals because "conditions for negotiations" were not yet ripe as revealed by Hanoi's general, Nugyen Van Vinh.[28] Mao once again was applying his protracted strategy to bog down the enemy. He believed, as he told Edgar Snow in January 1965, that the United States would lose its interest and withdraw in a short period of time.[29] Consequently, Hanoi should not negotiate a compromise, but fight until final victory.

But the Soviet Union acted to erode China's Vietnam policy. Moscow's "united action" proposal was warmly welcomed by the Vietnamese Communists. China's rejection of it only gave rise to Hanoi's resentment toward Peking. As the war escalated, Moscow offered more sophisticated weapons to Hanoi, rolled out the red carpet for Le Duan at the 23rd Congress of the CPSU in 1966, and supported Hanoi's peace feelers throughout 1967.† It was only

---

*In September 1965, Lin Piao unequivocally sent a message to the Vietnamese: "Revolution or people's war in any country is the business of the masses in that country and should be carried out primarily by their own efforts; there is no other way."[26]

†In January 1967, Pham Van Dong, in his interview with Harrison E. Salisbury, softened Hanoi's position on negotiations by saying that Hanoi's four conditions of 1965 were basic conditions for the settlement of Vietnam problems, not for peace talks.[30] In early February of the same year, Foreign Minister Ngyuen Duy Trinh listed a bombing halt as the only condition for peace negotiations. Trinh's statement was repeated in October 1967 and January 1968. Moscow supported Hanoi's stand. As Premier Kosygin said in February in London, cessation of American bombing was "necessary in order to enable talks to take place."[31]

natural, therefore, when President Lyndon Johnson made his offer
for peace negotiations on March 31, 1968,[32] that it was accepted by
Hanoi but denounced by Peking as a "new fraud."[33] Angered at
Hanoi's defiance, China imposed a complete news blackout on the
Paris talks for seven months. It also reduced news reports in Jen-
min jih-pao on Vietnam from several items per day to almost none.
Prior to the Nixon Administration, China's policy toward the United
States in Vietnam seemed to have reached a stalemate. Meanwhile,
Soviet pressures were ever increasing. To break down the wall of
isolation, Peking took the initiative to propose on November 26,
1968 to negotiate with the United States for "an agreement on the
five principles of peaceful coexistence."[34]

The proposed meeting was canceled by Peking because the
United States granted political asylum to Liao Ho-shu, a defected
Chinese diplomat in the Netherlands; yet the timing, the manner,
and the intent-discussed substance of China's proposal tended to indicate a possibility of improving Sino-American relations. In public, Peking continued to rail at President Nixon as a "hypocrite" and
"a god of plague and war."[35] In secret, nevertheless, Peking reacted favorably to Washington's proposal for normalizing Sino-
American relationships. *

On the Vietnam issue, China remained silent. Until Ho Chi
Minh's death, Peking carried little news on Vietnam. What made
headlines in the Chinese press were the Sino-Soviet border conflicts
on the Ussuri River in March 1969. The clash led China to close
down the Sino-Soviet border traffic, which held up Soviet arms shipments to Vietnam for a period of time;† and Peking launched a nationwide war-preparation campaign directed against Russia. The slogan,
"pei-chan, pei-huang, wei jen-min" (be prepared against war, be
prepared against natural disasters, and do everything for the people)
was devised to serve the campaign. It is clear, therefore, that
China was then much more concerned over the Soviet threat in the
border area than over the United States in Vietnam.‡

---

*The information was given in December 1972 by a White House
staff member, who declined to go into details.

† L'Humanite (March 15, 1969), the French Communist Party
newspaper, denounced the Chinese curbs on Soviet aid shipments as
acts of "criminal character."

‡ There has been a thought that the Chinese military, which was
then led by Lin Piao, had planned the border conflict in order to gain
ascendancy over its rivals in domestic politics. Lin Piao was chosen,
over Chou En-lai and others, as Mao's successor at the Ninth Party
Congress in April 1969, one month after the border conflict.[36]

Alexei Kosygin met with Chou En-lai in Peking a few days after Ho Chi Minh's funeral in September 1969. The Soviet premier offered a three-point program for relaxing Sino-Soviet tensions: border talks, resumption of the exchange of ambassadors, and trade negotiations. Before long, China agreed to talks and exchange of envoys. But Kosygin's visit at this juncture emphasized the serious tension between China and the Soviet Union. *

Three weeks after Ho's funeral, Pham Van Dong visited Chou En-lai for the celebration of China's twentieth anniversary on October 1. The Vietnamese delegation was well received, and a new Chinese aid agreement was signed. Peking joined with the Hanoi delegation in calling President Nixon "a fool if he thinks he can end the war without complete and unconditional withdrawal."[39] Moreover, on his return from Europe in late October, Pham Van Dong held further talks with Chou in Peking; China once again pledged its firm support for Vietnam and insisted on U.S. unconditional withdrawal.[40] But China resumed the Warsaw talks on January 20, 1970, and the United States continued its troops withdrawal without Communist challenge.†

The Cambodian Incursion, Spring 1970

The Cambodian coup in March 1970 presented a greater crisis for the Vietnamese Communists and Prince Sihanouk than for China.

---

*Rumors were much in the air at that time that a Sino-Soviet war might break out. It was quite possible that Kosygin's meeting with Chou was designed to deliver a Soviet ultimatum to China. "It is a typical Soviet practice," as Zbigniew Brzezinski observes, "to have grave warnings delivered by the more moderate Soviet leaders in order to give these warnings greater credibility."[37] After Kosygin's visit, China improved state-to-state relations with Russia by resuming border talks and exchanging ambassadors. But for the ideological dispute, China made no retreat. As Mao told Edgar Snow in December 1970, the ideological polemics could go on for 9,000 years if not 10,000.[38]

†By December 1969, General Giap decided to adopt a combined strategy of protracted warfare and flexible offensive.[41] Le Duan, first secretary of the Lao Dong party (Party chief today), also advocated a similar flexible strategy toward South Vietnam. In his important article published in February on the fortieth anniversary of the Party, he discussed a score of topics, from socialism and revolution in Vietnam to industrialization. On Hanoi's war strategy, he suggested a temporary military deescalation, a protracted guerrilla warfare, and a flexible strategy.[42]

For a week, the Vietnamese Communists held formal meetings with General Lon Nol in Phnom Penh on the Cambodian sanctuary issue. The meeting broke off on March 23. The same day Sihanouk announced in Peking that he would organize a new national union government and a liberation army against the Lon Nol regime. Hanoi and the Vietcong immediately declared their support for Sihanouk and withdrew their diplomats from Phnom Penh, and Peking began to criticize Lon Nol on April 16. [43]

In late April, the summit conference of the Indo-Chinese Peoples opened in a China-Lao-Vietnam border area. At its end, Chou En-lai flew in from Peking. As Chou clearly indicated at his banquet for the participants of the conference, China would provide a powerful support for them and would fight together with them for their common cause. To the Communists, the polarization in Indochina between the revolutionaries and the imperialists-reactionaries now became clear and simple. In holding a common cause, China could now ally with the three Indochinese revolutionary peoples; and by joining the Vietnamese Communists' rejection of peace feelers from Russia and France, China sided closer with the Indochinese peoples than the Soviet Union. This was what China officially stated as "a completely new stage."[44]

The Cambodian incursion in early May prompted both Russia and China to condemn the United States. At a surprise news conference, Kosygin criticized Nixon's policy and raised doubts about Soviet-American negotiations.

China's response was more violent and merits a little more detail here for the convenience of later analysis. On May 6, Jen-min jih-pao devoted three and one-half pages (out of six) to cover the incursion. * In a few days, China granted its formal recognition to Sihanouk's regime, severed (together with North Vietnam and North Korea) diplomatic relations with the Lon Nol government, and withdrew its personnel from Phnom Penh. Moreover, a Chinese Communist special force of 4,200 men reportedly entered Cambodia. [45] On May 11, Mao Tse-tung held "a very cordial and friendly" talk with Le Duan, who just came to Peking after a three-week stay in Moscow. Beginning in mid-May, thousands of Chinese armed personnel moved, for at least ten days, to the Sino-Vietnamese border. On May 19, Peking canceled the scheduled Warsaw talks on May 20. To cap these intensive developments, Mao issued a personal statement on May 20 accusing the United States of "brazenly" invading Cambodia and urging

---

*The regular May 15 issue of Peking Review, not the special issue of May 8 on the Indochina summit conference, also devoted 20 out of 39 1/2 pages [51 percent] to cover the incursion.

the people of the world to unite and defeat the American aggressors and their lackeys. [46] Then a wave of massive demonstrations of hundreds of thousands of people swept over Peking, Tientsin, Shanghai, and other cities in support of Mao's statement. The anti-American campaign reached a new peak. Undoubtedly, the incursion had inflicted considerable damage on the Vietnamese Communist forces in the five-year-old sanctuary areas, * but it turned out to be a windfall to China. China's behavior won a good friendship with Sihanouk and alarmed Moscow.

In sharp language, Pravda on May 18 attacked Peking for seeking domination in Asia. [48] Radio Moscow also railed at Mao for his "encouraging" U.S. aggression in Indochina. [49] Moreover, Moscow issued an unusual warning to the Indochinese Communists and revolutionaries that if they let their action be dictated by Peking, they would be led to "defeat," and that the lesson of the defeat of the Indonesian Communist Party (PKI) was still fresh. [50] Bitter over Moscow's non-recognition of his regime in exile, Sihanouk refused to accept Soviet offer of aid. Surprisingly to many, he viewed Russia's conflict with China as being motivated by racism, a fear of a "yellow peril" embodied in China. [51] Cambodia has become a new factor in Sino-Soviet rivalry.

But there was an undercurrent of a Sino-American rapprochement beneath Peking's violent attacks on the United States. For in mid-June, when American troops were evacuating from Cambodia, Chou En-lai reportedly was to have told Eastern European diplomats in Peking that China looked forward to the resumption of the Warsaw talks. [52]

The Laos Operation, February-April 1971

From late November to early December of 1970, top American officials repeatedly warned Hanoi of bombing reprisal in North Vietnam if Hanoi stepped up fighting in the South. On December 10, Hanoi issued a Party-government joint appeal to the people for continuing war until final victory. [53] Unprecedentedly, the appeal was submitted on the following day to Chou En-lai by Hanoi's ambassador in Peking. China then stated on December 13 its support for the Hanoi appeal. [54]

---

*Of all the accounts on the incursion, the most convincing is probably the report written by Louis Wiznitzer, a Brazilian journalist. His informants were Hanoi's delegates to the Paris peace talks. [47]

One month after the appeal was made public, tensions mounted. At first, the United States increased its air raids in Laos, and then, in early February 1971, the U.S. Air Force assisted Saigon troops in invading Laos along Route 9. Twenty thousand Saigon soldiers were used and approximately 9,000 American troops were also involved. Hanoi decided to fight. A reinforcement of two regiments moved in, engaging in a heavy battle--"much worse than Tet!"[55]

As the tension grew, Peking expressed its concern. After some public exchanges, China told Washington on February 14 that "the war adventure of U.S. imperialism in Laos definitely poses a grave threat to China."[56]

To make the situation worse, Nixon refused to rule out a wider U.S. air war or a Saigon push to North Vietnam, which alarmed both Xuan Thuy and Mrs. Nguyen Thi Binh to issue warnings to Washington. They stated that the U.S. actions had posed a threat to China and that China "would not remain idle." Peking echoed immediately.[57] From the end of February to early March, invasion rumors spread in Saigon.[58] To prepare against a possible invasion and to make a psychological maneuver, Hanoi appealed to China by inviting Chou En-lai for a secret talk.

Chou En-lai visited Hanoi from March 5 to 8. In a joint communique, he and Pham Van Dong emphatically stated that the Laos operation "menaces the security of North Vietnam" and China. They warned that if the United States expanded its war in Indochina, China was determined to take all necessary measures to support the Indochinese peoples, "not flinching even from the greatest national sacrifices."[59] It seems that China was prepared to help defend North Vietnam if needed.

Mao may have been perturbed by the Laos operation, but he did not really consider the move as a threat to Chinese security. He knew Nixon was deescalating the war and he was "fairly confident of Nixon's limited intentions in Laos."[60] Perceiving a rapid development in a Sino-American thaw, his move was only to satisfy Hanoi psychologically.

As events turned out, the Communists fought well, and Saigon troops evacuated completely from Laos in early April.* By that time, the intriguing ping-pong diplomacy was already under way.

---

*The Communists claimed to have won four battles in a week (March 16-22), eliminating more than five regiments of Saigon troops.[61] One year later, the New York _Times_ carried a similar story of the Communist victory of the Laos operation.[62]

Nixon's Visit to China

The Sino-Soviet border conflict in March 1969 must have prompted Mao to review his Soviet policy. Meanwhile, he must have been attracted by Nixon's desire for a rapprochement that was secretly relayed to him immediately after the conflict. A sketch of the events leading to the new development is roughly reconstructed as follows:

In late March 1969, Nixon informed China via President de Gaulle's ambassador in Peking that he was withdrawing from Vietnam and was desirous of normal relations with China. A favorable response came back. In June 1969, Nixon began to withdraw troops from Vietnam and in July acted to relax curbs on China travel and trade. In early August when Nixon visited Romania, he further asked the Romanian leaders to convey his relations-improvement message to Peking. In December of the same year, the United States further eased restrictions against China trade.

In January 1970, the Warsaw talks resumed after almost two years of suspension, to be followed by a second meeting in February. One month later the United States again eased China travel curbs, permitting trips for any "legitimate purpose." The Cambodia incursion interrupted the Warsaw dialogue. But when it was just over, Nixon, in an interview with news commentator Howard K. Smith on July 1, reaffirmed his desire to improve relations with China. Meanwhile, Secretary of State William Rogers appealed to China in Tokyo for a settlement in Vietnam. In the same month, China released the Most Reverend James Edward Walsh after his 12-year imprisonment.

By December 1970, Mao must have been generally convinced of Nixon's seriousness in improving relations with China. When, therefore, Edgar Snow saw him on December 18, 1970, he expressed welcome to Nixon's visit to China. [63] The Laos operation, albeit disturbing, did not destroy the foundation of the coming rapprochement. On March 15, 1971, two days before the Chinese table-tennis team left for Japan, the United States lifted bans on travel to China. Then Mao overruled any doubts of the Peking officials on granting a visa to the American table-tennis team to visit China. "So," as Chou En-lai said, "with one sentence of Chairman Mao's, we invited the U.S. table-tennis team." [64]

Nixon immediately eased further China trade embargo, allowing nonstrategic exports to China. Before long, a small flow of visitors to China followed. Then came the surprise news in July 1971 of Nixon's scheduled visit to China.

It is unnecessary to dwell upon Nixon's visit and the well-known Shanghai Communique of February 1972. Two aspects in the communique, however, are of special concern. The first is on Indochina.

The United States stressed the principle of self-determination and the significance of the U.S. withdrawal. China, on the other hand, expressed its firm support to the Indochinese people for the attainment of their goals according to the Joint Declaration of the Summit Conference of the Indochinese Peoples in April 1970.

The second aspect is on Taiwan. The United States "acknowledges that all Chinese on either side of the Taiwan Strait maintain there is but one China and that Taiwan is a part of China. The United States Government does not challenge that position."[65] Furthermore, Washington promised to withdraw its forces from the island as "the tension in the area diminishes," but expressed its interest in the peaceful settlement on the Taiwan issue.

It is true that after the Nixon visit, American officials sought to reassure the rest of Asia that the U.S.-Taiwan treaty of 1954 was intact and that the Shanghai Communique on eventual withdrawal of forces did not alter the capacities of the United States to help defend Taiwan.[66] But the rapprochement brought a series of international blows to Taiwan, including its ouster from the United Nations and the establishment of liaison offices in Peking and Washington.

The Spring Offensive and Cease-fire Agreements, 1972-73

The stormy spring 1972 offensive of the Communists in South Vietnam on three fronts (north, central, and south) scored an early victory. By early May, Anloc, Quangtri, and several other cities fell. Saigon was under the Communist threat.*

---

*Many American officials held an unconvincing view that this Communist offensive was a go-for-broke campaign. Its motives, however, can be summarized as follows:

1. To occupy one or two provinces (such as Quangtri or Hue) and establish the capital of the Provisional Revolutionary Government of the Republic of South Vietnam there
2. To overthrow or threaten to overthrow the Nguyen Van Thieu government
3. To gain strength in the Paris peace talks
4. To use up the heavy and more sophisticated weapons already in North Vietnam (note that about 600 tanks were used in this offensive, of which approximately 425 were destroyed) so as to ask new Soviet military aid
5. To undermine Sino-American rapprochements and Soviet-American detente.

To meet the crisis, on May 8 Nixon ordered the mining and blockading of North Vietnamese ports and the bombing of rail lines and other targets. It was a drastic reescalation, taking the risk of breaking his scheduled Russia visit. As a result, the Soviets made new protests and speeded up Vietnam aid. But all Soviet supports to Vietnam turned sour due to Moscow's continuing welcome of Nixon's visit in late May. *

Had it not been for the rapprochement, China would certainly have perceived the reescalation as a more serious "threat" than ever to its security. The Chinese foreign ministry issued only one mild protest statement on June 13. After Henry Kissinger's visit to Peking on June 20, China became silent. There were no personal statements from Mao and no mass demonstrations. China's long-practiced militancy had been defused by Nixon's new China policy. China's response was its continuing support for the Vietnamese Communist cause and Chou En-lai's advice to Nixon to follow President Dwight Eisenhower's example in Korea to end the Vietnam War. Meanwhile, China quietly but speedily helped build two plastic pipelines for fuel supplies to Hanoi.

By December, many factors had pushed Hanoi closer than ever to agreeing to a cease-fire pact: Nixon's surprise counteroffensive of bombings and blockading, China's and Russia's accommodations with the United States, the failure of the Communist offensive, the U.S. compromise peace offer of May 8, and the severe damage in the North under bombings and blockade. But the extremely destructive bombing in December was the decisive force that compelled the Hanoi leaders to sign the Vietnam peace accord in January 1973. China, contrary to the past, made no serious protest against the massive air raids other than its urge for a peaceful settlement. As it envisaged its enemy now shifting from its south to its north, the order of the day for Peking was the promotion of Sino-American relations. †

---

*Note that Premier Phan Van Dong and General Vo Nguyen Giap did not come out to welcome President Nikolai Podgorny in Hanoi in June--an unprecedented action and therefore a snub to the Soviet leader.

†For instance, in late December Chou En-lai asked Marilyn Berger to report his message to the American people that the December bombings imperiled Sino-American relations. [67]

SINO-AMERICAN RAPPROCHEMENT AND THE END
OF THE VIETNAM WAR, 1973-75

The Sino-American rapprochement made a speedy move in
1973. Beginning with Mao's two-hour meeting with Kissinger on February 17, China played an active role in promoting the rapprochement. During Kissinger's February visit, China and the United
States decided to establish a liaison office in each other's capital.
This decision, without any condition attached, was obviously a Peking
compromise. With an eye on some dissents, Chou En-lai had to explain the move at the Tenth Party Congress in August 1973. He said
that "necessary compromises between revolutionary countries and
imperialist countries must be distinguished from collusion and compromise between Soviet revisionism and U.S. imperialism."[68] He
cited the example of the Brest-Litovsk Treaty to justify the Sino-
American new ties.

During Kissinger's November visit, Mao again held a talk with
him. They pushed the two nations closer to full diplomatic relations.
The Watergate affair puzzled Peking about American political stability. But Kissinger was quick to reassure the Peking leaders that
"no matter what happens in the United States in the future," the
American policy toward China would remain constant.[69] In such a
conciliatory and cooperative spirit, cultural and scientific exchanges
were increased, trade was surging, and Kissinger was able to hold
several talks with Le Duc Tho in February, May, June, and December on the "peace agreement without peace" situation in Vietnam.

In 1974-75, however, Sino-American relations declined. Generally speaking, two important events led to this reverse development: the reinforcement of U.S.-Taiwan diplomatic ties and the
further development of the U.S.-Soviet detente. The U.S. failure
in Vietnam and the Watergate scandal also had some unfavorable impact on the delicate rapprochement.

Peking was unhappy over the appointment of Leonard Unger in
February 1974 to succeed Walter P. McConaughy as the American
ambassador to Taiwan. Rumors had spread in both Washington and
Taipei for some time that McConaughy would be the last American
ambassador to Taipei. But the Unger appointment set the rumors at
rest. Worse still, Washington agreed to Taipei in the same month
to open two new general consulates in this country. Peking filed
protests. Kissinger's explanation satisfied no one when he said that
he had not had much to do with Unger's appointment and that he was
not informed about the new Taiwan consulates.

During his visit to China in September 1974, Senator William
Fulbright detected China's unappreciative attitude toward the U.S.-
Soviet talks on the limitation of nuclear arms.[70] The Ford-Brezhnev

meeting at Vladivostok in November of the same year was even more
unwelcome to Peking leaders. China, therefore, gave a cold shoulder to Kissinger on his visit immediately after the Vladivostok meeting, and Mao did not receive him. To show its displeasure, China
canceled two orders in January and February 1975 for total U.S.
wheat purchase for the year.

The sweeping Communist victory in Vietnam in the spring of
1975 reflected the total failure of U.S. involvement in Indochina.
Riding on the tide of the American defeat, China smoothly achieved
a major diplomatic gain by establishing full relations with Thailand
and the Philippines. The trend of conciliation with China, a logical
development of disappointment with the United States and of desire
for accommodation with Peking, ran through Southeast Asia. Peking
regarded the United States as a "wounded tiger," considerably hurt
by its Vietnam defeat and the Watergate affair.[71]

Meanwhile, the progress of the American-Soviet det ente
alarmed Peking. Its spokesman bluntly warned President Gerald
Ford during the latter's visit in December 1975 that "rhetoric about
'detente' cannot cover up the stark reality of the growing danger of
war."[72] This language served to state clearly that Peking's prime
motive for a close relationship with the United States was to use
Washington as a counterweight against Moscow.

CONCLUSIONS

On the basis of the preceding discussions, a few observations
can be made. These analyses develop from the attempt to answer
the three questions raised at the outset of this chapter within the context of the principle of the four analytic elements.

Intensity of China's Support for Vietnam
Against the United States

Whether or not the Vietnam War presented a threat to China
was judged mainly by China's consideration of its national interests,
nationalistic concept, and the viewpoint of contradiction. Prior to
1971, occasional massive military strikes, such as the Cambodia
incursion and Laos operation discussed earlier, were conceived as
threats to China's security. National interests were the top priority
of policy deliberation; contradiction theory and nationalist sentiment
also played an important role. These strikes often stimulated China
to respond to the United States in an emotional and violent way. On
the other hand, the regular fighting in South Vietnam was considered

only a hostile act to China, not a threat; while tensions remained, China's response was less emotional and in lower level. Thus, the interaction was sometimes violent, sometimes quiet, sometimes high, sometimes low. In this context, it is significant to see further the intensity of China's support for Vietnam in opposition to the United States as shown in Jen-min jih-pao.

Prior to the Paris peace talks, Jen-min jih-pao carried almost one item each day--news story, statement, or comment--in support of the Vietnam War. After the talks began, coverage dropped to almost nil. From January to August of 1969, the Party organ carried supporting items only one to five days monthly (that is, one or five support-days monthly). In September and October, the monthly support-day rose to 17 and 15, respectively and then maintained an average of seven for four months. Beginning at the latter half of March 1970 (the Cambodia coup) to December 1972, the support-day increased, ranging from 13 to 31 monthly in addition to occasional editorials or statements.

The trend shown in Figure 1 is self-explanatory. First, China intensified its response to the United States by increasing its support for both North Vietnam and the Vietcong (as well as other Indochinese insurgent groups) after the Cambodian coup. It had never dropped lower than 13. This indicates that Peking resumed its normal relationship with Hanoi after March 1970, and that Ho Chi Minh's death (in September 1969), unlike some news reports indicated, did not serve as a factor for intensifying Peking's support. It only provided Peking with an opportunity to improve Sino-Vietnamese relations. Second, the intensity of support for the Vietcong had been slightly lower than that for North Vietnam. Contrary to some analysis, this suggests that China had kept its support for these two Vietnamese authorities relatively in balance. Consequently, it is argued that Peking had not sought to exploit any disagreements between North Vietnam and the Vietcong in their war with the United States.

Characteristics of Mao's Strategy

The question of what forces had persuaded China to disentangle the Sino-American relations from the Vietnam War also should be analyzed by the four elements.

Beginning in March 1969, three important events developed within four months: the Sino-Soviet Ussiri conflict, the beginning of U.S. troops withdrawal from Vietnam, and Nixon's messages to Peking for improving Sino-American relations. These developments must have convinced the Peking leaders of the fact that the threat to

FIGURE 1

The Trend of the Intensity of Support, 1969-72

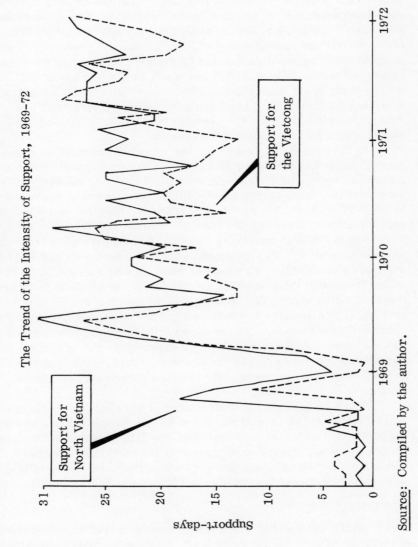

Source: Compiled by the author.

China had now shifted from the South to the North. The Soviet threat
was real. It posed the biggest problem to China. Japan was an
American ally and looked to Washington for leadership in East Asia.
If post-Cultural Revolution China remained in diplomatic isolation,
Peking might continue to have three potential enemies: the Soviet
Union and the United States and Japan. Against this background, a
rapprochement with the United States, which would be followed by a
thaw with Japan and a clarified position on Taiwan as part of China,
presented an attractive solution to the deadlock. This solution might
displease Vietnam, but Peking placed the security of its northern
frontier and the strengthening of its international position in a higher
position than the possible damage to Vietnam by a Sino-American
rapprochement. In fact, it did not result in any damage at all. Here
we see that, apart from the consideration of the factors of national
interests and ideological implications in disentangling new Sino-
American relations from the Vietnam issue, Mao's strategy has
played a crucial role in this development.

   In the process of developing the rapprochement, Mao showed
unequivocally his characteristics of caution, cooperation (alliance),
and concentration of strike. As discussed earlier, his pragmatic,
step-by-step, from-unofficial-to-official approach to rapprochement
in 1969-72 revealed his cautious character. Mao had employed it in
past situations, including his struggle against Lin Piao. *

   His success in reversing Peking's position from confrontation
to accommodation with Washington and Tokyo demonstrated his needs
and ability to establish a rapprochement. To be sure, it is neither a
united front with the United States and Japan nor an alliance by traditional Western standards. But insofar as Mao's strategy is concerned, it is a cooperation developing from his concept of united front
to meet China's needs. Mao realized fully that the United States and
Japan did not hold the same strategy for cooperation as China's. Yet
there were common grounds for accommodation. One of these
grounds was the concern of their common adversary, the Soviet
Union.

   Mao then revealed another aspect of his character--concentra-
tion of strike at one direction. Since he has succeeded in reducing
the hostilities of his former opponent (the United States), Mao now
concentrates his efforts on dealing with the remaining adversary.
China's fear of Russia, particularly since 1969, has necessitated
such an international lineup. During President Ford's visit to China

---

   *In the case of Lin Piao, Mao's tactics were "throwing rocks,
blending sand and digging at the wall." It was a highly tactical step-
by-step approach to his success. [73]

in December 1975, the Peking leadership was able to reach an understanding with the American president, which was expressed publicly later, that they entertained a mutual interest in countering any expansion of Soviet influence in the Pacific, Western Europe, and Angola. [74] This was a gain to Peking in terms of Mao's international united front against the Soviet Union. In addition, Peking's insistence on the insertion of an antihegemony clause in a future Sino-Japanese treaty is another attempt to oppose the Soviet Union. Moreover, China's strengthening of the Sino-French relationship and its efforts to open up relations with the European Common Market, an opportunity that the Kremlin passed up earlier, are aimed at an increasing international confrontation with Russia. So are China's campaigns in the Middle East and Angola. Unless unexpected factors develop, China's all-out struggle with the Soviet Union will remain in force for some time.

"Alliance and Struggle" with the United States

What are the implications of the Sino-American rapprochement? An effective detente (as well as rapprochement) requires two conditions: pressure and cooperation. Pressure comes from one's adversary; cooperation is room for accommodation with one's detente partners. Soviet pressure on China had grown strong enough to help isolate the People's Republic. During the process of responding to Washington's desire for a better relationship, Peking has found considerable room for Sino-American accommodation, such as trade, cultural and scientific exchanges, security of the Far East, and a common adversary--the Soviet Union. On these aims, China undoubtedly has placed high priority.

The element of national interest may be considered to be more important than the others. And yet the factor of ideology that polarizes the United States and China into two different worlds predetermined some limits to the relations between the two countries. On the one hand, China has benefited enormously from the rapprochement, such as UN membership, obtaining more than 50 nations' diplomatic recognition, trade and cultural-scientific exchanges with the United States, and, above all, higher international position and prestige. On the other hand, the American-Soviet detente continues to advance, Peking and Washington still have not established a full diplomatic relationship, and the Taiwan issue remains unsettled. In favorable situations, China shows a cooperative and friendly attitude toward the United States. In unfavorable situations, China turns cool and harsh. China's relations with the United States are both cooperative and critical, as dictated by the tactic of the combination of "alliance and struggle."

Immediately after Kissinger's first visit to Peking in 1971, a well-intended article was published in Hung-ch'i (Red Flag) in August 1971.[75] It stressed the importance of Mao's tactic of the combination of "alliance and struggle" toward the Kuomintang during the Sino-Japanese War, as elaborated in Mao's article "On Policy,"[76] and urged the necessity of restudying this article in order to attain an "all-round and integrated understanding of the Party's policies and tactics." The theses of alliance and struggle and of the exploitation of international contradictions through the Sino-American rapprochement were constantly repeated in the Hung-ch'i article and the secret Kunming Documents of March 1973.[77]

Thus, when Nixon visited and cooperated with China in 1972, Peking was enthusiastic and cooperative (alliance-cooperation); when the American-Soviet detente developed well, Peking denounced the superpowers' hegemony (struggle-criticism); when the United States rapidly promoted trade and cultural-scientific exchanges with China, Peking compromised on the diplomatic liaison office (alliance-cooperation); and when the United States made the Leonard Unger appointment for Taiwan and further advanced the American-Soviet detente, China showed no reluctance to express its displeasure to the United States (struggle-criticism). Nevertheless, since Peking realizes fully that cooperation with the United States is a necessity for its confrontation with the Soviet Union, the Sino-American rapprochement will be carried on in a form of more "alliance" and less "struggle."

In sum, China's response to the United States in 1969-75 has developed from a time of hostility during the Vietnam War to present-day reconciliation. Despite basic differences between Peking and Washington, the two sides have learned to understand each other's perceptions of areas of interest. When their interests converge, a better relationship develops. Insofar as China's interests are concerned, Sino-American rapprochement is the best strategy for China to deal with several crucial problems, such as the Soviet issue, the status of Taiwan, the plans for a rapid industrialization, and the promotion of international leadership. For mutual benefit, improvement of relations is expected to continue in the future.

NOTES

1. For the model, see Ole R. Holsti, Robert C. North, and Richard A. Brody, "Perception and Action in the 1914 Crisis," in Quantitative International Politics: Insights and Evidence, ed. J. David Singer (New York: The Free Press, 1968); and Robert Jervis, "The Costs of the Quantitative Study of International Relations," in

Contending Approaches to International Politics, ed. Klaus Knorr and James N. Rosenau (Princeton, N.J.: Princeton University Press, 1969).

2. King C. Chen, "Peking's Strategy in Indochina," Yale Review, June 1965, p. 550.

3. Mao Tse-tung, "On Contradiction," in Selected Works (Peking: Foreign Languages Press, 1965), vol. 1, pp. 318, 330.

4. Mao Tse-tung, "On the People's Democratic Dictatorship," in Selected Works (Peking: Foreign Languages Press, 1961), vol. 1.

5. Peking Review, January 24, 1964, p. 7. For the origin of Mao's "intermediate zone" concept, see Anna Louise Strong, "The Thought of Mao Tse-tung," Amerasia 11, no. 6 (June 1947): 161-62.

6. Lin Piao, "Report to the Ninth National Congress of the Communist Party of China," Peking Review, April 30, 1969, p. 31.

7. See the "Kunming Documents," Chinese Law and Government 8, no. 1 (Spring 1975): 30-60.

8. Harold C. Hinton properly describes the Sino-Soviet armed conflict as a clash of nationalism in "Conflict on the Ussuri: A Clash of Nationalism," Problems of Communism 20, nos. 1-2 (January-April 1971).

9. Unlike Glenn D. Paige on Harry Truman's decision on Korea (The Korean Decision [New York: The Free Press, 1968]), the outsiders of Peking's decision-making circle will probably have no opportunity at all to gain access to any significant data on Mao's decisions on major international issues. Allen S. Whiting's work on Peking's decision to enter the Korean War (China Crosses the Yalu [New York: Macmillan, 1960]) was done largely through content analysis.

10. The psychological factor is certainly an important determinant of policy formulation. See Richard C. Snyder et al., Foreign Policy Decision-Making (New York: The Free Press, 1962), p. 140; and Joseph de Rivera, The Psychological Dimension of Foreign Policy (Columbus, Ohio: Charles E. Merrill, 1968), chap. 5.

11. Mao Tse-tung, "Concentrate a Superior Force to Destroy the Enemy Forces One by One," in Selected Works (Peking: Foreign Languages Press, 1961), vol. 4, p. 104.

12. Mao Tse-tung, "On Policy," in Selected Works (Peking: Foreign Languages Press, 1965), vol. 2, pp. 442-43.

13. Kung Ch'u, "Ts'an-chia Chung-kung wu-chuang tou-cheng chi-shih" [Records of My Participation in Chinese Communist Armed Struggles], Ming Pao (Hong Kong), no. 71 (November 1971): 94-98.

14. For James Reston's interview with Chou En-lai and Chou's view of Japan in 1971, see Frank Ching, ed., Report from China (New York: Avon Books, 1972), pp. 92-95.

15. Richard M. Nixon, "Asia after Viet Nam," Foreign Affairs 46, no. 1 (October 1967): 113-14.
16. Richard M. Nixon, U.S. Foreign Policy for the 1970's: Building for Peace (Washington, D.C.: U.S. Government Printing Office, February 25, 1970), pp. 10-14; U.S. Foreign Policy, 1969-1970: A Report of the Secretary of State (Washington, D.C.: Department of State Publication 8575, March 1971), pp. 36-39.
17. Nixon, U.S. Foreign Policy for the 1970's, op. cit., p. 15.
18. Ibid., p. 62.
19. United States Foreign Policy, 1971: A Report of the Secretary of State (Washington, D.C.: Department of State Publication 8634, March 1972), p. 71.
20. Ibid., p. 72.
21. Raphael Littauer and Norman Uphoff, eds., with a preface by Neil Sheehan, The Air War in Indochina, rev. ed. (Boston: Beacon Press, 1972).
22. Edgar Snow, "Interview with Mao," New Republic, February 27, 1965, pp. 17-23.
23. See, for instance, Uri Ra'anan, "Peking's Foreign Policy 'Debate,' 1965-1966," and Donald Zagoria, "The Strategic Debate in Peking," both in China in Crisis, vol. 2, China's Policies in Asia and America's Alternatives, ed. Tang Tsou (Chicago: University of Chicago Press, 1968); and Michael Yahuda, "Kremlinology and the Chinese Strategic Debate, 1965-66," China Quarterly, January-March 1972.
24. See Snow, op. cit.; Lin Piao, "Long Live the Victory of People's War!" Peking Review, September 3, 1965; and Chou En-lai's statement in Peking Review, no. 20 (May 13, 1966): 5.
25. "Refutation of the New Leaders of the CPSU on 'United Action,'" Peking Review, November 12, 1965.
26. Lin Piao, "Long Live the Victory," op. cit., p. 19.
27. Allen S. Whiting, "How We Almost Went to War with China," Look, April 29, 1969, pp. 76-77; Richard M. Bueschel, Communist Chinese Air Power (New York: Praeger, 1968), p. 83; Hanoi Radio, July 3, 1965; New York Times, August 12, 1964, July 18, 1965; Jen-min jih-pao, December 6, 1965.
28. Copies of General Nguyen Van Vinh's speech were circulated in Saigan and Washington; see, for instance, Beverly Deepe, "How Hanoi Looks at Negotiating," Christian Science Monitor, May 9, 1968, p. 14.
29. Snow, op. cit.
30. New York Times, January 8, 1967, p. 34.
31. New York Times, February 9, 1967, p. 1.
32. L. B. Johnson, The Vantage Point (New York: Holt, Rinehart and Winston, 1971), p. 435.

33. For the DRV government's statement of acceptance, see Hanoi Radio, April 3, 1968; for Peking's denunciation of the peace talks proposal, see "U.S. Imperialist Chieftain Johnson Tries New Fraud," Peking Review, no. 15 (April 12, 1968): 14-15.

34. Radio Peking, November 26, 1968.

35. Jen-min jih-pao, February 19, 1969; New China News Agency, July 29, 1969.

36. Consult Thomas W. Robinson, "The Sino-Soviet Border Dispute," American Political Science Review, December 1972, pp. 1175-1202.

37. Zbigniew Brzezinski, "The Competitive Relationship," Research Institute on Communist Affairs Monograph (New York: Columbia University, 1972), p. 29n.

38. Edgar Snow, "A Conversation with Mao Tse-tung," Life, April 30, 1971, p. 48.

39. New China News Agency, September 26, 1969.

40. Jen-min jih-pao, October 26, 1969. On September 16, Nixon had announced another withdrawal of 35,000 troops from Vietnam.

41. See Vo Nugyen Giap, National Liberation War in Viet Nam: General Line--Strategy--Tactics (Hanoi: Foreign Languages Publishing House, 1971. This pamphlet was first published in seven articles between December 14 and 20, 1969 in Nhan Dan and Quan Doi Nhan Dan (People's Army).

42. See "Under the Glorious Banner of the Party, for Independence, Freedom and Socialist, Let Us Advance and Achieve New Victories," Nhan Dan, February 14, 1970, excerpted in Viet-Nam Courier, February 23, March 2, 9, 16, 1970. See also Viet-Nam Documents and Research Notes, document no. 77 (Saigon: American Embassy, April 1970).

43. Peking's minor criticism of the Lon Nol regime began in the occasional column "International Review" in Jen-min jih-pao: "Condemn the Atrocities of the Cambodian Rightist Clique, Running Dog of U.S. Imperialism," April 16, 1970, p. 6.

44. "The Statement of the Government of the People's Republic of China," Jen-min jih-pao, April 29, 1970.

45. New York Times, May 9, 1970, p. 2.

46. Jen-min jih-pao, May 21, 1970.

47. See Louis Wiznitzer, "How War Looks to North Vietnamese Envoys," Christian Science Monitor, April 21, 1971, pp. 1-2.

48. Pravda, May 18, 1970, reported in New York Times, May 19, 1970, p. 1.

49. Radio Moscow, in Mandarin to China, May 21, 1970.

50. M. Ukraintsev, "Asia and the Peking Empire-Builders," New Times (Moscow), June 9, 1970, p. 15. It should be noted that Moscow also granted new aid to North Vietnam on June 11, 1970.

51. Alessandro Casella, "In Peking, Monseigneur Talks About 'His' Communists, the Future of Cambodia, Nixon and the Death of Kings," New York Times Magazine, January 23, 1972, p. 9.

52. New York Times, June 18, 1970, p. 9.

53. Radio Hanoi, December 10, 1970.

54. Jen-min jih-pao, December 14, 1970.

55. Commented by General Frederick C. Weyand, deputy commander of U.S. forces in Vietnam, New York Times, March 2, 1971, p. 4.

56. Commentator, "Don't Lose Your Head, Nixon," Jen-min jih-pao, February 20, 1971.

57. Ibid.

58. New York Times, February 26 and 28, 1971.

59. "Joint Communique of the Central Committee of the Communist Party of China and the Government of the People's Republic of China, and the Central Committee of the Viet Nam Workers' Party and the Government of the Democratic Republic of Viet Nam," Jen-min jih-pao, March 11, 1971; Peking Review, March 12, 1971.

60. Ross Terrill, 800,000,000, The Real China (New York: Delta, 1972), pp. 145-46.

61. Jen-min jih-pao, March 25, 1971.

62. New York Times, March 12, 1972, p. 2.

63. Snow, "A Conversation with Mao," op. cit.

64. The Committee of Concerned Asian Scholars, China! Inside the People's Republic (New York: Bantam, 1972), p. 345. Also see Chou En-lai's statement to American newsmen, Detroit News, October 9, 1972, p. 1.

65. Peking Review, March 3, 1972, p. 5.

66. Lucian W. Pye, "China and the United States: A New Phase," Annals of the American Academy of Political and Social Science 402 (July 1972): 101.

67. See Marilyn Berger's report in Washington Post, December 29, 1972, p. 1.

68. Chou En-lai, "Report to the Tenth National Congress of the Communist Party of China," Peking Review, nos. 35-36 (September 7, 1973): 24.

69. New York Times, November 15, 1973, p. 8.

70. Christian Science Monitor, September 9, 1974, p. 2.

71. New York Times, October 24, 1975, p. 6.

72. Peking Review (December 5, 1975), p. 8.

73. For a summary of the tactics from secret papers, see New York Times, December 17, 1972, p. 3. For a detailed treatment on the Lin Piao case, see Michael Y. M. Kau, ed., The Lin Piao Affairs: Powers Politics and Military Coup (White Plains, N.Y.: International Arts and Sciences Press, 1975).

74. New York Times, December 5, 1975, p. 1.

75. "T'uan-chieh jen-min chan-sheng ti-jen ti ch'iang-ta wu-ch'i: Hsieh-hsi 'Lun cheng-ts'e'" [A Powerful Weapon to Unite the People and Defeat the Enemy: A Study of 'On Policy'], Hung-ch'i [Red Flag], no. 9 (August 2, 1971): 10-17.

76. Mao Tse-tung, "On Policy," op. cit., pp. 442-43.

77. "Kunming Documents," op. cit.

5

CHINA AND JAPAN
SINCE NORMALIZATION
A. M. Halpern

This chapter is limited to the presentation of a number of propositions concerning Chinese policy toward Japan beginning with the normalization of diplomatic relations in September 1972. It is obvious that over this span of time, as before normalization, Chinese policy toward Japan operated on several levels. For convenience, the chapter will distinguish two levels, that of direct bilateral negotiations and that of the PRC's dealing with Japan as a factor in the total context of international relations. Probably everybody will accept the proposition that activities on the two levels are linked. In the present period, however, the nature of the linkage is not as easily discernible as in past periods. As a generalization, it is suggested that an indirect linkage exists between the two levels but not necessarily between particular facets of one with particular activities on the other. In other words, while the overall pattern of bilateral relations is reflective of China's general strategy, no specific single strategic objective appears to determine directly a specific Chinese negotiatory maneuver.

The quality of the available evidence is uneven. Even before normalization, but especially since then, much more detailed, though still incomplete information is provided by Japanese sources than

---

The author wishes to express his appreciation of a grant from the Earhart Foundation which materially assisted the research on which this chapter is based. An earlier draft version of this chapter was presented at the Washington and Southeast Regional Seminar on China, October 24, 1975.

by Chinese.* This situation is regarded as significant in its own right, and will be commented on below.

THE NORMALIZATION PROCESS

The relevant questions concerning the normalization in September 1972 relate to timing, style, and strategic calculations. In July 1972, immediately after the resignation of Prime Minister Eisaku Sato and the assumption of office by Prime Minister Kakuei Tanaka, the Japanese were taken by surprise by clear signs that the PRC wished to move rapidly toward normalization of relations rather than let time pass. Many Japanese interpreted the PRC's eagerness as indicative of some weakness and therefore an advantage to Japan's bargaining position. Some speculated that China was in need of Japanese help in promoting economic development, others that China needed to normalize relations during the brief interval while Mao Tse-tung and Chou En-lai remained healthy and active, and still others that the Chinese knew they had to move fast in order to avoid risking a sudden shift in volatile Japanese public opinion.

In retrospect, these interpretations appear faulty. A more tenable interpretation is that the Chinese saw a set of circumstances as favorable to themselves as could be expected. Following their entry into the United Nations (October 1971) and the issuance of the Shanghai communique (February 1972), the Chinese had established the new pattern in their foreign policy and found their international prestige at a peak. Japan, in contrast, though largely recovered from the Nixon shocks, was still reappraising its foreign policy. There was general recognition that, in the wake of the U.S. shift in its China policy, a change in Japan's China policy was on the way. Politically, the change was positively welcomed by the opposition parties and by large elements of the governing Liberal-Democratic Party (LDP). The pro-Taiwan elements of the LDP accepted it grudgingly. Public opinion was overwhelmingly disposed toward normalization. Acceptance of this change as inevitable by the business community in the waning days of the Sato Administration created support for Tanaka in his rivalry with Takeo Fukuda over the

---

*The American Embassy, Tokyo, provides coverage of the Japanese daily and periodical press through two series of translations, the Daily Summary of the Japanese Press and Summaries of Selected Japanese Magazines. These are the main sources of references cited in this chapter.

succession to Sato. The belief that Tanaka would be better placed than Fukuda to carry out the necessary shift in policy was an important factor influencing the choice of business circles.

The Chinese were fully briefed on these developments. They were well aware of the positions taken by the opposition parties through conversations with official missions of these parties who had visited China throughout the year prior to Tanaka's accession. In addition, a number of conservative politicians and representatives of Japanese business groups had visited China with the purpose of mutual sounding out of views. Thus, as of early July, the Chinese could be sure that Japan's new political leadership was committed to normalization. The same pattern of communication persisted throughout July and August. Furthermore, in these same months, qualified representatives of the PRC government were in Tokyo, where they could be consulted for clarification of the Chinese position. *

The content of the Tanaka-Chou communique of September 1972 indicates that the Chinese maintained bargaining strength. Both before and after Tanaka's accession virtually all Japanese discussion of policy toward China revolved around the question of how Japan could meet the conditions that the PRC specified as necessary for normalization. In substance, Japan conceded to all these demands, of which the most important was termination of Japan's diplomatic relations with Taipei and acknowledgment of PRC sovereignty over Taiwan. The PRC accepted wording and procedures that enabled Japan to meet these demands with a minimum of complications, thereby validating assurances given privately that it would refrain from creating embarrassment for the new prime minister and his associates. †

---

*Details of a number of these behind-the-scenes communications were made public after the publication of the Tanaka-Chou communique. On the day the communique was released, Asahi published a detailed account of the activities of Yoshimi Furui and Seiichi Tagawa of the Liberal Democratic party, Yoshikatsu Takeiri of the Komei party, and Kozo Sasaki of the Japanese Socialist party. Furui published his own account of his and others' activities.[1] The visit to China by Takeo Miki in April 1972, though obviously undertaken with serious intent, has never been described fully in public.

†For the communique and associated documents see Peking Review, October 6, 1972. On the matter of sovereignty over Taiwan, the wording refers to Japan's obligations under Article 8 of the Potsdam Declaration, which in turn refers to the Cairo Declaration of 1943. In substance, Japan acknowledged that Taiwan

On the Chinese side, the basis of the new relationship with
Japan was the full development of the PRC's post-Cultural Revolution foreign policy. The pattern is complex, and one could choose
any portion of it as a point of departure. A major element is neutralization of the ability of the Soviet Union to threaten Chinese interests. Rapprochement with the United States, based on U.S. interest
in a balance that would avoid the potential for catastrophe inherent
in a Sino-Soviet war, was necessary for this purpose. The Sino-
American rapprochement, however, touches other matters as well.
The nonhegemony clause of the Shanghai communique can be considered as renunciation by both parties of the ambition to maintain
spheres of influence in Asia. It implies further that both parties
accept, albeit with differences of emphasis and detail, maintenance
of the independence of the various countries of Asia as a desirable
goal. The Chinese pattern includes identification of the PRC as a
developing country with interests that coincide with those of other
developing countries (the Third World) and rejection of the concept
of a socialist camp. Among Third World interests, the Chinese include opposition to the two superpowers, singly or jointly. In sum,
the ruling concept of current Chinese foreign policy is multipolarity,
conceived in terms sufficiently close to those employed by Henry
Kissinger to sustain a meeting of minds. In a multipolar world,
China would function neither as a nunior ally of a greater power nor
as the domineering leader of a bloc but as an independent factor in
world affairs, taking the course its interests indicate in each case.
    The Sino-American understanding not only precipitated a
change in Japan's policy toward China but put the PRC in a position
to consider the problem of Japan more calmly. Once the coordination of American and Japanese policies toward China was broken,
the Japanese were both free to and forced to deal with China autono-
mously. China had the advantage of dealing with a Japan no longer

---

belongs to China, thus departing from its previously held position
that while Japan had renounced all right and title in the 1951 San
Francisco Peace Treaty, sovereignty had not been transferred to
any other power but remained undetermined. Although the PRC had
originally demanded that Japan abrogate its 1952 peace treaty with
the Republic of China, the PRC accepted instead a statement to the
press by Masayoshi Ohira, separate from the joint communique, to
the effect that that treaty had "expired." On the vexed question of
whether or not a state of war had continued to exist between Japan
and the PRC, the Chinese agreed to a reference in the joint communique to termination of "the abnormal state of affairs" that had obtained between Japan and themselves.

constrained by or supported by its ally. How apprehensive the
Chinese ever actually were about the resurgence of Japanese mili-
tarism--the most prominent single theme in Chinese commentary on
Japan up to mid-September 1971--remains a matter of conjecture.
Rapprochement with the United States reduced Chinese anxiety over
Japan's potential role as an adjunct to an anti-Chinese American
strategy. The danger of conflict between China and the United States
or Japan over Taiwan was effectively reduced, and the revelation
on July 4, 1972, of the North-South Korean joint communique indicated the possibility of a similar reduction of the danger on the
Korean peninsula. Thus, any rapid movement by Japan toward developing a "forward defense" structure capable of intervening in
these areas was virtually eliminated. Furthermore, if the Chinese
ever had really been worried that Japan might emerge as an expansionist military power apart from its ally, the new situation (including normalization) provided checks against such a development. At
the least, the prospect of a militarized Japan was postponed for
approximately a decade.

Under these circumstances, for the PRC normalization involved no disadvantages and some worthwhile advantages. In the
short run, it made it possible to regularize on an official basis
aspects of the Sino-Japanese relationship that had been carried on
unofficially or semiofficially. In the long run, it promoted the establishment of an international role for Japan that was likely to suit
China's preferred strategy.

SINCE NORMALIZATION

As noted earlier, the Chinese press's coverage of Japanese
affairs has declined remarkably since normalization. Not only the
charges of resurgent Japanese militarism but a variety of other
allegations of dastardly actions or intent (for example, in relation
to Taiwan, Korea, and Southeast Asia) are conspicuously absent.
The most frequent theme in Peking Review references to Japan in
1975 was sympathy for Japan in the face of Soviet harassment of
Japanese fishing vessels and support of the legitimacy of Japan's
claim to the southern Kuriles. The Japan Communist Party is still
occasionally the subject of casual insults but no longer is treated as
a serious bete noire. There are no detailed analyses of Japan's
domestic politics. Such analyses were never frequent but were
indicative, when they were made, of a real degree of concern. The
September 1970 analysis of the Japanese polity, which served as the
doctrinal underpinning of the PRC's propaganda campaign against
the revival of Japanese militarism,[2] has long been obsolete, and no

alternate analysis has been published. One could speculate that the group of Japan experts who have resumed control of the formulation and implementation of the PRC's policy toward Japan* either feel no need for such a declaration or consider that the Japanese polity is currently changing in ways whose outcome is not entirely predictable. On a less grandiose level, the New China News Agency's report[3] of the result of the December 1972 Japanese Lower House election was noticeably curt, even in comparison with the brief treatment such elections have normally received.†

China's handling of a Japanese Socialist Party (JSP) delegation in May 1975 provides an interesting example of restraint The delegation was headed by the party chairman, Narita Tomomi, but was influenced by younger socialist dietmen belonging to the "New Current Group." The visit and talks with representatives of the China-Japan Friendship Association coincided with one of the more delicate phases of negotiations between the Chinese and Japanese governments concerning the content of a treaty of peace and friendship. On the point at issue--whether or not an article dealing with joint opposition to hegemony on the part of third powers should be included in the text of the treaty--the JSP subscribed to a joint statement in which the PRC's position was fully endorsed. The New China News Agency published the text of the statement, but the Peking Review gave the visit only cursory treatment and did not print the text of the statement--the first time it had failed to publish the result of talks with a JSP delegation.[4] Although the statement aroused a variety of reactions, Peking did nothing to exploit it to further advantage.‡

This negative evidence, I believe, can support a number of propositions. First, normalization entailed a shift by the PRC from primary reliance on "people's diplomacy" in its approach to Japan to emphasis on official communication. While the tactic of fostering popular pressure on the government to change its China policy became

---

*After a period of eclipse during and after the Cultural Revolution.

†The election resulted in striking gains for the JCP and losses for the LDP. Since the election was the first test after normalization of Prime Minister Tanaka's strength, and since the result made it necessary for Tanaka to come to terms with Fukuda in order to operate his party and government effectively, it must be assumed that the PRC took it more seriously than NCNA coverage indicated.

‡The Soviet Union was outraged at what it considered Narita's perfidy. Within the JSP, the incident exacerbated feelings between the pro-China and pro-Soviet wings, as well as within the Central Executive Committee, which nevertheless approved the statement.[5]

unnecessary once the policy was changed, the Chinese have by no means forgotten those who stood by them in the past. They regularly refer to "old friends" whom they still esteem--for example, the Japan-China Cultural Exchange Organization, the Japan-China Friendship Association (orthodox), as well as specific individuals-- at the same time that they show appreciation of "new friends," among whom they include former Prime Minister Tanaka, former Foreign Minister (now Finance Minister) Masayoshi Ohira, Speaker of the House of Councillors Kenzo Kono, and Shigeru Hori. Only when the Chinese feel some uncertainty about the attitudes of new friends do they call on old friends to provide illumination.

Second, China now accepts the existing distribution of power in Japan, political as well as economic, as a fact of life and no longer actively attempts to modify that distribution. A partial qualification, to be examined below, must be noted. The PRC was very satisfied with the Tanaka-Ohira combination but is less satisfied with the present group of influential men centered on Prime Minister Miki. The difference is one of relatively small degree, and its effect on operations is debatable.

Third, the PRC has done nothing to impede the growth of official channels of communication and the substitution of these for private channels. Embassies of each country were established fairly promptly, in March 1973, with personnel selected by both with careful attention to expertise. Both ambassadors have been accorded adequate responsibility. Two major Chinese missions made extended visits to Japan in 1974, one led by Liao Ch'eng-chih and the other by Vice Minister for Foreign Affairs Han Nien-lung. *

Fourth, the priority of Japan as a foreign policy target was distinctly lowered after normalization. Perhaps it might be more accurate to say that the priority of foreign policy in general has declined, since even Chinese opposition to the superpowers and support of the Third World look more like a posture than a positive policy. As for Japan, the PRC now clearly classifies it as a component of the "Second World" along with the Western European countries. The PRC further seems satisfied with the postnormalization state of its relations with Japan. A small piece of positive evidence in this

---

*Ambassador Heishiro Ogawa, who at one time served as consul general in Hong Kong, is a specialist on Sino-Soviet affairs. His staff drew on the experience of the China Section of the Bureau of Asian Affairs. Ambassador Ch'en Ch'u's staff members are described in Asahi, January 14, 1973. Liao Ch'eng-chih has long (except for the Cultural Revolution interlude) been the key figure among the PRC's Japan experts.

regard is the reference made to Japan in Chou En-lai's speech at the Fourth National People's Congress in January 1975. The comment was brief: "We are ready to work together with the Japanese Government and people to promote friendly and good-neighbourly relations between the two countries on the basis of the Sino-Japanese Joint Statement." It represented, however, a more forthcoming attitude toward Japan than was shown to any other country. Furthermore, Chou did not directly couple Japan with other "Second World" countries whom he offered to support "in their struggle against superpower control, threats and bullying."[6]

Fifth, in place of the direct pressures exerted by the PRC during the Sato Administration--whether through denunciations, demands, or the mobilization of pro-Chinese forces in Japan through people's diplomacy--Chinese pressure is now exerted gently and indirectly. The Chinese let their attitude be known through Japanese correspondents stationed in Peking or through comments made to Japanese of some political standing who visit China in nonofficial capacities.

Sixth--and here there is some positive evidence--the Chinese no longer regard Japan as a military threat either in itself or as an ally of the United States. The first solid indication of the revised Chinese estimate was given early in 1973, through comments made by Chou En-lai to a visiting conservative politician, Takeo Kimura, repeated by Liao Ch'eng-chih in an interview with a group of Yomiuri reporters, and again confirmed late in the year by comments made by Foreign Minister Chi P'eng-fei to a delegation of the Foreign Affairs Committee of the Lower House of the Japanese Diet.* According to these statements the substance of the PRC's declared position was the following: The danger of revival of militarism is low, since the Japanese people will resist it; Japan as an independent country is entitled to a defense capability, but the PRC does not endorse Japan's Fourth Defense Buildup Plan; since there is a threat to Japan from the USSR, Japan needs to remain under the U.S. nuclear umbrella; the Japan-U.S. Mutual Security Treaty remains objectionable in

---

*Kimura's account of his talks with Chou was widely reported in the Japanese press on January 27, 1973. Of particular interest is an interview with Kimura reported in Sankei, January 29, 1973. Chi's remarks, made on October 12, were reported in Asahi, October 16, but more extensively in an article written by Eiichi Nagasue for Kyoto DSP, the organ paper of the Kyoto prefectural branch of the Democratic Socialist Party.[7] Nagasue, one of the DSP's recognized theorists on military affairs, was a member of the Japanese delegation, and Chi had singled him out as a special target of his remarks.

principle, but since in practice it poses no threat to China there is
no need to abrogate it.

This position is obviously a total departure, even though with
reservations, from that taken by the PRC in 1970-71. It also re-
verses the PRC's advocacy over many years of neutralism and rejection of military alliance as the proper policy for Japan. Though
Chou was subsequently inactive and Chi P'eng-fei was replaced as
foreign minister by Ch'iao Kuan-hua, the position outlined by Chou
and Chi has not been altered.*

OPERATIONAL AGREEMENTS

At the time of normalization, Prime Minister Tanaka proposed
that a number of agreements on technical aspects of Sino-Japanese
relations be concluded. At the time, Chou En-lai dismissed these
questions as "trifles." Settlement of these "operational agreements"
was therefore deferred until after the appointment of ambassadors.
When Heishiro Ogawa was appointed as Japan's ambassador, he made
it known that the Japanese approach would be to conclude these
agreements--on aviation, trade, shipping, and fisheries, in that
order--as the prelude to a treaty of peace and friendship provided
for in the Tanaka-Chou joint communique. While things did not proceed in quite that way, the implementation of the premises of normalization was on the whole in accord with the PRC's guidelines as
posited above.

The PRC treated three of the operational agreements as no
more than that--as technical or administrative matters with no political admixture. In regard to the remaining question--the aviation
agreement, chronologically the first to be taken up--the Chinese
introduced a political condition.

The trade agreement was signed in Peking on January 5, 1974
in the midst of stormy debates in Japan over the political aspect of
the aviation agreement. The trade agreement, valid for three years
and subject to automatic extension, is wholly technical in content.
Its central provisions concern reciprocal most-favored-nation treatment. In addition, it establishes a Sino-Japanese governmental
mixed committee empowered to make recommendations for further
implementation. [8] With this, the former Memorandum Trade Office,

---

*The execution of the Fourth Defense Plan has fallen well short
of the original schedule. The major obstacle to its progress is not
political but the impact of inflation on a static budget.

which had for years served as one of the two major channels for
trade negotiations, and, as many suppose, functioned also as a
quasiofficial political pipeline, was dissolved. The mixed committee has displayed little activity. A Japan-China Economic Association (headed by Yoshihiro Inayama, chairman of the board of Nippon
Steel Corporation) was formed in November 1972 to serve as a channel for private-level trade discussions. The Japan International
Trade Promotion Association (JITPA headed by Aiichiro Fujiyama)
continues to serve the needs of smaller Japanese industries. The
sometime rivalry between these two Japanese channels, which in
the past the PRC was able to fan for its own purposes, has largely
moderated.

Trade volume, slow to grow at first, then expanded at an accelerating rate and with an accelerating imbalance in favor of Japan.
Volume increased from $1.1 billion in 1972 to $2 billion in 1973,
$3.3 billion in 1974, and $3.8 billion in 1975, with Japan recording
a positive balance of $118 million in 1972, $67 million in 1973, $683
million in 1974, and $730 million in 1975.* The acceleration in both
aspects is partially to be discounted as accruing from the rapid rate
of inflation of Japanese prices.

Among Japanese exports, steel and machinery are now prominent. On the Chinese side, oil occupies an increasing place.[9] Japanese imports of oil from China amounted to 1 million tons in 1973
and over 4 million tons (less than the originally contracted amount
of approximately 4.9 million tons) in 1974, an amount expected to
rise to over 7 million tons in 1975. For the present, Japan is the
most suitable buyer of Chinese oil. Because of its high wax content,
Chinese oil is difficult for the refineries of other Asian buyers to
handle. Japanese refineries are equipped to handle it, though only
for a limited type of use.

The future of Chinese exports of oil to Japan is difficult to
foresee, except that there is general agreement that the amount will
increase steadily. The trade is desirable from the Japanese standpoint as in diversifying its sources of supply, even if not to the point
of eliminating dependence on the Middle East. The remaining problem for Japan is to reach a long-term agreement to ensure a stable
supply. At the end of 1975, negotiations to this end were under way.
On the Chinese side, oil is the most promising source of foreign
exchange. The trade in oil is therefore mutually advantageous.

_____

*All figures are approximate and drawn from various Japanese
press accounts of periodic reports by JETRO [Japan External Trade
Recovery Organization]. The figures are sufficiently reliable as indicators of trends.

Some observers have speculated that Japan could become so dependent on Chinese oil that the PRC would acquire strong leverage that could be used to extort political concessions from Japan. The possibility cannot be dismissed, but the factors bearing on it are many and complex. [10]

The shipping agreement, signed November 13, 1974, also provides for most-favored-nation treatment. At some points in the negotiations, the PRC showed signs of raising a political condition concerning the display of the Chinese Nationalist flag by Taiwan vessels entering Japanese ports, but in the face of Japanese adherence to the principle of free navigation and the maintenance of existing practice, the PRC yielded the point. The fisheries agreement, designed to replace a long-existing private agreement, took the longest period of negotiation. Besides various technical issues, such as allowable horsepower of ship engines, size of net meshes, and so on, the main obstacle was the PRC's desire to establish a military guard line. Eventually, the Chinese met Japanese desires, and the agreement was signed on August 15, 1975, at a time when negotiations on the treaty of peace and friendship were seemingly at a deadlock. [11]

The reasonableness and spirit of accommodation of the PRC on these three operational agreements contrast with its apparent intransigence on the aviation agreement and the friendship treaty. In each case the Chinese set a political condition that aroused strong opposition of the most conservative elements of the Liberal Democratic party. The opposition was predictable in the case of the aviation agreement but perhaps somewhat fortuitous in the case of the friendship treaty. The motives of the Chinese in each case are obscure, and it is also possible that their stubbornness was in part a reaction to the appearance of opposition. By the same token, their reasonableness in other cases may be partly accounted for by the fact that they offered no occasion for domestic controversy in Japan, and the negotiations were thus insulated from an extraneous political action-reaction pattern.

The controversy that broke out in connection with the aviation agreement had nothing to do with the initiation of regular air transportation. Both sides desired this traffic, and repeatedly said so. In the simplest terms, the issue for the Chinese was whether Japan would fulfill its declaration in the Tanaka-Chou communique to respect the PRC's position on the sovereignty of Taiwan. The aviation question provided the earliest opportunity for a test. The Chinese suggested several formulas by which to avoid the possibility that PRC and Nationalist flag-carrying aircraft would stand side by side on Japanese airfields. The formula finally adopted was proposed by Foreign Minister Ohira in order to meet Chinese demands. It

entailed a declaration by Japan that, consequent to its termination
of diplomatic relations with Taipei, it no longer regarded the Nationalist flag as the banner of a nation.

For the Japanese, there was a question of the PRC's living up
to assurances privately given at the time of normalization that China
would refrain from disrupting Japan's commercial relations with
Taiwan. The aviation issue was the occasion for reviving intraparty
political conflict between the pro-Taiwan hawks and the pro-PRC
doves in the LDP. It was at this point, in mid-1973, that an anti-
Tanaka cross-factional group of younger right-wing LDP Diet mem-
bers--the Seirankai--was formed, which then spearheaded the opposition together with the already existing Nikka Rengo (Association
for Promoting Japan-Republic of China Relations, headed by Nadao
Hirokichi). The agreement was signed on April 20, 1974. When the
Lower House vote on ratification took place, some 80 LDP representatives absented themselves from the Diet in a massive display
of opposition, equal to a similar maneuver in 1956 on the occasion
of the ratification of the Soviet-Japanese agreement on resumption
of diplomatic relations and not matched since that time. Taipei then
immediately retaliated by canceling China Airlines flights to Japan
and prohibiting Japan Airlines not only from flying to Taiwan but
from overflying its territory. The cost to China Airlines was
measurable, but the financial damage to Japan Airlines was far
greater.

It is hard to believe that Peking did not foresee, even if not
in full detail, the domestic political impact on Japan of Ohira's formula. The pro-Taiwan hawks had been quiescent at the time of
normalization, but it was known that they nursed resentment. While
the PRC's insistence that a matter of principle was involved can be
taken as genuine, one must conclude that, however favorably the
Chinese looked on the Tanaka-Ohira governing combination, they
deliberately took the first occasion to set a test of Tanaka's ability
to deliver. Ohira delivered, but he and Tanaka were left to take the
consequences. Ohira was criticized on a number of grounds: that
the agreement itself was lopsidedly disadvantageous to Japan's
aviation interests; that Ohira had grievously misread Taipei's attitude; and that if there had been a problem of translating Peking's
principles into a suitable formula for compromise, it was a dilemma for the Chinese, not for the Japanese government, to resolve.
All of this contributed to weakening the Tanaka government. *

---

*The problems thus created, however, in no way can be taken
as decisive for the fate of the Tanaka government, whose many difficulties stemmed from other sources. The Chinese repeatedly have

The suspension of air traffic between Japan and Taiwan lasted for a little over a year. On July 1, 1975, Foreign Minister Miyazawa Kiichi stated in the Diet that although Japan did not recognize the Nationalist flag as the flag of a nation, there were many countries that did so recognize it, and in that sense it had some standing. On July 9, an agreement for resumption of civil air service on a private commercial basis was signed between nongovernmental organizations established on both sides in December 1972 to manage commercial relations between them.[12] The Japanese government regarded the agreement as being "within the framework of the Japan-China Joint Communique." From Peking, Liao Ch'eng-chih promptly criticized the agreement as "tantamount to trampling down" the joint communique.[13] The Japanese interpreted Liao's remarks, apparently correctly, as statements for the record, which would not be followed by any retaliatory action.

PEACE AND FRIENDSHIP TREATY

Shortly after the ratification of the aviation agreement, the Chinese, perhaps as a gesture of compensation, let it be known that they were ready to proceed on a treaty of peace and friendship without waiting for the completion of other operational agreements. The Chinese gave indications of a desire to move quickly and smoothly, but again a question of Chinese principles impeded progress. In November 1974, Han Nien-lung visited Tokyo and conveyed to Vice Minister for Foreign Affairs Fumihiko Toge the PRC's ideas regarding the content of the treaty. Included in this content was the Chinese proposal that the hegemony clause (Article 7) of the Tanaka-Chou communique be incorporated as an article in the treaty. This Chinese proposal was not publicized at the time.

Soon after Han Nien-lung's visit, Tanaka was forced to resign the prime ministry. In the ensuing reorganization, Takeo Miki became prime minister and formed a new government markedly less desirable in Chinese eyes. The influence of Tanaka and Ohira declined severely. Miki himself had proven his enthusiasm for good relations with China, but his position depended on the cooperation of Takeo Fukuda, Etsusaburo Shiina, and Hirokichi Nadao, who did not share Miki's enthusiasm and were inclined to be supportive of Taiwan. Negotiations were suspended while the new government put itself in order.

---

displayed appreciation of Tanaka as a Japanese leader, sometimes citing him as an example Miki could well follow.

When talks were resumed in early February 1975, Han Nien-lung's proposal became publicly known, and once again domestic controversy rose to the surface. Soviet Ambassador Oleg Troyanovsky informed leading Japanese politicians that his government regarded the proposal, which contains a reference to joint opposition to the hegemony of third powers, as hostile toward the Soviet Union. This consideration carried weight with Japanese business circles and conservative politicians.* The foreign ministry also resisted the Chinese proposal as possibly productive of contradictions with Japan's policy of nonhostility to any country and, in any case, as ambiguous in view of the absence of any strict definition of acts that were to be construed as hegemonic. Almost unanimously the press, including papers usually in sympathy with the Chinese position, supported the foreign ministry. Those who favored yielding to the PRC were some elements of the political left (not including the Communist Party) and some LDP doves. After several rounds of negotiations between Ambassador Ch'en Ch'u and Togo, the Japanese government made a counterproposal involving the substitution of a statement in the treaty's preamble for an article in the text, but this was declined by Peking.

Chinese motives and tactics are rather obscure. At an early point in the negotiations, the Chinese had let it be known that they were willing to omit territorial questions from the treaty. Since these could have raised potentially controversial issues relating to Taiwan and the Senkaku (Tiao Yu) islands, the Japanese were much relieved that the questions could be bypassed. On the hegemony clause, the Chinese position is that an important matter of principle is involved--of sufficient importance in their eyes to have been incorporated in the preamble of their constitution as adopted by the National People's Congress (NPC) in January 1975--on which they cannot compromise. They further argue that both the Shanghai communique and the Tanaka-Chou communique contain the language they propose to include in the treaty and that, in fact, this language was first proposed by the United States. The Chinese show no particular elation at the political confusion the question has evoked in Japan. It is possible that in this case, as in the case of the aviation agreement, the opposition in Japan has had the effect of hardening Chinese attitudes. Nevertheless, one can make a case for the theory that,

---

*It is clear that it is the anti-Soviet thrust rather than the renunciation of hegemonic ambitions that is the source of difficulty. Such staunch conservatives as Nadao and Shiina at times have indicated that they would accept a joint Sino-Japanese renunciation of hegemony if the provision for opposition to the hegemony of the superpowers were omitted.

at least after February 1975, the Chinese have wittingly used the issue as a test of Miki's ability to govern.

It is not at all clear that the Chinese anticipated or deliberately set out to create these problems for Miki, but once they manifested themselves the Chinese did nothing to moderate them. Chinese pressure has been delicate. There have been no official statements or fulminations in the press. PRC spokesmen on several occasions have stated that "the heavens will not fall" if the treaty is not concluded soon. The Chinese attitude has been disclosed through conversations, including some by former vice premier Teng Hsiao-p'ing, with various Japanese visitors to China, nonofficial for the most part. To such visitors Teng has stressed, without apparent truculence, the advantages to Japan of acceding, the disadvantages of declining, and, of particular relevance, has several times stated that the central question is whether Miki has the courage to insist on getting the action he wants and which he knows is right.

The nearest thing to a display of exasperation by Teng Hsiao-p'ing came in statements to a group of Japanese newsmen on July 21, 1975. On this occasion he identified Japanese opponents of the hegemony clause as being of "three kinds: (1) forces seeking revival of militarism, (2) persons who are afraid of the Soviet Union, and (3) those who are playing with the tactics of diplomacy." He warned that carrying out "balanced diplomacy by using cheap tricks" would be useless; Japan could not succeed in playing off the PRC and the Soviet Union against each other. At the same time, Teng described the difference over the hegemony clause as "but a small episode . . . not very important," and declared that the PRC would "wait indefinitely" for the Japanese government to come round.[14]

The question had become something of a political football in Japan. Soon after taking office, Prime Minister Miki had listed conclusion of the treaty as a priority item in his foreign policy program. Failure to progress is a setback to the program but of less consequence than Miki's failure to obtain ratification by the Diet of the Nuclear Non-Proliferation Treaty, and the foreign policy program as a whole was of lower priority than Miki's domestic legislation. Still, Miki showed a strong desire to arrive at a conclusion. In mid-May he transmitted to Peking through Ambassador Ogawa a personal four-point statement confirming his own enthusiasm for the treaty and his determination not to retreat from the basic principles of the 1972 joint communique. The foreign ministry, bypassed in this procedure, was confused by and resentful of what it regarded as a private demarche incompatible with its own approach, which it believed it had adopted with the prime minister's full knowledge and approval.[15] The Chinese response to Miki was entirely negative, and responsibility for further action reverted to the foreign ministry.

The Soviet press continued to publish objections to the hegemony clause. Japanese who saw no reason to antagonize the Soviets continued to oppose it. A number of Japanese not directly involved took the attitude that the government had somehow bungled, that the problem could have been resolved by intelligent handling from the outset.

By midsummer, it appeared that negotiations had returned to the original starting point. In late September, Foreign Minister Miyazawa held two long conversations with Foreign Minister Chiao Kuan-hua in New York, where both were attending the UN General Assembly session. The atmosphere reportedly was friendly, although there was no immediate concrete result. After returning home, however, Miyazawa on several occasions hinted at the possibility that the Japanese might clarify their understanding that a hegemony clause was not directed against a third country, that it did not call for joint action, but stated a principle applicable to all international relations and was in conformity with the UN Charter. If the PRC (by some unspecified procedure) should acknowledge the validity of this understanding, the wording of the clause would be reduced to a mere technicality.[16]

The original intent was that the treaty should serve as the culmination of a series of postnormalization developments, which, taken in toto, would confirm the transition of Sino-Japanese relations to a state of mutual goodwill and advantage and would serve to initiate the next period in the relationship. Although some of the lust has been rubbed off, the treaty still contains promise of fulfilling this function. No firm prediction concerning the date of signature or the precise contents can be made as this is written. But the process has been started, in accordance with the desires of both sides, and it is more reasonable to suppose that the common desire persists than that it does not. The desire is apparently stronger on the Japanese than on the Chinese, so that a Japanese concession is somewhat more likely than a Chinese. On the other hand, the issue is not vital to either side. Both are in a position to carry on constructive relations not substantially affected by the absence of this treaty.

There is one missing piece in the puzzle. When a matter is controversial in Japan, it is comparatively easy to identify the issue, the parties involved, and the variety and intensity of their interests. In the light of events in China over the last decade, it is safer to assume the existence of domestic controversy than to ignore it. But the parties, issues, and interests are most difficult to pin down. One can suggest that Chinese strategy and behavior vis-a-vis Japan have been materially affected by internal politics, but one cannot satisfactorily demonstrate what the effect has been. This aspect of

the problem became even harder to analyze after the death of Chou
En-lai in January 1976. It had been expected, in Japan as elsewhere,
that Teng Hsiao-p'ing would quickly succeed Chou as premier.
While PRC policy toward Japan might then be modified because of
differences in Chou's and Teng's personal styles, the basic line and
premises were expected to persist. The ascent of Hua Kuo-feng
does not necessarily account for the failure of the Chinese to show
any response to Miyazawa's four points. The internal power struggle also does not necessarily presage a radically new approach to
Japan. The events of early 1976 do, however, introduce some new
uncertainties.

CHINESE STRATEGIC CALCULATIONS

There is a rather widely accepted formulation of Chinese foreign policy according to which the overriding objective of the PRC
is the containment (or countercontainment) of the Soviet Union, including prevention of the growth of Soviet influence in Asia. For
this purpose the PRC finds a continued U.S. military presence in
Asia desirable and positively tolerates the existing national security
relationship between the United States and Japan. At the same time,
the PRC has a definite interest in impeding the development of
closer relations between Japan and the USSR and an equal interest
in drawing Japan closer to itself as against the USSR.
     This is an appealingly simple formula, easily translatable
into a two-dimensional diagram. There is also evidence that supports it and hardly any evidence to the contrary. Even if one accepts the formula, however, there is a need for finer definitions.
How much urgency attaches to the various Chinese objectives?
What actions is the PRC ready and able to take, what costs is it
willing to pay, and how likely is it to succeed? How stable is the
current pattern? Is the present pattern a constellation of interde-
pendent factors such that a change in any of them would stimulate
changes in all the others?
     A factor to be considered is the overall shape of Japan's for-
eign policy and the way it meshes with China's. The Japanese have
rejected the concept of a quadrilateral balance of power in Asia.
Insofar as there is a balance of power in the region, they treat it as
a triangular balance--United States-China-Soviet Union--to which
they are tangentially related. The overriding consideration for
Japan is to preserve an intimate and mutually beneficial relationship with the United States. Toward the PRC and the USSR, Japan
holds to a posture of equidistance, developing its relations with
both while avoiding any form of cooperation with one that could be

to the detriment of the other. Japan also seeks to diversify and to broaden the scope of its relations with countries other than the three major powers, primarily in the hope of attaining long-term stability of sources of supply of natural resources vital to its economy. The Asian-Pacific area is an especially attractive area of opportunity for Japan. Finally, Japan adheres to nonuse of military means.

If one compares this pattern with the Chinese pattern described earlier in this chapter, superficially there appear to be few or no common elements. On the other hand, the respective definitions of interests and objectives, reflecting different national situations and divergent doctrinal perspectives, exhibit no points of necessary conflict but rather a certain complementarity.

With regard to equidistance, the Chinese have not found it necessary to take significant action to reinforce the Japanese position. It was the Japanese who took care to explore Chinese reactions to any developments in Japanese-Soviet relations that Peking might find undesirable. A case in point is the negotiations relating to Tyumen oil and the method of transporting it by a rail line to be newly built in Siberia close to the Russo-Chinese border. It was a Japanese negotiator, Kogoro Uemura, then chairman of Keidanren (Federation of Economic Organizations of Japan), who on his initiative undertook a trip to Peking to get some measure of the Chinese view. The Chinese did not need to intervene actively but limited themselves to sage warnings about the untrustworthiness of the Soviets--something they themselves had learned through bitter experience. The Soviet proposal was not adopted for a number of reasons, one of which was the negative attitude of the PRC.

By the same token, the Soviet Union, while it made its position on the hegemony clause emphatically clear, did not have to resort to extraordinary steps or offer to take retaliatory measures in order to stimulate Japanese resistance to the Chinese. The equidistance posture is self-generated and self-sustaining. The PRC and the Soviet Union enjoy the privilege of defining the limits of their satisfaction with it. Throughout 1975, the Soviets had made their dislike of the hegemony clause fully known by way of verbal communications, some by their ambassador in Japan to selected Japanese political figures and some through comments to Japanese visitors to the Soviet Union, as well as by a number of emphatically worded articles in the Soviet press. These measures were effective enough to impede Japan's full acceptance of the Chinese formula.

It was surprising therefore that Foreign Minister A. A. Gromyko, during an official visit to Japan in January 1976--very soon after the death of Chou En-lai--chose to increase the pressure by letting it be known that the Soviet Union might "reconsider" its relations with Japan if Japan agreed to incorporate the hegemony

clause. The move was counterproductive. It brought forth from
Miki and Miyazawa sharply worded comments, the gist of which was
that the Sino-Soviet controversy was an affair of those two countries
only and that Japan did not intend to become involved in it. Japan,
their statements indicated, would conduct its relations with both
countries in the ways best calculated to serve Japanese interests.
Miki further stated that his determination to proceed with the treaty
with China had been fortified by Gromyko's unseemly behavior.

These reactions were far from constituting a declaration that
the policy of equidistance was to be jettisoned. At most, they could
be taken as portending a change in tone, namely, in future, Japan
would no longer refrain from serving its own purposes out of fear of
giving offense to either disputant. It appeared that Gromyko had
created an opening for Miki and the Chinese that they could not have
created by themselves. In the situation that arose in China following
Chou's death, the Chinese did not make use of the opening.

China's view of Japanese activities in Southeast Asia is less
easy to diagnose. In Southeast Asia China is proceeding methodically
to establish new relations and revive interrupted ones where already
the Japanese presence is well entrenched. The few relevant bits of
evidence indicate some Chinese concern over future divergence of
interests in the area. Chou En-lai had dropped a critical remark or
two concerning the exploitative character of Japanese enterprise in
the area, and Teng Hsiao-p'ing had noted, among other advantages
to Japan of the hegemony clause, that a clear Sino-Japanese declaration would reassure the Southeast Asian countries. There seems
little cogency to these observations. Immediately after Sino-Japanese
normalization, there was some apprehension in Southeast Asia over
potential collaboration between the two Asian giants at the expense
of lesser countries. The course of Sino-Japanese relations since
then has largely allayed these fears. Both China and Japan are
conscious that their Southeast Asian interests may diverge at some
future time, but not necessarily to the point of producing conflict.

The present constellation, which confers a high degree of
tenability on both Chinese and Japanese policies, could be disturbed
by a significant change in Sino-Soviet relations. A number of sce-
narios can be generated on the hypothesis of improvement and an
equal number on the hypothesis of deterioration. The details are
too numerous to be considered in the scope of the present study. In
either hypothesis, the foreseeable outcome is likely to be less com-
fortable for Japan than the present situation and to involve stronger
pressures by China to align Japan with itself. Somewhat similar
effects could be produced by an accelerated withdrawal of the United
States in Asia or by a more forceful Soviet program to strengthen
its influence in Asia.

Various possible alternatives to the present Asian balance have been discussed. One possibility is a Sino-Japanese condominium over Asia. This would appear to require a significant U.S. disengagement as a condition and a Soviet effort to fill the vacuum as a stimulus. Another possibility is a triangular American-Japanese-Chinese alliance to contain the Soviet Union. It is difficult to establish, under foreseeable conditions, the compelling advantage to the three countries of a formal alliance as against ad hoc coordination in case of need.

In sum, the present constellation permits a mutually profitable relationship to exist between China and Japan. The mutuality is not perfect. A nice judgment is required to determine whether or not the value of Japan's contribution to China's economic development compensates for the imbalance in trade. On the political level, China enjoys some ability to constrain some of Japan's actions, while Japan has no equivalent influence on China. There are latent sources of difficulty relating to, for example, the ultimate resolution of the status of Taiwan or, more remotely, the situation on the Korean peninsula. No initiative is likely to be taken by Japan that would risk creating a crisis in these situations. A chinese initiative is conceivable.

Leaving aside the possibility of an abrupt change in the PRC's total strategy, which might ensue in the course of a post-Mao succession struggle, the basic fact is that it is not Japan that has the capability of posing critical problems for China. Rather, it is the two superpowers. The Chinese approach to Japan therefore is likely to be regulated within a triangle, with Japan located sometimes inside and sometimes outside the perimeter.

BILATERAL RELATIONS AND
STRATEGIC CALCULATIONS

At the onset of this chapter, the question was raised of how Chinese direct relations with Japan are related to Chinese total foreign political strategy. The answer remains unclear. As compared with previous phases of Chinese foreign policy, the connection between the two aspects appears less close than ever before. One might conclude that the present pattern of Chinese objectives, qualified by the observation that the priority of foreign policy is lower than usual and that no objective is now pursued with excessive vigor, permits the Chinese an unusual freedom of action vis-a-vis Japan in matters where expediency is allowed to rule. The major obstacles to smooth development in technical matters arise when the dynamic of Japanese domestic politics creates problems of amour propre for the Chinese. The existence of a similar dynamic in Chinese domestic politics can be inferred but not demonstrated.

The present constellation is productive in the limited sphere of bilateral relations. The congruence of Chinese and Japanese major objectives, dissimilar as they are when viewed in the abstract, contributes to this result. The future may be clouded. In particular, Japan's foreign policy is in one degree or another hostage to developments in Chinese domestic politics, Sino-Soviet relations, and U.S. policy toward Asia, especially toward China. Therefore, there are ways in which the present status could be disturbed, with outcomes that seem to forebode increased levels of tension and decreased payoff to all concerned. Such eventualities, however, with apologies to one of Peking's favorite slogans, are not independent of man's will.

NOTES

1. Yoshimi Furui, "Nitchu Kokko Seijoha no Hiwa" [Secret Story of the Normalization of Sino-Japanese Relations], Chuo Koran, December 1973.

2. "Down with Revived Japanese Militarism," joint editorial, People's Daily and Liberation Army Daily, September 3, 1970, in Peking Review, September 4, 1970.

3. New China News Agency, Peking, December 12, 1972.

4. For the text, see New China News Agency, Peking, May 12, 1975. The visit is described in Peking Review, May 16, 1975.

5. For a pointed editorial comment, which takes Narita to task for failing to understand that normalization had rendered "people's diplomacy" techniques obsolescent, see Nihon Keizai, May 14, 1975.

6. Chou En-lai, "Report on the Work of the Government," in Documents of the First Session of the Fourth National People's Congress of the People's Republic of China (Peking: Foreign Languages Press, 1975).

7. See Mainichi, December 17, 1973, for an account of the Nagasue article.

8. For the text of the trade agreement, see Nihon Keizai, January 6, 1974.

9. In January-September 1975, steel accounted for 35.4 percent of Japan's exports to China, while crude oil accounted for 46.7 percent of Japan's imports from China. See Japan Times, October 31, 1975, quoting a JETRO report.

10. The difficulties of determining the size of Chinese reserves, future production, and export capability are analyzed in Kambara

Tetsu, "The Petroleum Industry in China," The China Quarterly,
October-December 1974. Accounts of Sino-Japanese negotiations on
trade in various commodities since normalization depict both sides
as sharp bargainers, but reflect no direct influence of political considerations.

11. For the text of the shipping agreement, see Yomiuri,
November 13, 1974. For the main contents of the fisheries agree-
ment, see Nihon Keizai, August 15, 1975; and for a discussion of
PRC concessions see Sankei, August 17, 1975.

12. For the text of the agreement, see Asahi, July 10, 1975.

13. See Japanese press, July 8, 1975, and on.

14. Kyodo News Service dispatch from Peking, July 21, in
Sankei, July 22, 1975.

15. See Japanese press, May 16, 1975 and on; see also summary article, Japan Times, May 19, 1975.

16. See Japanese press, September 24, 1975 and on, but especially Japan Times, September 26 and 29, October 2 and 3, and
November 8, 1975.

KOREA IN CHINA'S FOREIGN POLICY
Chün-tu Hsüeh

China's foreign policy toward Korea is influenced by the following basic factors: historic relations between the two countries, the principles of proletarian internationalism, China's concern with its security because of geographic proximity, the common problems of the unification of a divided country, and the maintenance of the balance of power in East Asia, that is, China's relations with Japan, the United States, and the Soviet Union. Apart from national security, these factors do not always carry the same weight in the formation of China's policy toward Korea. One consideration may exercise stronger influence at one time, while the interplay of other factors may be decisive at other times. A change in one of these variables or the interaction of China's relations with other powers may result in policy changes by all the actors concerned with the Korean Peninsula. Needless to say, Korea's own decisions cannot be completely ignored. This chapter first will analyze China's policy toward Korea within the above framework and then discuss Korea's response to the Sino-American rapprochement.

TRADITIONAL CHINESE-KOREAN RELATIONS

It is well known that the traditional relations between China and the states surrounding it--Korea, Burma, Annam (Vietnam), and others--constituted an international system based on concepts

---

This chapter is a revised version of a paper presented at the Sixty-ninth Annual Meeting of the American Political Science Association, New Orleans, September 4-8, 1973.

distinctively different from the Western system of international law.
China was a "superior state," while Korea and Vietnam were "dependent" or "subordinate states." The concept of dependent states can
be understood only in the context of the traditional Confucian cultural
relations, rather than by the Western legalistic concepts. Traditional
Sino-Korean relations were different from the suzerain-protectorate
or suzerain-vassal relationship, which involve legal implications,
including certain obligations on the part of the suzerain state to manage the foreign and military affairs of the vassal state.

Several official statements and incidents may be cited to illustrate this point. In 1591, the king of Korea replied to Hideyoshi, the
Japanese warrior who had aspired to rule East Asia from Peking, in
these words:

> You stated in your letter that you were planning
> to invade the supreme nation [China] and re-
> quested that our Kingdom join in your military
> undertaking. . . . We cannot even understand
> how you have dared to plan such an undertaking
> and make such a request of us. . . . For
> thousands of years, from the time . . . the
> founder of the Kingdom of Korea received the in-
> vestiture from the Chou dynasty, up to our own
> time. . . . Our two nations have acted as a
> single family, maintaining the relationship of
> father and son as well as that of ruler and sub-
> ject. . . . We shall certainly not desert "our
> lord and father" nation. . . .[1]

The famous and favorite statement often repeated by China's
Foreign Office in the 1870s also puzzled the Western International
lawyers: "Korea, though a dependence of China, is completely
autonomous in her policies, religion, prohibition, and orders. China
has never interfered [with] it."[2] Indeed, in the old international order of East Asia, China exercised power with restraint. As U.S.
Minister George F. Seward wrote in 1879:

> It is not too much to say that it has been within
> the power of China for a very long period to over-
> run and subdue these petty states. . . . A great
> people filling all their territory to the limit of its
> sustaining power, but remaining for centuries
> self-contained, regardful of their own dignity and
> place, but regardful also of the rights of the petty
> powers about them, is a spectacle not very common

in the history of the world. It is one upon which
we may pause to raise the question whether a
state capable of such conduct has not, for some
reason, a poise and balance of judgment and tem-
per greater than we have been in the habit of
attributing to her, and which entitles her to a
large measure of respect and esteem.[3]

For two centuries prior to the 1870s China had seldom interfered with Korea's internal or foreign affairs, in spite of their nominal tributary relations. The change of policy was partly due to a
response to foreign design in Korea. A direct interference in Korea's
domestic politics occurred in 1882, when China sent troops to Korea
to restore order. China took hostage of the regent, who was the
father of the king and leader of the conservative faction. Three years
later, when China decided to permit the regent to return to Korea,
the Peking imperial edict (September 20, 1885) declared:

The Court is aware that filial piety is the most
important virtue and that in the dependent state
that virtue is regarded highly. . . . The Board
of Rites should inform the said [Korean] King that
[the release of his father] is our extraordinary
benevolent act. . . . The said King should carefully take lesson from the past mistakes and . . .
devote [his] whole heart in the administration.[4]

It is probably impossible to find any similar statements defining the relations of two countries in Western international law.
It should be stressed, however, that Western scholars have
often tended to overemphasize the concept of the Middle Kingdom,
and of the inequality of nations of the tributary system as if it were
the only international system that China recognized and practiced.
As a result, Chinese international posture has often been distorted.
In the 1950s, some leading scholars in Chinese studies went so far
as to say that it was one of the reasons why the West could not get
along with the People's Republic of China. The fact of the matter is
that for more than a century since 1842, China never had been accepted as an equal in the "family of nations," and that one of the
main objectives of China in modern time has been to achieve equality.
Furthermore, Russia was not included among the list of tributaries
in an official Chinese document published in 1820, and it is doubtful
that missions from the West at the end of the eighteenth century and
throughout the nineteenth century were so considered by the Manchu
government.[5]

PROLETARIAN INTERNATIONALISM

Since the inauguration of the Democratic People's Republic of Korea (DPRK) in 1948 and the establishment of the People's Republic of China (PRC) in 1949, Korea, or at least its northern part, has remained culturally and politically orientated toward China after the interval of half a century. Of course, the common ideology shared by the two countries now is communism rather than Confucianism. Nevertheless, since the 1950s, the regional international international system of East Asia, as far as China, North Korea, and part of Indochina are concerned, is in some respects reminiscent of the historic Confucian system of the family of nations. As Chou En-lai remarked during Kim Il Sung's visit to China in July 1961: "China and Korea are real brothers in a big family of Socialism, and friendship between the two peoples is a tested one through bitter struggle." During his visit to Pyongyang in April 1970, Premier Chou described relations between the two countries in these words:

> China and Korea are neighbours linked by mountains
> and rivers. There exists a traditional militant
> friendship between the Chinese and Korean peoples.
> The friendship cemented with blood was forged and
> has grown in the course of the protracted struggle
> against our common enemies, U.S. and Japanese
> imperialism. The militant friendship between the
> Chinese and Korean peoples is the embodiment of
> the intimate relationship of our two peoples who
> share weal and woe and are as closely linked as
> lips and teeth. [6]

And it was perhaps more than rhetoric when Kim Il Sung, at the banquet given for Premier Chou, stated that "Korea and China are friendly neighbours linked together as blood and flesh," and that "the people of the two countries are brothers bound by deep-rooted friendship ties."[7] In April 1975, the general secretary of the Workers' Party of Korea and president of the DPRK said during his visit to Peking: "Korea-China friendship is a militant friendship between class brothers based on Marxism-Leninism and proletarian internationalism."[8]

While the description of relations between China and Korea in terms of "father and son" or "elder brother and younger brother" reflects the traditional Confucian concept of the family of nations in the old traditional order of East Asia, Korea and China are now on equal terms as "class brothers." It may not be too far-fetched to suggest that "brotherhood" is akin to the concept of fraternal inter-

national socialist solidarity, and by and large China has served as a
model for the development of Korea (DPRK) since the 1950s as it did
in the imperial past. Although these and other aspects of the traditional Chinese-Korean relationship continue, there is a qualitative
difference between the traditional government and social structures
of China and Korea and their contemporary socialist systems.

With some exceptions, notably the Cultural Revolution, North
Korea has generally followed domestic and foreign policies parallel
to China's. For example, DPRK's basic policy during the post-
Korean war development period (1953-56) was "to learn from the
Soviet Union." After 1956, the policies of economic development in
North Korea were largely based on the Maoist model of development.
The collectivization drive, the Chollima (flying horse) movement,
and the Chongsan-ni method seemed to emulate Chinese procedures
developed during the Great Leap Forward. In addition, the amalga-
mation of the cooperative farms at the level of the basic administrative unit (ri) in North Korea followed the unification of the administrative tasks of the hsiang (Chinese equivalent of the North Korean ri)
government and of the commune in China. Both countries subsequently shifted to the policy of self-reliance.

On the occasion of Chou En-lai's first state visit to Korea in
1958, Kim Il Sung presented a theoretical rationale for the acceptance of the Chinese model. He stated that the contribution of the
Chinese Communist leadership to Marxism and Leninism was the
creative application of Marxism-Leninism to the concrete conditions
of China that the people in North Korea "must not only admire and
praise but also learn" in order to build socialism in North Korea.[9]
For his own reasons, Kim Il Sung also had reservations about Nikita
Khrushchev's denunciation of Stalin. Thus, perhaps one may argue
that the Korean emulation of China today is quite similar in some respects to Chinese-Korean traditional relations.[10]

Of course, the times have changed. Learning is no longer one-
sided, as illustrated by Chou En-lai's assertion during his visit to
Korea in February 1958:

> In recent years, there have been great develop-
> ments of economic, cultural, scientific and tech-
> nological mutual assistance and cooperation be-
> tween our two countries. This relationship should
> unquestionably continue. We should especially pay
> attention to help each other and learn from each
> other in technological matters. I trust that learn-
> ing from each other and encouraging each other in
> the construction of socialism will further consoli-
> date and develop our cooperative relationship on

the basis of our brotherly ties and enhance the
economic growth of our two countries. [11]

The relations between North Korea and China are conducted
under the fundamental principles of proletarian internationalism, [12]
including solidarity and fraternal union among the workers of all nations and countries in the fight for their common aims, proletarian
solidarity in the fight against the exploiters, the equality of nations,
and discharge of the international duty toward the international proletariat by the working class of every country. As a result of the
formation of the world socialist system, proletarian solidarity has
added a new form in the concept of socialist solidarity, which is expressed through moral and material assistance among the socialist
countries and nations. The basic principles of socialist internationalism have become the cornerstone of the relationships between the
socialist nations. According to Soviet sources, the basic principles
are ideological and political unity, mutual fraternal aid and support,
national equality, state independence and sovereignty, and the international duty of the people of every socialist country toward the world
socialist community and the international working class. [13] The fact
that the socialist camp no longer exists does not necessarily mean
that these basic principles should completely be discarded.

Relations between socialist countries are international relations of a new type. On the whole, relations between the PRC and
the DPRK have conformed to the "principles of complete equality,
respect for territorial integrity, sovereignty and independence, and
non-interference in each other's internal affairs, and . . . on the
principles of mutual support and mutual assistance in accordance
with proletarian internationalism." [14] China did not interfere with
internal affairs of North Korea even when the Yenan faction of the
Korean Workers' Party was purged. [15] Of course, China does not
recognize the "Brezhnev doctrine," or practice it in Korea. On
Party relations, there are no longer "superior" and "subordinate"
parties in the Communist movement; all Communist parties are "independent and equal," and their relations are based on "proletarian
internationalism and mutual assistance." [16]

CHINA'S SECURITY AND THE BUFFER STATE

Korea is located on the border of northeast China. The two
countries are separated by the Yalu River. Relations between them,
as between the Chinese and Vietnamese, often have been described
as close as "lips and teeth." The analogy is indicative of the Chinese
view of Korea as a buffer state, vital to China's national security.

Within 60 years (1894-1953), three major wars were fought in East Asia because of Korea, two of which involved China directly. China was forced to fight the Japanese in 1894-95, when Japan attempted to dominate Korea. In 1950, China chose to send "volunteers" to fight against the United States in order to save North Korea and to counter America's threat. At that time, North Korea was actually the responsibility of the Soviet Union.[17] Perceiving Korea as the "lips" to China's "teeth," Peking found it necessary to intervene. The intervention fully demonstrated not only "proletarian internationalism" but also China's perception of Korea's importance to China's security. Although China had reestablished itself as a major power in East Asia after World War II, it was the Korean War that most enhanced its international status prior to its acquisition of nuclear weapons.

Korea is a classic example of a buffer state in East Asian politics.[18] Many aspects of the Korean War have remained obscure, but one thing that appears quite clear is that China was unjustly condemned as an aggressor by the United Nations, and that the Chinese intervention was actually motivated by fear of America's threat to Chinese security.[19] When the United States ignored the repeated private and public warnings that China would "not sit idly by" if U.S. forces crossed the 38th parallel, it became imperative for China to move in to preserve North Korea's position as a buffer state. The intervention served both China's national interests and the ideological demand for international socialist solidarity.

The term "buffer state" is primarily a British-Indian coinage, minted perhaps in the 1880s; and it did much to solidify the system of alliances ringing the Indian subcontinent on the landward side.[20] In this context, there are two features of the idea of the buffer state. First, the buffer is geographically interposed between the potential enemy and the area to be defended; second, the region must, in some sense, be a protectorate. This principle of defense involves staving off an enemy's advance by interposing a protective zone.

The characteristics of buffer protectorates include nonoccupation of the buffer; diminution of sovereignty, that is, the buffer should exclude other foreign influence; and no interference with law and custom. Buffer states, as so conceived, are not satellites, which can serve as bridgeheads to facilitate aggression; they rule out partition or any form of breakup enforced by the great powers on either flank; and the system has nothing in common with neutrality or neutralization.*

---

*Neutralization, which is forced on a weaker power, as it was on Belgium from 1839 onward, "has never been a practical method of statecraft in Asia." The general practice has been to play one group against another.[21]

But identification of the buffer with the formal protectorate is too limited. Siam (Thailand) served as a buffer between French Indochina and British Burma, but it was not a protectorate of either Britain or France. Buffer states are usually weak states that provide military security for their more powerful contiguous states. They are erected to maintain the balance of power by their powerful neighbors. *

In Asia, Afghanistan, Vietnam, Siam, and Korea served as buffer states at various times. In fact, Korea and Vietnam are outstanding examples of buffer states in the second half of the twentieth century. The concept reemerged during the Korean War of 1950 and the Vietnam War in the 1960s. In some respects, Vietnam and Korea occupy similar positions in China's foreign policy.†

PEKING, PYONGYANG, AND THE TAIWAN QUESTION

Although China's influence in Korea was naturally enhanced as a result of the Korean War, China seemed not to have made any special effort to increase its influence at the expenses of the Soviets in the years immediately after the war. China had reservations concerning Nikita Khrushchev's denunciation of Stalin, but relations between the two countries remained friendly. No noticeable power struggle over Korea occurred. Indeed, China had intended to withdraw all its troops from Korea earlier than 1958. By October 1954,

---

*The outstanding examples of buffer states in Europe were Belgium and Switzerland. By article VII of the Treaty of 1829, the great powers recognized and collectively guaranteed Belgium as an "independent and perpetually neutral" state. Belgium was a buffer state between France and Germany until 1914 when the treaty was considered by the Germans as a "scrap of paper." Switzerland, whose neutral status was proclaimed by the great powers at the Congress of Vienna in 1815, has served successfully ever since as a buffer between Austria, Italy, France, and Germany.[22]

†Geographically, Vietnam is on the border of southwest China, separated by low mountains and jungle and a well-defined barrier marked by passes such as the "Suppressing the South Pass," which was renamed "Friendship Pass" by the Chinese Communists in 1953. Populated by non-Chinese but ruled by China in early times and subsequently a tributary state until the French conquest in the nineteenth century, Vietnam was the only country in Southeast Asia that had adopted the institutions and beliefs of the Confucian ideology.

China had already withdrawn 87,900 men, and an additional 52,200
were pulled out between April and October 1955. The final withdrawal was delayed until October 1958 because of an urgent request
by the Pyongyang government. [23]

As Sino-Soviet relations began to deteriorate after 1959, Peking
began to pay special attention to Pyongyang as China sought ideological and political allies in the dispute. At first, the North Koreans
scrupulously avoided taking sides in the Sino-Soviet conflict. The
concept of self-reliance and independence became the symbol of
North Korea's neutrality. After 1960, Kim Il Sung slowly gravitated
toward the Chinese position, partly because he favored Mao's militant approach to world problems over Khrushchev's strategy of peaceful coexistence, the Soviet stand on the Sino-Indian border conflict,
in the Cuban crisis of 1962, and the Soviet attempt to seek a detente
with the United States.

While the Soviet Union terminated economic and military aid
to Pyongyang between late 1962 and 1965,* the Chinese supplied
$150 million in loans for the first three years of the Korean Economic
Plan for 1961-67. [25] The Chinese aid was given at the time when
China itself was in great need of economic resources as a result of
the Great Leap Forward.

During the Cultural Revolution, China was too preoccupied with
internal affairs to have an effective foreign policy. Soviet aid to
North Korea was resumed by the Soviet leaders who overthrew
Khrushchev. Attacks on Kim Il Sung by Red Guard posters appeared
to be unauthorized activities by the ultraleftists rather than a change
of policy. The recall of the Chinese ambassador to Korea had no
more significance than being part of the general recall of all but one
of their ambassadors. Nevertheless, relations between the two countries remained at an all-time low.

But, interestingly enough, North Korea adopted a hard-line
foreign policy parallel to China's even though there was little likelihood of coordination and consultation between the two countries at
that time. This hard-line approach was a reaction to the 1965 South
Korea-Japanese treaty and the possible revival of Japanese militarism. Pyongyang's militant posture was shown by the significant increase of alleged "subversive" activities in South Korea in 1967 and
1968, and the attempted assassination of Park Chung Hee in January

---

*The Nodong Sinmun editorial of October 28, 1963 remarked:
"Today some people . . . have unilaterally repealed their agreements
with fraternal countries and have virtually cut off the relations for
economic and technical cooperation." Apparently, the "people" that
the KWP organ referred to were the Russians. [24]

1968 (a mission Pyongyang has maintained was the work of South
Korean guerrillas), the seizure of the U.S.S. Pueblo two days later,
and the downing of a U.S. reconnaissance aircraft in April 1969. [26]

China's moves to improve its relations with North Korea after
the Cultural Revolution were consistent with its general pattern of
behavior toward many foreign countries. The warming trend was
signaled by the following events: a visit to China by President Choe
Yong-kun of North Korea on China's National Day (October 1, 1969),
the sending of a Chinese ambassador to Pyongyang in March 1970,
and a visit by Premier Chou En-lai to Pyongyang in April 1970. The
Chinese-Korean joint communique subsequently stressed the revival
of Japanese militarism, calling it a "dangerous force of aggression
in Asia." The communique called for further consolidation of friendship and unity between the two peoples based on their common struggle
against American imperialism in Korea, Vietnam, and Taiwan. [27]
This statement was a direct response to the Nixon-Sato communique
of November 1969, in which the Japanese prime minister stated that
"the Republic of Korea was essential to Japan's own security" and
that "the maintenance of peace and security in the Taiwan area was
also a most important factor for the security of Japan." [28] Peking
was also aware of the Soviet attempt to contain China through a "system of collective security in Asia," which was formally proposed by
CPSU Central Committee General Secretary L. I. Brezhnev in June
1969 at the international Communist party meeting in Moscow.

As the world entered the 1970s, all the major powers concerned
with Korea favored detente in the peninsula. Shortly before the announcement in July 1971 that President Richard Nixon was to visit
China in 1972, the Chinese delegate to the Korean Armistice Commission attended a meeting for the first time since August 1966. In
an interview with James Reston in August 1971, Chou En-lai repeated
that "a way should be found to bring about a rapprochement between
the two sides in Korea and to move toward a peaceful unification of
Korea." Furthermore, the "Korean question is also linked up with
the problem of Japanese militarism." [29]

In the Shanghai communique issued at the end of President
Nixon's visit to China in February 1972, Peking declared its firm
support of the DPRK's "eight-point program for the peaceful unification of Korea" and its stand for the abolition of the U.N. Commission
for the Unification and Rehabilitation of Korea, while the United States
pledged that it would "support efforts of the Republic of Korea to seek
a relaxation of tension and increase communications in the Korean
peninsula." [30] And a People's Daily (Jen-min jih-pao) editorial
promptly endorsed the July 4, 1972 Joint Statement of the North and
South. [31]

Although not in the same sense as Korea, Vietnam (before unification in 1976), or Germany, China is a divided country. Therefore, Peking must take Taiwan into account in the formulation of its
policy toward Korea. As early as 1950, as a result of President
Harry Truman's decision to send the Seventh Fleet to the Taiwan
Straits after the outbreak of the Korean War, the Peking government
had considered the "U.S. armed intervention of Korea and aggression on Taiwan of China" to be two "serious and closely related"
problems.[32] Indeed, the dialogues and negotiations in the Korean
Peninsula may establish the direction and reveal the thinking of the
Peking leaders on the unification of Taiwan. Both Taiwan and South
Korea are supported by the United States. As a corollary of the
Sino-American rapprochement, Peking naturally favors relaxation of
tension in the Korean Peninsula. As the tension in Asia diminishes,
the United States will have to live up to its commitments in the
Shanghai communique.

In the communique, the United States "reaffirms its interest in
a peaceful settlement of the Taiwan question by the Chinese themselves . . . [and] the ultimate objective of the withdrawal of all U.S.
forces and military installations from Taiwan. In the meantime, it
will progressively reduce its forces and military installations on
Taiwan as the tension in the area diminishes." The relaxation of
tension in the Korean Peninsula (as well as in Indochina), therefore,
has direct bearing on the withdrawal of America's military presence
in Taiwan. The Korean dialogues should create a favorable atmosphere for discussion of the reunification of the divided countries.[33]

Subsequently, Peking's peaceful overtures to Taiwan have been
intensified. The publicity given to Chang Shih-chao's trip to Hong
Kong in May 1973 was the most dramatic move by Peking,[34] followed
by the release of massive "war criminals" and KMT agents in 1975.
Peking and Pyongyang appeared to have acted in concert concerning
their respective unification problems. When Kim Il Sung put forward
a new policy line embodied in five propositions in June 1973, it was
promptly supported by China the next day.[35]

Apparently, there had been close consultation and coordination
before the new line was advanced, and China certainly had Taiwan in
mind. In fact, on many occasions Taiwan was mentioned when the
Korean unification problem was being discussed.[36] Of course, there
are significant differences between South Korea and Taiwan with respect to their adversaries. South and North Korea may be considered almost equals, but Taiwan is merely a province of China. In
terms of population, territory, and military strength, Taiwan can
hardly be compared with the mainland. Hence, the unification of
China can only mean the "absorption" or "liberation" of the province
by Peking. This was one of the reasons that Taiwan did not follow

South Korea's flexible policy in response to the Sino-American rapprochement.* Furthermore, both Koreas appear to have tolerated
"dual recognition,"† except for the U.N. where the North has consistently opposed Seoul's "two Koreas" approach, while Peking insisted that it would not establish diplomatic relations with any country that still recognizes the Republic of China on Taiwan.

Another consideration that may relate to the Taiwan question
involves the long-standing relations between South Korea and Taiwan:
The unification of Korea on terms advocated by Pyongyang and Peking
would deprive Taiwan of one of its moral allies and further isolate
the regime there. In any event, Korean unification is likely viewed
by Peking as a long-term problem rather than a priority in its global
foreign policy.[39] But, unlike the Russians, the Chinese have to pay
much more attention to Korea for reasons other than that of Sino-
Soviet rivalry.

BALANCE OF POWER

Chinese foreign policy toward Korea may also be viewed in the
context of China's relations with Japan, the United States, and the
Soviet Union, as well as their bilateral relations with each other and
Korea. As mentioned earlier, Peking made no special effort to increase its influence in North Korea at the expense of Moscow during
the period of Sino-Soviet "solidarity" in the 1950s. It was only after

---

*According to a resolution adopted by the Standing Committee
of the Kuomintang's Central Committee, June 27, 1973, "the Administration adheres to the anti-Communist national policy under
which no contact will be sought with the Chinese or Russian Communists."[37] This stand subsequently has been reiterated on numerous
occasions.

†Kenya and Uganda have established diplomatic relations with
both North and South Korea, as well as Jamaica and Venezuela since
October 1974. Other countries having diplomatic relations, or hav-
ing announced intention to establish relations with both North and
South, include Afghanistan, Argentina, Bangladesh, Burma, Camer-
oon, Costa Rica, Denmark, Finland, Gabon, Gambia, Iceland,
India, Indonesia, Iran, Jordan, Liberia, Madagascar, Malaysia,
Maldives, Malta, Mauritius, Nepal, Norway, Rwanda, Senegal,
Sierra Leone, Singapore, Sweden, Tunisia, Upper Volta, and Zaire.
South Korea maintains consulates, while North Korea has embassies
in Pakistan and Egypt. South Korea maintains an embassy, while
North Korea has a consular office in Uruguay.[38]

the deterioration of the relationship that China began to woo North
Korea in order to win an ideological and political ally in the dispute
with the Soviet Union.

It has been mentioned that China favored relaxation of tension
in the Korean Peninsula as a result of the Sino-American rapprochement. Japan's role in Korea always has been of great concern to
China. After the establishment of diplomatic relations between Japan
and Korea in 1965, there has been an increasing economic dominance
of South Korea by Japan. The Nixon Doctrine (July 1969) expected
Japan to play a leading role in Asia. The Nixon-Sato communique
(November 1969) stated that the Republic of Korea was "essential" to
Japan's own security and that Taiwan was "a most important factor
for" the security of Japan. These developments partly account for
Premier Chou En-lai's visit to Pyongyang in April 1970 and a subsequent exchange of visits by the army chiefs of the PRC and DPRK.

China has toned down its attack on the revival of Japanese militarism since the establishment of relations between the two countries
in September 1972. However, Peking's reticence on the subject does
not mean indifference. Peking cannot support a united Korea that
would be primarily responsive to Japan and serve once again as a
springboard for Japan's aggressive continental policy; nor can China
support a policy that would cause communism in Korea to come under
Soviet rule, as in the case of Outer Mongolia. It would also be unacceptable for China to support the unification of Korea, which would
constitute the triumph of South Korea. Any one of these developments would upset the existing balance of power in the area and
threaten China's security. Although the Korean Peninsula is barely
larger than Minnesota, the combined population of South (33 million)
and North (15 million) would make Korea the sixteenth most populous
nation in the world, only a little behind Italy, the United Kingdom,
and France. Furthermore, the combined armed forces of North and
South, totaling more than 1 million, would place Korea's as the fifth
largest in the world's standing armies.*

While China's intervention in the Korean War was motivated by
concern for national security, America's response to the outbreak of
the Korean War also can be explained partially by its concern for the
security of Japan, which was recognized as a vital U.S. interest.
The U.S. response was also based on the premise that the war was

---

*It is interesting to note that Korea had no military tradition
and that Korea's armed forces had been exceedingly feeble for more
than 200 years before the Japanese occupation. It is the United
States, however, that is partly responsible for the militarized policy in South Korea since the 1960s.[40]

a part of a pattern of international Communist expansion and aggression, and that Korea was a "dagger aimed at the heart of Japan"--a perception used by the Japanese in the past to rationalize their aggression. But North Korea had neither the intention nor the capability of throwing a dagger at Japan's heart. On the contrary, it was Korea that was used by the Japanese as a springboard for continental expansion.

Historically, both China and Korea have been victims of Japanese aggression. The rise of Japan received initial blessings from the Western powers, until they, too, became victims of Japanese militarism. At times, many Asians questioned the U.S. policy of rearming Japan and encouraging the Japanese to take up more "responsibilities" in Korea. As one Korean scholar remarked in 1972:

> American policy these days seems to be just a
> repetition of what America did from 1900 to 1907.
> At that time they were always saying that Korean
> security was not that important for the defense of
> the U.S., so they had to get the Japanese to take
> over the Korean security problem. Now the Ameri-
> cans are beginning to withdraw from the Korean
> peninsula--so it appears to be exactly the same
> pattern. [41]

He also stated that "if the Japanese are going to get very strong militarily, then probably the situation is returning to the 1894-1895 pattern."[42] Undoubtedly this will be true if China and the Soviet Union are unable to maintain their powerful positions in the future. As a result of Sino-American rapprochement and the Vietnam debacle, however, Washington no longer encourages Japan to take up more "responsibilities." But, economically, South Korea will be likely to move from the American orbit to the Japanese orbit if it has not already done so. It looks as if the United States fought the Korean War in order to benefit the Japanese. Japanese economic penetration will inevitably be followed by political influence if not ultimate military control. *

---

*Japanese influence in Korea may also be "invited" by Korean leaders in their power struggle. It is quite common in Korean history for one political faction to invite foreign powers to help defeat its rivals. The activities of Kim Dae Jung, the opposition party presidential candidate and rival of Park Chung Hee, signaled the return of this characteristic of Korean tradition. Kim was active in the United States and Japan, and before he was kidnapped in Tokyo

KOREA'S RESPONSE TO THE
SINO-AMERICAN RAPPROCHEMENT

"The Korean people," declared an editorial of the People's Daily, "are the masters of Korea."[44] Nevertheless, Korea is inevitably affected by the decisions of great powers. As one observer remarked: "The Future of Korea as well as her past is inextricably tied to her geographical position."[45] Historically, Korea has always had to contend with the power rivalries of its neighbors--Russia, China, and Japan. Japanese aggression toward Korea led to the Sino-Japanese War of 1894-95. It was followed by a decade of Russo-Japanese rivalry that culminated in the Russo-Japanese War of 1904-05. After years of championing Korea's independence, Japan finally annexed the country in 1910. After World War II, the United States and the USSR replaced Japan as the dominant powers in the peninsula.

Korea has good reasons to be suspicious of great powers. After all, until after the surrender of Japan, "Koreans played no part whatsoever in planning or decision making regarding Korea's future."[46] Furthermore, the country was divided by the United States and the Soviet Union in 1945. The leaders of the South and the North owed their existence to their respective mentors, and the DPRK was saved from almost certain annihilation only by the timely intervention of China in 1950. As a result of the resumption of diplomatic relations between Japan and South Korea in 1965, Japan once again plays an increasingly important role in the Korean Peninsula.

Although Kim Il Sung declared in September 1971 that the change in Sino-American relations would have "no direct relation to us,"[47] it is obvious that the Sino-American rapprochement has had a profound effect on Korea. In fact, by the time Chairman Mao had decided to welcome President Nixon to visit China,[48] North Korea was also beginning to change its militant posture to a more moderate stance toward South Korea. In his report to the Fifth Congress of the Korean Workers' Party,[49] Kim Il Sung called for a people's democratic revolution in South Korea based on the concept of a united front, a strategy that he had tried in 1954-56 when China adopted a conciliatory posture after the Korean War.

During the dramatic visit of America's ping-pong team to China, Foreign Minister Ho Dam proposed an eight-point unification

---

and shipped back to Seoul, he was drafting a speech that reportedly predicted the eventual overthrow of the Park regime and asked Japan to give "moral support to the democratic forces in South Korea."[43]

formula at the Supreme People's Assembly of the DPRK on April 12, 1971.[50] The proposal was promptly endorsed by the Chinese.*

After Henry Kissinger's secret visit to Peking, followed by the joint announcement on July 15, 1971 that President Nixon had been invited to visit China, Norodom Sihanouk flew to Pyongyang from Peking. At the mass rally in Pyongyang to welcome the Cambodian leader on August 6, 1971, Kim Il Sung characterized Nixon's forthcoming visit as "a trip of defeat, not the march of a victor."[52] At the same time, he also expressed his willingness to make contact with the political leaders of South Korea, including the Democratic Republican Party in power. This view was expressed again in his interview with <u>Yomiuri Shinbun</u> reporters on January 10, 1972. In the same interview he also expressed his willingness to improve North Korea's relations with the United States and Japan.[53]

The Third Plenum of the KWP (Korean Workers' Party) Central Committee adopted a resolution in November 1971 concerning Sino-American relations and the improvement of relations between Japan and North Korea through the mechanism of the newly formed Japan-North Korean Parliamentary League. It was clear that North Korea had decided to improve its relations with South Korea, the United States, and Japan. The basic objectives of the DPRK's policy toward Japan include promotion of trade, establishment of diplomatic relations, and strengthening of pro-Communist Korean residents organizations in Japan.[54]

In May 1972, Kim Il Sung discussed unification problems with Harrison E. Salisbury and his colleague, John Lee, who were the first two non-Communist Americans to visit Pyongyang in 24 years.[55]

---

*The eight-point unification formula included total withdrawal of U.S. troops; mutual reduction of the respective armed forces of North and South Korea to 100,000 or less each after the U.S. departure; termination of the ROK-U.S. mutual defense pact and the ROK-Japan treaty; establishment of a unified central government by holding a free North-South election; assurance of full freedom of political activity and the unconditional release of all political prisoners in the South; establishment of a confederation of North and South Korea as a transitional step, leaving the differing social systems intact; promotion of trade, economic cooperation, and interchange and cooperation in science, culture, the arts, and physical culture, establishment of mail exchanges, and permission for travel between the two sides; and holding a political consultative conference with all political parties and public organizations from both sides in attendance to negotiate the programs outlined above.[51]

Initially, South Korea was apprehensive about the Sino-American rapprochement, as illustrated by the comment made by the Korean ambassador to the United States concerning President Nixon's announcement of his forthcoming trip to China: "while we welcome this dialogue between these two world giants, at the same time we are understandably in a quandary as to the future of our peninsula vis-a-vis the policies of the United States, China, the Soviet Union and Japan."[56] However, South Korea fully realized that the United States could not be expected to continue to assume the burden that it had in the past, and that "there are limits to what the United States may be expected to do, limits not by lack of good will or good faith, but by changes in the times and circumstances."[57]

Based on the "rapidly changing international structure about us," Park Chung Hee proclaimed a state of national emergency in December 1971, and declared martial law in October 1972 in South Korea. In his announcement of "Extraordinary Measures" on October 17, 1972, Park warned that "we must guard ourselves against the possibility that the interests of the third or smaller countries might be sacrificed for the relaxation of tension between big powers."[

The immediate result of the changing international situation was the Red Cross talks, and the secret South-North dialogues that resulted in the joint communique of July 4, 1972.* Both sides expressed the common desire to achieve the peaceful reunification of the country at the earliest possible date, and agreed to promote the unification of the country on three principles: by Koreans themselves "without reliance upon outside force or its interference," by peaceful means, and by transcending the differences of ideology, ideal, and system. The two sides agreed to take a number of steps, including refraining from slandering and committing armed provocations, installing permanent direct telephone links between Pyongyang and Seoul, and forming a North-South coordination committee.[59]

---

*On August 12, 1971, the president of the South Korean Red Cross proposed that direct negotiations be held to search for ways to unite families who had been separated by division of Korea. Numerous talks subsequently were held at Panmunjom. Just prior to the conclusion of the preliminary talks, another channel of communication was opened. Early in May 1972, Lee Hu Rak, director of the South Korean Central Intelligence Agency, secretly visited North Korea, where he met Premier Kim Il Sung and Kim's younger brother, Kim Yong-chu, to discuss a broad range of political issues. Then Second Vice Premier Pak Song-chol traveled to Seoul to meet South Korean President Park Chung Hee. From these meetings came the July 4, 1972 communique.

After the joint communique of July 4, 1972, the South Korean press promptly began to refer to North Korea as "pukhan" (North Korea) instead of the "Northern Puppet," a term that had been used for years in South Korea. At the same time, the North Korean reference to the other half of the country was changed from the "U.S. imperialists and their lackeys" to "the South Korean rulers" or "the South Korean authorities." Through a new constitution adopted on December 27, 1972, Kim Il Sung became the DPRK president, and the official capital was changed to Pyongyang from the earlier designation, "Seoul."[60]

The Sino-American rapprochement was a gain for Peking and, by extension, for Pyongyang. Before December 1970, only 58 countries had diplomatic relations with the People's Republic of China; since then more than 50 additional countries have recognized Peking. The DPRK also has broken out of its previous international isolation. Between 1948 and 1970, only 31 countries had established diplomatic relations with North Korea. Since then, it has been recognized by more than 12 states. In June 1973, it was granted permanent observer's status at the United Nations.

The DPRK's position on U.N. membership, however, is different from that of the ROK (Republic of Korea). On June 23, 1973, Park Chung Hee dropped its long-standing opposition to Pyongyang's participation in the U.N. debates on Korea. He declared that he would not object to the simultaneous entry of North and South Korea into the U.N. as full-fledged members. Within hours, however, Kim Il Sung rejected the proposal. He suggested instead that the North and South should not seek separate entrances to the world organization, but should join the U.N. under the single name of the "Confederal Republic of Koryo."*

---

*He also put forward the following proposals: remove the state military confrontation and ease tension between the North and South; realize collaboration and interchange in all political, military, diplomatic, economic, and cultural fields; and solve the question of reunification of the country by convening a national assembly composed of representatives of people of all strata, political parties, and social organizations in the North and South. Furthermore, he demanded that the United States withdraw its troops from South Korea at the earliest date (but did not make this a precondition), and that the U.N. Commission for the Unification and Rehabilitation of Korea (UNCURK) be dissolved.[61] Commenting on Kim Il Sung's proposal on the establishment of the Confederal Republic of Koryo, the South Korean ambassador to France told me in Paris in July 1973 that it was "a big joke." The U.N. General Assembly subsequently (November 1973) dissolved the UNCURK.[62]

Geographically and militarily, North Korea is in a somewhat advantageous position. The country is supported by China and the Soviet Union, the two continental powers that border North Korea. The treaties between the DPRK and its two allies (July 1961) call for immediate military and other assistance in case of military attack from any nation. South Korea, on the other hand, is supported by two maritime powers--the United States and Japan--separated from the peninsula by sea. The Korean-American mutual defense treaty of 1953 provides that in the event of an armed attack, each party "would act to meet the common danger in accordance with its constitutional processes."[63] The Japan-ROK treaty of 1965 contains an ambiguous article that provides the basis for the speculation that the Japanese government "self-defense" force might come to the aid of the ROK within the framework of the U.N. forces.*

The two Koreas reacted differently to the establishment of diplomatic relations between China and Japan in 1972. Seoul was concerned about whether or not Tokyo would honor the 1965 ROK-Japan treaty, while Pyongyang enthusiastically pursued the new development in Sino-Japanese relations. As a corollary to this development, the DPRK is prepared to promote friendship with the ruling Liberal Democratic Party of Japan, and to develop trade, travel, and cultural exchange with Japan before diplomatic ties are established--a Peking-Washington model. Since September 1971, the Japanese press and politicians have been invited to visit Pyongyang. A close examination of policies and statements emanating from Pyongyang and Peking "suggest that North Korea intends to follow a set of policies complementary to those of the Chinese People's Republic, with some of the same basic tactics being pursued."[66]

It is interesting to note that there has not yet been any significant improvement in relations between Peking and Seoul or between North Korea and the United States. In March 1973, a statement issued by the ROK's foreign ministry revealed that South Korea was ready to negotiate with the People's Republic of China concerning jurisdiction over off-shore oil exploitation of the Yellow Sea and the East China Sea. This was a reply to Peking's charges that South

---

*The government of Japan denied having made such a commitment.[64] According to Article III of the treaty, the signatories confirm that the government of the Republic of Korea is the only legal government in Korea as specified in resolution 195 (III) of the U.N. General Assembly. This ambiguous formula was designed to meet the ROK government's claim that it was the legitimate government of all Korea while at the same time avoid the implication that Japan recognized the ROK jurisdiction over North Korea.[65]

Korea had allowed foreign oil companies to search for oil in China's coastal areas. It was the first time South Korea used the official national designation of China. [67] This was a significant indication of South Korea's attitude, but Peking made no response. Peking is opposed to a two Koreas policy, and it will be unlikely to establish any official contacts with Seoul. When North Korean Vice Premier and Foreign Minister Ho Dam proposed to replace the existing military armistice agreement with a peace agreement with the United States in March 1974, [68] the State Department reacted coolly to the suggestion. [69] The U.S. government gave no answer to the proposal. [70] Washington's basic policy is to support the dual entry of both South and North Korea into the United Nations without prejudice to their eventual reunification. If North Korea and its allies would improve their relations with South Korea, the United States would be prepared to take similar reciprocal actions. Furthermore, the United States would not discuss security arrangements on the Korean Peninsula without South Korea's participation; nor would the United States agree to terminate the UN command without new arrangements which would preserve or replace the armistice on a new, permanent legal basis. Washington repeatedly proposed that the United States, PRC, North Korea, and South Korea hold a conference to find a solution acceptable to all parties. [71]

CONCLUSIONS

There is no doubt that the Sino-American rapprochement was the underlying factor in the initiation of the dialogue between the DPRK and ROK.* However, there are no signs of early unification. The breakthrough was remarkable, but the dialogues soon deteriorated. By the spring of 1974, harsh words again were exchanged and tensions were renewed. Both regimes want unification--but on different terms. Meanwhile, Pyongyang wants the complete withdrawal of foreign troops from the peninsula, while Seoul favors the conclusion of a non-aggression pact for peaceful coexistence between the South and North.

----

*On June 1, 1972, I arrived at Seoul where I talked to some of the officials on the National Unification Board. I got the impression that they were extremely suspicious of North Korea, and they asked me a number of questions concerning the mission of George C. Marshall, who was sent to China by President Truman to mediate negotiations between the Kuomintang and the Chinese Communists in December 1945. I did not know then that the South and the North were engaged in the secret negotiation that resulted in the July 4 joint communique.

The latter proposal, which was made by Park Chung Hee on January 18, 1974, was rejected by the North as a "two Koreas plot."[72] Park's earlier suggestion (June 1973) for both governments to join the United Nations was also condemned by Kim Il Sung as a policy of "fixing and perpetuating the national division,"[73] a policy attributed by the North Korean leader as the "main difficulty" for the detente between the South and the North after their joint statement of July 1972.[74]

The future of Korea is closely related to the future interaction among the major powers concerned with the Korean Peninsula. The two conflicting resolutions on Korea submitted by Algeria and the United States with other countries respectively and adopted by the UN General Assembly in November 1975 indicated some basic differences of views between different powers on the issue.[75] Given the same trend of the international situation, neither China, the United States, nor the Soviet Union desires a war in Korea or increased tension in the area.[76] When Kim Il Sung visited Peking in the wake of the Vietnam debacle in April 1975, there was a serious concern in Washington and Seoul for the Korean situation, but it turned out to be a false alarm. * China and the Soviet Union no longer take concerted policy on Korea, but they share some common goals, such as peaceful unification of Korea. Although the Russians have also supported a series of moves taken by North Korea since 1971,[78] the Soviet policy today is in favor of maintaining the status quo.[79] The Koreans, of course, are capable of taking independent action, but it is unlikely that either North Korea or South Korea can wage a civil war on a sustained basis without assistance and support from their respective allies. It appears that two Koreas will continue to exist on a semipermanent basis while working out a formula of unification. Both sides will continue to stress the need for the common goal, while accusing each other of the violation of their agreement or bad faith.

It goes without saying that a unified Korea oriented to one side would be unacceptable by the other. But it is doubtful that Korea could be neutralized and excluded from power bloc struggles.[80] The DPRK's confederation proposal seems to present a realistic formula that would permit the temporary continuation and coexistence of two separate systems and two different ways of life, while, at the same time, fulfilling the desire of the Korean people for the ultimate unification of their country. Furthermore, it would maintain the existing balance of power in the area.

---

*It has been suggested that Kim's visit was not necessarily initiated by the DPRK leader: if the North Koreans wanted to use the Indochina situation to further their revolutionary strategy toward South Korea, Kim would have also visited Moscow.[77]

The objective of China's foreign policy both ideologically and in terms of security consideration is to establish a united Communist Korea friendly to Peking or, alternatively, as a modus vivendi, a divided Korea in which the South need not be a Communist but should be free from foreign troops. While South Korea and the United States might be prepared to formalize Korea's division on the German model, Peking and Pyongyang are absolutely opposed to the two Koreas policy. They maintain that U.S. forces should be withdrawn from South Korea and that the Korean question should be resolved by the Korean people themselves, free from any foreign interference. [81]

The PRC and the DPRK share the same ideology, and their chief respective domestic rivals, Taiwan and South Korea, are supported by the United States and economically influenced by Japan. Both Peking and Pyongyang hope that the Sino-American rapprochement will encourage Washington to withdraw from the area. They believe that once interference from outside forces ends, the Chinese and the Korean peoples will be able to resolve their respective problems of unification. China is greatly concerned with the influence of the Soviet Union in North Korea and the potential future role of Taiwan, as well as American and Japanese influence in Taiwan and the Korean Peninsula. Chinese foreign policy toward Korea is determined to a large extent by the interactions among these variables.

NOTES

1. Quoted in M. Frederick Nelson, Korea and the Old Orders in Eastern Asia (1945; reprint ed., New York: Russell & Russell, 1967), p. 76.

2. Quoted in Frederick Foo Chien, The Opening of Korea (Hamden, Conn.: Shoe String Press, 1967), p. 16. According to Chien, the origin of this statement by China's Foreign Office (Tsung-li Yamen) is probably to be found in answers the Foreign Office gave to Minister Williams of the United States and Minister Rutherford Alcock of England regarding their requests for the Foreign Office to ask Korea why the nationals of their two countries had been mistreated. See the correspondence between the Yamen and the two ministers in March 1869, Ch'ing-tai ch'ou-pan i-wu shih-mo: T'ung-ch'ih ch'ao [History of the Management of Barbarian Affairs during the T'ung-chih Reign] (Peiping: National Palace Museum, 1929-30), vol. 57, pp. 23-28 (hereafter cited as IWSM). Earlier, in May 1867, the Yamen, in conversation with the French minister, had made the same statement when France asked for permission to preach in Korea, ibid., vol. 42, p. 54; Chien, op. cit., pp. 214-15.

3. Seward to Evarts, December 11, 1879, in Papers Relating
to the Foreign Relations of the United States, 1861-1928 (Washington,
1862-1943), 1880, p. 179, quoted in Nelson, op. cit., p. 106.

4. National Palace Museum, ed., Ch'ing Kuang-hsu ch'ao
Chung-Jih chiao-she shih-liao [Documents on Sino-Japanese Rela-
tions, Kuang-hsu Reign] (Peiping, 1932), vol. 8, p. 41, quoted in
Chien, op. cit., p. 189.

5. G. Jamieson, "The Tributary Nations of China," China
Review 12 (1883): 96. For an inquiry of legal equality among the
feudal states, see Shih-tsai Chen, "The Equality of States in Ancient
China," American Journal of International Law 35 (1941): 641-50.
See also Richard L. Walker, The Multi-State System of Ancient
China (Hamden, Conn.: Shoe String Press, 1953). It may be mentioned that, although the equality of states has been regarded as a
basic principle of modern international law, it is also a question
much disputed in academic circles ever since the last quarter of
the nineteenth century. Chen, op. cit., pp. 641-42.

6. Chou En-lai, Peking Review, April 10, 1970, p. 14.

7. Ibid., p. 11.

8. DPRK Office of the Permanent Observer to the United Nations, press release, April 1975, p. 3.

9. Quoted in Ilpyong J. Kim, "The Chinese Communist Relations with North Korea," Journal of Asiatic Studies 3, no. 4 (December 1970): 65.

10. Cf. Glenn D. Paige, "North Korea and the Emulation of
Russian and Chinese Behavior," in Communist Strategies in Asia,
ed. A. Doak Barnett (New York: Praeger, 1963), pp. 228-58.

11. Chung-hua jen-min kung-ho-kuo tui-wai kuan-hsi wen-
chien chi [Collected Documents on Foreign Relations of the People's
Republic of China], vol. 5 (Peking: Shih-chieh chih-shih she, 1959),
p. 34. Cf. Ilpyong Kim, op. cit., p. 66.

12. Joint communique, April 7, 1970, Peking Review, April
10, 1970, p. 5.

13. Marxism-Leninism on Proletarian Internationalism (Moscow: Progress Publishers, 1972), pp. 16, 25. The first part of this
book contains the writings and speeches of Marx, Engels, and Lenin
on proletarian internationalism, followed in the second part by ex-
tracts from the writings and speeches of the leaders of the international Communist movement excluding Chinese leaders. The new
Soviet interpretations of the question of internationalism based on
"a correct principles attitude towards the Soviet Union," and "limited sovereignty" are, of course, unacceptable to Chinese leaders.

14. A Proposal Concerning the General Line of the International Communist Movement: Letter of the Central Committee of
the Communist Party of China in Reply to the Letter of the Central

Committee of the Communist Party of the Soviet Union, June 14, 1963 (Peking: Foreign Languages Press, 1963), p. 45.

15. Robert A. Scalapino and Chong-Sik Lee, Communism in Korea (Berkeley: University of California Press, 1972), pt. 1, pp. 512-24.

16. A position taken by the CPSU and endorsed by the Chinese Communist Party; see A Proposal Concerning the General Line of the International Communist Movement, op. cit., p. 47.

17. The Soviet advisers, who were with the North Korean army, were recalled shortly before the outbreak of the war in order to avoid their capture, which might have precipitated a Soviet-American confrontation. See Khrushchev Remembers (New York: Bantam, 1971), p. 403.

18. For a brief and unsatisfactory discussion of Korea from the standpoint of the buffer state concept and the balance of power, see Hans J. Morgenthau, Politics Among Nations, 5th ed. (New York: Knopf, 1973), pp. 176-77; see also Ku Kwhan Sul, "Some Bases for Negotiation of Buffer States: The Korean Case," mimeographed (Cambridge, Mass.: Center for International Affairs, Harvard University, 1965).

19. In an article written several days after the outbreak of the Korean War, and published in the New York Sheng-huo tsa-chih [Life Magazine] 1, no. 4 (July 16, 1950), I concluded that should the U.S. forces march north of the 38th parallel, "the war would be enlarged." The article is included in Chün-tu Hsüeh, Shih-nien tsa-lu [Selected Writings of a Decade] (Hong Kong: Universal Book Company, 1964), pp. 143-47. For the origin and other aspects of the Korean War, see Khrushchev Remembers, op. cit., pp. 400-07; I. F. Stone, The Hidden History of the Korean War (New York: Monthly Review, 1952); and Allen S. Whiting, China Crosses the Yalu (New York: Macmillan, 1960).

20. "Buffer States: Their Historic Service to Peace," Round Table, September 1955, p. 334.

21. Ibid., p. 341.

22. Frederick H. Hartmann, The Relations of Nations, 4th ed. (New York: Macmillan, 1973), pp. 320-31. Cf. Morgenthau, op. cit., pp. 176-77.

23. Broadcast of the Pyongyang Domestic Service in Korean, October 8, 1969, cited by Rinn-sup Shinn, "Changing Perspectives in North Korea: Foreign and Reunification Policies," Problems of Communism, January-February 1973, p. 58.

24. Quoted in Joungwon Alexander Kim, "Soviet Policy in North Korea," World Politics 22, no. 2 (January 1970): 249-50. See also Myung Kun Yiu, "Sino-Soviet Rivalry in North Korea Since 1954" (Ph.D. dissertation, University of Maryland, 1969).

25. Rinn-sup Shinn et al., Area Handbook for North Korea
(Washington, D.C.: U.S. Government Printing Office, 1969), pp.
204-305. According to the same source, between 1961 and 1965,
the Soviet Union provided some $56 million worth of goods on a long-
term loan basis.
26. For a list of activities considered subversive by North
Korea in 1965-72 based on UN sources, see Rinn-sup Shinn, "Changing Perspectives in North Korea," op. cit., p. 61.
27. See Peking Review, April 10, 1970, pp. 3-5, 6-24, for
other related reports and documents. In the joint communique issued
at the end of the visit of the Rumanian delegation headed by Chief of
State Nicolae Ceausescu on June 15, 1971, Kim Il Sung again opposed
the revival of Japanese militarism. For the text of the communique,
see Rodong Shinmun, June 15, 1971.
28. United States Foreign Policy, 1969-1970: A Report of the
Secretary of State (Washington, D.C.: U.S. Government Printing
Office, 1971), p. 503.
29. Frank Ching, ed., The New York Times Report from
China (New York: Avon, 1971), p. 105. The Jen-min jih-pao editorial of January 29, 1972 appealed for the peaceful unification of
Korea.
30. For the text of the Shanghai communique, see Peking Review, March 3, 1972.
31. Editorial, "A Good Beginning," Jen-min jih-pao [People's
Daily], July 9, 1972.
32. Chou En-lai, telegram to UN Secretary-General Lie,
November 11, 1950. The Information Department of the Chinese
People's Anti-America and Aid-Korea Headquarters, ed., Wei-ta ti
k'ang-Mei yuan-Chao yun-tung [The Great Anti-America and Aid-
Korea Movement] (Peking: People's Publishing House, 1954), pp.
42-43.
33. Chün-tu Hsüeh, "The Shanghai Communique: Its Significance and Interpretation," Asia Quarterly (Brussels), no. 4 (1973):
279-85. See also Chün-tu Hsüeh, "Nixon's Visit to China and Asian
Politics," Joongang Ilbo [Central Daily News], Seoul, February 29,
1972 (in Korean).
34. Peking Review, June 1, 1973, p. 4. Subsequently, numerous articles speculating on Chang's mission have been published
abroad. He was a follower and close friend of Huang Hsing in the
Republican revolutionary movement that overthrew the Manchu dy-
nasty. I saw him again in Peking on November 3, 1971. One of his
daughters is now married to Foreign Minister Ch'iao kuan-hua.
For a biographical sketch of Chang Shih-chao (1881-1973), see Howard
L. Boorman, Biographical Dictionary of Republican China (New York:
Columbia University Press, 1967-71), vol. 1, pp. 105-09.

35. The support was expressed by Premier Chou En-lai at a banquet given by Colonel Moussa Traore, head of state and president of the government of Mali, June 24, 1973; Peking Review, June 29, 1973, p. 5.

36. For example, see editorials, Jen-min jih-pao, June 25, 1973 and June 25, 1975; Peking Review, June 29, 1973, p. 7; and Peking Review, June 27, 1975, p. 5; see also Joint Communique of the Government of the People's Republic of China and the Government of the Democratic People's Republic of Korea, Peking Review, April 10, 1970, pp. 4-5; May 2, 1975, p. 10.

37. Chung-yang jih-pao [Central Daily News], Taipei, June 28, 1973.

38. For details, see "reference materials" on "The Korea Question in the United Nations" (in Korean), issued by the ROK Ministry of Foreign Affairs, November 19, 1975.

39. For a discussion of this point, see Harold Hinton, "Communist China and the Problem of Korean Unification," International Conference on the Problem of Korean Unification, August 1970: Report (Seoul: Asiatic Research Center, 1971).

40. See Gregory Henderson, "Korea in United States Policy" (Paper presented at the 69th Annual Meeting of the American Political Science Association, New Orleans, September 1973), pp. 7-8.

41. Soon Sung Cho, in Major Powers and Korea, ed. Young Kim (Silver Spring, Md.: Research Institute of Korean Affairs, 1973), p. 61.

42. Ibid., p. 60. Cho also stated that "encouraging Japanese military defense is actually intensifying the tensions in Asia, and there is nothing to gain from it." Ibid.

43. Don Oberdorfer, "The Case of the Kidnapped Korean," Washington Post, August 26, 1973, p. C3.

44. Peking Review, April 20, 1973, pp. 12-13, in English.

45. David I. Steinberg, Korea: Nexus of East Asia (New York: American-Asian Education Exchange, 1968), p. 39.

46. Gregory Henderson, "Korea," in Divided Nations in a Divided World, ed. Gregory Henderson, Richard Ned Lebow, and John G. Stoessinger (New York: David McKay, 1974), p. 49.

47. Kim Il Sung, interview with managing editor, Ashai Shimbun, September 25, 1971. For the text of the interview, see Journal of Korean Affairs, October 1971, pp. 49-52.

48. Edgar Snow, The Long Revolution (New York: Random House, 1972), pp. 171-72.

49. Kim Il Sung, "Report to the Fifth Congress of the Korean Workers' Party," Workers' Daily, November 3, 1970.

50. See KCNA, Pyongyang broadcast, April 12, 1971, in English.

51. Editorial, Jen-min jih-pao, April 15, 1971; Peking Review, April 23, 1971, pp. 11-12. See also Ch'iao Kuan-hua, speech at the

26th General Assembly of the United Nations, November 15, 1971; Peking Review, November 19, 1971, p. 8.

52. KCNA International Service (Pyongyang), August 6, 1971, as monitored by FBIS; quoted in Byung Chul Koh, "North Korea's Unification Strategy: An Assessment," in Government and Politics of Korea, ed. Se-jin Kim and Chang-hyun Cho (Silver Spring, Md.: Research Institute on Korean Affairs, 1972), p. 273. For an excerpt of the speech, see Kim Il Sung, For the Independent Peaceful Reunification of Korea (New York: International Publishers, 1975), pp. 139-41. Comments on Nixon's trip were deleted from the excerpt. For a discussion of Korea's reaction, see Roy U.T. Kim, "The Four Powers and the Korean Detente" (Paper presented at the International Studies Association Convention, New York, March 1973), pp. 6-9. It may be noted that North Korea reacted rather mildly to Nixon's visit to Moscow in 1972, and Kim Il Sung welcomed the Soviet-American joint communique.

53. Yomiuri Shinbun, January 11, 1972; Kim Il Sung, For the Independent Peaceful Reunification of Korea, op. cit., pp. 151-56.

54. Young Hoon Kang, "North Korean Policy Objectives Toward Japan," Journal of Korean Affairs 4, no. 3 (October 1974): 33.

55. Kim Il Sung, For the Independent Peaceful Reunification of Korea, op. cit., pp. 157-72. Harrison E. Salisbury, To Peking and Beyond (New York: Quadrangle, 1973), chaps. 16 and 17. On January 10, 1971, and again on May 26, 1971, Kim Il Sung expounded the following stands: to conclude a peace agreement and to have a political consultation conference, and to establish a confederation system in Korea. For the earlier theme of peaceful unification as an internal issue to be decided by the Koreans themselves, see Kim Il Sung, "Report of the Central Committee of the Workers' Party of Korea to the Fourth Congress," Documents of the Fourth Congress of the Workers' Party of Korea (Pyongyang: Foreign Languages Publishing House, 1961), pp. 96-97. The Fourth Congress resolution, dated September 17, 1961, declared that "the withdrawal of the U.S. armed forces from South Korea [is] the prerequisite to North-South general election." Ibid., p. 363. In a reply to the President of Korean Affairs Institute in Washington, dated January 8, 1965, Kim Il Sung stated: "We have proposed time and again that if the South Korean authorities cannot accept the confederation, the nation's tribulations caused by the division should be lessened even a little by effecting North-South economic and cultural intercourse, leaving aside the political questions for the time being." Korean News, no. 2 (1965), p. 3.

56. Dong Jo Kim, address at the National War College, March 8, 1972; Korean Report, Spring 1972, p. 11. Kim "applauded President Nixon's efforts to ease world tensions." Ibid., p. 13.

57. Thaw Versus Freeze in Korea (Seoul: Ministry of Culture and Information [December 1971 or 1972], p. 10. See also "Special Statement by President Park on the Declaration of a State of National Emergency," December 6, 1971, ibid., p. 25.

58. Korean Report, Winter 1972, p. 3. For the South Korean official views and related documents of the "October Revitalizing Reforms," see Korean Quarterly, Winter 1972-73.

59. For the text of the joint communique, see Peking Review, July 14, 1972, pp. 8, 12.

60. Article 149 of the Socialist Constitution of the Democratic People's Republic of Korea. For the text of the new constitution, see the Pyongyang Times, December 30, 1972. Article 103 of the 1948 constitution of the DPRK designated Seoul as the capital of the country.

61. Peking Review, June 29, 1973, p. 6. For the full text of Kim's speech, see The People's Korea, June 27, 1973. For the concept of the "confederation," see Kim Il Sung, For the Independent Peaceful Reunification of Korea, op. cit., pp. 194-95.

62. For an account of the Korean question debated for the first time by the representatives of North and South Korea in the UN in the fall of 1973, see B. C. Koh, "The United Nations and the Politics of Korean Reunification," Journal of Korean Affairs 3, no. 4 (January 1974): 37-56. On various aspects of the unification expressed by non-Communist Korean scholars in 1970, see C. I. Eugene Kim, ed., Korean Unification: Problems and Prospects (Kalamazoo, Mich.: Korea Research and Publications, 1973).

63. Department of State Bulletin, October 12, 1953, p. 484.

64. For a discussion of security aspect of the ROK-Japan treaty, see Kwan Ha Yim, "Korea in Japanese Foreign Policy" (Paper presented at the Annual Meeting of the American Political Science Association, New Orleans, September 1973).

65. Shigeru Oda, "The Normalization of Relations with the Republic of Korea," American Journal of International Law 61 (1967): 41. For an analysis of the Korean alliances, see Astri Suhrke, "Gratuity or Tyranny," World Politics 25, no. 4 (July 1973): 508-32.

66. Robert A. Scalapino, "Changing Relations Between the United States and the Chinese People's Republic and the Impact Upon the Republic of Korea," statement before the Subcommittee on Asian and Pacific Affairs, U.S. House of Representatives Committee on Foreign Affairs, May 4, 1972; Korean Affairs, April 1972, p. 26.

67. Korea Week, March 31, 1973.

68. For a summary report of Ho Dam's proposal made at the Third Session of the Fifth Supreme People's Assembly, and a letter of Supreme People's Assembly to the U.S. Congress, proposing to conclude a peace agreement to replace the Korean Armistice Agreement, see the Pyongyang Times, March 30, 1974.

69. Washington Post, March 26, 1974, p. A14.

70. DPRK Office of the Permanent Observer to the United Nations, press release, August 7, 1974. South Korean Defense Minister Suh Jyong Chul suggested that the North Korean direct approach to the United States was "designed to make possible the estrangement" of the U.S.-ROK relations. News Conference by Secretary James R. Schlesinger and Defense Minister Suh Jyong Chul, Seoul, August 27, 1975, press release, U.S. Department of Defense.

71. Secretary Henry Kissinger, statement to the UN General Assembly, September 22, 1975. Also his speech before the Downtown Rotary Club and the Chamber of Commerce, Seattle, Washington, July 22, 1976; see U.S. Department of State, Bureau of Public Affairs, Office of Media Service, PR 351, pp. 5-6.

72. Editorial, Nodong Shinmum, January 26, 1974.

73. Kim Il Sung, answers to the questions raised by l'Unita, organ of the Italian Communist Party, in the Pyongyang Times, April 16, 1974; also his earlier answers to the questions put by the chief editor of Yugoslav newspaper Veceruje Novosti. See the Pyongyang Times, March 16, 1974.

74. On the occasion of the second anniversary of the North-South joint statement (July 4, 1972), the Rodong Shinmun published an article, "Reunification or Division," on July 3, 1974, discussing the unification issue in great length. For an English version of the article, see the Pyongyang Times, July 20, 1974. Cf. Chong-Sik Lee, "The Impact of the Sino-American Detente on Korea," in Sino-American Detente and Its Policy Implications, ed. Gene T. Hsiao (New York: Praeger, 1974), pp. 194-95.

75. For the differences of the two resolutions on Korea, see Peking Review, August 22, 1975, pp. 13-14; and Huang Hua, speech at the UN, Peking Review, November 28, 1975, pp. 11-12.

76. George Ginsburgs, "The U.S.S.R. and the Issue of Korean Reunification," International Conference on the Problem of Korean Unification, August 1970: Report (Seoul: Asiatic Research Center, 1971).

77. Young Hoon Kang, "Kim Il Sung's Trip to Peking," Journal of Korean Affairs 5, no. 1 (April 1975): 47-51. In May 1976, British Foreign Secretary Anthony Crosland was reportedly told in Peking that all talk of a new war in Korea was "out of the question." Washington Post, May 12, 1976, p. A19.

78. Charles McLane, "Soviet Policy Toward Korea," in Major Powers and Korea, ed. Young C. Kim (Silver Spring, Md.: Research Institute on Korean Affairs, 1973), pp. 10-11. Cf. Jane P. Shapiro, "Soviet Policy Toward North Korea and Korean Unification," Pacific Affairs (Vancouver) 48, no. 3 (Fall 1975): 351-52.

79. William Spahr, "The Military Security Aspects of Soviet Relations with North Korea," Journal of Korean Affairs 4, no. 1 (April 1974): 7.

80. Cf. Steinberg, op. cit., p. 8; and Henderson, op. cit., p. 15.

81. Joint Communique of the PRC and the DPRK, April 26, 1975, in Peking Review, May 2, 1975, p. 9.

7

THE PALESTINIANS AND CHINA'S FOREIGN POLICY
Yitzhak Shichor

INTRODUCTION

In 1974, ten years after its formation by the First Arab Summit Conference, the Palestine Liberation Organization (PLO) was reaffirmed as the sole representative of the Palestinians by another Arab summit conference in Rabat, Morocco. As a result of this decision, and of a decade of Palestinian political and military activity, PLO Chairman Yasser Arafat was invited for the first time by the United Nations General Assembly to take part in the debate on the Palestine problem, and several governments felt it necessary to accept, or at least to consider, the establishment of official PLO missions in their countries.

China was far better prepared for such an eventuality. Already in 1964-65 China was the first non-Arab government not only to recognize the PLO but also to permit it to open a permanent quasi-diplomatic office in Peking. In the following decade, China paid much attention to Palestinian affairs, which included extensive coverage of guerrilla operations; welcoming delegations; training guerrilla groups; extending military and other material aid; and, last but not least, fully supporting Palestinian claims and methods. By these actions, China anticipated not only all the non-Arab countries but even most of the Arab countries themselves.

Research for this chapter was facilitated by grants from Lady Davis Fellowship Trust and Leonard Davis Institute for International Relations, the Hebrew University of Jerusalem, and the Kadoorie Family Fund for Chinese Studies (a project of the Fund for Higher Education in Israel), to which the author is deeply grateful.

China's apparently considerable commitment to the Palestinians lent itself to some misconceptions. One myth, which still persisted in the early 1970s, was that of Peking pulling the strings behind the Palestine liberation movement, or even behind the radical Arab states. Furthermore, some observers were led to believe, particularly after the Soviet "betrayal" of the Arabs in June 1967, that China's "infiltration" into the Middle East was growing so rapidly that it would ultimately replace the Soviet presence.[1]

In fact, China's relations with the Palestinians were carried out within strict limits and, far from being taken for granted, were subject to review and reconsideration from time to time. The Chinese, of course, reiterated that China's stand on the Palestine problem had never changed. Yet, the Chinese always regarded the Palestine problem not as an isolated and independent local problem but as an integral part of the general situation in the Middle East and, more important, in the world as a whole.

China's attitude on the Palestine problem has changed, therefore, like its policies on many other issues. Some basic predispositions, which had been formulated first in the mid-1950s, were not modified throughout the whole period and are still valid. Others, however, underwent complete transformation, reflecting not only local developments but especially China's response to new global power relationships and constellations.

For these reasons it is difficult to discuss, and impossible to understand, China's Palestine policy as separated from Sino-Arab relations, Sino-Soviet relations, or Peking's perception of world affairs as a whole at a given time. It is proposed, therefore, to analyze China's changing attitude on the Palestine problem, as well as the development of China's actual relations with the Palestinians, against the background of international affairs as interpreted by the Chinese, from the 1950s to the present.

THE BEGINNINGS OF CHINA'S MIDDLE
EAST FOREIGN POLICY

China first became interested in the Palestine problem and in the Arab-Israeli conflict in the mid-1950s. At that time, Peking took a more relaxed view of world affairs as compared with previous years. After the end of the Korean and French Indochina wars in 1953-54, China began to believe that the imperialist camp was on the defensive. This did not mean that the West had abandoned its "aggressive plans"; on the contrary, Peking perceived constant indications of Western attempts to gain control over the Asian countries that could serve the imperialists as a springboard for attacking the socialist camp.

To frustrate these attempts has been one of China's basic foreign policy objectives, and the methods employed to achieve this
objective varied according to Peking' perception of the world situation. In the mid-1950s, China laid the emphasis not on armed
struggle but on organizing the Asian and African countries. This
was due to China's conviction that the newly independent bourgeois-
nationalist governments, previously suspected of being lackeys of
imperialism, might become part of a united front against colonialism and the West. To this end, and also in order to break its diplomatic isolation, China adopted a moderate foreign policy and was
predisposed to improve and establish relations with almost any of
these countries.

Although the Soviet Union was slow to endorse Peking's analysis of the international situation, Peking was hopeful that the new
Soviet leadership that had emerged in the mid-1950s would play a
positive and constructive role (particularly with regard to economic
and military assistance) within the anti-imperialist front. China,
therefore, despite some disagreement and suspicion, paid full public
tribute to Soviet foreign policy, including that in the Middle East.

The situation in the Middle East was regarded by the Chinese
as a precise reflection of the global situation. Because of its strategic location and rich oil resources, China regarded the Middle East
as a crucial link in Western attempts to forge a ring around China,
the Soviet Union, and the people's democracies. However, in China's
view, the threat to the socialist camp was still remote as compared
with the imminent danger to the Asian and African countries. China
insisted that Western-sponsored military pacts were directed primarily against the local peoples themselves and that, in fact, almost any problem in the Middle East (as elsewhere) had been manu-
factured by the colonialist powers to ensure their predominance.
They thought that driving imperialism out was an essential preliminary step toward the solution of these problems. Britain, the old
colonialist power in the Middle East, was now perceived by China
as being on the decline, while the United States, the new colonialist
power, was penetrating the region instead. From Peking's point of
view, the deepening "contradictions" among the Western powers,
which were most evident in their contest to control the Middle East,
enhanced the ability of the Middle East peoples to achieve complete
national independence.

Against this background, China moved to improve relations
with the Middle East countries, including Israel. Despite their
awareness of Israel's affiliation with the West, the Chinese considered Israel one of the newly independent countries that had been
oppressed by imperialism. There were then good prospects of establishing full diplomatic relations with Israel, and exchanges took

place toward this end.[2] By late 1954, the attitude of some Arab governments, notably those of Egypt, Syria, and Yemen, had become more favorable to the People's Republic of China (PRC), a change which Peking, despite its reservations, undoubtedly welcomed and wished to cultivate.

China's position on the Palestine problem in the mid-1950s fully reflected both these global and local circumstances, as well as the political stability within China.

China's basic view was, and still is, that the Arab-Israeli conflict and the Palestine problem both had been created as a result of the Anglo-American contest to gain control over the Middle East. The Chinese believed that as early as World War I Britain had given the Jews and the Arabs contradictory promises concerning their national aspirations in Palestine. After the Second World War, when its rule in Palestine became unstable, Britain tried to delay the solution of the problem and to use the United Nations to maintain its power.[3] "When the establishment of the Republic of Israel was proclaimed, Britain instigated the Arab League states to attack Israel, while the United States was secretly aiding Israel."[4] But the imperialists were not only "contending" to gain power but also "colluding"--together with the "reactionary Arab regimes"--to exploit the Arab-Israeli conflict in order to curb the genuine people's liberation struggle and to divert the people's hatred of colonialism against Israel.[5]

Thus, the Arab-Israeli dispute and the Palestine problem were considered not only the product of imperialism but also as a major pretext for the imperialists' presence and interference in the internal affairs of the Middle East countries. A further deterioration of the Arab-Israeli conflict was seen by the Chinese as "one of the most dangerous factors in the Middle East region." Such a deterioration had to be avoided: "The Chinese people very much hope that together the parties concerned could urge to achieve a peaceful settlement of the Palestine problem, with respect for and in line with the national interest standpoint of both the Arab and the Israeli sides, without letting the colonialists seize the opportunity to interfere in the Near East. . ."[6] [emphasis added]. In the absence of foreign intervention, said the Chinese, the parties concerned could negotiate directly on a basis of equality and according to United Nations principles.

It appears that in the mid-1950s, China regarded the United Nations 1947 Partition Plan as the ultimate solution of the Palestine problem, especially since this plan was regarded as a distinctively Soviet contribution:

The Soviet Union, loyal to the defense of weak and
small nations, did not accept the imperialist oppressive policy and proposed to establish in
Palestine one Jewish-Arab independent and democratic state; if this plan could not be realized,
then two independent-democratic states should be
established--one state for the Jewish people and
the other for the Arabs. On the basis of the
Soviet proposal the United Nations formulated the
Palestine Partition Plan, and on 29 November 1947
the United Nations General Assembly passed the
Palestine Partition Resolution. [7]

China was well aware of the fact that the Partition Plan had not
been carried out. On their maps, however, the Chinese showed, as
a rule, the partition borders along with the actual borders agreed
upon by Israel and the Arab states. Peking also fairly consistently
used on its maps the term "Palestine" together with the name "Israel,"
probably accepting the Soviet definition of Palestine as those areas
outside Israel (Pa-le-ssu-tan ch'u I-ssu-lieh ti ti-ch'u). [8] Quite often
when the Chinese were naming the countries of the Middle East they
mentioned Israel as well as Palestine, as two different countries. [9]
In any case, in the mid-1950s, the Chinese did not hold Israel
the sole nation responsible for not implementing the Partition Plan's
provision for an Arab state in Palestine: "Places inhabited by Palestinian Arabs were part of what had been occupied by Jordan, Egypt
and Israel"[10] [emphasis added]. Thus, China's attitude toward the
Palestine problem was, at least from Peking's point of view, carefully balanced. All the blame for the Palestine problem was put on
the imperialist powers, whereas Israel and the Arab states were
equally responsible for the failure to establish a Palestine state. The
Chinese tried to maintain this balanced stand during the Bandung
Conference, but their attempts have, in my view, been misinterpreted
for a long time, and thus need some elaboration.
There is no doubt that by late 1954, and probably even earlier,
Peking had become aware of the Arabs' extreme hostility toward
Israel and of the unanimous stand on the Palestine question of the
otherwise disunited Arab countries. However, the Arab hostility to
Israel was interpreted by Peking primarily as a product of "imperialist instigation and interference." At the same time, furthermore,
negotiations were taking place with Israeli representatives with a
view, on the Chinese side, to establishing full diplomatic relations.
It seems, therefore, highly improbable that, at that stage, Peking
decided to support the Arab side in the Arab-Israeli conflict in order
to win the goodwill of the Arab and other Muslim countries. There

was no indication of any Chinese intention to exploit the Arab-Israeli conflict, especially as there was not even a hint of a forthcoming Arab diplomatic recognition of the PRC. Events, however, pushed the Chinese, who had very little choice, into a position that appeared to be pro-Arab.

When the question of who was to be invited to Bandung was discussed at the second meeting of the Colombo powers at Bogor, Indonesia, in late December 1954, the Chinese found themselves indirectly involved in Arab-Israeli relations, on the Arab side. On December 20, 1954, the secretary general of the Arab League submitted a note to the conference sponsors that read in part: "It is known that this conference will be a regional one. It has been the policy of the Arab States not to participate in any regional conference where Israel is represented. The Arab States do not have any doubt that Israel will not be invited to this conference and will not participate therein."[11] This stand was strongly supported by Pakistan, which, however, was opposed to inviting the PRC. In the face of Indian and Burmese pressure and in order to avoid the undermining of Asian solidarity, Pakistan withdrew its opposition. "As a consolation prize for agreeing to the inclusion of Peking, the others agreed to her demand to exclude Israel. . . ."[12]

Apparently Peking had some reservations about the resolutions reached at Bogor:

> . . . The Asian-African conference should not be an exclusive regional bloc. . . . The five Prime Ministers declared that in seeking to convene the Asian-African conference, they were not activated by any desire for exclusiveness in respect to membership in the conference. We support this statement. Based on this statement, we consider that the door of the conference is open to those Asian and African countries that were not invited to it.[13]

China's comments could have represented no more than lip service to the principle of universality, once Peking itself had been invited. Yet, even if they reflected genuine uneasiness, in the final analysis China was no less interested, but probably more so than the five Colombo powers in the success of the conference and in demonstrating Asian-African "solidarity." To achieve these objectives "certain variations and minor modifications" were appropriate so that the nonparticipation of Israel was insignificant and very easily approved of by Peking.

Indeed, in early April, China supported for the first time a resolution in favor of the Palestinians and condemning Israel by name, a resolution by the leftist Conference of the Asian Countries in New Delhi and one that was much more forcefully worded than the rather moderate Bandung resolution on the same issue. * Despite this and other gestures toward the Arabs, however, Kuo Mo-jo, leader of the Chinese delegation to New Delhi, still insisted that international problems--specifically, the relations between China and Japan and China and Thailand, and those among the Middle East countries-- should be solved on the basis of the Five Principles of peaceful co- existence. [15]

China also adhered to this formula in Bandung. In the first two days of the conference, the Palestinian issue was raised by at least seven speakers. Chou En-lai had additional opportunities to hear about this subject in his private conversations with Nasser and with Ahmad Shuqayri (then Syria's ambassador to Egypt and vice chairman of the Syrian delegation to Bandung, who later became chairman of the Palestine Liberation Organization). Shuqayri presented the main Arab arguments on the Palestine issue at the conference, and ex- pended considerable effort to acquaint Chou En-lai with the details of the Palestine problem. [16]

In public, however, Chou En-lai tried to remain uncommitted, and referred to this issue only in his prepared speech of April 19, 1955, when he remarked briefly that "the problem of Arab refugees of Palestine still remains to be solved."[17] He completely ignored the Palestine question in the speech he actually delivered. But Chou En-lai could no longer evade the Palestine question when it was raised in the secret sessions of the Political Committee (consisting exclusively of the heads of delegations) on April 20 and 21. The de- bate centered around the draft resolution proposed by the Afghani delegation: "In view of the existing tension in the Middle East caused by the situation in Palestine and of the dangers of that tension to world peace, the Asian-African Conference declares its support of the rights of the Arab people of Palestine and calls for the imple- mentation of the United Nations resolutions on Palestine."[18]

Chou En-lai apparently said that he was inclined to support this resolution, except as regards the call to the UN, since China, not then a member of the UN, did not know the full contents of its

------

*The resolution said: "We also condemn pressure of all types that is being exerted by certain powers, especially through Israel and Turkey, to coerce the Arab countries to join military blocs. . . . This conference expresses its sympathies for the plight of the Arab refugees and upholds their right to return to Palestine. This con- ference condemns the aggressive policy of the ruling circles of Israel."[14]

resolutions (although all of the UN resolutions on Palestine were distributed to all of the Bandung delegates). He then suggested that the reference to the UN be replaced by a "world appeal" by the conference for the cause of the Palestine Arab refugees. He also pointed out that the problem of Palestine was the result of foreign intervention. [19]

A subcommittee consisting of the delegates of eight countries, including the PRC, was set up to draft the final resolution. It was within this framework that Chou En-lai compared the question of Palestine to that of Taiwan and maintained that it would be settled only when outside factors responsible for the "Palestine tragedy" would disappear. [20] However, the only addition to the final resolution approved by the subcommittee was: "And the achievement of the peaceful settlement of the Palestine question."

Several accounts of the conference have suggested that the Chinese outdid the Arabs in their attempts to condemn Israel and that they urged the adoption of a more forcefully worded proposal than that introduced by Afghanistan and supported by the Arab states. [21] This Chinese stand was said to have been appreciated fully by the Syrian delegation, [22] as well as by the former mufti of Jerusalem, Hajj 'Amin al-Husayni. *

Yet, closer examination of China's attitude on the Palestine problem during the conference, as well as afterward, reveals that there was very little new in it and that it did not deviate from China's previous views on Arab-Israeli relations.

During the conference the Chinese omitted in their reports such extremist pronouncements as "Palestine must be returned to the Arabs." [23] In a leading article in the People's Daily summing up the conference, Peking repeatedly said that "the rights of the Arab people in Palestine should be respected, and the question of Palestine should be peacefully settled according to the principle of the settlement of disputes by the people themselves." [24]

This issue was elaborated in a more comprehensive commentary on the Palestine question published after the conference. Following a brief presentation of the history of Jews and Arabs in

---

*He appeared in the Political Committee meeting on the 20th and later joined the Yemeni delegation, and, according to Dawn (Pakistan) of April 25, 1955, told Chou En-lai: "I thank you heartily for your defense of the Palestine question which was put forth in your excellent speech at the General Assembly and to the Political Committee." Chou En-lai replied: "We support all Arab problems in general and that of Palestine in particular as we do support the struggle of all enslaved peoples."

Palestine the Chinese, as in the past, blamed Britain and the United States for instigating the conflict. Peking again noted that the Republic of Israel had been proclaimed "on the basis of the UN Partition Plan" but the Palestinian Arab state could not have been established ". . . because the territories which, according to the UN Partition Plan, belonged to the Palestinian Arab state had been occupied by Israel, Jordan and other countries [Egypt]." Britain and the United States, in order to strengthen their position in the Middle East, exploited the refugee problem so as to increase the hostility between Israel and the Arabs, eventually provoking armed incidents. "It was precisely in view of this kind of situation that the Asian-African Conference declared support of the rights of the Palestinian Arab people and, furthermore, of seeking the implementation of the UN resolutions in order to reach a peaceful settlement of the Palestine problem."[25]

Thus, even after Bandung had brought them closer to the Arabs, the Chinese still maintained that foreign imperialist interference had been the ultimate cause of the Palestine problem; that the plight of the Palestinian refugees was not the fault of Israel alone but of some Arab countries as well; and that a possible settlement should follow the lines of the UN Partition Plan through direct negotiations rather than by the use of arms.

That China tried to keep its balanced position was also confirmed after the conference by Yao Chung-ming, China's ambassador to Burma, who joined Chou En-lai on his way back from Bandung. He reassured Israel that Chou En-lai had had no intention of alienating Israel in Bandung; he said that Chou En-lai had tried to evade the issue but could not forestall unanimity by dissociating himself from the resolution; that he had not mentioned Israel by name; and, finally, that rapprochement between China and the Arabs would not be accomplished at the expense of Israel, with which China still wished to maintain friendly relations.[26] There is little reason to doubt the sincerity of this explanation, which reflected China's basic attitude toward Israel until the Suez crisis in late 1956, at least.

On the whole, however, for China, the Palestine issue was of minor importance in the context of the Bandung Conference. In Chou En-lai's long report on the conference to the National People's Congress (NPC) his only reference to that issue was: "In the Resolution on Other Problems, the Asian-African Conference supported the right of Arab people of Palestine. . . ."[27]

If the Chinese had expected that by siding with the Arabs on the Palestine issue they would improve their relations with Arab countries other than those that had already moved in this direction (Egypt, Syria, Yemen), they were probably disappointed.

After the Bandung Conference, in late 1955, and particularly in mid-1956, there were further indications of China's interest in forming relations with Israel.* It is quite obvious that, at that time, China regarded the Arab-Israeli conflict as an embarrassment rather than as an asset. The persistence of the conflict vitiated China's basic design in the Middle East, namely, the withdrawal of the West. It also complicated China's relations with the Middle East states. For these reasons, China was in favor of settling this conflict as soon as possible; outside interference would have led only to war, which in turn would have led to further interference and to the consolidation of Western predominance in the Middle East: "Originally, the Arab-Israeli conflict, provided it stayed under the direction of a correct national policy, could have absolutely been solved. However, being under the conspiracy and provocations of Anglo-American imperialism, Arab-Israeli relations will only worsen more and more, leading eventually to the outbreak of war."[29] This was written at least half a year before war broke out on October 29, 1956. Following that war, China's rather moderate attitude toward Israel changed and became considerably more hostile, although not yet as uncompromising an approach as characterized the mid-1960s.

By early 1957, China had begun to perceive a shift from relaxation to tension in the world situation. There were many indications in the Chinese view that the West was again on the offensive, particularly against the Third World, but also against the socialist camp. Such Middle Eastern developments as the Suez invasion, the Eisenhower Doctrine, the Western pressure on Jordan and Lebanon, and the large-scale British operations in South Arabia confirmed Peking's analysis. China's position in the Middle East had also changed. Egypt, Syria, and Yemen had recognized China and had established full diplomatic, cultural, and economic relations with Peking. All these developments affected China's hitherto relatively balanced stand on the Arab-Israel conflict and the Palestine problem.†

---

*Although they did not mention Israel by name, the Chinese reiterated their wish to improve ties with countries that had not yet established diplomatic relations with the PRC [such as Israel and Ceylon]. They also declared: "We are against placing our friendly relations with certain countries [for example, the Arab countries] on the basis of excluding other countries [for example, Israel]."[28]

†For example, whereas until the 1956 war, China had said that, in May 1948, under the instigation of colonialism, the Arabs had attacked Israel, or that a war had "broken out," it now said that "Israel, immediately after its proclamation, started a war against its neighbouring Arab countries."[30]

From late 1956 on, China began to regard Israel as an instrument used by Western imperialism to exert pressure on the Arab countries and thereby to maintain tension in the Middle East. This was the first time that the Chinese named Israel a "tool" (kung-chu) of imperialist aggression[31] (although in the crisis itself Israel's role was described by Peking as merely "unwise" and was always conceived of by Peking as subsidiary and marginal to the role of Britain and France). What really irritated the Chinese was Israel's refusal to withdraw from Sinai and Gaza. China strongly rejected the idea that the securing of free navigation in the Suez Canal for Israel should be a precondition for the withdrawal of Israeli troops. China insisted that, even after Israel's withdrawal, passage should not be granted to Israeli ships before an attempt was made to solve the Arab refugee question.[32]

In this connection, a Chinese trade union leader declared in Egypt that the Chinese people were with the Palestinian Arabs in their struggle for human rights. The joint statement issued by the Chinese and Arab trade union representatives said that "the Chinese trade unions . . . sympathize with and support the struggle for human rights of the Arab people in Palestine."[33] This was, in fact, the first expression of China's belief that the Palestine problem was at the root of Arab-Israeli relations and that the settlement of no other aspect of the conflict should precede the settlement of the Palestine problem.

Still, China's view of a possible settlement remained unchanged. Burhan Shahidi, chairman of the China Islamic Association, who played an important role in Sino-Arab relations, reaffirmed China's basic stand that, in order to settle the dispute, all the resolutions of the Bandung Conference and the relevant United Nations resolutions must be observed strictly by the parties concerned.[34] Thus, despite the events of late 1956 and China's increased hostility toward Israel, a somewhat balanced view of the Palestine issue (which China still regarded as essentially one of the refugees) was maintained. This basic stand was maintained, with few exceptions, until the mid-1960s, when China's attitude on the Palestine problem was reformulated.

A RADICALIZATION OF CHINA'S FOREIGN POLICY

In the mid-1960s, the world situation, from Peking's point of view, was completely different. United States imperialism was now considered as being on the offensive in Asia, Africa, and Latin America. The Soviet Union was no longer China's ally but rather its enemy, which acted in collusion with the United States in order

to expand Soviet control over the Third World. To counter imperialist aggression and to undermine the Soviet position, China urged
the Third World peoples to wage armed struggle and people's wars.
As it had in the mid-1950s, China regarded Asian-African unity as
a vital precondition of victory. Much of Peking's foreign policy efforts were devoted to winning the support of Asian and African governments for a second Asian-African (Bandung) conference that
would exclude the Soviet Union and adopt a militant attitude toward
the United States. These attempts failed completely. Once more
(as in the late 1950s) China realized that some national-bourgeois
governments tended to crack under outside pressure and could not
be considered as partners in the anti-imperialist struggle. As a
result, China's relations with many Asian and African countries
deteriorated considerably, and Peking began to cultivate sub- or
supragovernmental national liberation movements and revolutionary
organizations. The political upheaval that began to sweep across
China by late 1965 also contributed to the radicalization of China's
foreign policy.

China's Middle East policy was again a precise reflection of
its global analysis. As in the past, the Middle East was regarded
by China as a crucial battlefield against imperialism: "The Middle
East figures prominently in the U.S. global strategy. . . . Just because the U.S. has a big stake in its oil, and because it has 'strategic interests' in the Middle East, any single spark of revolution, or
any anti-imperialist outcry in this region will send cold shivers down
the backs of the Americans in the White House."[35]

In addition, China thought that the Arab countries, particularly
Egypt, occupied a central position within the Asian-African world,
not only in geographic but in political terms as well. Because of
their growing dependence on the Soviet Union, the Arabs could frustrate both of China's aims--the exclusion of Moscow from the conference and the launching of militant opposition to the United States,
an opposition that Moscow preferred to avoid. It was necessary,
therefore, for China to win the support of the Arabs, lest its policy
meet with failure.

China began its most energetic campaign in the Middle East in
late 1963. This campaign, which gathered momentum as the forthcoming conference approached, consisted of diplomatic and political
efforts (including unprecedentedly frequent visits by Chinese leaders
to the Middle East) as well as various economic appeals (growth in
China's imports from the Middle East and unprecedentedly large aid
offers). It was against this background that the Chinese again became interested in the Palestine problem. They not only adopted,
almost in its entirety, the Arab stand on the problem but also established relations with the PLO, newly created by the Arab governments.

It took China some time to redevelop its interest in the Palestine question. In their exchanges with Arab leaders in the latter half of 1963, the Chinese apparently evaded the matter. Their few remarks on the Palestine issue were rather brief and vague, and neither implicated nor even mentioned Israel, for example: "The Chinese side reiterate its support . . . for the rights of the Arab people in Palestine."[36] Chou En-lai, who was visiting Egypt in late 1963, made the one brief remark devoted to the Palestine issue in his long press conference: "The Chinese people have always stood firmly behind the Arabs in Palestine in their just struggle for their legitimate rights. Our diplomatic actions have testified to this."[37] The joint communique stated that "the Chinese side declared its full support to the people of Palestine in restoring their legitimate rights and in returning to their homeland."[38]

Gradually, however, China's stand on the Palestine problem underwent considerable change. In the mid-1950s, China conceived of the problem mainly as an international dispute among Asian-African countries with local or regional significance at best. China believed that both Israel and the Arab countries shared some of the blame for not complying with the United Nations Partition Plan; the contradictions between Israel and the Arabs, of which Peking had definitely been aware, were perceived as basically nonantagonistic. Peaceful coexistence still applied, in China's view, to Arab-Israeli relations. Hence, Peking thought, the Palestine problem should have been settled politically through direct negotiation between the parties concerned, without foreign interference and according to UN resolutions, primarily the 1947 Partition Plan. This position that Peking accepted and endorsed was also the Soviet one; the blame for creating the problem and preventing its settlement fell entirely on the West.

By the mid-1960s, China's views had become completely different. The Palestine problem was no longer seen as merely an international dispute concerning refugees, but as a manifestation of the national liberation struggle of a distinct Palestinian people. The significance of this struggle extended far beyond the Middle East, having become part of the front against U.S. imperialism. Typically, the Chinese analyzed the Palestine problem in relation to themselves, and regarded the Palestinian and Arab peoples' struggle "as a great assistance to themselves in their opposition to U.S. imperialist aggression."[39] When the PLO delegation visited China in March 1965, Mao told its members: "Imperialism is afraid of China and the Arabs. Israel and Formosa are bases of imperialism in Asia. You are the front gate of the great continent, and we are the rear. They created Israel for you, and Formosa for us."[40] China was no longer interested in relations with Israel, which was no longer

considered to be a Third World country but rather an extension of
U.S. imperialism. Hence, in China's view, the contradictions
between Israel and the Arabs, particularly the Palestinians, had
become antagonistic and irreconcilable. From the mid-1960s,
therefore, the Chinese rejected any suggestion that the Palestine
question should be settled peacefully. [41] People's armed struggle
was regarded as the only way to settle the Palestine problem. Chou
En-lai explained the logic of China's stand:

> Countries whose territories had been invaded and
> occupied by imperialism, . . . naturally had every
> right to recover their lost territories by any means.
> To ask those countries which were subjected to ag-
> gression to renounce the use of force in any circum-
> stances was in fact to ask the people of all countries
> to renounce their struggle against the imperialist
> policies of aggression and war, placing themselves
> at the mercy of imperialism and submitting to im-
> perialist enslavement. [42]

Obviously, under these circumstances, China no longer regarded the
United Nations as suitable for and capable of contributing to the settlement of the Palestine question. In China's retrospective view, the
United Nations had been manipulated by Western imperialism not only
to create the Palestine problem but also to prevent its settlement. [43]
However, Anglo-American manipulation was no longer regarded as
the sole obstacle to the settlement of the Palestine question. From
mid-1966 on, Peking began to stress Soviet-American schemes as the
main reasons for the persistence of the Arab-Israeli conflict:

> US imperialism . . . uses the softening tactics, try-
> ing by every means to bring the Arab people to a
> "reconciliation" with the Zionists and an acceptance
> of the status quo of Israel, in other words, an ac-
> ceptance of the humiliating position of the victimized
> Palestinian Arabs.
>   It must be pointed out that the revisionist lead-
> ing group of the Soviet Union is a partner of the US
> in the latter's criminal plan against the Arabs. It is
> a well-known fact that the Soviet revisionists are
> linked with the Israeli Zionists. . . . Obviously, a
> conspiracy is afoot in which the Soviet revisionist
> leading group works hand in glove with the US im-
> perialists in betraying the Palestinian and Arab
> peoples' interests and their anti-imperialist
> struggle. [44]

The once acceptable 1947 Partition Resolution was no longer attributed to the Soviet Union, and was completely rejected in the mid-1960s as an Anglo-American fabrication. China offered no alternative plan for settlement other than support for the Palestinians in their struggle to restore their legitimate rights and to return to, or recover, their homeland. Although the Chinese have never denied in public Israel's right to exist, their own comments[45] and certainly their quotation of Palestinian statements have left little doubt that Peking would have welcomed a total Palestinian victory. *

These considerations provided the basis for a significant change in China's relations with the Palestinians. Whereas, in the mid-1950s, Peking had confined itself to rare and casual verbal support of the Palestinians' right to return to their homeland, and any Chinese gesture toward the Palestinians had been made indirectly through the Arab governments, beginning in the mid-1960s, China dealt directly with the Palestine liberation movement and systematically extended to the Palestinians both verbal and material support.

China's interest and involvement in the Palestinian liberation movement began to grow after the First Arab Summit Conference (January 1964) had recommended the formation of a distinct Palestinian entity. Chou En-lai, then in Somalia, acclaimed the decision: "We are glad to see the growing spirit of solidarity and cooperation among the Arab countries. China has always supported the Palestine people's just struggle for the restoration of their proper rights and for return to their homeland. "[47] Ahmad Shuyayri, who had been entrusted by the Arab leaders with organizing the Palestinians, immediately called on the Chinese ambassador in Cairo to convey the Palestine people's gratitude for China's support of the Palestine cause. [48]

In March 1964, China's press began to express extensive support of the Palestinians, and huge demonstrations were held in Peking. Among those present were two Palestinian guests from the Palestine Bureau in Algiers (possibly a Fatah branch). †

---

*For example, "The Palestinian people are more convinced than ever that people's liberation war is the only way to eliminate the colonialist base--Israel--and to liberate Palestine completely" [emphasis added]. [46]

†The Chinese, who named the guests as Muhammad Khalil and Muhammad Rif'at, gave no clue to their real identity. The sound of these names and other evidence suggest that they were Khalil al-Wazir and Yasser Arafat, leaders of Fatah in its early organizational stages in Algeria. Without mentioning these names Dawn (Pakistan) of March 28, 1964 reported that they had come from the Palestine

In May 1964, the PLO was established; in March 1965, its
first delegation, headed by Shuqayri, arrived in China. Throughout
the visit, the Chinese media discussed Middle Eastern and particularly Palestinian affairs in numerous articles and commentaries.
China's top leaders, including Mao Tse-tung, met the delegation for
talks. Judging from the wording of the joint statement published
during the visit, mutual understanding was quite extensive: "The
two parties agreed that the PLO shall set up a mission in Peking to
strengthen mutual cooperation. The Chinese people will make every
effort to support the Arab people of Palestine in their struggle to return to their homeland by all means, political and otherwise."[50]

It should be stressed that the initiative to establish relations
between China and the PLO apparently had come from the latter.
According to Shuqayri, the Chinese invited the PLO delegation only
after he himself told the Chinese ambassador in Cairo of his desire
to visit China. Similarly, it was Shuqayri's own suggestion that a
PLO mission should be opened in Peking and that China should supply
the PLO with military aid as well as with training for its members.[51]

Nevertheless, this was probably the strongest public commitment ever made by Peking toward the Palestinians. In addition to
their approval of the opening of a PLO office with quasi-diplomatic
status in Peking, the Chinese privately agreed to provide arms and
training. On May 15, 1965, Palestine Day was celebrated in China
for the first time; the celebrations took place thereafter yearly until
1971.

China's demonstration of friendship and support for the new-
born PLO seemed somewhat exaggerated. In 1965, the PLO was not
yet a national movement and, more important, it was not yet engaged
in a genuine liberation war. Oman and Aden were then regarded as
centers of people's armed struggle, but not Palestine.[52] Moreover,
the PLO intentionally had no socialist pretensions and the image of
its leader, Ahmad Shuqayri, was far from that of a revolutionary or
a socialist leader. He suggested that training PLO members in China
was necessary before starting a people's war in Palestine. Mao
Tse-tung's view on the need of foreigners to come from abroad for
training in China was reportedly as follows:

> All things can be divided. Imperialism is also
> a thing, it also can be divided, it also can be

Bureau in Algeria, which, according to them, was the strongest
private organization after the Arab League struggling for the Palestine cause. Other sources confirmed that Khalil al-Wazir had visited China at that time.[49]

extinguished bit by bit. . . . This principle is very
simple, there is nothing deep and mysterious about
it. There is no need to read boring books, those
who fight also do away with reading books. All the
time we fought we did not read books. Read only a
little, much reading is no good.

The battlefield is a school. I am not opposed
to military schools. They can be conducted. However, they should not last too long. If they go for
two or three years, that is too long. Several months
is enough. . . . The important thing is battlefield
training. . . .

There are some foreign people studying in
China military matters. We advise them to go
back, there is no need to study too long. Several
months is quite enough, all classroom lectures are
of no use. To go back and take part in fighting is
more useful.[53]

According to another account, he said:

Do not tell me that you have read this or that opinion
in my books. You have your war and we have ours.
You must make the principles and ideology on which
your war stands. Books obstruct the view if piled
up before the eye. What is important is to begin
action with faith. Faith in victory is the first element of victory--in fact, it may mean victory itself.[54]

Yet, despite having been aware of the PLO's shortcomings,
the Chinese responded positively to the Palestinians' initiative and
to their specific requests. China's decision to support the PLO
could not have been influenced by any Chinese "model" of revolutionary experience or by pure revolutionary and ideological considerations. Like most other foreign policy decisions, it involved a
wide range of interests reflecting China's basic analysis of a given
international situation, and the developments in the Asian-African
world, the Middle East, and China itself.

A full decade before many countries in the world, including
the Arab countries, did so, China had realized that the Palestine
problem was the crux of the Middle East question as well as the way
to the settlement of the Arab-Israeli conflict, and furthermore, that
the PLO was the true representative of the Palestinian people.
Therefore, although the PLO was not yet a revolutionary movement

in the mid-1960s, it undoubtedly had, in China's view, a strong national and revolutionary potential. China's support of the Palestinian cause and of the PLO could promote both short-term and long-term Chinese foreign policy objectives.

In the first place, the Palestinians were firmly opposed to the United States. At a time when Peking believed U.S. imperialism was making repeated attempts to expand its control over the Third World, the PLO, committed to armed struggle against the United States and its "tool of aggression" Israel, could not only cause concern but could even harm and undermine American interests in an extremely important and sensitive area.

Second, although the PLO tried repeatedly to obtain the approval and support of the Soviet Union, it was consistently rejected or ignored.[55] Furthermore, the Soviets not only disapproved of the PLO and its methods but still maintained full diplomatic relations with Israel. China's recognition and support of the PLO and the Palestinian cause were, very possibly, also intended to weaken Moscow's hitherto predominant position in the Arab world.

Finally, China was well aware of the fact that the PLO had been sponsored and created by the Arab governments and that it apparently enjoyed their unanimous support. As the only non-Arab country to have so acted, China's alignment with the Arab governments on this sensitive issue was clearly intended to please them and to gain their support for one of China's most urgent short-term objectives: the convening of the Second Bandung Conference, which, without Soviet participation, would urge armed struggle against "US imperialism" throughout the Third World.

Already by the end of 1965, it had become clear that the Chinese had failed completely to achieve their short-term objectives. The much-prepared Asian-African conference was postponed indefinitely. China no doubt underestimated the Arabs', including the Palestinians', predisposition toward the Soviet Union. The Arab governments were reluctant, to say the least, to relinquish the material advantages of Soviet friendship by excluding Moscow from the proposed conference. They were ready to forgo the conference altogether lest it turn into a battlefield between China and the Soviet Union.

China also misinterpreted the Arab governments' stand on the Palestine issue. The Arab governments, which since 1948 had monopolised (and in fact neglected) the management of Palestinian affairs, had no intention in the mid-1960s of providing their new creation, the PLO, with unlimited freedom of action and exclusive responsibility to "liberate" Palestine. There was no unanimous agreement among the Arab leaders on the PLO's future course of action and they, particularly Nasser, preferred to keep the PLO under close control.

The generous offer of political indoctrination and of military aid made by China to the PLO in order to gain the goodwill of the Arab governments had, therefore, complications. It not only threatened to reduce the PLO dependence upon the Arab governments but had also been made without consulting senior Arab leaders, primarily Nasser. When in Peking, Shuqayri instructed the Chinese to deliver arms shipments for the PLO directly to Alexandria, without first obtaining Nasser's approval. The Egyptian ambassador in China warned him of the seriousness of this omission. Nasser was indeed furious, and refused to receive Shuqayri after the latter's return from China.[56]

By the end of 1965 and early 1966, China's relations with the Arab governments were cool again. As the attempted united front from above collapsed, China turned to achieve its foreign policy plans by relying more and more on national liberation movements. The failure of China's Palestine policy to win the goodwill of the Arab leaders did not discourage the Chinese from continuing their support of the Palestinians, since China's interest in the Palestinians had not been based on short-term expediency alone. Despite the upheavals of the Cultural Revolution there was Chinese verbal encouragement, initial shipments of Chinese arms (rifles, mines, explosives, hand grenades, and machine guns) reached Palestinian hands, and the first groups of Palestinians (probably no more than a few dozen) returned to the Middle East after having been trained on Chinese soil.

Following the June 1967 war, the Chinese probably felt that their investment in the Palestinians had not been in vain. In Peking's view, the war confirmed China's analysis of the Middle East situation and provided crystal-clear evidence that, so long as the two superpowers were involved in Middle Eastern affairs, no settlement would be reached; that the conventional strategy employed by the Arab governments and dictated by the Soviets had failed completely; and that an independent Palestinian people's war should become the spearhead of the struggle against Israel, a war fully supported by the Arab governments.[57]

Although the Arabs were defeated in the war, their defeat provided the Palestinians with an important asset for people's war: a potential base inside enemy-occupied territory. As early as 1965, the Chinese chief of staff had advised the visiting PLO delegation that it should have a base inside Israel because operations from outside would only enrage Israel and lead it to carry out retaliation operations against the Arab countries.* Israel's occupation of large

---

*He pointed out that the Galilee mountains were of great military advantage, being close to vital Israeli targets, as well as to Syria and Lebanon, where rear bases could be established.[58]

Palestinian-inhabited areas was thus of immense revolutionary significance from Peking's point of view. This opportunity to launch a genuine Palestinian armed struggle, based on and assisted by the local population, coincided with the revolutionary outbursts in China as the Cultural Revolution reached its climax, and raised China's ideological and revolutionary expectations of the Palestinians.

Very soon, however, China's hopes for an independent, Maoist-style Palestinian people's war inside Israel began to be shattered. Within a few months, Israel's reprisals and countermeasures brought guerrilla activities inside the Israeli-administered territories to a virtual standstill. Palestinian raids from outside Israel's borders followed by Israeli retaliations were thereafter curbed, and in some cases stopped altogether, by the Arab governments themselves.

These governments, still under Soviet influence, could not be reconciled with either a people's war strategy or with the Palestinians playing the central role in the struggle against Israel. This view was expressed, sometimes indirectly, on many occasions. For example, a number of articles in al-Ahram by Muhammad Hasanyn Haykal, then editor of this influential and semiofficial Egyptian daily and a close friend of Nasser, repeatedly downgraded the importance of the Palestinian organizations, stressing their marginal and secondary role. [59]

For their part, the Palestinians remained dependent upon the Arab regimes. Some organizations were no more than agents or representatives of certain Arab governments, while practically all of them operated under their auspices, and often at their mercy. Disillusioned, Na'if Hawatma, leader of the People's Democratic Front for the Liberation of Palestine, admitted that "in its present conditions, the resistance movement is more like a bargaining card in the hands of the Arab regimes rather than a revolutionary vanguard capable of liberating Palestine, let alone the Arab homeland." [60]

Involved in the question of the Palestinians' exposure to outside manipulations was China's grave anxiety about the growing influence of the Soviet Union on the Arabs and, at least indirectly, on the Palestinians as well. However, the quantity and quality of the Soviet aid to the Arabs were in sharp contrast to what China could and did offer. So, despite their relatively close relations with the Chinese, the Palestinians, including the radicals, never turned their backs on the Russians. At the beginning of 1967, Shafiq al-Hut, chairman of the PLO Beirut Office, plainly argued: "If Peking supports unrestrictedly Arab right to restore Palestine in theory there is, however, no doubt that in practice it is Moscow that can translate this support into a language of international value" [emphasis added]. [61]

Another result of the 1967 war that frustrated China's expectations was the disintegration of the Palestine liberation movement into smaller factional organizations. Although some of these factions, particularly the People's Front for the Liberation of Palestine and the People's Democratic Front for the Liberation of Palestine, claimed to be Marxist-Leninist, China apparently always preferred to deal with the main organizations, PLO and Fatah. The radical and leftist groups never regarded Mao Tse-tung's thought as the only and exclusive guide to revolution; they were small, detached from the masses, often persecuted and outlawed, and fomented subdivision of the Palestine liberation movement. Furthermore, they gave first priority to what China considered only a secondary and subsequent goal: the overthrowing of the existing Arab regimes and the starting of a social and political revolution.

Fatah, on the other hand, deliberately rejected Marxism-Leninism; studied the Chinese revolutionary experience along with the Vietnamese, the Cuban, and other models; and even claimed to have an "original" revolutionary trial that preceded the Chinese.[62] Nonetheless, it was Fatah that obtained most of China's attention, support, and encouragement, because of its large popular basis and its primary concern with the national rather than the sociopolitical task.

Thus, China's support of national liberation movements was not determined by their revolutionary character or their conformity to the Maoist model alone, but by considerations influenced by the local situation and, more important, the international one.

A NEW STATUS AND A NEW FOREIGN POLICY

By the late 1960s, as the Cultural Revolution was subsiding, China began to perceive a major change in the world situation. This change emerged, in Peking's view, out of three different but complementary trends: increased belligerency of the Soviet Union in Europe, the Middle East and Asia, ultimately directed at China; indications of America's readiness to lessen its political and military involvement, particularly in Asia; and a growing desire for liberation and independence manifested by the peoples of the vast intermediate zone, who rejected the hegemony of both superpowers.

While China's relations with the Soviet Union deteriorated drastically, the Chinese succeeded simultaneously in establishing or improving relations with most of the world, including the United States, and the PRC was admitted to the United Nations and, as a permanent member, to the Security Council. Their new status in the world and their relatively moderate foreign policy compelled the

Chinese to become more selective in their support of national liberation movements and revolutionary organizations.

China's Middle East policy has been dictated, since the early
1970s, by these considerations and particularly by Chinese fear of
the Soviet Union. Whereas in the past the Middle East was considered by the Chinese as an important link in the projected American
encirclement of China, the Middle East is now regarded as part of
the Soviet attempt to outflank China from the South, while the Soviet
military buildup along China's northern frontiers constitutes a direct
threat on another front. To be sure, both Moscow and Washington
have been accused by the Chinese of "contending and colluding" in
the Middle East, yet today China seems much more concerned about
the Soviet position in the Middle East than about that of the United
States. This concern, as well as China's new position in world
affairs, is reflected in Peking's approach to the Palestine problem
and to the Arab-Israeli conflict in recent years.

The Chinese still condemn Zionism and Western imperialism
for creating the Palestine problem and the two superpowers for preventing its settlement: "It is mainly due to the obstruction and
sabotage by the two superpowers, the United States and the Soviet
Union, that the Palestinian people's national rights have not been
restored over a long period."[63] However, a careful examination of
Chinese commentaries and speeches on the Palestine problem reveals that the Soviet Union has been condemned much more, and in
stronger terms, than the United States:

> Social-imperialism has always been colluding with
> US imperialism and hostile to the Palestinian people.
> It has wildly slandered and abused the Palestinian
> people's armed struggle as "terrorist operations,"
> thus revealing its fear of and hatred for the Pales-
> tinian people's armed struggle and greatly discredit-
> ing itself. Recently, it has changed its tactics and
> hypocritically pretended to "support" the Palestin-
> ian people's armed struggle. It is clear to every-
> one that its aim is merely to place the Palestinian
> armed forces under its control, using them as
> capital in making dirty deals with US imperialism
> in the Middle East, so as to realize its criminal
> plot of stamping out the Palestinian armed struggle
> and divide up the Middle East with US imperialism.[64]

Under such circumstances China still insists that armed struggle is the only way to settle both the Palestine problem and the
Arab-Israeli conflict, so long as three other fundamental principles

are closely observed: noninterference from outside, unity among the Palestinians and the Arabs, and self-reliance. In this respect little has changed in China's position on the Middle East question since 1967, a position that has been repeated persistently to the present:

> The essence of the Middle East question is aggression versus anti-aggression and a question of the Palestinian and other Arab peoples fighting for national liberation. There is certainly no room for compromise on this question. The restoration of the Palestinian people's right to national existence and the Arab countries' struggle to recover their lost territories constitute an integral whole. As long as the lost territories of the Arab states are not recovered and the Palestinian people's national right is not restored, there can be no true settlement of the so-called Middle East question."[65]

Yet, although repeating this view over and over again, the Chinese never have elaborated on the meaning of such key phrases as "the restoration of the Palestinian people's right to national existence" or "recovery of the lost territories," thus leaving some room for maneuver and change. One change, though still marginal, can be found in Peking's attitude toward Israel.

In recent years there were signs and hints of slight moderation of the Chinese attitude toward Israel, spelled out in private talks as well as in public pronouncements. One remarkable indication is the change of style, which is less rude and insulting than it used to be. Terms like "a dagger thrust into the Arab hearts," "tool of aggression," or "running dog of U.S. imperialism" with which the Chinese usually referred to Israel in the 1960s no longer appear.

Although the Chinese still refuse to have any contact with either the government or the people of Israel, they began definitely to distinguish between the two, something very rarely done before. After China's admission to the United Nations, Chou En-lai was quoted as saying: "Among the 76 countries which voted for the Albanian resolution there are, of course, some countries which cannot have official governmental relations with China although their peoples are friendly with the Chinese people. One example is Israel. This does not mean that we cannot become friendly with the Jewish people."[66] China's representatives in the United Nations reiterated several times that the Chinese were "not opposed to the Jewish people or to the people of Israel" but only "to Israeli Zionist policies of aggression and expansion."[67]

Some visitors to China in recent years, such as Anthony
Wedgwood-Benn, Pietro Nenni, Pierre Mendes-France, Giuseppe
Medici, and others, have shared the impression that the Chinese
had admitted, sometimes in marked embarrassment, that, although
the establishment of the state of Israel had been a grave mistake
from the very beginning, Israel's right to exist must be reckoned
with and recognized post-factum.[68]

All this may lead to the conclusion that, in China's view, the
"restoration of Palestinian national rights" does not necessarily involve the destruction of the state of Israel.

This change of attitude, as well as China's admission to the
United Nations and the recently increased influence of Third World
countries on UN policy and resolutions, might lead the Chinese to a
reinterpretation of the United Nations' role in the Palestine problem.

China's basic stand has been, since the mid-1960s, that "the
United Nations, manipulated by the U.S. imperialists and the Soviet
revisionists, has become their tool for undermining the people's
revolutionary struggle in various countries and is absolutely unreliable."[69] Nothing much changed in that opinion after the PRC
joined the United Nations. Although raising the Palestine issue in
almost every debate on the Middle East, the Chinese nonetheless
abstained from most votes, repeatedly indicating that Israel had not
been firmly condemned and that the restoration of the Palestinians'
legitimate rights had not been mentioned or taken into account sufficiently.

However, after the United Nations General Assembly invited
the representatives of the Palestinian people to take part for the
first time in the discussion of the Palestine question, the Chinese
apparently began to adopt a more flexible attitude toward the United
Nations: "We maintain that the United Nations must rectify its past
unjust attitude on the Palestine question and adopt a just resolution
on this question to recognize the Palestinian people's national rights
and support their restoration."[70] Altogether, however, the Chinese
stand on the Palestine problem was only marginally affected by
Peking's new analysis of the world situation. The actual relations
between China and the Palestinians were influenced much more by
this.

There was no apparent reason why Peking should downgrade
the Palestine liberation movement that was fighting Israel, a state
definitely not on Peking's list of countries with which it wished to
improve relations. Also, the priority given to improving relations
with the Arab governments should not have been contradictory, but
rather complementary, to a simultaneous cultivation of the Palestinians. Indeed, it seems as if in the early 1970s China's relations
with the Palestinians were still flourishing: the New China News

Agency and the Chinese press continued to support the Palestinians; leaders and delegations representing almost all the Palestinian organizations visited China frequently; China was still providing the Palestinians with both training and arms.

Nevertheless, many indications showed that the content, intensity, and scope of China's rhetorical support and material assistance to the Palestinians had declined considerably.[71] The most obvious indication was the reduced Chinese coverage of Palestinian operations. The Chinese became much more selective in their reports. In some cases they deliberately avoided quoting news of Palestinian achievements.[72] When the Chinese did refer to the Palestinians, they maintained that Palestinian victory could be achieved only subject to certain conditions:

> We are convinced that the Palestinian people will surely smash any military attacks . . . and win victory in their national liberation war provided they keep to the road of armed struggle and, along with other Arab people, fight a protracted people's war against imperialism and Zionism resolutely by closing their ranks, working ceaselessly to build up their strength self-reliantly, maintaining vigilance, fearing no difficulty and refusing to be duped.[73]

Quite often, the Chinese referred to "twists and turns," "difficulties," "temporary difficulties," "difficult circumstances," or even "the most difficult circumstances" that the Palestinians were encountering in their struggle.

It seems, therefore, that Peking was well aware of the basic weaknesses of the Palestine liberation movement. Of these, prolonged stagnation and lack of unity were particularly criticized by Premier Chou En-lai when he met journalists from 11 Arab countries who were on a visit to China during "Palestine International Week" in May 1971. He was quoted as saying that he did not understand the meaning of the "temporary retreat in the Palestinian struggle, which could imply that there was no conflict with the enemy." There was no room to retreat, he stressed, and unity was essential as a primary condition for victory.[74] Later, in a provocative and frank interview, Chou En-lai indirectly admitted that he considered the liberation movement in the Middle East to be on the wane.[75]

China's dissatisfaction with the Palestinians was expressed also in deeds. Chinese arms supplies, which in any case "have accounted for only a small percentage of the armoury of the Palestinian guerrillas,"[76] were now further reduced. Some Palestinians

admitted that the Chinese had not fulfilled their own pledges, even
minor ones, and sources in Beirut said that actual Chinese aid was
less than a quarter of what had been promised.[77] Other Chinese
gestures of solidarity with the Palestinians also disappeared. "Palestine Day," celebrated in China every year since 1965, was last
observed in May 1971. "Palestine International Week," introduced
in May 1971, was not repeated.

Similar downgrading was reflected in the treatment accorded
by the Chinese to Palestinian leaders and delegations. Yasser
Arafat, Fatah leader and, since early 1969, PLO chairman, paid
his first visit to China in March 1970, precisely five years after his
predecessor's visit. There were many differences between the two
visits. Arafat came to China only after he had spent 12 days in
Moscow a month earlier (he had made a visit to Moscow in 1968 as
well); he was received in China mainly by "deputies" rather than by
leaders of high rank and was not received by Chairman Mao, who
shortly afterward received several Arab leaders. In addition, the
People's Daily did not publish either an editorial or a commentary
concerning Arafat's visit, no joint communique was issued, and no
tangible results could be noticed following the visit.

There was also a marked difference between China's response
to the October 1973 War and to the June 1967 War as far as the
Palestinians were concerned. In 1967, Chou En-lai had met the PLO
representative along with other Arab ambassadors, and sent messages of support to the heads of the Arab states, as well as to PLO
Chairman Shuqayri. In 1973, the PLO representative was not
present at Chou's meeting with the Arab ambassadors and no message of support was sent to Arafat.

This and other evidence suggest that China was not so enthusiastic about Shuqayri's replacement by Arafat as might have been
assumed. China's reservations about the Palestine liberation movement and its new leadership probably increased further after terror
had been introduced by both the radical and the moderate Palestinian
organizations. From the beginning, Peking ignored almost completely Palestinian acts of terror, in itself an obvious sign of dis-
approval. Later, Chinese diplomats and leaders privately criticized
Palestinian terrorism,[78] and Ch'iao Kuan-hua, then vice foreign
minister and chairman of China's delegation to the United Nations,
publicly clarified the Chinese position: "The Chinese Government has
always opposed assassination and hijacking of individuals as a means
for waging political struggles and is also opposed to terrorist acts
by individuals or a handful of people divorced from the masses, because they are harmful to the cause of national liberation and people's revolution. "[79]

CONCLUSIONS

To sum up, China's fundamental stand on the Palestine problem has never changed. The Chinese have always believed that foreign powers had created the problem and sustained it throughout the
years in order to attain a dominant position in the Middle East. The
Palestine problem, therefore, has always been analyzed by the
Chinese not as a local Middle Eastern issue but as an issue of international significance that reflects the resistance of local people
either to imperialism (British, American, West German) or social-
imperialism (Soviet). Consequently, Peking has always insisted that
the Palestine problem should be settled within the Middle East context and without intervention from outside. These fundamental concepts were valid in the 1950s and still are.

While China's strategic overview remained relatively solid,
policies and tactics were frequently changed. And since the Chinese
perceived the Palestine problem from the international point of view,
these changes should be understood not merely as a response and
reaction to developments in the Middle East or in terms of China's
internal affairs, but primarily against the background of China's
periodically revised analysis of the world situation.

In the mid-1950s, in light of their perceived relaxation of international tension, the Chinese advocated a peaceful political settlement of the Palestine problem according to UN resolutions. Peking
criticized Israel as well as the Arab governments for not complying
with these resolutions, but still held the Western powers as ultimately
responsible for the grave situation in the Middle East.

Since the mid-1960s, however, when the Chinese believed they
were facing the combined hostility of the United States and the Soviet
Union, and with the emergence of the Palestine liberation movement,
China's views on the Palestine problem have changed considerably.
The Chinese not only urged the Palestinians to adopt the strategy of
armed struggle and people's war against Israel (and, in fact, against
Western imperialism at large) but also established formal and regu-
lar regulations with the Palestine liberation movement.

Apart from some Asian liberation movements, in which the
Chinese had a special and direct interest due to geographic proximity,
in the last decade, the Palestine liberation movement has received
more consistent Chinese attention, sympathy, and support than any
other liberation organization. Yet China's policy toward and relations with the Palestinians could not be fully explained and understood within the exclusive framework of Peking's revolutionary
strategy. As we have seen, the Palestine liberation movement has
infringed upon most of the requirements of the "Maoist revolutionary
model." Basic Chinese principles, such as Communist leadership,

unity, independence, self-reliance, people's war inside enemy-occupied territory, and so on, were completely forgone by the Palestinians.

On the other hand, China's relations with the Palestinians have never been motivated by pragmatic considerations alone, although in 1964-65 such considerations played a significant role in China's initial association with the PLO. Apart from intending to win the goodwill of the Arab governments, the Chinese supported and encouraged the Palestine liberation movement whenever they felt that the Palestinians maintained or intensified their opposition, not to Israel, but to the superpowers: the United States, the Soviet Union, or both.

This does not mean, however, that China was deeply involved in or unreservedly committed to the Palestine cause. In the first place, the circumstances imposed their own limitations: geographic distance, limited Chinese economic and military capabilities, Soviet predominance in the Middle East, and some Arabs' and even Palestinians' fears of possible Chinese subversion. Second, there was never any indication of a Chinese intention to become more involved in the Palestine liberation struggle. Such involvement is incompatible not only with China's revolutionary doctrines that a people's war must be fought by the peoples concerned but also with China's actual international behavior in the past.

Nevertheless, China has been portrayed for a long time as a disruptive force in the Middle East, stimulating Arab and Palestinian radicalism and militancy, and as responsible for the deterioration of Arab-Israeli relations. This image was created, deliberately or unintentionally, in different quarters, because of various factors. First, Chinese propaganda itself apparently supported the Palestinians fully, continuously reporting Palestinian "victories" and exaggerating the revolutionary potential of the situation in the Middle East. Second, Soviet propaganda stressed the aggressive, subversive, and irresponsible aspects and possible effects of China's behavior in the Middle East. [80] Third, some circles in pro-Western Middle Eastern states (such as Jordan, Lebanon, Saudi-Arabia, and Israel), as have particularly those of Taiwan, have repeatedly warned against the expansion of Chinese communism and its disruptive consequences. Finally, the radical Arab states, particularly Syria, as well as the Palestinians themselves, have contributed to the image of China's inflated influence in the Middle East by paying frequent tribute to Mao's works and principles and by "disclosing" and proclaiming China's "unconditional" readiness to supply the Palestinians with arms and training.

However, there is no evidence of a Chinese attempt to control the Palestine liberation movement through those Palestinians who

underwent military and ideological training in China or of a prefer-
ential treatment accorded to Chinese-trained Palestinians after their
return. Judging from their military operations, it seems that China's
revolutionary doctrines had a very limited effect on the Palestinians
compared with the practical skills they acquired. There is also no
indication that, apart from their overt relationship with the PLO
and Fatah, the Chinese covertly supported the more radical Palestinian groups or regarded them as the real core of the Palestine
liberation movement in the long-term perspective.

Improved Sino-American relations since 1971, as well as
China's conviction of the crucial importance of Second and Third
World countries in resisting superpower hegemony, brought about a
decisive change in China's position in the world. The Middle East,
which had played a marginal role in China's world outlook after the
Cultural Revolution, became extremely important in the early 1970s.
China's renewed interest in the Middle East was based on two major
observations: First, the Middle East has become a primary target
of Soviet expansion and thus a crucial battlefield and focal point in
the struggle between the superpowers for the control of Europe,
Asia, and Africa. Second, some Middle East governments, notably
Egypt and Iran, revealed obvious signs of disillusionment by the
Soviets, and indeed by Soviet-American collaboration, and took
measures to increase their own independence, unity, and influence.

China's perception of the central role played by the Middle
East governments in the resistance to superpower hegemony, and
particularly to Soviet intervention, led to a significant change in its
attitude toward national liberation movements in the Middle East.
The Chinese had come to realize that some governments that were
threatened by national liberation movements provided a more reliable and effective barrier against American and particularly Soviet
expansion than the revolutionaries who fought them; in fact, those
governments even made some valuable contribution to uniting the
Second and Third World countries against the superpowers. Accordingly, the Chinese adopted a more flexible stand on armed struggle.
Implicitly, they began to advise the liberation movements in the
Middle East to hold negotiations along with launching armed struggle.
This approach conformed to China's revolutionary doctrine based on
the Chinese Communist revolutionary experience that political bargaining is an intrinsic part of the military and political struggle.

Thus, China's relations with the Palestinians had their ups
and downs in the last decade, having been conditioned by many factors, including, primarily, the world situation, but also the Middle
East situation and the situation in China itself. But China's analysis
of the origins, nature, and possible settlement of the Palestine problem remained highly consistent to this very day. China's Palestine

policy should, therefore, be understood fundamentally in terms of this consistent strategic analysis rather than in terms of unstable tactical relations.

NOTES

1. For example, see R. Medzini, "China and the Palestinians --A Developing Relationship?" New Middle East, no. 32 (May 1971): 37.

2. For more details, see Michael Brecher, Israel, the Korean War and China: Images, Decisions and Consequences (Jerusalem: Jerusalem Academic Press, 1974).

3. Shih-chieh chih-shih shou-ts'e 1955 [World Knowledge Handbook] (Peking: Shih-chieh chih-shih she, 1955), p. 448.

4. Yang Hsueh-ch'un, "Hsia-ai min-tsu-chu-i t'ung-chih hsia ti I-ssu-lieh" [Israel Under the Rule of Narrow-Minded Nationalism] Shih-chieh chih-shih [World Knowledge], no. 9 (February 25, 1953): 20 (hereafter cited as SCCS).

5. Shih-chieh chih-shih shou-ts'e 1955, pp. 451, 860; Chung Lin, "Chung-chin-tung kuo-chia ti min-tsu chieh-fang yun-tung" [The National Liberation Movement of Middle and Near Eastern Countries], SCCS, no. 3 (February 5, 1955): 14.

6. "Wei-le Chin-tung ti ho-p'ing ho an-ch'uan" [For Peace and Security in the Near East], Kuang-ming jih-pao, April 21, 1956, p. 4. See also "Mei-kuo pu-ying kan-she Pa-le-ssu-tan chu-shih" [The US Should Not Interfere in the Situation in Palestine], Jen-min jih-pao [People's Daily], October 1, 1955 (hereafter cited as JMJP); Kung-jen jih-pao, November 13, 1955, in BBC, Summary of World Broadcasts, Far East, no. 510, p. 6 (hereafter cited as SWB/FE); Ta-kung pao, November 15, 1955, SWB/FE, no. 511, p. 6; "Observer," JMJP, April 20, 1956, SWB/FE, no. 555, p. 3.

7. Shih-chieh chih-shih shou-ts'e 1955, p. 448.

8. "'Chung-tung' ho 'Chin-tung'" [Middle East and Near East], SCCS, no. 23 (December 1951): 9.

9. For example, Li Ping, Jen-shih wo-men ti shih-chieh [Recognize Our World] (Peking: Kung-jen ch'u-pan she, 1952), p. 34.

10. Shih-chieh chih-shih shou-ts'e 1955, p. 451. See also P'ei Min, "Pa-le-ssu-tan wen-t'i" [The Palestine Problem], SCCS, no. 10 (May 20, 1955): 32-33.

11. Mohamed Abdel Khalek Hassouna, The First Asian-African Conference Held at Bandung, Indonesia (April 18-24, 1955), report submitted to the League of the Arab States' Council (Cairo: Imprimerie Misr, 1955), p. 22.

12. David Kimche, The Afro-Asian Movement, Ideology and Foreign Policy of the Third World (Jerusalem: Israel Universities Press, 1973), p. 52.

13. JMJP, January 5, 1955, SWB/FE, no. 421 (January 11, 1955): 7.

14. New China News Agency, April 10, 1955, SWB/FE, no. 448 (April 14, 1955): 21 (hereafter cited as NCNA).

15. NCNA, April 8, 1955, SWB/FE, no. 448 (April 14, 1955): 10.

16. Ahmad al-Shuqayri, Min al-Qimma 'ila 'l'Hazima [From Zenith to Defeat] (Beirut: Dar al-'Awda, 1971), p. 218; and Munazzamat al-Tahrir al-Filastiniyya, Munazzamat al-Tahrir al-Filastiniyya wa-Jumhuriyyat al-Sin al-Sha'abiyya [The Palestine Liberation Organization and the People's Republic of China] (n.p., n.d.), pp. 23-24. See also New York Times, April 21, 1955.

17. NCNA, April 19, 1955, SWB/FE, no. 451 (April 26, 1955): 13.

18. Indian Information Service, April 21, 1955, ibid., p. 18; Hassouna, First Asian-African Conference, op. cit., p. 94.

19. "Chou Backs Arabs on Israel Dispute," New York Times, April 21, 1955.

20. Hassouna, op. cit., p. 119; George McTurnan Kahin, The Asian-African Conference, Bandung, Indonesia, April 1955 (Ithaca, N.Y.: Cornell University Press, 1956), p. 16; G. H. Jansen, Zionism, Israel and Asian Nationalism (Beirut: Institute for Palestine Studies, 1971), p. 258.

21. For example, Kimche, op. cit., p. 67, based on conference documents AAC/SR/2 and AAC/C.R./3.

22. Kahin, op. cit., p. 16.

23. Compare, for example, the Indian Information Service report of the speech of Lebanon's premier, April 20, 1955, with that of NCNA, SWB/FE, no. 451 (April 26, 1955): 10.

24. JMJP, April 25, 1955, SWB/FE, no. 453 (May 3, 1955): 19.

25. P'ei Min, op. cit., pp. 32-33.

26. David Hacohen, Yoman Burma [Burmese Diary] (Tel Aviv: Am Oved, 1963), pp. 479-80 (in Hebrew).

27. "Premier Chou En-lai's Report on the Asian-African Conference" (delivered at the meeting of the Standing Committee of the National People's Congress on May 13, 1955), NCNA, Daily Bulletin, supplement no. 226 (May 19, 1955): 4.

28. See, for example, Chou En-lai, "The Present International Situation, China's Foreign Policy and the Question of the Liberation of Taiwan" (Speech delivered at the National People's Congress, June 28, 1956), NCNA, Daily Bulletin, supplement no. 245 (June 29, 1956): 6, 8; Liu Shao-ch'i, "The Political Report of

the Central Committee of the Communist Party of China to the 8th
National Congress of the Party, September 15, 1956," in Eighth
National Congress of the Communist Party of China (Peking: Foreign
Languages press, 1956), vol. 1, Documents, p. 93; Ch'en Yi, "The
Present International Situation and Our Foreign Policy, September 25,
1956," speech, ibid., vol. 2, p. 345. See also "What Kind of a
Country Is Israel?" Ta-kung pao, December 7, 1955, as summarized
in China News Analysis (Hong Kong), no. 116 (January 20, 1956): 6.

29. P'ei Min, "I-ssu-lieh" [Israel], in Chung-chin-tung lieh-
kuo chih [Records of the Various Countries of the Middle and Near
East] (Peking: Shih-chieh chih-shih she, 1956), pp. 175-77.

30. See "Pa-le-ssu-tan wen-t'i" [The Palestine Problem],
Shih-chieh chih-shih shou-ts'e 1957, pp. 910-11.

31. In Chou En-lai's message to Nasser, dated November 10,
1956. Chinese text in Jen-min shou-ts'e 1957 [People's Handbook]
(Peking: Ta-kung pao she, 1957), p. 406. English text in SWB/FE,
no. 613 (November 15, 1956): 2.

32. See Ta-kung pao, February 17, 1957, SWB/FE, no. 640
(February 21, 1957): 4; Peking home service, April 3, 1957,
SWB/FE, no. 653 (April 9, 1957): 4.

33. NCNA (Cairo), April 16, 1957, in U.S. Consulate General,
Hong Kong, Survey of China Mainland Press, no. 1515 (April 24,
1957): 35 (hereafter cited as SCMP); NCNA (Cairo), April 18, 1957,
SCMP, No. 1516 (April 25, 1957): 54. See also JMJP, November 14,
1957, SWB/FE, 717 (November 19, 1957): 5.

34. NCNA, June 16, 1957, SWB/FE, no. 674 (June 20, 1957):
2. On Burhan Shahidi (Pao Erh-han), see Donald W. Klein and
Anne B. Clark, Biographic Dictionary of Chinese Communism,
1921-1965 (Cambridge, Mass.: Harvard University Press, 1971),
pp. 5-9. See also Francois Joyaux, "Les Musulmans de Chine et
la Diplomatie de Peking," L'Afrique et l'Asie, no. 77 (ler. trimestre,
1967): 17-24.

35. NCNA, May 4, 1966, SWB/FE/2155/A4/1.

36. "Sino-U.A.R. Joint Communique," NCNA, April 25,
1963, SCMP, no. 2969, pp. 37-38.

37. "Premier Chou En-lai's Press Conference," Peking
Review, no. 52 (December 27, 1963): 12.

38. Ibid., p. 11.

39. Editorial, JMJP, March 17, 1964; SWB/FE/1509/A4/1.

40. Al-Anwar (Beirut), April 6, 1965 (from NCNA), quoted
by John K. Cooley, Green March, Black September, The Story of
the Palestinian Arabs (London: Frank Cass, 1973), p. 176. See
also Al-Hawadith (Beirut), April 30, 1965.

41. For example, Peking Review, no. 19 (May 7, 1965): 4,
condemning Bourguiba's proposal for Arab-Israeli peaceful coexis-

tence; and NCNA, May 4, 1966, SWB/FE/2155/A4/1, denouncing
Soviet proposals for peaceful settlement of the conflict.

42. "Premier Chou En-Lai Reports on the Results of His Visit
to 14 Countries," Peking Review, no. 18 (May 1, 1964): 12.

43. This view was reinforced by Indonesia's withdrawal from
the UN early in 1965. See, for example, "The United Nations--Tool
of U.S. Imperialist Aggression," Peking Review, no. 3 (January 15,
1965): 14; "Justice Cannot Be Upheld in U.N.," Peking Review, no.
4 (January 22, 1965): 13; "U.N. Must Be Thoroughly Reorganised,"
Peking Review, no. 5 (January 29, 1965): 6.

44. Editorial, JMJP, May 15, 1966, SWB/FE/2164/A4/3.

45. For example, Commentator, "Break This Aggressor
Dagger Israel Into Pieces," JMJP, November 16, 1966, SWB/FE/
2319/A4/1.

46. Statement from the Peking office of the PLO, NCNA,
November 10, 1966, SWB/FE/2316/A4/2.

47. Press Conference in Mogadishu (Somalia), NCNA, February 3, 1964, SCMP, no. 3157, p. 33.

48. NCNA, February 5, 1964, SWB/FE/1486/A4/1.

49. See Ehud Ya'ari, Fatah (Tel Aviv, 1970), pp. 27-28, 227;
Cooley, Green March, Black September, op. cit., p. 91. On January 16, 1973, the Egyptian daily al-Jumhuriyya said that both Abu-
'Amar and Abu-Jihad had visited China in 1964. These have been the
pseudonyms of Yasser Arafat and Khalil al-Wazir.

50. "Joint Statement of the Chinese People's Institute of
Foreign Affairs and the PLO," JMJP, March 23, 1965, SCMP,
no. 3425, p. 36.

51. Shuqayri, Min al-Qimma ila 'l-Hazima, op. cit., pp. 219,
229.

52. Peter Van Ness, Revolution and Chinese Foreign Policy
(Berkeley: University of California Press, 1971), Chap. 4, especially pp. 85-86 and 92-93.

53. "You Fight Your Way, We Fight Ours," a Talk with the
Palestine Liberation Organisation Delegation (March 1965), in
Mao Tse-tung ssu-hsiang wan-sui [Long Live Mao Tse-tung's
Thought] (n.p., August 1969), pp. 614-15. English translation in
Miscellany of Mao Tse-tung Thought, Joint Publication Research
Service, no. 61269-2 (February 20, 1974): 447-48 (hereafter cited
as JPRS). Part of the talk is also in Mao Tse-tung wen-hsuan
[Selected Writings of Mao Tse-tung] (n.p., n.d.), translated in
Translations on Communist China, no. 90, JPRS, no. 49826
(February 12, 1970): 23.

54. Quoted in Cooley, Green March, Black September, op.
cit., p. 176. Cf. Shuqayri, Min al-Qimma ila 'l-Hazima, op. cit.,
p. 260.

55. Shuqayri, ibid., pp. 269-71. Shuqayri and other Palestinian leaders were very careful not to alienate the Soviets. They paid frequent tribute to the positive contribution of the USSR toward the Palestinians, especially in the United Nations and the Security Council (where China, of course, had no say before 1971). See, for example, Markaz al-Abhath, Munazzamat al-Tahrir al-Filastiniyya [PLO Research Center], Yawmiyat Filastiniyya [Palestine Diary] (1965): 204, 252.

56. Shuqayri, Min al-Qimma ila 'l-Hazima, op. cit., pp. 233, 269-70.

57. Chou T'ien-chi'ih, "Lessons of the Arab War Against Aggression," Hung Ch'i [Red Flag], no. 13 (August 17, 1967): 51-57, translated in Peking Review, no. 37 (September 8, 1967): 22-26.

58. See Shuqayri, Min al-Qimma ila 'l-Hazima, op. cit., pp. 237-38.

59. See al-Ahram, September 15, 1967, January 18 and 26, August 15, and September 19, 1968.

60. Al-Sayyad (Lebanon), January 30, 1969.

61. Al-Hawadith (Lebanon), February 3, 1967; and other Arab newspapers of that date. See also Yawmiyat Filastiniyya, February 15, 1967.

62. Y. Harkabi, "Fedayeen Action and Arab Strategy," Adelphi Papers, no. 53 (December 1968).

63. Commentator, "National Rights of Pal estinian People Must Be Fully Restored," JMJP, November 27, 1974, Peking Review, no. 48 (November 29, 1974): 11.

64. Commentary, "The Armed Struggle of the Palestinian People Is Forging Ahead in Victory," JMJP, January 7, 1970, SWB/FE/3274/A4/1. See also Huang Hua's speech on the Palestine question in the United Nations, November 18, 1974, Peking Review, no. 48 (November 29, 1974): 13.

65. "U.N. Security Council Debate of Middle East Situation," Peking Review, no. 25 (June 22, 1973): 11.

66. Interview on October 28, 1971, Asahi Shimbun, November 6, 1971.

67. For example, "Chiao Kuan-hua's Speech on Middle East Question," Peking Review, no. 51 (December 17, 1971): 9; "Huang Hua's Speech on Palestine Question," Peking Review, no. 48 (November 29, 1974): 13.

68. Pierre Mendes-France, Dialogues avec l'Asie d'Aujourd'hui (Paris: Editions Gallimard, 1972), pp. 147, 150-51. See also Francesco Gozzano (who accompanied Pietro Nenni on his tour to China and participated in Nenni's talks with Chou En-lai and other Chinese leaders), "China's Stand on the Middle East," New Outlook (Tel Aviv) 15, no. 1 (1972): 41.

69. NCNA, June 5, 1969, SWB/FE/3093/A4/2.

70. "Huang Hua's Speech," Peking Review, no. 48 (November 29, 1974): 13.

71. Abdullah Schleifer, "La Percee Chinoise au Proche-Orient," Jeune Afrique, no. 537 (April 20, 1971): 41.

72. Washington Post, February 6, 1971.

73. Chinese Deputy Chief of Staff, in Peking Banquet for Fatah Delegation, NCNA, September 21, 1971, SWB/FE/3676/A4/2.

74. Al-kifah (Lebanon), quoted by the Middle East News Agency, May 10, 1971.

75. Muhammad Hasanyn Haykal, "A Long Debate with Chou En-lai," al-Anwar (Lebanon), February 23, 1973.

76. "Arab Guerrillas Look to China," Times (London), August 19, 1970.

77. New York Times, February 10, 1971.

78. For example, Christian Science Monitor, November 5, 1970.

79. New York Times, October 4, November 22, 1972.

80. For example, "The Middle East: Soviet Anxieties," Mizan 9, no. 4 (July-August 1967): 146-52; D. Volsky, "Middle East Schemes of Peking," New Times (Moscow), January 22, 1969; "Moscow Comments on Maoist Foreign Policy," Chinese Communist Affairs: Facts and Features (Taipei) 2, no. 2 (April 2, 1969): 2; "The Kremlin Arabian Nightmare," New York Times, January 18, 1971.

CHINA'S FOREIGN RELATIONS
WITH LATIN AMERICA
Robert L. Worden

CHINESE PERSPECTIVES OF LATIN AMERICA

The Latin America policy of the People's Republic of China (PRC)* can be divided chronologically into two definitive periods closely related to PRC policy toward the United States: the 1949-71 anti-United States united front period and the post-1971 period of emerging rapprochement with the United States. The former period was the period of a concerted anti-United States policy. Mao Tse-tung, on the eve of his birthday in 1947, set the tone for China's long-range Latin America perspective that was to remain substantially unchanged until the 1970s. He said, "The people of Latin America are not slaves obedient to U.S. imperialism."[1] During this period of enmity between the PRC and the United States, and most specifically since the late 1950s, Chinese advocacy of wars of national liberation in Latin America was the main policy theme.

Within this theme there were two major currents: the championing of the theme of "people's war" for use in Latin America and consolidation of a united front against the United States and its imperialist lackeys." In the Chinese perspective, these lackeys were the prevalently right-wing governments of the Latin American

---

*It should be noted that PRC Latin America affairs are dealt with through the American and Oceanic Affairs Department of the Ministry of Foreign Affairs, and that, in the Chinese perspective, Latin America consists of all countries and territories in Central, South, and Caribbean America, including present and former colonies of Spain, Portugal, Britain, France, and Holland, as well as Puerto Rico and other U.S. possessions.

republics that depended, usually out of necessity, on U.S. military and economic aid.

Chinese policy in this period put Latin America in the context of the hou-yuan--the backyard--of the United States, an area downtrodden and exploited by "Yankee imperialism" because of its geographic proximity to the leading imperialist power. Chinese foreign policy makers perceived that U.S.-Latin American interests were closely intertwined, whether by choice or necessity, and that charges of "imperialist aggression" in Latin America could be used as a valuable and credible propaganda weapon in the worldwide anti-U.S. campaign.

The Latin American peoples were in need of "liberation" from both the U.S. imperialists and local reactionary rule, and the Chinese willingly provided their own revolutionary experience as a model, co-equally for a time with the Cuban model, as the most effective means of bringing about this liberation.

One of the basic factors that the PRC chose to consider in formulating a foreign policy toward Latin America was a sense of commonality in the pre-1949 situation in China and the then-current situation in Latin America. They viewed the Latin American countries as being ruled by essentially feudal and reactionary governments which were ultimately controlled and supported by the neocolonialist United States. They also gave consideration to the socioeconomic system in most Latin American countries: the blocs of poor peasants, Indians, and blacks; the concentration of wealth and power among a small number of politically conservative leaders; and the dependence on trade with, and economic development by, American-owned companies and U.S. government aid programs. Additionally, a factor the Chinese could not fail to notice was the tradition in Latin America of revolutionary violence as a means of obtaining political power--a perfect example of Mao's adage that political power grows out of the barrel of a gun.

Latin America, in the Chinese view, suffered from many of the same types of neocolonial, feudal, and reactionary ills that China had endured before 1949. Thus, the PRC had a dual goal in its Latin America policy: to provide the Chinese model to the Latin American left to "liberate" their countries and, at the same time, to create discord in the backyard of the United States.[2] There were, of course, many legitimate or formal contacts between Latin America and China during this time, resulting in trade and cultural exchange. The overwhelming thrust of the pre-1971 period was, however, based more on militant political policies than on economics or culture.

PRC foreign relations in the early years were concerned first with the "fraternal" Communist countries of Eastern Europe and Asia and later with the emerging nations of Asia and Africa. It was not until the mid- and late 1950s that a gradual awakening of Chinese interest in Latin America was brought about by such events as the anti-Communist coup d'etat in Guatemala in 1954 and the seizure of power by Fidel Castro in Cuba in 1959. It was just several years prior to Castro's success that Latin America had been elevated to a place in China's Third World aphorism "Asia, Africa, and Latin America." Over the years, Latin America has figuratively and literally maintained a quantitative third place in China's Third World relations. In news reportage in the Chinese press, trade, exchanges of all types, involvement in political, economic, and cultural affairs, Latin America has consistently ranked behind Asia and Africa.[3]

In the second period, generally 1971 and thereafter, China's Latin American policy experienced a marked shift away from advocacy of violent upheaval and, in turn, stressed that government-to-government contacts were more fruitful. This exchange coincided with the general easing of tensions between the PRC and the United States.

After 1971, the PRC addressed itself to support of various issues of regional political and economic interest to the actual leadership elements in Latin America--a contrast with the past when Peking gave most of its support to the potential and generally radical leftist leaders on a national level. Among issues supported by the PRC were the 200-nautical-mile territorial sea limit or exclusive economic zone, economic independence, the Latin American nuclear-weapon-free zone, and Third World economic and political rights in general.

In the 1970s, the PRC departed from ideological demands and open support of the left in exchange for formal diplomatic relations and support of many of the same governments that the Latin American left opposed. By the end of 1974, the PRC had full diplomatic relations with ten Latin American nations.*

Most Latin American nations had satisfactory relations with the Republic of China government on Taiwan and generally followed

---

*Cuba (1960), Chile (1970), Peru (1971), Mexico (1972), Argentina (1972), Guyana (1972), Jamaica (1972), Trinidad and Tobago (1974), Venezuela (1974), and Brazil (1974). No new diplomatic recognition occurred in 1975. Taiwan has steadily lost diplomatic ground in Latin America in the 1970s. In 1960, 100 percent, or 21, of the independent republics had diplomatic relations with Taipei. By 1974, the figures had dropped to 50 percent, or 13, of the republics and newly independent states in the region. Three countries--Bahamas, Ecuador, and Grenada--had relations with neither government through mid-1975. The remainder of the decade should show similar decline in favor of Peking in formal government-to-government relations between Taiwan and Latin American countries.

the cold war policies of the United States toward the PRC. Latin American voting patterns on UN questions concerning the PRC between 1950 and 1971 verify this phenomenon. Except for Cuba (since 1960), Latin American governments followed the U.S. line of anti-PRC votes until 1970 when Chile sided with Cuba for the first time. Until that time, the Latin American nations voted in a nearly uniform bloc against resolutions favoring the seating of Peking. Even as the U.S. policy of preventing the PRC from obtaining the seat of China was waning and Third World nations were voting in increasing numbers in favor of Peking, the Latin Americans continued to follow Washington's line. Other than Cuba, and Chile in 1970, the uniformity was broken only by a few abstentions over the 21-year period of attempts to seat the PRC in the UN.

In the final round of voting in October 1971, however, seven Latin American nations voted to oust Taipei and seat Peking. Five other Latin American nations abstained.[4] Of these 12 countries, only two, Cuba and Chile, had diplomatic relations with Peking at the time of the voting and six others, Peru, Mexico, Argentina, Guyana, Jamaica, and Trinidad and Tobago, established relations thereafter. In addition, two staunch opponents of the PRC seating, Brazil and Venezuela, also established relations with the PRC.

The move to establish formal diplomatic relations, accompanied by a growth in bilateral trade and economic cooperation, was an indication of fundamental change in PRC foreign policy not only in Latin America but on a worldwide scale. Empathy for Third World causes gained Peking more friends than did some 20 years of advocacy of violence.

In accord with this policy shift was considerably less anti-U.S. propaganda vis-a-vis Latin America. Critical comments in the post-1971 period tended to dwell more on the evils perpetuated in Latin America by the American capitalist system than on U.S. government policies, per se.

Transcending both periods and with increasing frequency and emphasis since the mid-1960s was a significant rise in anti-Soviet polemics in the context of Latin America. In the pre-1971 era, the Sino-Soviet dispute was primarily manifested in the competition for allegiances with the Latin American Communist parties. After 1971, in an era when both the PRC and the USSR deemphasized their fraternal connections with the generally illegal Latin American left, the PRC launched an anti-Soviet campaign which rivaled the anti-U.S. movements of the 1950s and 1970s. The USSR was presented as the primary threat to Latin American security in the 1970s and beyond and virtually replaced the United States in China's campaign to identify the "enemies" of Latin America.[5]

A parallel dispute between the PRC and Cuba affected Chinese Latin America policy after the mid-1960s. It lacked the bitterness and extent of the dispute between Peking and Moscow and centered around the mentorship of the wars of national liberation.

MAJOR FOREIGN POLICY ISSUES: WARS OF NATIONAL LIBERATION

In the 1960s, the most frequently addressed issue in the Latin America policy of the PRC was the "wars of national liberation." In the post-"Bandung Spirit" phase of policy, the Chinese turned more and more toward advocating and supporting armed violence--the "people's wars"--and Latin America seemed a natural breeding ground for Mao Tse-tung's guerrilla and political strategies. Many similarities can be drawn between preliberation China and Latin America: guerrilla forces holding forth in mountain retreats, large pockets of poor peasants, primarily agrarian and foreign-controlled protoindustrial economies, U.S.-backed right-wing governments, and a current of discontent, if not periodic open warfare, among the real or imagined representatives of the masses. Latin America has a well-known revolutionary tradition of its own, and it was, indeed, a violent upheaval in Cuba that initially sharpened China's focus on prospects in Latin America. Following the Cuban revolution there were a number of other armed conflicts in Latin America that the Chinese propagandists perceived as a regionwide war of national liberation and a united-front struggle against "U.S. imperialism and its lackeys." A 1963 Chinese survey of the "national-democratic" movements in Latin America clearly stated that "people from all walks of life in many Latin American countries have formed united fronts and are increasingly organizing joint action."[6]

After Castro's triumphant entry into Havana in January 1959, the PRC announced "the heartfelt solidarity of China's population with the heroic struggle of the Cuban people," and pledged its "firm support" to the revolutionary movement.[7] In April of the same year, Premier Chou En-lai told the Second National People's Congress that as a matter of foreign policy China was "ready to give support and assistance to the fullest extent of [its] capabilities to all national independence movements in Asia, Africa and Latin America."[8] In the same context, Lin Piao, then minister of national defense, was to write six years later that it was the "internationalist duty" of socialist countries to support the "people's revolutionary struggles" in Third World areas like Latin America.[9]

Although most of the Latin American countries had been independent of Spain since the 1820s, the Chinese perceived that "national independence" was still wanting in the region. The "people" needed to be freed from the joint bonds of U.S. imperialism and domestic reactionary rule of both economic and political servitude. The Cuban revolution was seen as the model for the hoped-for united struggle against the United States and the local reactionary regime. When Castro made his Second Havana Declaration in February 1962, a call for a continental fight against the common U.S. enemy, the Chinese announced that there were "two roads" for the Latin American peoples to follow: "One is the road taken by Cuba . . . the other is to bow to U.S. rule and remain forever its vassals."[10] It was the first road that the Chinese were seeking to support as a means for liberation in Latin America. Although Chinese policy toward Cuba was to change by the mid-1960s, that of the early 1960s was intimately bound up with Castro's revolution.

During the 1960s, there was not an armed movement of any consequence in Latin America that did not receive at least implicit support from Peking.[11] Until the Sino-Cuban rift opened in 1966, the Chinese held up Castro's revolution as a model to Latin American revolutionaries and were in turn gratified by the assurances of men like Ernesto "Che" Guevara who said that, during the guerrilla warfare days in the Sierra Maestra, Mao's works were "spread widely among commanders on the front and were called 'food from China'. . . ."[12]

Except for Chinese-run guerrilla training schools, at least one allegedly in Cuba, and the rest in China, and whatever secret military agreements that may have been made, most of China's support of wars of national liberation was of a moral and propagandistic nature.[13] All elements of the Chinese media were used to champion the Cuban revolution as an example for other Latin Americans. Articles and books written by Castro and Guevara were translated and published in China for both domestic and foreign consumption.[14] Both Guevara and Cuban President Osvaldo Dorticos visited the PRC amid great fanfare in November 1960 and September-October 1961, respectively.

The Chinese had high hopes for the example provided by the Cuban revolution. Speaking at a press conference in Algiers during his 1963 African tour, Premier Chou En-lai emphatically stated: "the Cuban people . . . have pointed out for the peoples of other Latin American countries the path for armed struggle to break away from imperialist control and attain national liberation. With the emergence of revolutionary Cuba, there will appear in Latin America a second and third Cuba."[15] But Peking eventually grew tired of giving Castro and his followers such broad support, especially as ideological differences became apparent.[16]

During and after the period of Sino-Cuban cordiality (ending in 1965-66), the Chinese gave verbal and written support to rebel movements in Argentina, Bolivia, Brazil, Colombia, the Dominican Republic, Ecuador, Guatemala, Peru, Uruguay, and Venezuela on a relatively wide basis. Central American and other Latin American countries and colonies did not escape Peking's notice, and unrest in those areas was given periodic publicity. Chile and Mexico, the PRC's main Latin American friends in terms of potential trade and cordial relations, were generally spared from the national liberation support policy.

Various pro-PRC Communist Party organizations in Latin America advocated revolution but few became involved in actual fighting as called for in the Chinese theory of people's war. The only case of a Chinese-inspired people's war led by an established Communist Party was the one inconclusively conducted (circa 1968-70) by the Ejercito Popular de Liberacion (People's Liberation Army), the military wing of the pro-Peking Communist Party of Colombia (Marxist-Leninist).[17] Earlier, the Chinese had put great store in the guerrillas of the Fuerzas Armadas de Liberacion Nacional (Armed Forces of National Liberation, or FALN) of Venezuela, which had a flurry of revolutionary activity in 1963. The FALN movement had direct ties to Castro's government, and in light of a number of successful forays, the Chinese saw "a new situation . . . arising in the surging national and democratic movements in Latin America."[18] In the case of Bolivia, the pro-Peking Communist Party of Bolivia (Marxist-Leninist) called for "armed struggle" and "people's liberation" but failed to collaborate with the faltering forces of a transplanted Che Guevara in southeastern Bolivia.[19] Peking's support became moot as the armed movements throughout the region were crushed or forced underground by civilian governments and military dictatorships alike.

The PRC had been heartened by the Cuban success and looked forward to other wars of national liberation in Latin America. Its foreign policy for the region, or at least selected parts of the region, was formed around support of the insurgents who, when they came to power, could be expected to align themselves with Peking. The general failure of the Latin American movements in the 1960s obviated the Peking strategy.

In the post-1971 period, the policy became passe. Peking turned to more open and formal methods of international contact, and refrained from overt support to insurgents in the Latin American countries with which it had diplomatic or at least friendly relations and even in those countries not receptive to PRC overtures. The main evidence in support of this belief was the absence of publicity of armed movements in the countries in the aforementioned categories, with the notable exception of Brazil in February 1974.[20]

200-Nautical-Mile Maritime Zone

As a major foreign policy theme, support of the Latin American claims to territorial sea rights came only after the Cultural Revolution and at a time of growing publicity and acceptance of the issue in the Third World. One of the earliest mentions of China's stand on the issue, and which can be accepted as an indication of the emergence of a new policy line, appeared in a <u>Jen-min jih-pao</u> <u>(People's Daily)</u> editorial in November 1970. The editorial attacked the United States for its years of "wanton plundering" of the maritime resources of the Latin American nations and for "behaving just like pirates on the high sea," and stated Peking's support of the 200-nautical-mile limit. [21]

The Latin American stand on the 200-nautical-mile limit had been initiated by Chile and Peru in 1947 in a quest to protect their fishing rights. By August 1967, 14 Latin American nations had signed a joint declaration reaffirming the right to fix the limits of their own territorial waters. China's support of this issue was not only a measure that encouraged good relations with Latin America but was a convenient mode of criticism of the two superpowers--the United States and the USSR--which had carried out "frenzied plundering" of the territorial waters of the countries in the region. [22]

The joint communique establishing diplomatic relations between the PRC and Peru in November 1971 was the first bilateral agreement signed by China that formally recognized the 200-mile limit. [23] Subsequent communiques with Argentina and Mexico also stated China's recognition of the 200-mile limit, as have numerous speeches made by Chinese representatives at the UN and especially at the 1974 Third United Nations Law of the Sea Conference held in Caracas, Venezuela. [24]

The Soviet Union challenged the Chinese position on the 200-mile limit at the Caracas conference by saying that Peking had attempted "to sidetrack the conference not only to prevent a successful solution to [maritime] problems but [also to] produce chaos on the seas. . . ." [25] The Soviet stand on the 200-nautical-mile limit was that it should be resolved only in conjunction with the "established principles" of freedom of navigation and the free passage of all ships through international straits. The Chinese saw this as Moscow's means of clouding the real issue, which was the territorial integrity of Third World maritime zones.

The motives for Chinese support of the sea limit policy considered not only goodwill but economic and defensive contingencies as well. The economic importance of the policy was reflected in the move by the PRC to conclude favorable maritime trade and transport agreements with Chile and Peru, the major maritime nations of

South America. Trade with these nations, developed mostly after
PRC recognition of the 200-mile limit, could eventually lead to subsequent agreements calling on Chinese technology and aid for additional exploitation of maritime and subsea mineral resources in the
territorial waters and maritime economic zones of the Latin America
and Third World nations.

PRC foreign policy makers also recognized the defensive advantages of a 200-mile limit. Such a limit, pending universal recognition, could legally keep alien war vessels at a much greater distance than the currently recognized 3- or 12-mile limit. In this regard, the 200-mile-limit policy was coordinated with another policy
issue--nuclear-weapon-free zones.

The PRC has had territorial sea problems of its own and will
have more in the future. Insular territories beyond the Asian continental shelf and in surrounding seas are an integral part of Chinese
defensive and economic needs. An ulterior motivation for support
of the Latin American sea limit certainly was the Chinese hope for
reciprocal support in times of need. The establishment of the precedent of 200-nautical-mile sea limits would be of great benefit to China
when the time came for it to press for such a limit in its own behalf.

                        Economic Independence

The 200-nautical-mile limit was actually part of and coordinated
with a more general policy, that of economic independence for Latin
American and other Third World countries. The PRC axiom that the
political independence of a country is imperative on economic independence was used to explain the need for the economic struggle Peking
supported in the underdeveloped countries of the world. The quest
for economic independence was also viewed as a "component part of
the national-liberation movement in Latin America."[26] In the period
when Chinese support for military struggles against established governments shifted to support of those governments that stood against
the developed nations, Peking gave added attention to an analysis of
Latin America's economy.

That analysis had deep roots in the PRC view of international
economic cooperation, which it stipulated should be based on principles of "equality and mutual benefit" and "independence in foreign
trade."[27] These principles conformed to the "Bandung Spirit,"
which called for "mutual benefit and mutual respect" in economic
matters and for attaching no conditions detrimental to the trading
partner and demanding no privileges of that partner. Soon after the
Bandung conference, China announced its desire to help other underdeveloped countries achieve economic independence in compliance

with these principles. Its support of the principle of economic independence has been widely circulated and increasingly focused in its analysis over the years.[28]

As in other foreign policy areas, the PRC took note of only the Asian and African countries in economic matters until the mid-1950s. The year 1956 was noted by Peking for its "marked development" in economic relations with Latin America even though these countries were still viewed as having capitalist economic systems rather than the developing economies of what was later to be called the Third World.[29]

By the late 1950s, the PRC analysis of the Latin American economy was based on its close ties with the economy of the United States. The United States was charged with trying to offset its own recession by shifting its problems onto Latin America (a charge renewed in the 1970s vis-a-vis both the United States and the USSR). This was accomplished by cutting prices on imports, stiffening import quotas, raising tariff duties, and dumping surplus products at high prices on Latin American markets, according to the PRC analysis. These actions, in turn, only served to aggravate "popular bitterness and resentment" in Latin America against the United States and contributed to the movement to oppose the "U.S.-Wall Street" exploitation of the region's economic resources.[30]

The Cuban revolution was cited as an "example for other Latin American peoples to follow in their fight to free themselves from U.S. economic exploitation and win themselves independence in economic development."[31] Primary in the Cuban economic model was the eradication of semifeudal land relations through land reform and nationalization of all U.S. enterprises. The least developed Latin American countries fit well into this model, as they, as Cuba had been, were viewed as the victims of American monopolist and imperialist exploitation: forced to grow monocrops (sugar, bananas, coffee, and so on), with feudal modes of production, national industrial development held in check, and basically economically backward.

By the mid-1960s, when Peking's use of the Cuban example had been severely moderated, the Vietnam War was said to have been a major cause of continued U.S. economic penetration of the region. American investments increased as war needs necessitated "plunder" of petroleum, copper, bauxite, and other strategic materials from Latin America. The United States called for "economic integration" and development of "joint enterprises," terms abhorrent in the Chinese perspective. The United States used the Alliance for Progress, labeled by Peking as a "plan of aggression" and a "scheme of economic plunder" by Washington, but, in the last analysis, a failure.[32] As the Indochina War and the domestic situation resulting from the Cultural Revolution caused Peking to focus on problems closer to

home, little was said in regard to the economic independence of
Latin America in the late 1960s. What scant attention was paid to
the region was devoted to the wars of national liberation and the destruction of existing socioeconomic-political systems. If anything,
the economies of Latin America were seen as having "gone from bad
to worse" due to U.S. problems at home and abroad and its continued
support for the rightist governments that followed Washington's example in fiscal and political affairs.[33]

In the 1970s, interest in the Latin American economy reemerged.
Peking's analysis was still based on the principles of mutual benefit
used in its own expanding foreign trade with Latin America, and the
role of the United States in exploiting its backyard had been complicated by its contention with the USSR in the region. A new focus,
however, was put on the means for attaining economic independence.
The emphasis was put on suggesting specific actions to be taken
against the developed countries, particularly the United States and
the Soviet Union, and encouraging unity and cooperation among the
under- and lesser developed nations carrying out economic actions.

The Chinese advised Latin Americans to demand recovery of
their natural resources, develop basic industries, enhance the role
of national capital, change from single-product economies, and
strengthen political and economic cooperation. Leading among the
methods of attaining economic independence was nationalization, or
at least reduction of control of foreign-owned mines, plantations,
and industries. Whether by legislation, negotiation, or outright
seizure, expropriation of resources and modes of production was
considered essential. The examples of Chile, Mexico, Peru, and
Venezuela in this regard were particularly praised. Planned economies, such as those of Guyana, Jamaica, and Trinidad and Tobago,
were also cited. In short, the Latin Americans were being told to
strive for one of the PRC's most hallowed achievements--self-
reliance.[34]

Somewhat apart from the Chinese principle of self-reliance
was Peking's advocacy of regional cooperation among Latin American
countries in economic and trade relations and coordination with the
Afro-Asian countries in areas of strategy. What China referred to
as a united front against the United States in 1971[35] turned into a
proliferation of area organizations aimed at obtaining economic independence for the region. Among the groups given support in the
Chinese media were the Andean Pact Organization, the Caribbean
Free Trade Association (CARIFTRA), the Caribbean Community
(CARIBCOM), the Multinational Caribbean Shipping Company, and
the Latin American and Caribbean Confederation of Small and
Medium-Sized Industry. The Organization of Petroleum Exporting
Countries (OPEC), of which Ecuador and Venezuela are members,

was widely supported by the PRC in its media and at the UN. This regional cooperation, ideally using "natural resources as a weapon," called for a reaffirmation of an inter-American economic system without U.S. participation or Soviet intrusion.*

The PRC motivation in aiding and advising Latin America in its quest for economic independence played on Latin American desires for such status dating from Hispanic and British colonial days. It was an issue in which the Latin Americans had a lengthy and, in the 1970s, relatively successful struggle. In the PRC analysis, it was a struggle very similar to that which the Chinese people had in achieving self-reliance. In the 1970s, the Chinese found their advices closely coinciding with Latin American actions, which, as a result, helped them win friends in some formerly hostile governments, such as Brazil, Peru, and Venezuela. It was an issue in which Peking found itself supporting not only national but regional level organizations and advising them on methods that could lead to the development of economies independent of the superpowers and big-power capitalist countries in general.

Nuclear-Weapon-Free Zone

PRC support of a nuclear-weapon-free zone in Latin America dates from 1963, a year before China detonated its first nuclear device. It was also at a time when China was developing its nuclear capability and beginning openly to oppose the Soviet position on disarmament and nonproliferation. Coincidental with the 1963 signing of the Nuclear Test Ban Treaty between the United States and the USSR, the PRC called for the creation of a nuclear-weapon-free zone that would encompass Asia, Africa, the Pacific area, Central Europe, and Latin America.[37] A multilateral initiative among the Latin American nations, led by Mexico, resulted in a November 1963 resolution submitted to the UN General Assembly by 12 Latin American governments also calling for such a zone.

After the detonation of China's first nuclear device in 1964, Chou En-lai made a policy statement that held through to the 1970s that testing and development of nuclear power by China was entirely for defense against the nuclear threat of the superpowers, that China has consistently stood for the complete prohibition and thorough

---

*The Andean Pact Organization, founded in May 1969, has been frequently cited for making "positive progress" in promoting balanced and coordinated development and economic integration in Latin America.[36]

destruction of nuclear weapons, and that a summit meeting of all countries of the world should be held to discuss the question and, as a first step, to reach an agreement on the nonuse of nuclear weapons.[38] The advocacy of the nuclear-weapon-free zone is the logical evolutionary stage in China's avowed antinuclear warfare policy.

The nuclear-weapon-free zone issue was implicitly renewed as a leading foreign policy line for Latin America in then Vice Minister of Foreign Affairs Ch'iao Kuan-hua's first speech to the UN General Assembly on November 15, 1971. Ch'iao expressed his government's irreversible position on the development of nuclear defenses while standing for "breaking the nuclear monopoly and ultimately eliminating nuclear weapons and nuclear war" and stated the necessity of convening an international conference to "reach an agreement on the nonuse of nuclear weapons."[39]

Chinese support of the issue was an easy and effective means of developing friendships with certain Latin American governments. In keeping with Mexico's leading role in the effort to establish a nuclear-weapon-free zone, the issue was noted when diplomatic relations were established between the PRC and Mexico. The Chinese explicitly supported the "just position of Mexico and the other Latin American states on the establishment of a nuclear-weapon-free zone in Latin America. . . ."[40]

On August 21, 1973, the PRC signed Additional Protocol II of the 1967 Treaty for the Prohibition of Nuclear Weapons in Latin America (also known as the Treaty of Tlatelolco).[41] The treaty prohibits the testing, use, production, and possession of nuclear weapons by Latin American countries as well as the introduction, stockpiling, installation, and deployment of any nuclear weapons on their territories. Additional Protocol II to the treaty requests nuclear powers not to take any action in contravention of the treaty, nor to use or threaten to use nuclear weapons against any of the signatories.

The signing was not without some difficulties on the Chinese side since the Protocol related to the nonproliferation and partial test ban treaties. A visit to China by Mexican President Luis Echeverria in April 1973 softened Chinese resistance to the Protocol, and Chou En-lai promised that the PRC would sign. He said, however, that doing so "would not prejudice China's consistent position against the Treaty on Nonproliferation and the Partial Test Ban Treaty."[42]

China felt, at that time, as it had for the previous decade, that it was compelled to develop its own nuclear weapons for defensive purposes. Although China's mode of signing was seemingly inconsistent with the spirit of the treaty, Latin American response to China's move was positive and drew praise from various government officials and international organizations.[43]

The Chinese stand on the Latin American nuclear-weapon-free zone related to PRC national security interests and its desire for leadership of the Third World. The Chinese, viewing the U.S.-USSR attempts to prevent nuclear proliferation as elements of a scheme to dominate the world, adopted the position that Chinese proliferation was necessary as a means of deterring a superpower attack or threat of attack, thus hastening the day when nuclear weapons could be totally eliminated. [44]

While China's nuclear policy did not condemn nuclear proliferation by other countries, it professed to back firmly those nations that stood against the development of nuclear arms. In its double-edged policy, the Chinese stood opposed to expansion of U.S. and Soviet "nuclear hegemony" (to do so being to the PRC's own defensive advantage), while supporting, and thus gaining the friendship of, countries similarly opposed. The PRC welcomed Latin American efforts to establish the nuclear-free zone in the region through an international agreement that implied the right of Latin American nations to demand the dismantling of foreign military bases in the region and to refrain from consenting to the establishment of new ones. The major reason for PRC resistance to signing Additional Protocol II of the Treaty of Tlatelolco and the insistence on opposing the test ban and nonproliferation treaties was its stand against superpower nuclear superiority.

A September 1973 Jen-min jih-pao editorial perceived that, while locked in a "fierce nuclear arms race," the superpowers were "scrambling for spheres of influence and practicing nuclear blackmail and nuclear threat" against Latin America. [45] What was a threat to Latin America could, of course, be construed as a potential threat to China itself. In seeking nuclear equity, the Chinese felt that by all means they must also seek to limit the scope of superpower nuclear strength.

The Soviet position is that, since the 1950s, it had advanced the idea of setting up nuclear-free zones and favored such a zone in Latin America. In Moscow's view, however, the Treaty of Tlatelolco was ineffective in that it did not forbid the transit of nuclear weapons across the territories of signatory states and the use of those states of nuclear explosions for peaceful purposes. Using this rationale, the Soviets declared it was "impossible" for it to sign the treaty. [46] It is notable that the Soviets sided with Cuba in refusing to participate in the Treaty of Tlatelolco.

Anti-USSR

Whereas the United States was considered in Chinese foreign policy to be the primary target in Latin America in the pre-1971 era, the USSR, either in contention or collusion with the United States, was considered the major threat to Latin American state sovereignty and economic independence in the 1970s. In the earlier period, PRC anti-Soviet attitudes centered more on ideological issues construed as anti-China, such as the policies in dealing with Cuba, support of Latin American revolutions, and contention between pro-CCP and pro-CPSU Latin American Communist and leftist parties. In the post-1971 period, anti-Soviet attitudes are those involving Soviet actions considered to be anti-Latin America. The direction of the earlier period has been changed: contact with and support of Latin American governments are favored and the previous PRC antiestablishment issues have been subdued or modified.

In the 1960s, there were radical differences in Chinese and Soviet Latin America policies, although ultimate ambitions and fundamental ideological assessments had somewhat similar conclusions. Both sides hoped for the eventual socialization of Latin America with political and economic alignments with Communist nations in the meantime. The Soviets, learning from the lessons of Comintern days, took flexible and cautious means in trying to establish a pattern of friendly relations with a hostile and generally anti-Communist Latin America. Direct advocacy of violent revolutionary upheaval was no longer a part of Soviet foreign policy. For most of the 1960s, as pointed out above, it definitely was in China's scheme.

The Cuban revolution provided somewhat of a dilemma for the Soviet Union and a boon for China. The Soviets were gratified by the success of Castro in bringing a socialist and anti-U.S. government to power in the Caribbean and pleased at the opportunity of gaining a foothold on the doorstep of the United States. Large quantities of aid, so badly needed by Cuba, were certain to cause resentment and suspicion in Latin American anti-Communist circles and objections from the United States, and yet that aid was exactly what Cuba, as a potential Communist nation, needed. On ideological and strategic grounds, the Soviet Union saw advantage in giving financial aid and moral support to Castro on a large-scale basis. Heavy grants of military aid resulted in the October 1962 confrontation between the United States and the USSR--the Cuban missile crisis--and a setback for the Soviet Union's foreign policy in Cuba and Latin America in general.

For the Chinese, the Cuban revolution was ideally suited to their policy. Castro was a guerrilla fighter with a Marxist background, a leader of peasants, and an implicit advocate of Mao-like military strategy. While the PRC was unable to give the kind and volume of aid as had the Soviets, it did give small amounts of financial assistance and large amounts of ideological support by equating the Chinese and Cuban revolutions as models applicable to all of

Latin America. This type of support, which was generally wanting
in Soviet policies toward Cuba, was welcomed by a hemispheric-
minded Castro. The Chinese were able to obtain a dual usage--doing
Castro an ideological favor while presenting opposition to the Soviets.

The distinctions between the Chinese-Cuban model and the
Soviet "revisionist" model were publicized, more so toward the mid-
point of the decade, in an effort to disinterest the Latin American
left in the Soviets and to encourage alignment with Peking, at least
indirectly, for a time, through Havana. The latter point, if it existed at all, was wishful thinking on the part of Peking. Cuba was
and continues to be heavily dependent on the USSR in many ways,
and Castro, from the onset, has proven to be a man of independent
action and independent political thinking.

While both the PRC and the USSR became involved in Cuba,
their modes were thus different and incompatible: Soviet economic
and military aid versus revolutionary and anti-Soviet ideological of-
ferings from the Chinese. The former intended to strengthen a fledg-
ling socialist state; the latter attempted to use Cuba to export its
revolutionary ideology throughout the region. Revolution, civil wars,
coups, and armed violence have been a tradition in Latin America,
thus making the Chinese and Cuban revolutions relatively acceptable
modes of obtaining power. The similarity between the economic and
class structures of Latin America and China has also given weight to
the Chinese opinion that their model was more suitable to the region
than that of Moscow. As Edward Taborsky wrote, the Chinese appeal
made "the most credible ring in the ears of the most impatient and
most leftist . . . of Latin American revolutionaries."[47]

The missile crisis "brought sharply into focus the emergence
of Latin America as still another area of serious political conflict
between the PRC and the Soviet Union."[48] Although Peking sided
with Moscow and Havana during the crisis, the Chinese soon thereafter categorized the Soviet backoff during the confrontation with the
United States as a betrayal of Cuba.[49] What followed was a period of
Cuban disenchantment with the USSR and relative harmony with China
until 1965. For Cuba, the time was opportune for at least a slight
shift toward China. The Sino-Soviet dispute was in full force with
the two Communist powers seeking influence against each other.
Castro was able to take advantage of the rift by gaining support from
Peking so as not to continue to be so predominantly reliant on Moscow. At the same time, the Soviet Union, although more critical of
Castro than in the past, yet not wanting to lose its Caribbean foothold, continued to pour military and economic support into Havana.

One of the most obvious manifestations of the Sino-Soviet dispute in the pre-1971 period, and that which has undergone perhaps
the closest empirical scrutiny, is the alignment of the Latin American

left with the CCP, the CPSU, or neither. Latin American political organizations present a diverse study in fragmentation. The diversity vis-a-vis the PRC and the USSR on the Latin American left, and particularly among the Communist Parties, can generally be said to have begun as soon as a point of departure between Peking and Moscow could be discerned by third parties.

In theory and practice, the Latin American Communist Parties had long followed orthodox Marxist-Leninist doctrine that the industrial proletariat was the decisive force in the socialist revolution. Thus, Communist and leftist groups had been almost exclusively urban and mainly interested in trade union activities, and, for the most part, followed the ideological lead of Moscow. These groups traditionally were disunited and weak and frequently illegal.

These Soviet-oriented parties were unsuited to the needs and expectations of China as a would-be world Communist leader. Immediately after the Twentieth Congress of the CPSU in 1956 (at which Khrushchev announced de-Stalinization), the Chinese began an effort to divert loyalties of the Communist Parties throughout the world to Peking. Eleven Latin American Communist Parties responded to invitations to send delegations to the Eighth Congress of the Chinese Communist Party in September 1956, and, in March 1959, 12 Communist Party leaders from Latin America toured China and were received by Chairman Mao at Chengchou.[50] (It should be pointed out that in the 1950s and 1960s, Mao, Liu Shao-ch'i, and Chou En-lai either jointly or individually received almost all such visitors to China to win mass alignment.)[51] As one analyst said, "the Chinese [had] provided an important facade for a Marxist approval to revolution that [was] fresher and less tarnished than [had] been provided by the older party organizations."[52]

As radical factions (usually styled Marxist-Leninist) split away from the orthodox parties, Peking announced its support by explicit recognition of the splinter groups. Such Chinese foreign language journals as Pekin Informa (the Spanish-language edition of Peking Review distributed in Latin America) frequently published news items about and communiques and messages from these Marxist-Leninist parties, thus giving them a sense of legitimacy. The existence of the orthodox, pro-CPSU organizations was totally ignored. Even though complicated by pro-Castro and Trotskyite parties, dual alliances, and total membership rolls in favor of the Soviet groups, there were slightly more Communist and leftist parties with loyalties to Peking than to Moscow by the early 1970s. Study shows that, in the early 1970s, 19 parties were pro-Chinese as compared with 17 pro-Soviet parties. Seven others were at least partially pro-Chinese (in combination with Castroite and Trotskyite allegiances) with only two partially pro-Soviet groups in this category. Membership figures

by far favor Moscow and continue to overshadow Peking's successes.[5]
Since the seating of the PRC in the UN, formal relations with Latin
American governments, and softening of anti-U.S. policies, the ties
with the Latin American parties are still deemed important although
they are less frequently acknowledged.

A shift has been seen from presenting the Soviet Union to the
Latin American Communists and leftists as a revisionist ideological
renegade to presenting them as "social-imperialist" and even "social-
fascist" aggressors who violate the territorial seas and threaten the
region with nuclear weapons and economic exploitation. The United
States commits the same crimes according to Chinese policy, but
being a neocolonialist power on the decline, such can be expected.
For the Soviets, such conduct is unforgivable.[54]

In 1968, the Soviet Union was characterized in Chinese propaganda as the "No. 1 accomplice of U.S. imperialism." By the following year, Soviet Latin America strategy was shown by the Chinese
as having become increasingly dependent on "taking the cunning
schemes of U.S. imperialism as its example." By 1973, the PRC
charged that the USSR not only had disregarded repeatedly Latin
American positions on the nuclear-weapon-free zone, the 200-
nautical-mile territorial sea, and economic rights but also posed
as "a menace to the peace and security of Latin America" by sending a nuclear-armed naval force into the territorial waters of several Caribbean nations.[55]

For their part, the Soviets assess Peking's Latin America
strategy in the 1970s as "rapprochement with the imperialist camp"
and as a "hegemonistic plan" that includes efforts to form blocs with
the "most reactionary and anti-Communist forces on the continent."[56]

Anti-United States

PRC Latin America policy vis-a-vis the United States always
has been predicated on the perception of a common enemy to both
the Chinese and the Latin Americans. Mao Tse-tung's statement
quoted at the beginning of this chapter was apt in regard to Chinese
attitudes toward U.S. involvement in Latin America. The theme
was continued in a 1964 Jen-min jih-pao editorial, which said: "U.S.
imperialism is the sworn enemy of the Latin American peoples and
. . . no illusions must be entertained about this ferocious enemy."[57]
Cognizance of the Latin American resentment, or at least suspicion,
of the "colossus of the North" was not difficult for the PRC. They
have sought, first through support of leftist revolutions and political
groups and later through cooperation with Latin American governments and commercial establishments, to offset the overwhelming

economic and political effects of the United States. As a result, the
Chinese hoped to gain valuable Third World friends and trading partners at the expense of the United States. In the post-1971 period,
there may be considerably less motivation to outdo the United States
as more essentially economic contacts are being made and Sino-U.S.
rapprochement softens antagonisms on a multilateral basis.

In the period when legitimate and formal contacts were few or
nonexistent, the Chinese carried out virulent attacks in their media
against the U.S. presence and activities in Latin America. Anti-
U.S. mass rallies in Chinese cities and Mao Tse-tung statements
followed such U.S. involvements in the region as the Bay of Pigs
(Playa Giron) invasion in 1961, the Panama Canal Zone riots in
1964, and the Dominican Republic intrusion in 1965. Latin American
visitors to China were usually invited to participate and address such
rallies and relay their own experiences in suffering at the hands of
Americans or fighting against the United States and its "neo-colonial
lackeys." Detailed chronologies of protest and violence were published when such U.S. leaders as Eisenhower, Nixon, and Kennedy
visited Latin America. [58] The efforts, however, had influence primarily on the Chinese population at home and only secondarily on the
relatively small readership of exported Chinese propaganda abroad.
Latin American revolutionaries returning from Peking were perhaps
the greatest beneficiaries of the Chinese effort but were hardly in a
position to influence favorably the actual holders of power in their
homelands. It was, nevertheless, a method of exporting revolutionary ideology and stirring up anti-U.S. feelings in Latin America and
at the same time gaining Peking-leaning followers in the region.

The traditionally anti-Communist governments of Latin America
were aware of all the reasons for anti-U.S. attitudes in their own region and did not need a distant advocate of agrarian unrest to remind
them. It was only through the cultivated Chinese efforts of the 1970s
to support favored issues of specific Latin American governments,
to offer generous trade and interest-free aid terms, and to adjust
previous policies to accommodate a wide spectrum of Latin American
political philosophies that the Chinese were able to present themselves as an alternative to the United States.

Sino-American rapprochement has produced both relief and
positive reaction in Latin America. With their erstwhile mentor,
the United States, no longer the world's leading advocate of containment of the PRC, most Latin American countries began to make independent judgments toward Peking. Some might believe that Latin
America, in keeping with its pattern of following the U.S. foreign
policy lines, still does so in the post-1971 period by moving closer
to China. In the mid-1970s, recognition of the PRC has become an
acceptable policy for even such governments as that of Brazil (which

at one time had been the PRC's greatest nemesis in Latin America),
and with Chinese trade and technical cooperation agreements on the
increase, it is seen that the Latin Americans have gone beyond the
liaison office phase of the United States.

Chinese opposition to the United States vis-a-vis Latin America
continues to exist in the post-1971 period, but is generally voiced in
formal debates in the UN on issues better appreciated by the Latin
Americans than were the revolutionary polemics of old.

ESTABLISHMENT OF RELATIONS

The general trend of PRC recognition strategy in Latin America
is similar to that used in the rest of the world in the 1970s. Informal
contacts are initiated, often starting with exchanges of "friendship
delegations"--frequently those sponsored by the China-Latin America
Friendship Association or the binational friendship association of a
particular Latin American country. * The Chile-China Cultural Institute, for example, was instrumental in lobbying in favor of the
PRC since the 1950s (it is also significant in that the late Salvador
Allende, leader of a 1954 congressional delegation to Peking, was
its honorary president in 1959). Other informal and friendly relations are developed with athletic organizations, medical personnel,
academic institutions, the entertainment and cultural fields, and
trade organizations. Eventually government-to-government contacts
are initiated. As a pattern, this seems to hold true for the early
recognitions of the PRC.

A trend toward more immediate government-to-government
contacts in the prerecognition stage has become more evident in the
mid-1970s. The lengthy procession of "friendship delegations" of

---

*The China-Latin America Friendship Association was estab-
lished on March 16, 1960 under the joint sponsorship of the All-China
Federation of Trade Unions, the China Peace Committee, the Chinese
People's Association for Cultural Relations with Foreign Countries,
the China Council for the Promotion of International Trade, the Chinese People's Institute of Foreign Affairs, the Red Cross Society of
China, and various national professional and mass organizations. A
leading literary figure, Chu Tu-nan, was chosen as association president, along with six vice presidents, most prominent of whom was the
writer Chou Erh-fu.[59] Since 1952, at least 18 friendship associations
have been founded in 11 Latin American countries. In some countries
that changed Taipei's representative for Peking's, local Chinese cultural centers experienced pro-PRC evolutions.

the late 1960s and early 1970s has been bypassed in favor of direct exchanges of official government missions. Venezuela and Brazil followed this pattern prior to formal recognition, and countries not having diplomatic relations with the PRC, such as Costa Rica, Ecuador, Panama, and Colombia (at the time of writing) followed a similar pattern.

A pattern, correlated with PRC worldwide, economic-oriented policies of the 1970s, is the establishment of trade relations prior to diplomatic relations with the countries of Latin America. Trade agreements between a Latin American nation and one of China's state-owned import/export corporations have almost always preceded diplomatic exchanges. This point is well illustrated in the case of Brazil. Vice Minister of Foreign Trade Ch'en Chien was sent to Brasilia in August 1974 ostensibly to sign a major import-export agreement. He stayed on after the signing ceremony to make final arrangements for diplomatic recognition several days later. While other countries' recognition did not follow so close upon commercial negotiations, eight of the first ten Latin American nations to recognize the PRC followed this sequence.*

The modes of mutual PRC-Latin American recognition have demonstrated a nonrigid and evolving formula of initial relations. A study of the joint communiques issued by the PRC and the first ten Latin American countries to establish relations with Peking illustrates this fluid trend in recognition policy. [60]

Cuba (September 28, 1960), as in most cases in PRC-Latin American relations, was the exception to any trend. Being first did not mean the setting of precedents. Not only did ten years intervene until the next recognition but the new Cuban government was a revolutionary and socialist organization much to China's liking. A communique announcing formalization of relations made mention only that the two countries were doing so "to further develop the relations of friendship and co-operation already existing between two fraternal peoples." The curt announcement addressed no issues or interests, implying only Peking's recognition of Cuba's recently attained socialist-state status.

The next two communiques, those of Chile (December 15, 1970) and Peru (November 2, 1971), followed the then-current trend

---

*Jamaica and Trinidad and Tobago were the two exceptions and the Jamaicans have since signed a technical cooperation agreement and the Trinidadians have negotiated a trade agreement. Lack of a contract with one of the Chinese national import-export corporations does not preclude trade with the PRC either directly or through a third party.

of Chinese insistence that the other nation "take note" of the Peking
stand on Taiwan as an inalienable part of China and recognition of
the PRC as the "sole, legal government" of China. Peru obtained
PRC recognition of its sovereignty over a 200-nautical-mile maritime zone. Mexico (February 14, 1972) won Chinese support of the
nuclear-weapon-free zone in Latin America, a favorite project of
the Mexican president. No mention was made, however, of Taiwan
or "sole legal" government.

Development of trade was the major aspect of the next two communiques: Argentina (February 19, 1972) and Guyana (June 27, 1972).
While the former "took note" and recognized the PRC as the "sole
legal" government of China, and both Argentina and Guyana agreed to
take "active measures" in expanding trade, the latter document was
based purely on the development of trade as stipulated in a previous
economic agreement of November 14, 1971. The only Latin America
issue addressed was that on the 200-nautical-mile limit in the Argen-
tine communique.

The last four communiques in the sample—Jamaica (November
21, 1972), Trinidad and Tobago (June 20, 1974), Venezuela (June 28,
1974), and Brazil (August 15, 1974)—indicated a changing trend. An
additional communique, that with the newly independent island of
Grenada (October 10, 1974) and that was signed but evidently abrogated almost immediately, conformed to the same trend. All contained a statement about the promotion of "friendly relations and cooperation" between the two countries (unlike Cuba, which established
relations between "two fraternal peoples"). The communiques of
Venezuela, Brazil, and Grenada showed a return to the PRC earlier
insistence, or at least the ability to win the concession, in isolating
further the Nationalist government, with both Venezuela and Brazil
"taking note" and recognizing the "sole legal" status of Peking.
Grenada recognized the "sole legal" status but "acknowledged,"
rather than took note of, the inalienability of Taiwan. Grenada's
communique also had a clause in it about the development of relations
for the "mutual advantage of both countries and peoples."

While these communiques represent an initial rather than a continuing indication of the status of Chinese relations with a particular
nation, they are of value in determining specific PRC policy toward the
country at the time of recognition, as well as illustrating the general
patterns of Peking's Latin America policy as it evolved. The following section surveys relations with the ten aforementioned countries
at the time of and since recognition in the hope of determining trends
in the continuing and evolving relations between those nations and
China.

REVIEW OF RELATIONS

Since the establishment of relations with the ten nations, there were varied responses to relations with the PRC. As seen from the communiques, the modes of establishment of relations were not uniform and the manner of continuing those relations was far from uniform. The PRC had relations with governments in Latin America ranging from Communist (Cuba) to those branded as fascist (Chile after Allende). Responses on both sides necessarily varied from one country to the next.

Cuba

Peking's Cuba policy was formulated around the realization of Cuba's political and economic vulnerability due to its close proximity to the United States. In order to prove that social problems could be overcome through socialist rule, strong support had to be given to the Caribbean country that exchanged a right-wing dictatorship for a revolutionary regime. Cuba was the second opportunity the PRC had had to embark on the route to normalization of relations with a Latin American nation. Earlier in the decade, Peking and the Jacobo Arbenz government of Guatemala had become increasingly friendly only to have the 1954 coup d'etat put a quick end to what China hoped would be its first diplomatic entry in Latin America. With Cuba, the Chinese moved slowly but assuredly. A New China News Agency office was established in Havana in April 1959 (the first in Latin America). In the summer of the same year, a Chinese delegation was sent to participate in July 26th National Day celebrations, and by December, a contract had been signed for a major Chinese purchase of sugar. Shortly thereafter, in February 1960, Minister of Foreign Affairs Ch'en Yi made a speech proclaiming support of the Cuban revolution. After the exchange of numerous delegations and the signing of another trade agreement, diplomatic recognition was established in September 1960.

It was only after the PRC had decided that Cuba was acceptable as a socialist and genuinely revolutionary country that progress was made toward recognition. The delegations exchanged during the summer of 1960 were mostly political in nature and helped Peking policy makers arrive at a decision finally to establish formal relations. Cuba proved to be a major foreign policy step for the PRC, but it was not until after the 1962 missile crisis between the United States and the USSR that Castro became disillusioned with reliance on Soviet aid and moved toward closer relations with China. When the time finally came, during the period of disillusionment, the Chinese were able to give aid commensurate with their means, but only a small portion of their miniscule foreign aid budget went to Cuba. In the years before and just after the missile crisis, the total U.S. $100 million in Chinese loans to Cuba between 1960 and 1963 represented only 8 percent of all loans (U.S. $1.224 billion) to all Communist countries in the same period. In the period from the missile crisis to the beginning of the Sino-Cuban rift (1963 to 1965), PRC-Cuba trade was unbalanced in China's favor and loans are not thought to have been any more substantial (possibly even less) than in the earlier period (1960-63). [61]

It was quickly proven that China had no great need for Cuba's major export, sugar, and Peking began to renege on previous assurances that consistently larger purchases would be made. Cuba, in turn, was in desperate need of Chinese rice and foodstuffs that China exchanged for sugar. As sugar purchases decreased so too did promised Chinese rice exports; Castro was furious. The Chinese were upset by Cuban payment deficits and rejected a Cuban move to make up the deficits with money from a Chinese economic development loan, and despite Chinese efforts in 1965 (the greatest year ever in Sino-Cuban trade) to expand both aid and trade from their end, the Cubans did not respond accordingly.

In the final analysis, it was not only these economic deficiencies that hindered cordial relations, although they played a major role in Castro's January 1966 denunciation of the PRC. Rather it was ideological jealousies over mentorship of the revolutions in Latin America and accusations of Chinese meddling in Cuban internal affairs through widespread distribution of propaganda that precipitated the rift.

The Cubans had asked the Chinese in the fall of 1965 to desist from further propagandizing the Cuban population with "subversive" and "anti-Soviet" literature. PRC-Cuba relations already were disrupted by ideological and organizational discord among Communist groups emerging as pro-PRC or pro-Cuba in other parts of Latin America. The problem of the Chinese propaganda being distributed in Cuba and the rest of Latin America was that it presented Mao, not Castro, as the mentor for Latin American and other Third World revolutions. Given Castro's determination to become an acknowledged leader of the Latin American liberation movements, a Sino-Cuban clash on theoretical as well as political grounds was inevitable. [62] The rift became open in 1966, causing China to lose some prestige in Latin America and for trade between the two nations to decrease. Castro denounced China during the Tricontinental Conference (Conference of Solidarity of the Peoples of Africa, Asia and Latin America) in Havana, providing a great embarrassment for China. [63]

By 1973, when relations were beginning to improve, China was negotiating for Brazilian sugar, resulting in a still weak state of economic affairs between China and Cuba. On the diplomatic front, Peking began an initiative in 1970 to reestablish full relations by sending a delegation of the China-Cuba Friendship Association to attend the Cuban National Day festivities in Havana. The group was the first Chinese representation, other than diplomatic (at the charge d'affaires ad interim level), to visit Cuba in five years. Friendly messages were exchanged and renewal of at least a formal cordiality was enhanced by the reappointment of ambassadors to both capitals in late 1970 and early 1971. Annual trade protocols were renewed on a regular basis despite the rift.

Chile

Chile, the second of the Latin American nations to establish diplomatic ties with the PRC, presents a case of policy adjustment indicative of the ministry of foreign affairs' diversity in the 1970s. During the Salvadore Allende regime, Chile-PRC relations were close, with trade and aid agreements flourishing. Allende was considered by the Chinese to be their friend, but as Chile became rife with economic and political problems, Peking was careful not to meddle in its internal affairs. China's reaction to the violent, right-wing coup d'etat that ended in Allende's death in September 1973 was drastically subdued compared with previous expressions of outrage over similar events in past decades. In the wake of the coup, the PRC remained one of only three Communist nations to continue relations with the military junta. To Peking's great satisfaction, the Soviet diplomats were expelled and relations unilaterally severed by Santiago on charges of internal interference. While expressing regret at Allende's untimely demise, Peking made only veiled references to the perpetrators of the coup, which had been "engineered by certain reactionary forces at home and abroad."[64] In keeping with subsequent PRC world policy, however, it was later charged that the coup was "a reflection of the intensified U.S.-Soviet rivalry for domination of Latin America."[65]

Full diplomatic relations with the junta were maintained, although in the years immediately following the coup, there were few notable government-to-government contacts and relations were subdued.

Because Peking's criticism of the junta was subdued, the Chinese themselves were criticized severely by Moscow for their continuance of relations with Santiago. The Soviets charged that "relations between China and Chilean fascism [were] becoming increasingly close" and that Peking planned to supply Santiago with arms "to be used to kill Chilean patriots."[66] While the latter charge seems to have been more a product of Sino-Soviet discord than of fact, the former was patently false. Contacts in the cultural, government, and political spheres, which were prolific during the Allende administration, became less than negligible after the coup. Trade, likewise, experienced a decrease. In somewhat of a departure from PRC Latin America policy in the 1970s was a slight undercurrent of support for the Chilean leftists. Periodic publicity was given to the illegal Chilean Communist Party (pro-Peking) and Jorge Palacios, a member of the Secretariat of the Central Committee of the Party, was a guest at 1975 May Day celebrations in Peking.[67]

The fact that relations between the two nations were not broken after the coup d'etat was evidence that the relationship (based primarily on copper and grain trade) was of mutual benefit. While politics caused the "friendship" between China and Chile to become muted, long-standing trade relations, although at a lower rate than in earlier years, continued.

Brazil

The establishment of relations between the PRC and Brazil was a particularly significant achievement for both nations. An international incident had been touched off in 1964 when nine PRC trade exhibition officials and New China News Agency journalists were arrested in conjunction with a military coup d'etat that overthrew the left-leaning government of President Joao Goulart. The nine were charged with sedition and espionage by the Brazilian junta, put on trial after six months' detention, and sentenced to ten years' imprisonment by a military tribunal. Shortly after the first anniversary of their arrest, the nine were expelled from Brazil.

The Chinese government had mounted a tremendous publicity campaign in behalf of the detainees, including notes of protest from the ministry of foreign affairs, mass rallies in Chinese cities, and sponsorship of an international jurists' group to observe the trial. Peking charged the collusion of Washington and Taipei with the junta in an "anti-China" campaign. The anti-China attitude of the Brazilian coup forces was charged by a number of factors. Goulart, as vice president of Brazil--the highest ranking Latin American government leader to visit the PRC at that time--had been in Peking in August 1961 when President Janio Quadros was overthrown by the military. Goulart was recalled to assume the presidency, and a period of relatively warm relations with China occurred despite diplomatic ties with Taipei. Brazil became one of the PRC's very few trading partners. A New China News Agency office and a commercial mission were opened in Rio de Janeiro, various delegations were exchanged, and plans were being made for a Chinese trade exhibition (with Chinese officials negotiating directly with Goulart) when the coup took place.

This friendliness between Goulart and a Communist nation only added to the wrath of conservative militarists who had also witnessed apparent collusion between Peking and the Peasants' League of Northeastern Brazil. League president Francisco Juliao had been a member of a parliamentary delegation to the PRC in 1960, and his wife and daughters had been received personally by Mao in 1962.[68] A letter, allegedly written by one of the trade officials, that purported to show the Chinese were considering training "special agents" for use in northeastern Brazil, was produced by the junta. Peking charged that the letter was a forgery of "U.S.-Chiang Kai-shek agents," but the military tribunal went ahead to convict the group of nine.[69]

The Brazilian military regime was a favorite target of Peking's throughout the following nine years, but as mutually favorable trade options developed, room was made within both governments for the establishment of diplomatic ties. After recognition, there was little interaction between the two governments other than the exchange of trade delegations, rightist military opposition being a hindrance to further or rapid development.[70]

Other Countries

Notable among PRC relations with other countries in Latin America was the exchange of high-level military delegations between China and Peru.* Such exchanges between the PRC and Latin America were unusual and, even though no publicly acknowledged military

---

*In April 1972, Madame Consuelo Gonzalez de Velasco, wife of the Peruvian president, visited China in company with General Javier Tantalean Vanini, the minister of fisheries, and Rear Admiral Alberto Jimenez de Lucio, minister of industry and commerce.[71] In October 1972, the Peruvian army chief of staff, Lieutenant-General Edgardo Mercado Jarrin, visited Peking.[72] In March 1974, Chinese Deputy Chief of Staff Hsiang Chung-hua visited Lima.[73] Additionally, military man, Pai Hsiang-kuo, filling in as minister of foreign trade, visited Lima to conclude a trade agreement in 1972. China also granted a U.S. $42 million interest-free loan and gave U.S. $500,000 in disaster relief to Peru.

agreements were made, the exchanges were significant because of their rarity.

An even higher level exchange of visits, characterizing the degree of relations between the two countries, took place with Mexico. As mentioned earlier, Mexico's President Echeverria traveled to China in April 1973 for a five-day tour. Two years later, Tachai model peasant leader, Vice Premier of the State Council and member of the CCP Politburo Ch'en Yung-kuei, returned the visit when he made a tour of agrarian areas of Mexico in March and April 1975.[74] The major diplomatic event accomplished in the period immediately after the establishment of relations was China's signing of Additional Protocol II of the Treaty of Tlatelolco. PRC relations with Mexico, dating from the 1950s, were similar to those with Chile (also dating from the 1950s) in its lack of support of insurgencies and in its generally pro-Mexican government views since the early period.

The relations formulated with the Cooperative Republic of Guyana, based primarily on trade, the keynote element in the joint communique establishing relations, continued to be of an economic nature in the following years. The Chinese sent trade delegations and textile and agricultural experts to Guyana and held an economic and trade exhibition in Georgetown. A March 1975 visit to Peking by Prime Minister L. F. S. Burnham resulted in a U.S. $10 million interest-free loan to Guyana. This was the second such loan, the first being a U.S. $26 million grant in 1972.[75]

Relations with Argentina, Jamaica, Trinidad and Tobago, and Venezuela in the period during which diplomatic relations were initiated had economic bases similar to that with Guyana. Economic and trade exhibitions were held in Buenos Aires (August 1973), Caracas (December 1974), and Kingston (March 1975). The high point of Chinese-Trinidad relations following establishment of formal ties were the two visits to Peking by Prime Minister Eric E. Williams in November 1974 and January 1975. The visits included talks with Chou En-lai and Teng Hsiao-p'ing and centered on mutual interest in the petroleum industry.[76] The Chinese showed similar interest in this regard toward Venezuela. *

---

*The leader of the delegation to the Chinese economic and trade exhibition in Caracas was Vice Minister of Fuel and Chemical Industries T'ang K'o. Shortly thereafter, the Permanent Secretary of the Venezuelan Front in Defense of Petroleum Anibal Martinez visited Peking.[77]

CONCLUSIONS

The Latin America policy of the PRC after its seating in the United Nations in 1971 was not based on the same types of alliances or united fronts that Peking had hoped would result in the heyday of its advocacy of the wars of national liberation. Neither did it seek to develop a network of interlocking pro-Mao Communist and leftist parties in the region, a virtually unobtainable task, as the PRC discovered, to direct from Peking. None of this is to say, however, that, after 1971, China had forsaken the concept of an international united front and no longer sought and took encouragement in the fraternal leanings of Latin American leftists and Communists toward Peking. The advocacy of armed revolution and the championing of people's war gradually diminished as tenets of Chinese foreign policy in the 1970s, particularly in the case of Latin America. Instead, support of the "just rights" and united struggles of the Latin American and Third World nations and peoples in the economic sphere, interwoven with other issues of national and regional interest, formed the elements of PRC policy in the post-1971 period.

The Chinese shifted from vociferous support of insurgencies to addressing themselves to such Latin American foreign policy thrusts as the 200-nautical-mile maritime zone, economic independence, and the nuclear-weapon-free zone. In general, the PRC stood ready to endorse the demands for economic independence and national sovereignty being made by the Third World peoples in international forums. At the same time, Peking encouraged the unity of the developing countries and led the attack against the accused major exploiters of the Third World, the United States and the USSR. While the thrust of China's attack changed from primarily anti-United States to primarily anti-USSR, a long record of anti-imperialism (in the Soviet context stated as anti-"social imperialism") continued to stand in the post-1971 period.

Trade and development of friendly government-to-government relations in Latin America were the major components of foreign policy in accord with the worldwide diplomatic initiative of post-Cultural Revolution China. China found trade and diplomatic relations to be the most compatible formula. The advocacy of the wars of national liberation and concurrent attempts to carry on at least low-level trade did not demonstrate a rational approach in statecraft in the estimation of the Latin American governments.

Foreign policies after 1971 were modified to complement Chinese internal policies. Just as domestic plans accentuated economic development, foreign policies emphasized sound diplomatic relations bolstered by aid, trade, and encouragement to developing countries in the economic sphere. All served as a means simultaneously to diminish superpower prestige and strength while building sound relations with Latin America as a part of the Third World.

NOTES

1. Mao Tse-tung, "The Present Situation and Our Tasks (December 15, 1947)," in Selected Works of Mao Tse-tung (Peking: Foreign Languages Press, 1961), vol. 4, p. 173.

2. The best description of the Chinese revolutionary model as it is applicable to Latin America is in Cecil Johnson, Communist China and Latin America, 1959-1967 (New York: Columbia University Press, 1970), chaps. 3 and 4.

3. For an analysis of the Chinese "three-world formula," see Peter Van Ness, "China and the Third World," Current History (Philadelphia) 67, no. 397 (September 1974): 106-09, 133. Van Ness's analysis is based partially on Teng Hsiao-p'ing's April 1974 speech at the UN Special Session on Raw Materials.

4. In favor were Chile, Cuba, Ecuador, Guyana, Mexico, Peru, and Trinidad and Tobago; abstaining were Argentina, Barbados, Colombia, Jamaica, and Panama. Analysis of the voting patterns was drawn from tabulations in Marjorie Ann Brown, Chinese Representation in the United Nations (Washington, D.C.: Library of Congress, Congressional Research Service, 71-228F, October 31, 1971); and "U.N. Role Calls on China," New York Times, October 26, 1971, p. 1.

5. For example, see "Rampant Counter-Revolutionary Acts by Soviet Revisionism in Latin America," Peking Review, no. 25 June 20, 1969, pp. 19-20; "NCNA Correspondent Notes Latin American View of USSR Policies," Paking NCNA broadcast, November 26, 1973, as quoted in Foreign Broadcast Information Service, Daily Report, People's Republic of China, December 5, 1973, pp. A13-15 (hereafter cited as FBIS/PRC); "USSR Steps Up Expansion into Latin America," Peking NCNA, May 22, 1974, as quoted in FBIS/PRC, May 22, 1974, pp. A22-23; and "Stepped-Up Soviet-U.S. Contention in Western Hemisphere," Peking Review, no. 22, May 31, 1974, pp. 22-24.

6. Lo Chi, "The Surging National Democratic Movements: Latin America on the March," Peking Review, no. 3, January 18, 1963, p. 8. The article analyzed that the "united front" had been strengthened by the U.S. naval blockade of Cuba during the 1962 missile crisis, which brought a "movement of protest" that "swept the whole of Latin America."

7. "Nationwide Rallies Demand: Imperialists Get Out of Asia, Africa and Latin America!" Peking Review, no. 4, January 27, 1959, pp. 9-10; and "Chinese People Support Anti-Imperialist Struggles in Cuba and Congo," Peking Review, no. 4, January 27, 1959, pp. 11-12.

8. Chou En-lai, Report on the Work of the Government (Speech delivered to the First Session of the Second National People's Congress, April 18, 1959) (Peking: Foreign Languages Press, 1959), p. 61.

9. Lin Piao, Long Live the Victory of People's War! (Peking: Foreign Languages Press, 1967), p. 49.

10. Editorial, Jen-min jih-pao, February 10, 1962, abridged English version in "Second Havana Declaration: Militant Banner of Unity of the Latin American Peoples," Peking Review, no. 7, February 16, 1962, pp. 8-10. In an "important" speech of February 12, 1962, Ch'en Yi made what amounted to a statement of official policy in expressing support, "on behalf of the Chinese Government and the Chinese people," of the Second Havana Declaration. See "Chinese Workers Warmly Acclaim and Support the Second Havana Declaration," The Chinese Trade Unions (Peking), no. 3 (March 1962): 2-3. A year later, the Chinese hailed the declaration as the "clarion call" for the liberation of Latin America. See Jen-min jih-pao, February 4, 1963, cited in "First Anniversary of the Second Havana Declaration," Peking Review, no. 6, February 8, 1963, p. 22.

11. See Peter Van Ness, Revolution and Chinese Foreign Policy, Peking's Support for Wars of Liberation (Berkeley: University of California Press, 1970), pp. 90, 93-94, 101.

12. "Land Reform--The Spearhead and the Banner of the Cuban Revolution," Shih-chieh chih-shih (Peking), June 5, 1959, p. 22; partially quoted in Johnson, op. cit., p. 136. In a documentary work on Guevara, editor Jay Mallin noted that it was uncertain whether Guevara knew of Mao's writings at the time of Castro's guerrilla campaign, but that Mao's (and Vo Nguyen Giap's) writings had considerable impact on his subsequent thinking and writing. See "Che" Guevara on Revolution, A Documentary Overview (New York: Delta Book, 1969), p. 29. It should also be noted that the first volume of Mao's works was not translated into Spanish and distributed in Latin America until around 1958. See "Chairman Mao's Works in Latin America," Peking Review, no. 38, November 18, 1958, p. 20.

13. The Huang Tao-pai School for Revolutionary Instruction was opened in Havana on February 14, 1962, sponsored by the Cuba-China Friendship Association and the Committee in Defense of Revolutionary Havana Province. Huang was a Chinese-Cuban revolutionary who died in 1930 while fighting against the Machado regime. See "Sino-Cuba Ties," Peking Review, no. 8, February 23, 1962, p. 21.

An article from Este y Oeste (Caracas), June 15-30, 1965, submitted
as testimony to the U.S. Senate Judiciary Committee, said that the
PRC had sent arms, munitions, and troops to Cuba "to help Castro
suppress the popular and military revolt." See Red Chinese Infiltration into Latin America (Washington, D.C.: U.S. Government Printing Office, 1965), p. 42. The Washington Post of August 5, 1972,
reported that a band of guerrillas connected with the Movimiento de
Izquierda Revolucionaria (Movement of the Revolutionary Left, or
MIR) and led by a man allegedly trained in China had been broken up
by the Peruvian army. A similar item was reported by the Monte-
video El Dia on May 22, 1973, about "Julian," a member of the Uru-
guayan MIR who reportedly had taken a guerrilla training course in
China in 1967. See "Combined Force Captures China-Trained Guerrilla," U.S. Joint Publications Research Service, Translations on
Latin America, no. 950, JPRS 59451, July 6, 1973, pp. 29-30. Although it is not known if he received training in China or from Chinese agents, one of the most well-known Latin American guerrilla
leaders until his death in May 1970 was the half-Chinese Yon Sosa,
head of the Fuerzas Armadas Rebeldes (Armed Rebel Movement, or
FAR) of Guatemala. Yon Sosa went by the sobriquet of "El Chino"
and his followers were known to have been heavily influenced by Chinese revolutionary experience. See Adolfo Gilly, "The Guerrilla
Movement in Guatemala," Monthly Review (New York), June 1965,
pp. 7-41. Gilly interviewed Yon Sosa in 1965.

14. Among the writings of Fidel Castro that were translated
into Chinese in the early 1960s were Revolutionary Works of Fidel
Castro, The Havana Declarations, and No One Can Stop the Cuban
People from Advancing. Guevara's writings include "Lydia," a description of a Cuban woman revolutionary, which appeared in Women
of China (Peking), no. 1 (1961): 24-25, as well as "Guerrilla Warfare:
A Means," Peking Review, no. 2, January 10, 1964.

15. "Premier Chou En-lai's Press Conference in Algiers
(December 26, 1963)," in Afro-Asian Solidarity Against Imperialism
(Peking: Foreign Languages Press, 1964), p. 77.

16. The publication of Ernesto "Che" Guevara's article,
"Guerrilla Warfare: A Means," Peking Review, no. 2, January 10,
1964, was suspected by Johnson (Communist China and Latin America,
op. cit., p. 155) as an indictment of the writer and the Cuban revolution in general because it contained what Peking held to be theoretical errors.

17. See "One More Spark: Guerrilla War in Colombia,"
Peking Review, no. 41, October 9, 1964, p. 24; "Colombia: One
Falls, Thousands More Arise," Peking Review, no. 11, March 11,
1966, which reported the death of leftist folk-hero Father Camilo
Torres; "Colombia: Growth of a Guerrilla Force," Peking Review,

no. 25, June 21, 1968, p. 31; "Colombia: People's Liberation Army
Fights Courageously," Peking Review, no. 26, September 3, 1969,
p. 30; and "Colombia P.L.A., Badly Batters the Enemy," Peking
Review, no. 10, March 6, 1970, pp. 27-28.

18. Yen Erh-wen, "National-Liberation Movement: Armed
Struggle Flames in Venezuela," Peking Review, no. 13, March 29,
1963, p. 14. Also see "Chinese Youth Will Forever Fight Side by
Side with Venezuelan Youth," Evergreen (Peking), no. 2 (1963): 28;
R. Montilla (secretary of the Communist Youth of Venezuela and a
visitor to China), "A Great Inspiration for Venezuelan Revolutionaries," Evergreen, no. 3 (1963): 31; "Speech by Madame Elena Garcia,
the Delegate from Venezuela" (at Great Hall of the People, Peking,
July 14, 1963), Women of China, no. 3 (1963): 34-35; "Armed Struggle in Venezuela, The Road to Liberation," Peking Review, no. 24,
June 12, 1964, p. 26; and "Latin America: Political Power from
Gun's Barrel," Peking Review, no. 15, April 9, 1965, p. 28, which
cited a women's guerrilla unit of the FALN.

19. See "Bolivia: Armed Struggle: The Only Path," Peking
Review, no. 18, April 28, 1967, p. 38. Johnson, Communist China
and Latin America, op. cit., pp. 224-25, points out that, in mid-
1965, the Communist movement in Bolivia came under the control of
pro-Chinese elements but that numerous arrests of the officials of
the Communist Party of Bolivia, including Jorge Echazu Alvarado,
an NCNA correspondent, so seriously weakened the movement that
neither the pro-Chinese nor the pro-Soviet Communists were able to
provide any significant help to Guevara. Lack of cooperation from
the Bolivian Communists was also cited in a diary kept by one of
Guevara's guerrilla band, see Mallin, "Che" Guevara, op. cit., p.
39. The Bolivian situation was also indicative of the three-way
Sino-Soviet-Cuban split, with none of the three able to gain the cooperation of the others.

20. See "Brazil: Peasants' Armed Struggle in Para State,"
Peking Review, no. 19, May 11, 1973, pp. 18-19; and Peking NCNA
broadcast, February 20, 1974, quoted in FBIS/PRC, March 5, 1974,
pp. A9-11, which mentions armed attacks on latifundists and defiance
of government troops in Para, Mato Grosso, and Ceara states in 1973.

21. See English translation, "Support Latin American Countries' Struggle to Defend Their Territorial Sea Rights," Peking Review, no. 48, November 27, 1970, pp. 7-8. A comprehensive survey and analysis of China's attitude toward the law of the sea is
Hungdah Chiu's "China and the Question of Territorial Sea," International Trade Law Journal (Baltimore) 1, no. 1 (Spring 1975): 29-77.

22. "Against the Superpowers Dominating the Oceans," Peking
Review, no. 5, January 29, 1971, p. 22.

23. "Joint Communique on Establishment of Diplomatic Relations Between China and Peru," Peking Review, no. 45, November 5, 1971, p. 5.

24. "Diplomatic Relations Established Between China and Argentina," and "Diplomatic Relations Established Between China and Mexico," Peking Review, nos. 7-8, February 25, 1972, pp. 25-26. Also see multipart collection of Chinese statements made at the conference, which can be found in China News Summary (Hong Kong), beginning in July 1974.

25. Leonid Nikolayev, "Useful Discussions," Pravda, August 31, 1974, p. 5, English translation in Current Digest of the Soviet Press (Columbus, Ohio) 26, no. 35 (September 25, 1974): 19. Among the numerous Chinese rebuttals of the Soviet position at Caracas were "USSR's Tricks of 'Recognizing' 200-Mile Economic Zone" and "Soviet Delegates Make Disgraceful Show at Caracas Conference," Ta Kung Pao Weekly Supplement (Hong Kong), July 11, 1974, p. 10; and "Deceptive Tricks of Soviet Social-Imperialism," Peking Review, no. 28, July 12, 1974, pp. 15-16. While not discussing the manifestations of the Sino-Soviet rivalry in Latin America, per se, a good summary of Soviet interests in the region can be found in James D. Theberge, The Soviet Presence in Latin America (New York: Crane, Russak & Company, 1974), a National Strategy Information Center "Strategy Paper."

26. "Latin American Countries Opposing Hegemony: Struggle for National Economic Development," Peking Review, no. 7, February 16, 1973, pp. 6-7, 12.

27. "For International Economic Co-operation," People's China, no. 6, March 16, 1952, p. 15; and Chi Chao-ting (General-Secretary, China Committee for the Promotion of International Trade), "China's Foreign Trade," People's China, no. 20, October 16, 1952, pp. 16-17, 33-35.

28. Yeh Chi-chiang (minister of foreign trade), "China's Economic Relations with Asian and African Countries: Progress and Prospects," People's China, no. 6, March 16, 1956, pp. 12-15.

29. "Closer Relations Between Nations," People's China, no. 6, March 16, 1956, pp. 16-17; and "Friends All Over the World," People's China, no. 6, March 16, 1957, p. 41.

30. "Latin America Nixes Nixon," Peking Review, no. 12, May 20, 1958, p. 3; and "Latin Americans vs. Wall Street," Peking Review, no. 25, August 19, 1958, p. 20, which cites the actions taken by Argentina, Brazil, Colombia, and Uruguay to "free themselves of Washington's control and end the plundering of their resources."

31. Chang Yeh, "Cuba's Economic Progress," Peking Review, no. 39, September 29, 1961, pp. 7-9. Also see Hsiao Ming, "Yankee

Imperialism and the 'Banana Republics,'" Peking Review, no. 14, April 5, 1963, pp. 17-19.

32. See Chian Jui-hsi, "U.S. Neo-Colonial Policy in Latin America," Peking Review, no. 34, August 24, 1962, pp. 9-12; "Sao Paulo Meeting: Shaky Alliance, No Progress," Peking Review, no. 48, November 29, 1963, pp. 24-25; "The Rio Conference: Carrot-and-Stick Policy Flops," Peking Review, no. 50, December 10, 1965, p. 21; and "U.S. Economic Penetration of Latin America in 1965," Peking Review, no. 5, January 28, 1966, pp. 17-18.

33. "U.S. Imperialism Steps Up Ruthless Plunder and Exploitation of Latin American People," Peking Review, no. 36, September 3, 1969, pp. 22, 31.

34. See editorial, Jen-min jih-pao, "Down with the Doctrine of Big-Nation Hegemony," translated in Peking Review, no. 5, January 29, 1971, pp. 6-7; "Latin America: Unite to Oppose Despotic Powers," Peking Review, no. 26, June 25, 1971, p. 13; "Latin America: U.S. 'New Economic Policy' Condemned," Peking Review, no. 39, September 24, 1971, pp. 19-20; "Latin America: Mounting Struggle to Defend National Independence and State Sovereignty," Peking Review, no. 43, October 22, 1971, pp. 13-14; "Latin American People's Struggle Against U.S. Imperialism Deepening," Peking Review, no. 4, January 28, 1972, pp. 17-18; "Latin America: Developing National Economy," Peking Review, no. 49, December 8, 1972, p. 21; "Support for Just Struggle of Latin American Countries and Peoples [Huang Hua's speech at UN Security Council meeting in Panama], Peking Review, no. 12, March 23, 1973, pp. 8-11; "Latin America: Struggle to Defend State Sovereignty," Peking Review, no. 30, July 27, 1973, pp. 14-15; "National-Liberation Struggle in the Caribbean," Peking Review, no. 2, January 11, 1974, pp. 9-11; "Latin American Countries' Efforts to Develop Their National Economies," Peking Review, no. 5, January 31, 1975, pp. 19, 23; and "Latin American Countries Develop Small and Medium-Sized Industries," Peking Review, no. 33, August 15, 1975, pp. 24-25.

35. "Down with the Doctrine of Big-Nation Hegemony," op. cit.

36. Peking Review contains many mentions of this organization, in particular, see "Andean Pact Organization: Five Years of Advance," Peking Review, no. 28, July 12, 1974, p. 21; and "Andean Pact Organization Plays an Active Role," Peking Review, no. 24, June 13, 1975, pp. 24-25.

37. Morton H. Halperin and Dwight H. Perkins, Communist China and Arms Control (Cambridge, Mass.: East Asia Research Center, Harvard University, 1965), pp. 118-19. As much as eight years earlier, it was declared that China would do its "very best to use atomic energy for the welfare of mankind." See Kuo Mo-jo, "Ban Atomic Weapons!" People's China, no. 6, March 16, 1955, pp. 3-5.

38. "Premier Chou Cables Government Heads of the World," Evergreen, no. 6 (1964): 3; and "PRC Reiterates Nuclear Policy at Stockholm Conference," Peking NCNA, June 16, 1972, FBIS/PRC, June 16, 1972, pp. A1-2.

39. "Speech by Chiao Kuan-hua, Chairman of the Delegation of the People's Republic of China," Peking Review, no. 47 (November 19, 1971, pp. 5-9.

40. "Diplomatic Relations Established Between China and Mexico," Peking Review, nos. 7-8, February 25, 1972, p. 26.

41. See "China Signs Additional Protocol II to Treaty for Prohibition of Nuclear Weapons in Latin America," Peking Review, nos. 35-36, September 7, 1973, p. 38.

42. "Joint Communique" (Shanghai, April 24, 1973), Peking Review, no. 17, April 27, 1973, pp. 6-7. For an earlier policy statement, see "Foreign Minister Chi Peng-fei's Statement: China Respects and Supports Proposition for Latin American Nuclear-Weapon-Free Zone," Peking Review, no. 47, November 24, 1972, pp. 7-8.

43. Statements of praise of China's signing by Mexican Foreign Minister Emilio O. Rabasa in "Government State Issued on L. A. Nuclear Arms Pact," Peking NCNA, August 22, 1973, as quoted in FBIS/PRC, August 23, 1973, pp. A1-2; and by Alfonso Benavides Correa, president of the Second General Conference of the Organization for the Prohibition of Nuclear Weapons in Latin America (OPANAL), and other OPANAL delegates, Peking NCNA, August 22, 1973, as quoted in FBIS/PRC, August 23, 1973, pp. A4-5.

44. Morton H. Halperin, China and Nuclear Proliferation (Chicago: University of Chicago Center for Policy Study, 1966), pp. 14-16; and "PRC Reiterates Policy at Stockholm Conference," op. cit.

45. "Support the Just Stand of Latin American Countries," translated from Jen-min jih-pao in Peking Review, nos. 35-36, September 7, 1973, p. 39.

46. M. Petrov, "Denuclearized Zone in Latin America," International Affairs (Moscow), no. 8 (August 1974): 43-51. Also see Yu. Ognev, "The Source Toward Disarmament and Peking's Position," Mirovaya Ekonomika I Mezhdunarodnyye Otnosheniya (Moscow), no. 8 (1973): 23-33, translated in U.S. Joint Publications Research Service, Translations on USSR Political and Sociological Affairs, no. 432, JPRS 60015, September 2, 1973, pp. 1-13.

47. Edward Taborsky, Communist Penetration of the Third World (New York: Robert Speller and Sons, 1973), p. 53.

48. Daniel Tretiak, "Sino-Soviet Rivalry in Latin America," Problems of Communism (Washington), January-February 1963, p. 26.

49. For Chinese support of Cuba, see "Chinese Government Statement in Support of Cuba's Struggle Against U.S. Imperialism, November 30, 1962," Peking Review, no. 49, December 7, 1962, pp. 8-9, which hailed the "staunch revolutionary will" of Cuba and the "heroic spirit" of all the people of the world who oppose imperialism and persevere in revolutionary struggle." Castro was glowingly called "a staunch Marxist-Leninist revolutionary fighter." No mention was made of the Soviet role in the conflict. For information on the Soviet "betrayal," see Kang Hsiao, "China and Cuba," Far Eastern Economic Review (Hong Kong) 38, no. 9 (November 29, 1962): 457-58.

50. See list in Eighth National Congress of the Communist Party of China (Peking: Foreign Languages Press, 1956), which included names of representatives from Argentina, Bolivia, Brazil, Chile, Costa Rica, Cuba, Ecuador, Guatemala, Mexico, Paraguay, and Peru; and "Chairman Mao Meets Leaders of Fraternal Latin American Parties," Peking Review, no. 10, March 10, 1959, pp. 10-11, which lists names of visitors from Argentina, Bolivia, Brazil, Chile, Colombia, Costa Rica, Cuba, Ecuador, Panama, Paraguay, Peru, and Venezuela.

51. Luis Aguilar, "Fragmentation of the Marxist Left," Problems of Communism (Washington), July-August 1970, pp. 1, 3.

52. William P. Garner, "The Sino-Soviet Ideological Struggle in Latin America," Journal of Inter-American Studies 10, no. 2 (April 1968): 244.

53. These statistics are based on the author's use of William R. Ratliff, ed., Yearbook on Latin American Communist Affairs (Stanford, Calif.: Hoover Institution Press, 1971); and Richard F. Starr, ed., Yearbook(s) on International Communist Affairs, 1973 and 1974 (Stanford, Calif.: Hoover Institution Press, 1973 and 1974). Tkachenko, "Peking's Latin American Strategy," op. cit., p. 72 charges that, in their "fight against the communist parties of Latin America. . . . the Chinese have allied themselves with Trotskyites, nationalists of every stripe, and extremists and peasant leaders" in Latin America.

54. See sources in note 5.

55. "Soviet Revisionists' Treachery Cannot Hold Back Surging Tide of Revolution," Peking Review, no. 5, February 2, 1968, pp. 29-30; "Soviet Revisionist New Tsars Use 'Aid' to Stretch Their Claws into Asia, Africa and Latin America," Peking Review, no. 28, July 11, 1969, pp. 24-26; and "Caribbean: Soviet Revisionists' Show of Force," Peking Review, no. 38, September 21, 1973, p. 23.

56. Cf. A. V. Kudryavtsev, "Certain Aspects of Peking's Latin America Policy," Latinskaya Amerika (Moscow), no. 3 (May-June 1975): 22-34, as translated in JPRS 65233, July 15, 1975, pp.

1-16; and V. Tkachenko, "Peking's Latin American Strategy," Inter-national Affairs (Moscow), no. 10 (October 1974): 7-78.

57. Jen-min jih-pao, April 30, 1964, English translation in "Lessons from Reactionary Military Coup in Brazil," Peking Review, no. 19, May 18, 1964, pp. 29-32.

58. For examples, see "Latin America," Evergreen (Peking), no. 2 (1962): 24-26; "Latin America on the Move," Peking Review, no. 2, January 12, 1962; "The New Upsurge of Struggle Among Latin American Youth and Students," Evergreen, nos. 4-5 (1962): 30-31; "For Your Reference: U.S. Political Intervention and Armed Sub-versions in Latin America," Peking Review, no. 22, May 28, 1965, p. 28; and for two maps highlighting armed movements in Latin America, see Evergreen, no. 2 (1963): 16; and Jen-min jih-pao, May 22, 1971.

59. See Chung-kuo shou tu ko chieh jen-min chu yuan La-ting Mei-chou (In Commemoration of the Meeting of the People of Various Circles of Peking in Support of the Latin American Peoples) (Peking: China-Latin America Friendship Association, 1960).

60. The partial or full texts of the communiques can all be found in the following issues of Peking Review: Cuba--no. 40, Octo-ber 4, 1960, p. 46; Chile--no. 2, January 8, 1971, p. 3; Peru--no. 45, November 5, 1971, p. 5; Mexico and Argentina--nos. 7-8, February 25, 1972, pp. 26-27; Guyana--no. 27, July 7, 1972, pp. 5, 18-19; Jamaica--no. 48, December 1, 1972, p. 4; Trinidad and Tobago--no. 26, June 28, 1974, pp. 3-4; Venezuela--no. 27, July 5, 1974, p. 5; and Brazil--no. 34, August 23, 1974, p. 4. Grenada's joint communique was broadcast by Peking NCNA, October 10, 1974 (FBIS/PRC, October 11, 1974, p. A15). A note was made by FBIS, however, that about one and a half hours after the announcement, NCNA transmitted a service message canceling the announcement. No further explanation was given. The Grenada communique has been included here inasmuch as it was a formally negotiated and signed agreement even though it later may have been abrogated.

61. See three publications by U.S. Congress, Joint Economic Committee: An Economic Profile of Mainland China (Washington, D.C.: U.S. Government Printing Office, 1967), p. 621; People's Republic of China: An Economic Assessment (Washington, D.C.: U.S. Government Printing Office, 1972), pp. 350 ff.; and China: A Reassessment of the Economy (Washington, D.C.: U.S. Government Printing Office, 1975), pp. 617 ff.; U.S. Department of State, Bureau of Intelligence and Research, Communist States and Developing Coun-tries: Aid and Trade in 1972 (RECS-10), June 15, 1973, Table 4; and Udo Weiss, "China's Aid to and Trade with the Developing Coun-tries of the Third World," Part II, "A Summary of Aid and Trade in 1972 and 1973 According to Geographic Regions," Asia Quarterly

(Brussels), no. 4 (1974): 304-09. In spite of the expansion of economic relations with Latin America in the 1970s, trade remained minimal. In 1973, only 1 percent of PRC total exports went to Latin America with 5.1 percent of its total imports coming from that region. See "China's Trading Partners, 1973," China Trade Report (Hong Kong) 13 (September 1975): 8.

62. Johnson, Communist China and Latin America, op. cit., p. 169. For a comprehensive collection of Sino-Cuban rift texts, see "Castro's Attack and Peking's Answer," Global Digest (Hong Kong) 3, no. 4 (1966): 92-138.

63. See U.S., Senate, Committee on the Judiciary, The Tricontinental Conference of African, Asian, and Latin American Peoples (Washington, D.C.: U.S. Government Printing Office, 1966), pp. 37-38 specifically on Chinese participation. Also see "Tricontinental: General Declaration of the First Conference," Tricontinental (Havana), no. 3 (November-December 1967): 101-12; and Elizabeth K. Valkenier, "Sino-Soviet Rivalry in the Third World," Current History 57, no. 338 (October 1969): 204. After the Tricontinental Conference and the Sino-Cuban rift began, the Cubans sought to glamorize the Vietnamese revolution. "The Vietnamese way" was the only way to "eliminate misery, hunger and win power" wrote a Cuban editorialist. See "Editor," Tricontinental (Havana), no. 3 (November-December 1967): 1-2. Che Guevara carried the analogy further, writing that "America, a forgotten continent in the world's more recent liberation struggles . . . has before it a task of great relevance: to create a Second and a Third Viet-Nam. . . ." The statement was somewhat reminiscent of an earlier one of Chou En-lai on Cuba (see above). See Che Guevara, "Message to the Tricontinental," Tricontinental, no. 14 (September-October 1969): 93. Other articles in the same journal hailed the successes of Kim Il Sung, but even general mention of China was avoided.

64. "Chile: Military Coup," Peking Review, no. 38, September 21, 1973, p. 22. For various analyses of the PRC reaction, see C. L. M., "Peiping's Reactions to the Chilean Coup D'etat," Issues and Studies (Taipei) 10, no. 2 (November 1973): 7-9; A. Istomin, "Rejoinder: Kindred Spirits," Pravda, December 8, 1973, p. 5, translated in The Current Digest of the Soviet Press (Columbus, Ohio) 25, no. 49 (January 2, 1974): 18; Robert L. Worden, "Chile and China," The New Leader (New York) 57, no. 2 (January 21, 1974): 4-5; and Felix Greene, "China and Chile," U.S.-China Friendship's Voice (Washington), Fall 1974, pp. 1, 4-5.

65. Peking NCNA broadcast, June 11, 1975, as quoted in FBIS/PRC, June 13, 1975, p. A5.

66. "Close Relations Between Peking Leaders and Chilean Fascism," Soviet News (Soviet Embassy, London), no. 5782 (April

22, 1975): 147. Also see election speech by Political Bureau member Mikhail Suslov, "Every Worker an Active Creator of History," Soviet News, no. 5789 (June 17, 1975): 209; and "Maoists Ties with Chilean Junta," Pravda, June 11, 1975, p. 5, as translated in The Current Digest of the Soviet Press (Columbus, Ohio) 27, no. 23 (July 2, 1975): 13; and "Maoists Are Friends of the Junta," Pravda, August 21, 1975, p. 5, as translated in Current Digest 27, no. 34 (September 17, 1975).

    67. See Peking NCNA broadcasts October 9, 1974, April 9, 1975, and May 1, 1975, as quoted in FBIS/PRC, October 10, 1974, April 11, 1975, and May 2, 1975.

    68. "Brazilian Parliamentary Delegation," Peking Review, no. 43, October 25, 1960, pp. 20-21; and Yuan Mu, "Friends from Across the Sea," Women of China (Peking), no. 3 (1962): 14-16.

    69. Chinese foreign-language sources on the affair include at least 28 articles from Peking Review between April 10, 1964 and April 30, 1965, as well as one article from China's Sports (Peking), no. 3 (1966): 25, which related how the prisoners kept physically fit while interned in Brazil. A case of similar charges but of much less international repercussion was in Colombia in 1973 when the Bogota government "invited to leave the country" five Chinese newsmen because of "their activities related to public order in the country." See "Chinese Newsmen," Washington Post, May 10, 1973.

    70. See Peking NCNA, November 12, 1974, as quoted in FBIS/PRC, November 15, 1974, p. A20; and Jornal do Brasil (Rio de Janeiro), April 9, 1975, p. 15, as quoted in FBIS/Latin America, April 11, 1975, p. D1.

    71. "Distinguished Guests from Peru Welcomed," Peking Review, no. 17, April 28, 1972, p. 4.

    72. "Peruvian Army Delegation," Peking Review, no. 44, November 3, 1972, p. 31.

    73. "News Brief," Peking Review, no. 13, March 29, 1974, p. 26.

    74. "Vice-Premier Chen Yung-kuei Visits Mexico," Peking Review, no. 14, April 4, 1975, pp. 3-4.

    75. For the October 1974 trade exhibition, see Peking NCNA, November 21, 1974, as quoted in FBIS/PRC, November 22, 1974, pp. A11-A12; for the Burnham visit, see "Prime Minister Burnham Visits China," Peking Review, no. 12, March 21, 1975, p. 3; for the loans, see USSR and the Third World, March-April 1972, p. 243; and Hong Kong AFP, March 14, 1975, as quoted in FBIS/PRC, March 17, 1975, p. A21.

    76. For the Williams' visits, see "Press Communique on the Visit to the People's Republic of China by Dr. Eric Williams, Prime Minister and Minister of External Affairs of Trinidad and Tobago,"

Peking Review, no. 46, November 15, 1974, pp. 8-9; and "Prime Minister Williams Visits China," Peking Review, no. 6, February 7, 1975, pp. 3-4.

77. See various NCNA broadcasts in FBIS/PRC, December 6-30, 1974, and Peking NCNA, May 1, 1975, as quoted in FBIS/PRC, May 6, 1975, p. A15.

9

THE PRC'S POLICY OF PROTECTING CHINESE NATIONALS ABROAD
Shao-chuan Leng

It is universally recognized that every state has a right of protection for its citizens abroad. However, much controversy has arisen as to when and how this right of protection may be exercised.[1] Often, political factors have been interwoven with the legal question of diplomatic protection. This is particularly true in the case of the overseas Chinese problem facing the People's Republic of China (PRC).

Since 1949, the PRC has made a wide range of claims against various countries in behalf of Chinese abroad.[2] Nowhere is the protection issue as sensitive as in Southeast Asia where there is a large concentration of overseas Chinese.*

Because of their numerical and economic strength, their strong cultural ties with China, and some ambiguity of their nationality, the Chinese living in Southeast Asia have posed a complicated problem between the PRC and its Asian neighbors. Although recent studies have exploded the myth that the Chinese abroad are Peking's "fifth column,"[4] the overseas Chinese in Southeast Asia, nevertheless, remain the targets of local resentment and suspicion and, at times, have been the victims of official persecution and mob violence. Consequently, what Peking has or has not done in their behalf is of special interest.

---

*There is no certainty about the precise number of overseas Chinese in Southeast Asia. Twenty-two million would appear to be the round figure currently used, including the population of Hong Kong and Macao. It is also unclear as to the actual percentage of the overseas Chinese that can legally be classified as Chinese nationals. This explains why in recent years Peking has been rather vague about the size of the overseas Chinese population.[3]

This chapter will trace the preliminary trend of the PRC's protection policy through a survey of its significant dealings with other Asian countries on this question. It will begin with an examination of Chinese efforts to resolve the dual nationality issue. Then it will study Peking's responses to the various forms of mistreatment of the Chinese abroad: restrictive and discriminatory measures, mob violence, and mass internment. Hopefully, this chapter will shed light not only on China's perception and exercise of the right of protection under international law but also its capacity to coordinate and reconcile its interest in the overseas Chinese and its broad foreign policy interest.

THE DUAL NATIONALITY ISSUE

The PRC's Common Program of 1949 (Article 58), its Constitution of 1954 (Article 98), and Constitution of 1975 (Article 27) promise protection to the legitimate rights and interests of Chinese residing abroad.[5] Aside from this legal commitment, certain political and economic considerations appear to have affected Peking's overseas Chinese policy. First, there is the KMT influence to combat among the Chinese abroad. Second, the overseas Chinese represent an important source of foreign exchange by way of annual remittances.* Third, the overseas Chinese may be used to promote better economic or political relations between China and the countries in which they reside.

During the early years of the People's Republic, Peking seemed to follow the practice of the Nationalist government to claim all people of Chinese blood as Chinese nationals, even though it abolished in 1949 the entire body of laws enacted by the Nationalist government, including the Nationality Law of 1929 based on the principle of jus sanguinus.[7] In its revolutionary mood, Peking took a militant stand on the protection of the Chinese abroad and also attempted to manipulate the overseas Chinese for political purposes.[8]

However, a marked shift from this militant position to a moderate one occurred in 1954 when Peking launched the policy of peaceful coexistence to win the friendship of the new states of Asia and Africa. Aware of the local populations' suspicion and hostility toward the Chinese in Southeast Asia, the PRC apparently decided

---

*There is no agreement among experts on the annual figures of overseas Chinese remittances. According to a conservative estimate, the remittances averaged over $44 million annually between 1950 and 1964.[6]

that a move must be made to clarify the overseas Chinese legal
status and to remove their "subversive" label if their legitimate interest and the overall interest of Chinese foreign policy were to be
genuinely served.

Peking's new approach to the overseas Chinese issue was first
underlined by a speech made by Chou En-lai on September 23, 1954.
Speaking before the First National People's Congress, the Chinese
premier expressed the hope that the Southeast Asian countries would
respect the legitimate rights and interests of the overseas Chinese.
To improve the situation, he promised that China would urge the
overseas Chinese to respect the laws and customs of the countries
of their residence, and was prepared to settle the question of their
nationality. [9]

The new line found its concrete manifestation in the conclusion
of the Sino-Indonesian Dual Nationality Treaty in April 1955. [10]
This treaty constituted a significant departure from the traditional
Chinese position in that it adopted the principle of voluntary option
to solve the dual nationality issue. According to its provisions, all
persons with dual nationality who had reached their maturity should
formally choose, on the basis of free will, the citizenship of either
China or Indonesia within two years after the exchange of the ratification (Articles 1-3). The choice of one of the nationalities would en-
tail the loss of the other (Article 4). Those who failed to choose
their nationality within the prescribed two-year period would retain
the nationality of their fathers. In case they had no legal relationship with their fathers or the nationality of their fathers were unknown, their mothers' national origin would determine their nationality (Article 5).

Under the treaty a person who chose the nationality of one
country would automatically lose it if he established permanent
residence abroad and regained the nationality of the other country
(Article 7). As for the nationality of a newly born child, the treaty
adhered to the jus sanguinus principle to prevent new problems of
dual nationality. It stipulated that a child born in one country would
acquire, upon his birth, the nationality of the other country if both
parents or the father held the nationality of the latter country (Article 8). Evidently, with a view to removing future friction and
ensuring better treatment of Chinese nationals in Indonesia, the
treaty stated that

> Each high Contracting Party agrees to encourage its
> own citizens residing in the other country . . . to
> respect the laws and social customs of the country
> in which they reside and not to take part in political
> activities of that country. Each high Contracting

Party affirms its willingness to protect according
to its laws the proper rights and interests of the
citizens of the other party residing in its territory [Article 11].

In an exchange of notes on June 3, 1955, which formed the
integral part of the treaty, China made a further concession to exempt from filing declarations a group of overseas Chinese who, in
the opinion of the Indonesian government, had already implicitly
abandoned the nationality of China by virtue of their social and political status. [11]

Whatever its imperfections, the treaty represented a considerable diplomatic achievement. [12] Chinese spokesmen pointed out
that such "reasonable" settlement of the dual nationality issue was in
the interest of the overseas Chinese and the interest of the policy of
peaceful coexistence. They also stated that the Sino-Indonesian
Treaty could serve as a precedent for the settlement of the dual
nationality issue between China and other countries in Southeast
Asia. [13]

However, strong objections to the treaty raised by a number
of Indonesian political parties and a dispute between the two countries
in 1954 over discriminatory measures against the Chinese in Indonesia led to a long delay in making the treaty effective. [14] The exchange of ratifications did not take place until January 1960, and
implementation did not begin until the signing of the supplementary
agreement in December 1960. Although a period of cordial Sino-
Indonesian relations ensued, the Communist coup of September 30,
1965 in Indonesia dramatically reversed the trend. The general
suspicion of Peking's alleged involvement in the coup created strong
anti-Chinese feelings in Indonesia, and popular pressure eventually
resulted in the unilateral abrogation of the Dual Nationality Treaty
by Djakarta on April 10, 1969. [15] Except for a New China News
Agency's Comment, the PRC, nevertheless, has chosen not to make
any official response to Indonesia's unilateral action. *

Although no similar nationality treaties have been concluded
between the PRC and other countries, Peking clearly has adopted

---

*It should be noted that the treaty was to last 20 years and was
to remain in force thereafter unless one of the parties requested its
termination (Article 14). In a statement on the Indonesian projected
measure to abrogate the treaty, the New China News Agency (November 14, 1968) accused the Indonesian regime of violating treaty
provisions and of depriving the Chinese born in Indonesia the right
to opt for Indonesian citizenship upon attaining maturity.

the principle of voluntary option as the means to settle the dual nationality issue. This principle was incorporated in a Sino-Nepalese
agreement on several matters in September 1956.[16] More important, it was expounded by Chou En-lai in his 1956 visit to Southeast
Asia. In an interview with David Marshall, former chief minister
of Singapore, on October 9, 1956, Chou stated that the Chinese government wished to see the Chinese in Singapore voluntarily obtain
Singapore citizenship and give complete loyalty to the country of
their residence in the interest of all concerned. He also added:
"Any Chinese resident who voluntarily obtains Singapore citizenship
will cease to possess Chinese nationality though, of course, his in-
inherent ethical and cultural affinity with China will continue to
exist."[17]

In a speech to the overseas Chinese in Burma in December 12,
1956, Chou repeated the same theme and added that those Chinese
who became Burmese citizens should no longer play a role in overseas Chinese organizations. Those who remained as Chinese nationals, Chou stressed, should obey local laws and refrain from
participating in local political activities.[18]

Undoubtedly, Chou's statements during his Southeast Asia
tour set the one of the PRC's overseas Chinese policy in recent
years and have since been echoed and elaborated by other Chinese
spokesmen. Two significant components of this policy have become
clear. One is the recognition of the right of the overseas Chinese
to renounce unilaterally Chinese nationality[19] and the other is the
urging of Chinese nationals abroad to respect local laws and customs
and to take no part in any political activity.[20]

Contrary to the allegations of its critics, this policy is not of
sacrificing the overseas Chinese for the sake of foreign policy
gains.[21] Rather, it is a rational and pragmatic policy to advance
the interest of the Chinese abroad through the removal of the dual
national issue and the improvement of relations between China and
its Asian neighbors. Given a favorable environment resulting from
Peking's enlightened policy, the overseas Chinese who have opted
for local nationality should have a better chance to enjoy their rights
as full-fledged citizens of the country of their residence without
having their allegiance under suspicion. By the same token, those
who remain as Chinese nationals should become less an object of
local hostility and discrimination; in case of flagrant injustice, the
Chinese government would have a clear-cut right of diplomatic protection without violating the principle of noninterference in internal
affairs of another country.[22]

RESTRICTIVE AND DISCRIMINATORY MEASURES
AGAINST CHINESE RESIDENTS

Despite these efforts to solve the dual nationality issue, the treatment of the overseas Chinese by the developing countries of Southeast Asia has continued to give rise to occasions for the PRC to exercise its right as well as to implement its pledge to protect Chinese residents abroad. The most common controversy has been over the restrictive and discriminatory measures undertaken by the nationalistic governments of the Southeast Asian countries against the Chinese minority in economic, political, and social fields of activity. Some of these governments have maintained diplomatic relations with Peking, while others have not.

In dealing with the latter, the PRC has been handicapped by a lack of official contact. Thus, protection offered to the overseas Chinese in such cases has taken either the form of verbal protests through the Jen-min jih-pao and the spokesmen of the Overseas Chinese Affairs Commission (OCAC) or that of resettlement of the overseas Chinese forced to return to China. Even during the early years of the PRC when the Peking government assumed a militant external posture, it did not go beyond the aforementioned position of protection in the face of the anti-Chinese policies (ranging from economic discrimination to political oppression) pursued in Thailand, the Philippines, Malaya, and French Vietnam.*

Illustrative is the following passage from a statement issued in October 1954 by Peking's Overseas Chinese Affairs Commission

---

*In its protests against these countries' discriminatory policies, the PRC used strong words along with vague threats but showed no sign of supporting them with action. Typical is the Jen-min jih-pao's denunciation of the Thai government on July 23, 1952 for its decision to raise the annual identification tax on Chinese residents. The paper warned the Thai government that "its vicious, unreasonable action is a serious encroachment on the right of several million Chinese residents in Thailand and will certainly not be tolerated by the Chinese people. The Thai government must end this ruthless persecution and extortion or it must hold itself responsible for the grave consequences resulting from this act of persecution of Chinese residents in Thailand."[23] In the case of Malaya, Peking did make an attempt in March 1951 to send an investigation team there. However this move was soon abandoned because of the British refusal.[24]

reviewing its own record in protecting Chinese residents abroad
during the first five years:

> At present, in the countries which have established
> friendly relations with our country, the condition
> of the overseas Chinese have seen some improve-
> ment. But in countries not friendly to us, the po-
> sition of overseas Chinese is a difficult one. . . .
> In Thailand, for instance, during the past
> few years, the 3,500,000 overseas Chinese there
> have been subjected repeatedly to large scale per-
> secution. Many overseas Chinese were deported
> or arrested. The Philippine government has also
> ceaselessly enforced acts against the Chinese,
> and the 180,000 overseas Chinese in that country
> have been subjected to persecution. . . . The
> overseas Chinese in French occupied areas in
> Vietnam also face serious difficulties. . . . The
> three million overseas Chinese in Malaya are not
> faring well either. During the past five years,
> between 400,000 and 500,000 Chinese have been
> detained in concentration camps provided by the
> Malayan government. Overseas Chinese un-
> reasonably deported from that area, according
> to official figures released by the Malayan author-
> ities alone, exceeded 24,000.
> During the past few years, our government
> has paid the closest attention to the difficult situ-
> ation of overseas Chinese. For the protection of
> the legitimate rights and interests of overseas
> Chinese, our government and our people have
> issued serious protests and statements against
> the acts of persecution of overseas Chinese on
> the part of certain countries. Serious concern
> has been felt for the persecuted overseas Chinese,
> and those forced to return to the country have
> been cared for and placed in jobs. [25]

Subsequently, the PRC took a less militant and more realistic
stand toward these countries on the overseas Chinese issue. This
was partly in line with its new policy position and partly because of
the realization that little could be done to influence those governments

that had diplomatic ties with the Chinese Nationalist government in Taiwan. *

Still, from time to time, the PRC responded to discriminatory actions against the overseas Chinese. For instance, after the Sarit coup in 1958, Thailand stepped up repressive measures against pro-Communist Chinese through a number of arrests, the search of Chinese schools, and the closing of several newspapers. In a statement issued on November 3, 1958, OCAC spokesmen protested against the "persecution" of Chinese residents by the Thai authorities and accused the latter of acting under the pressure of the United States. It was pointed out that China had all along persisted in the spirit of the Bandung Conference, advocated friendship between Asian and African countries, and directed the overseas Chinese to abide by the laws of the country where they were living, not to take part in local political disputes, and to engage in construction works beneficial to the local economy. But the Thai government, said the Chinese spokesmen, "ignored China's hitherto friendly attitude and the wishes of the peoples of these two countries, violated internationally established fundamental human rights, persecuted innocent overseas Chinese, and infringed upon the proper rights of the overseas Chinese."[27]

Peking's reaction to the forced naturalization of Chinese in South Vietnam is another case in point. In August 1956, Ngo Dinh Diem's government decreed that all local-born Chinese should be considered Vietnamese citizens. Then it followed up with another ordinance banning Chinese nationals from 11 retail trades and giving them from six months to a year to liquidate their business. These measures strained the friendly relations between Nationalist China and South Vietnam, and Taipei's representations failed to change Saigon's policy.[28] In May 1957, the PRC, through the OCAC and the Jen-min jih-pao, demanded of Diem's government the immediate withdrawal of its "unreasonable measures." Peking's main complaint was that Saigon acted on the nationality question without mutual consultation or taking into account the free wishes of Chinese residents. The unilateral action to force the overseas Chinese to change their nationality was "not only a wanton violation of the proper rights and interests of the overseas Chinese in South Vietnam but also a serious transgression of the principle of international law."[29]

---

*It should be noted that the Chinese Nationalists also have had no significant influence on those governments in protecting the overseas Chinese.[26]

In regard to the countries that the PRC had official relations with, there were, of course, more channels open for it to perform the protective function for its nationals. Its preference appeared to have been the use of goodwill and friendly relations as a means to promote the interest of the overseas Chinese. Diplomatic protests and representations were resorted to only when necessary and often on a selective basis. Cambodia and Indonesia may be cited as examples.

In the mid-1950s, the Cambodian government moved to close 16 economic occupations to Chinese aliens.[30] It also banned political activity in the Chinese schools.[31] The situation, however, subsequently improved as a result of the development of close ties between the PRC and Cambodia and Chou En-lai's urgings that Chinese residents in Cambodia should respect local laws and customs and refrain from all political activities in their host country.[32] Following the ouster of Prince Sihanouk by General Lon Nol in March 1970, some incidents of persecution of Chinese residents were reported, for example, the closing of Chinese schools and the compelling of Chinese residents to support the new regime. There was no official protest from Peking. Instead, the New China News Agency reported these incidents and labeled them not only a gross encroachment upon the legitimate rights and personal security of Chinese residents in Cambodia but also an attempt of the "right-wing clique" to undermine the traditional friendship between Chinese and Cambodian peoples.[33]

Between the signing of the Sino-Indonesian Dual Nationality Treaty in 1955 and the exchange of its ratification in 1960, a major dispute erupted between Peking and Djakarta over the treatment of the overseas Chinese. Since late 1957, the Indonesian government had been increasing its pressure against Chinese residents, initially against pro-KMT Chinese and later against all persons of Chinese ancestry. Numerous Chinese schools were closed and many Chinese newspapers were banned.[34] In November 1959, a far-reaching regulation was issued by Djakarta to ban Chinese aliens from retail trade in rural areas, and it was accompanied with an army decree ordering the Chinese to terminate residence in West Java.[35]

Since these measures affected 300,000 Chinese residents, the PRC had no choice but to respond. Vigorous protests through both diplomatic channels and news media were launched against the "imperialist-inspired" persecution of the Chinese. Officials of the Chinese embassy in Djakarta reportedly advised Chinese residents to resist the ban. On the other hand, the Indonesian government justified its measures on the grounds of national interest and accused the Chinese embassy of interference in Indonesia's internal affairs by ordering Chinese residents to defy the Indonesian authorities.[36]

In the early stage of this crisis of 1959-60, veiled threats were made by some Chinese spokesmen. For example, the editorial of the <u>Jen-min jih-pao</u> on December 12, 1959 declared that "It would be a grievous mistake for anyone to suppose that the Chinese government and the 650,000,000 Chinese people would watch their compatriots being subjected to unjustified discrimination and persecution abroad without doing anything."[37] However, at no time did the PRC officially threaten to break diplomatic ties with Indonesia or to contemplate the use of force. Its main means of protection for the overseas Chinese were to seek an amiable settlement of this dispute with Djakarta and to offer repatriation to those Chinese who had to leave Indonesia.

In a note to Indonesian Foreign Minister Subandrio on December 9, 1959, Chinese Foreign Minister Ch'en Yi proposed a three-point solution to the problem: the two countries should exchange without delay the instruments of ratification of the Dual Nationality Treaty of 1955; Indonesia should protect the rights of Chinese nationals; and arrangements should be made for repatriation to China of Chinese "who have become homeless and lost means of livelihood or who do not wish to remain in Indonesia."[38] In another note to Subandrio on December 24, Ch'en Yi reiterated the three-point proposal and defended the Chinese delegates' activities in Indonesia as legitimate:

> The execution by the Chinese representative organs
> in Indonesia of their duty to protect their own na-
> tionals, while the latter's proper rights and inter-
> ests are seriously impaired, can in no way be
> interpreted as agitation to incite overseas Chinese
> to defy the orders of the local government, even
> less it can be used justifiably as an excuse for
> placing discriminative restrictions on the Chinese
> diplomatic representative organs.[39]

The exchange of the instruments of ratification of the 1955 Treaty in January 1960 obviously helped to ease the tension. In his letter of March 15, 1960 to Subandrio, Ch'en Yi emphasized the PRC's repatriation effort and asked for Djakarta's cooperation:

> The Chinese government has repeatedly asked the
> Indonesian government to take up the responsibility
> of sending overseas Chinese back to China in ac-
> cordance with their own will, and has made prepa-
> rations for the reception and settlement of the
> returned overseas Chinese. Since the Indonesian

government has indicated that for the present it has difficulties in providing ships, the Chinese government has taken the initiative in sending ships to transport overseas Chinese back to China.[40]

By the end of 1960, the Sino-Indonesian dispute was practically over in the wake of the coming into force of the Dual Nationality Treaty, the relaxation of restrictive measures against the Chinese in Indonesia, and the repatriation of 100,000 overseas Chinese to the mainland.* Throughout the crisis the accent of the PRC's position was on negotiation rather than confrontation, and this approach eventually not only served its foreign policy interest of keeping Djakarta's friendship but also alleviated substantially the problems for Chinese residents in Indonesia, even though at the price of repatriating large numbers of overseas Chinese to China.

MOB VIOLENCE AND OTHER OUTRAGES AGAINST OVERSEAS CHINESE

While discriminatory measures against resident aliens may constitute a basis for international claims, the failure of a government to use "due diligence" to prevent mob violence against aliens is clearly a well-recognized ground of international responsibility.[43]† In the mid-1960s mob violence and other outrages against Chinese residents occurred in countries like Indonesia and Burma. Such incidents put to a severe test the PRC's policy of protecting the Chinese abroad.

Relations between Peking and Djakarta deteriorated rapidly following the failure of the Communist coup of October 1965 in Indonesia. The anti-Communist drive of the Indonesian army and the allegation of Peking's involvement in the coup inspired a rash of anti-China and anti-Chinese incidents throughout Indonesia. Except

---

*The numbers of Chinese who returned to China from Indonesia in 1960 were estimated between 94,000 and 100,000.[41] Officially, this dispute came to an end in April 1961 when Ch'en Yi visited Indonesia and signed a friendship treaty between the two countries.[42]

†Besides nonsuppression and nonpunishment of mob actions, wanton killing, unlawful arrest, imprisonment or detention, and unduly harsh, oppressive, or unjust treatment of aliens by local officials have been the basis of numerous international claims.[44]

for brief intervals, the violent campaign against the Chinese (regardless of their citizenship) continued through 1965-67. The Indonesian authorities not only arrested many Chinese nationals and closed Chinese schools but openly tolerated mob actions, including the beating and killing of Chinese, ransacking of Chinese shops and homes, and raiding of the Chinese embassy and consulates.[45]

Indonesia's anti-Chinese incidents reached a new height in 1967 with the formal removal of Sukarno from office. Army personnel intensified their extortion and intimidation of Chinese businessmen, police fire killed and wounded Chinese demonstrators, and rioting mobs indiscriminately attacked Chinese and their property.[46] In West Kalimantan alone, by the end of 1967, hundreds of Chinese had been slaughtered while tens of thousands had become refugees.[47]

Against the postcoup anti-Chinese campaign, the PRC issued a stream of diplomatic protests to the Indonesian government. In its protesting notes, Peking labeled the serious anti-Chinese incidents as a "brutal encroachment" upon the proper rights and interests of Chinese nationals and a "gross violation" of the elementary principles of international law and relations.[48] Repeatedly, it demanded that Djakarta immediately stop the persecution, punish the culprits and instigators, compensate for all Chinese losses, and safeguard the personal safety and property of all Chinese residents.[49]

In many of its notes issued in 1965 and 1966, the PRC accused the Indonesian authorities of nonsuppressing and even encouraging mob actions against the Chinese.[50] It compared the Indonesian persecution of the Chinese with the fascist atrocities against the Jews, and charged that the Indonesian army and policy directly participated in the looting and killing of Chinese nationals.[51]

Besides diplomatic protests, the PRC also withdrew its technical advisers and cut off aid to Indonesia in retaliation.[52] As these measures failed to change Djakarta's policy, Peking again offered to repatriate those Chinese (regardless of their citizenship) wishing to leave Indonesia. During the course of the repatriation, China complained about many obstacles placed by the Indonesian government to obstruct the departure of Chinese repatriates, for example, restrictions on the number of visas issued and on the effort of Chinese consular officials to facilitate repatriation arrangements.[53] Between October 1966 and October 1967, some 5,165 Chinese eventually were transported to China by Chinese ships.[54] In contrast to 1959-60, the number of Chinese who left Indonesia this time was much smaller.

One observer thinks that both Peking and the overseas Chinese apparently had some sobering second thoughts about the effectiveness of repatriation as a solution to Indonesia's periodic outburst of anti-Chinese sentiments.*

At no time during the dispute did Peking ever threaten to break diplomatic ties with Djakarta. However, in October 1967, official relations between the two countries were suspended when the Indonesian government withdrew its diplomats from Peking and the Chinese government followed suit by recalling its representatives from Indonesia. With the suspension of diplomatic ties with Djakarta, Chinese news media have become the main vehicle expressing Peking's indignation over the Indonesian persecution of Chinese residents. For example, a commentator of Jen-min jih-pao on February 4, 1968 charged that "the reactionary Suharto-Nasution regime in Indonesia recently perpetrated a shocking fascist atrocity by carrying out the massive slaughter and persecution of Chinese nationals in West Kalimantan" and warned that it owed "the Chinese people another blood debt."

Different from the Indonesia case, the 1967 anti-Chinese riots in Burma were directly related to the Cultural Revolution of China. The events that led to the spectacular reversal in Sino-Burmese relations followed the same pattern as the incidents in Macao, Hong Kong, Moscow, and elsewhere, typifying China's turbulent foreign relations during the Cultural Revolution.[56]

Until the dramatic change in 1967, Sino-Burmese friendly relations were considered as a model for Peking's policy of peaceful coexistence. However, a serious clash occurred in June 1967 between the Burmese authorities, who forbade schoolchildren to wear Mao Tse-tung's badges, and the defiant Chinese students, who insisted on bringing Maoist political material into the schools. This led to anti-Chinese riots in Rangoon in which Burmese mobs attacked

---

*According to David Mozingo,

As a result of the earlier experience Peking discovered that the number of repatriates was too large to handle and that it was wise to discourage others from coming. The overseas Chinese soon learned that remaining in Indonesia involves less severe adjustments than adapting to new life in China. Djakarta learned a few lessons too. Indonesia's economy can ill-afford the loss of the large numbers of Chinese who presently constitute an irreplaceable skill group. And finally, the 1959-60 experience taught Peking that her ability to coerce Djakarta by withdrawing the Chinese was not only limited, but also politically counterproductive.[55]

Chinese residents and the Chinese embassy. Eventually, one Chinese economic aid official and many overseas Chinese were killed.[57] Soon afterward, the PRC openly denounced the Ne Win government as a "reactionary band of fascist killers" and called for its overthrow by the Burmese Communist Party.[58]

In asserting the right to protect its nationals in Burma, the PRC issued numerous protests and statements through the second half of 1967 and the early months of 1968. First, it accused the Burmese government of engineering and inciting the anti-Chinese riots, and demanded an immediate stop to persecuting the Chinese, compensation for Chinese losses, and severe punishment for the culprits.[59] Second, China expressed its desire to ship medical and relief supplies to the Chinese in Burma. When permission was refused by Rangoon, it contended that the Burmese government had no justification whatsoever to refuse such arrangements "if it respects the right of a foreign government to protect its nationals and recognizes the most elementary norm of international relations."[60]

Peking's effort to send civil aircraft to Burma to bring wounded overseas Chinese back home for medical treatment was also frustrated by Rangoon's refusal; so was the attempt of many Chinese to make arrangements to return to China. The Burmese obstructions to such "legitimate" efforts were another subject of Chinese protests.[61] In addition, the PRC complained about the illegal arrest and detention of many Chinese by the Burmese authorities, and claimed that Burma used torture, secret trials, and other improper proceedings to prosecute the overseas Chinese.[62]

Mass demonstrations were organized by the Red Guards in Peking against the Burmese embassy during July 29-31, 1967.[63] The PRC also abrogated the Sino-Burmese agreement on economic and technical cooperation in October 1967.[64] But Peking never threatened the Burmese throughout the crisis with either the use of force or the break of diplomatic relations. Its verbal warnings were confined to such ambiguous statements as "the 700 million Chinese people stood pledged to support patriotic overseas Chinese in their struggle against fascist persecution; should the Burmese government continue its anti-Chinese criminal acts in disregard of our warnings, it must bear the full responsibility for all the grave consequences."[65] In late 1967 and early 1968, when the tension between the two countries began to ease, Peking reverted to the pre-Cultural Revolution position to remind Rangoon that Chinese in Burma had always been told to respect local laws and customs.[66]

MASS INTERNMENT OF CHINESE IN INDIA

Chinese residents in India have never posed a problem with the same magnitude as their counterparts in Southeast Asia. Although

New Delhi began to take measures against pro-Peking overseas Chinese in 1959, with the deterioration of Sino-Indian relations, it was the outbreak of the border war between the two countries in 1962 that prompted the Indian government to put persons of Chinese descent (citizens and aliens alike) under extensive control and regulation. A number of far-reaching orders issued in October-November 1962 authorized restrictions on movement, deprivation of certain basic rights of Indian citizenship, and arrest followed by either internment in camps or detention in prison.

One result was the mass arrest and internment of all Chinese residents in Assam and certain districts of West Bengal. By February 18, 1963, there were 2,165 Chinese interned at Deoli and Rajarthan and an additional 143 detained in local jails. The large number of other Chinese residents in India also suffered a variety of difficulties, including the loss of homes and businesses.[67]

In protests against India's mass internment of Chinese as a race, the PRC, too, asserted the right of protection without making distinction between dual nationals and persons who maintained only Chinese nationality. The Indian actions were frequently branded as a violation of accepted norms of international law and an encroachment on basic human rights.[68] Peking rejected India's "national security" justification and maintained that India's failure to meet the international obligation to protect foreign residents constituted "a serious international delinquency."[69]

Besides diplomatic protests, essays were published by Chinese scholars to support Peking's claims. Professor Chou Keng-sheng, in particular, wrote a lengthy article to attack the Indian position by referring not only to specific provisions of international conventions but also to the works of "bourgeois" authorities on international law.[70]

The PRC further clashed with India over the right of Chinese diplomats to visit the arrested Chinese and obtain information about them. The Indian government repeatedly rejected Chinese requests and allowed the exchange of information only through the medium of the International Committee of the Red Cross (ICRC). Peking, however, claimed that since the diplomatic relations were kept, Chinese diplomats should have direct contacts with the interned Chinese so as to exercise the right of diplomatic protection. By the same token, it challenged the ICRC's visits to the internment camp without its consent.[71]

During the dispute, the PRC also accused India of mistreatment of the interned Chinese and offered to repatriate all the internees and their dependents. After agreeing to the principle of voluntary repatriation, Peking sent repatriation ships to India on three separate occasions: April, May, and July 1963. Altogether these ships brought back to China 2,395 overseas Chinese, of whom

1,665 were internees and 730 were their dependents.[72] Some 594 Chinese internees, however, reportedly preferred confinement to India to repatriation.[73]

RECENT TRENDS

In line with the diplomatic initiatives undertaken since 1969, the PRC has recently shown greater moderation and pragmatism in its policy toward the overseas Chinese: to urge them to take the citizenship of the country of their residence and to adopt a low-key approach to racial problems involving Chinese residents abroad. Early 1972, for instance, the Chinese ambassador to Burma labeled dual nationality as an "illegal phenomenon" and said that after acquiring Burmese nationality, the Chinese in Burma "can enjoy full privileges as Burmese citizens and can serve local interests more effectively. This will be good for the overseas Chinese long-range survival and for the developments of friendly relations between Burma and China."[74] In a speech at a reception for overseas Chinese delegates on the eve of the twenty-third anniversary of the founding of the PRC, General Yeh Chien-ying had this to say:

> Many foreign friends of Chinese descent are also attending this reception today. You are kinsmen of the Chinese people. You have adopted the nationality of other countries of your own accord and we have no objection to your choice. We would like to see you make contributions to your countries and to the promotion of the friendship between the people of your countries and China.[75]

When bloody anti-Chinese riots broke out in Malaysia in May 1969, Peking handled the incidents with great restraint, only having them reported in the Jen-min jih-pao (May 20, 1969) as a news item without any official protest. By the same token, Chinese news media prudently chose not even to mention the racial violence that engulfed the Chinatown of Bangkok in July 1974.*

---

*In this delicate situation, Taipei was also very cautious in its attitude toward the racial incidents that occurred in Bangkok during July 3-6, 1974. Only after the riots were brought under control did Chung-yang jih-pao (Central Daily News) (July 8, 1974) report the appeal of the overseas Chinese leaders to Chinese residents in Thailand for cooperation with the Thai government to restore peace and order.

In an apparent move to dispel South Asian countries' fear of links between local Chinese residents and mainland China, the PRC has abolished the Overseas Chinese Affairs Commission and has dropped in its new constitution the overseas Chinese representation in the National People's Congress. [76] The Chou-Razak joint communique of May 1974 establishing Sino-Malaysian diplomatic ties contained a statement that further clarified the PRC's position toward the overseas Chinese:

> Both the Government of the People's Republic of China and the Government of Malaysia declare that they do not recognize dual nationality. Proceeding from this principle, the Chinese Government considers anyone of Chinese origin who has taken up of his own will or acquired Malaysian nationality is automatically forfeiting Chinese nationality. As for residents who retain Chinese nationality of their own will, the Chinese government acting in accordance with its consistent policy, will enjoin them to abide by the law of the Government of Malaysia, respect the customs and habits of the people there, and live in unity with them, and their proper rights and interests will be protected by the Government of China and respected by the Government of Malaysia. [77]

Although the Indonesians, who abrogated the 1955 Dual Nationality Treaty with China in 1969, may not be persuaded to cast aside their doubts about either Peking's intentions or the loyalty of the local Chinese, the Chou-Razak agreement seems to have set a pattern for resolving the overseas Chinese issue in Southeast Asia, namely, joint efforts to encourage the total assimilation of Chinese residents into local communities.

In April 1975, President Ferdinand Marcos issued an instruction to simplify procedures for acquiring Filipino citizenship by Chinese. Just before his trip to China, Marcos issued on June 6, 1975 a decree granting permanent residence to some 2,000 overstaying Chinese--another step toward the ultimate integration of thousands of overseas Chinese into Philippine society. [78] In his joint communique with Chou En-lai on June 9, 1975, normalizing Sino-Philippine relations, it was stated that both governments "consider any citizen of either country who acquires citizenship in the other country as automatically forfeiting his original citizenship. "[79]

The Sino-Thai joint communique of July 1, 1975, establishing diplomatic relations, also contained a provision concerning the overseas Chinese identical with the one cited in the Chou-Razak joint communique of 1974.[80] It is anticipated that over 300,000 Chinese residents in Thailand will become Thai citizens through simplified procedures for nationalization following the normalization of relations between Peking and Bangkok.[81]

CONCLUSIONS

The record of Peking's protecting Chinese nationals abroad is a mixed one. While officially committed to diplomatic protection, the PRC has fluctuated between hard and soft lines in its policy implementation. During 1949-53 and 1966-68, Peking adopted a militant posture in asserting the right of protection and in condemning foreign countries' mistreatment of overseas Chinese. In all the other years, however, it has been pragmatic, flexible, and selective in protecting nationals abroad.

One significant manifestation of Chinese pragmatism was the conclusion in 1955 of a dual nationality treaty with Indonesia. Although the treaty was later abrogated by Djakarta, Peking has continued to adhere to the twin policy lines developed in the mid-1950s: acceptance of the principle of voluntary option to settle the dual nationality issue and encouragement of the overseas Chinese to observe the laws and customs of the countries of their residence. This policy has recently been reaffirmed by the PRC when establishing diplomatic ties with Malaysia, the Philippines, and Thailand. In the long run, this enlightened approach will not only promote good relations between the PRC and its Asian neighbors but will also advance the genuine interest of the Chinese living in Southeast Asia.

In its controversies with other countries over the treatment of Chinese, the PRC has often evoked international law to boost its stand. The tendency is for official communications and pronouncements to dwell on generalities and for semiofficial spokesmen to provide detailed arguments and legal amplification. With respect to the methods of dispute resolution, Peking has shown a definite preference for bilateral negotiation and has consistently resisted the employment of an intermediary of third-party judgment.

When confronted with extreme provocations, the PRC has often coupled its protests with strong language and vague threats. Occasionally, it has used the cessation of economic and technical aid as retaliatory measures. But never has Peking threatened to use military force or to break diplomatic ties to back up its protests. At times, repatriation was resorted to as a form of protection, but, while offering temporary relief to the overseas Chinese under untenable conditions, it can hardly be used regularly for problem solving. Time and experience will eventually enable Peking to develop more effective means to protect Chinese nationals abroad. In the meantime, the PRC's current conciliatory policy toward the overseas Chinese issue is likely to create an atmosphere wherein occasions for diplomatic protection to arise may well be diminished.

NOTES

1. L. Oppenheim, International Law, 8th ed. (Lauterpacht) (London: Longmans, Green, 1955), vol. 1, pp. 686-87; W. G. Friedmann, O. J. Lissitzyn, and R. C. Pugh, International Law (St. Paul, Minn.: West Publishing Co., 1969), pp. 748-49. For special works on diplomatic protection and state responsibility regarding aliens, see E. M. Borchard, Diplomatic Protection of Citizens Abroad (New York: The Banks Law Publishing Company, 1915); F. S. Dunn, The Protection of Nationals (Baltimore: Johns Hopkins University Press, 1932); A. V. Freeman, The International Responsibility for Denial of Justice (London: Longmans, Green, 1938); and Gillian White, Nationalization of Foreign Property (New York: Praeger, 1961).

2. A number of such cases are available in Jerome A. Cohen and Hungdah Chiu, eds., People's China and International Law: A Documentary Study (Princeton, N.J.: Princeton University Press, 1974), vol. 1, chaps. 25, 26.

3. For the estimates of numbers of overseas Chinese in Southeast Asia, see Stephen Fitzgerald, China and the Overseas Chinese (Cambridge: Cambridge University Press, 1972), pp. 2-4, 196); Lea E. Williams, The Future of the Overseas Chinese in Southeast Asia (New York: McGraw-Hill, 1966), pp. 10-13.

4. For instance, Williams, op. cit.; and particularly Fitzgerald, op. cit.

5. The English texts of the Common Program and the constitution of 1954 are in A. P. Blaustein, ed., Fundamental Documents of Communist China (South Hackensack, N.J.: F. B. Rothman, 1962), pp. 1-53. For the constitution of 1975, see note 76 below.

6. Chun-hsi Wu, Dollars, Dependents and Dogma (Stanford, Calif.: Hoover Institution, 1967), p. 142.

7. Cohen and Chiu, op. cit., vol. 1, chap. 23, note following item 23-7; Tao-tai Hsia, "Settlement Between Communist China and Other Countries," Osteuropa Recht 2 (1965): 28, 34-35.

8. A. Doak Barnett, Communist China and Asia (New York: Harper, 1960), pp. 185-87.

9. Chou En-lai, "Report on the Work of the Government," People's China, no. 20 (1954): 24.

10. The Chinese text of the treaty is in Chung-hua jen-min
kung-ho kuo tiao-yueh chi, 1959 [Compilation of Treaties of the
People's Republic of China] (Peking, 1960), vol. 8, pp. 120-27
(hereafter cited as TYC). The English text is in Shao-chuan Leng
and Hungdah Chiu, eds., Law in Chinese Foreign Policy (Dobbs
Ferry, N.Y.: Oceana Publications, 1972), pp. 301-05.

11. "Exchange of Notes Between Indonesia and the People's
Republic of China on the Implementation of the Dual Nationality
Treaty, June 3, 1955," Ch'iao-wu cheng-t'se wen-chi [Collected
Documents on Overseas Chinese Policy] (Peking, 1957), pp. 29-33.

12. For various views on the treaty, see Barnett, op. cit.,
pp. 195-96; Fitzgerald, op. cit., pp. 107-10; Hsia, op. cit., pp.
32-36; David Mozingo, "The Sino-Indonesian Dual Nationality Treaty:
An Evaluation," Asian Forum, July/September 1970.

13. For instance, Wang Chi-yuan, "Nationality of Overseas
Chinese," People's China, no. 12 (1955): 9; "Another Example of
Resolving International Problems Through Peaceful Negotiations,"
editorial, Jen-min jih-pao [People's Daily], Peking, April 23, 1955.

14. David W. Willmatt, The National Status of the Chinese in
Indonesia: 1900-1958 (Ithaca, N.Y.: Cornell University Press,
pp. 44-66; D. P. Mozingo, Sino-Indonesian Relations: An Overview,
1955-1965 (Santa Monica, Calif.: Rand Corporation, 1965), pp. 22-29.

15. For the impact of the 1965 coup on the relations between
the two countries, see Justus M. Van der Kroef, "The Sino-Indonesian
Rupture," The China Quarterly, January-March 1968. According to
official Indonesian estimates in 1967, half of the 3 million persons of
Chinese origin were regarded as Chinese nationals and the other half
as Indonesian citizens. Ibid., p. 13.

16. "Sino-Nepalese Exchange of Notes on Several Matters Concerning Relations Between the People's Republic of China and the
Kingdom of Nepal, September 20, 1956," TYC, 1956 (1957), vol. 5,
pp. 7-9. For a discussion of this and other agreements between the
two countries, see Hsia, op. cit., pp. 28-30.

17. See Ch'iao-wu cheng t'se wen-chi, pp. 44-46, for the text
of Chou's interview with Marshall.

18. See ibid., pp. 1-10, for the text of Chou's speech.

19. Report by Fang Fang, vice chairman of the OCAC, to the
Chinese People's Political Consultative Conference, March 16, 1967,
in Jen-min shou tse, 1958 [People's Handbook] (Peking, 1958), p.
367; statement by Ho Hsiang-ning, chairman of the OCAC, 1949-59,
Ch'iao-wu pao [Overseas Chinese Affairs Journal], Peking, January
20, 1958, pp. 3-4. In an editorial, "Rational Settlement of the Dual
Nationality Problem of the Overseas Chinese," Jen-min jih-pao on
December 24, 1960 said that "it is irrational for the overseas Chinese to possess dual nationality."

20. Ho Hsiang-ning, New Year broadcast, January 1959, Ch'iao-wu cheng-ts'e wen-chi, p. 18; Liao Ch'eng chih (chairman of the OCAC since 1959), New Year broadcast, January 1966, New China News Agency, January 2, 1966.

21. For instance, during the Cultural Revolution, radical elements attacked Liao Ch'eng-chi's policy for overseas Chinese affairs as one of "capitulation" and of "betraying the interests of the overseas Chinese," Fitzgerald, op. cit., pp. 172-79.

22. For the Chinese approach to the principle of nonintervention, see Jerome A. Cohen, "China and Intervention: Theory and Practice," University of Pennsylvania Law Review (1973).

23. New China News Agency, July 23, 1952.

24. Fitzgerald, op. cit., pp. 95-96.

25. Jen-min jih-pao, October 6, 1954; for the English translation, see American Consulate General, Hong Kong, Current Background, no. 304 (November 10, 1954): 2-3.

26. Barnett, op. cit., p. 205.

27. New China News Agency, November 3, 1958. In the post-Bandung period, a treaty similar to the Sino-Indonesian Dual Nationality Treaty reportedly was offered to Thailand by the PRC, but Bangkok declined to discuss this issue with Peking. See David A. Wilson, China, Thailand and the Spirit of Bandung (Santa Monica, Calif.: Rand Corporation, 1962), pp. 56-57.

28. Bernard B. Fall, "Vietnam's Chinese Problem," Far Eastern Survey, May 1958, pp. 66-68.

29. Ho Hsiang-ning's statement and an editorial in Jen-min jih-pao, May 21, 1957; "Ngo Dinh Diem's Persecution of Overseas Chinese," People's China, no. 12 (1957): 40.

30. Barnett, op. cit., p. 206.

31. Michael Leifer, "Cambodia and China," in Policies Toward China: Views from Six Continents, ed. A. M. Halpern (New York: McGraw-Hill, 1965), p. 335.

32. Chou's advice to Chinese residents was contained in his joint statement with the premier of Cambodia on November 27, 1966. The text of the joint statement is in Jen-min shou-ts'e, 1958, p. 389.

33. New China News Agency, April 1 and 26, 1970.

34. Barnett, op. cit., pp. 206-07; William G. Skinner, "Overseas Chinese in Southeast Asia," Annals of the American Academy of Political and Social Science, January 1959, pp. 141-43.

35. Mozingo, Sino-Indonesian Relations, op. cit., p. 22; Justus M. Van der Kroef, "Indonesia's Economic Dilemma," Far Eastern Survey, April 1960, p. 58.

36. Indonesia--The Ban," Far Eastern Economic Review, December 24, 1959, pp. 1017-19; New York Times, November 18, 1959, p. 12; November 19, 1959, p. 3; December 12, 1959, p. 7; December 14, 1959, p. 3.

37. For similar statements also made by top officials of the All-China Federation of Returned Overseas Chinese, see New China News Agency, December 13 and December 16, 1959.

38. Jen-min jih-pao, December 12, 1959.

39. New China News Agency, December 25, 1959.

40. Ibid., March 17, 1960.

41. Fitzgerald, op. cit., p. 148; and Williams, op. cit., p. 66.

42. See Mary S. Somers Heidues, "Peking and the Overseas Chinese: The Malaysian Dispute," Asian Survey, May 1966, p. 284.

43. Oppenheim, op. cit., pp. 365-67; Friedmann, Lissitzyn, and Pugh, op. cit., pp. 782-96.

44. Herbert W. Briggs, ed., The Law of Nations, 2nd ed. (New York: Appleton-Century-Crofts, 1952), pp. 566-67.

45. David Mozingo, "China's Policy Toward Indonesia," in China's Policies in Asia and America's Alternatives, ed. Tang Tsou (Chicago: University of Chicago Press, 1958), pp. 344-45; Van der Kroef, "The Sino-Indonesian Rupture," op. cit., pp. 9, 16-17; China Quarterly, January-March 1966, p. 249, and April-June 1966, p. 223. In Medan, North Sumatra, for instance, some 200 Chinese of both Indonesian and Chinese citizenship were killed by Moslems using sticks and knives. See Donald Kirk, "Indonesia's Chinese Are People Without a Country," New York Times Magazine, October 23, 1966, p. 144.

46. The China Quarterly, July-September 1967, pp. 218-19; Van der Kroef, "The Sino-Indonesian Rupture, op. cit., pp. 16-19.

47. Ibid., p. 12.

48. Chinese protest of November 4, 1965, Peking Review, November 26, 1965, p. 21; Chinese protests of March 10, 1967, New China News Agency, March 13, 1967.

49. Chinese protest of November 27, 1965, Peking Review, December 3, 1965, p. 10; Chinese protest of March 10, 1966, ibid., March 18, 1966, pp. 5-6; Chinese protest of July 1, 1967, American Consulate General, Hong Kong, Survey of China Mainland Press, no. 3975 (July 7, 1967): 46.

50. Peking Review, November 26, 1965, pp. 21-22; ibid., December 3, 1965, pp. 9-10; ibid., March 18, 1966, pp. 5-6.

51. Survey of China Mainland Press, no. 3929 (May 1, 1967): 28; no. 3975 (July 7, 1967): 45-46.

52. Van der Kroef, "The Sino-Indonesian Rupture," op. cit., p. 21; Mozingo, "China's Policy Toward Indonesia," op. cit., p. 345.

53. Peking Review, April 7, 1967, p. 37; Jen-min jih-pao, September 25, 1967.

54. Van der Kroef, "The Sino-Indonesian Rupture," op. cit., p. 15; China Quarterly, July-September 1967, p. 219, October-December 1967, p. 193.

55. Mozingo, "China's Policy Toward Indonesia," op. cit.,
p. 346.

56. See, for example, Robert A. Scalapino, "The Cultural
Revolution and Chinese Foreign Policy," Current Scene, August 1,
1968.

57. New York Times, June 27, 1967, p. 3; June 24, 1967, p.
3; June 24, 1967, p. 1; Peter Van Ness, Revolution and Chinese Foreign Policy (Berkeley: University of California Press, 1970), pp.
225-26.

58. Ibid., p. 226; "From Coexistence to Condemnation; the
New Chinese View of Burma," Current Scene, October 17, 1967, pp.
22, 5-6.

59. Chinese protest, June 28, 1967, New China News Agency,
June 28, 1967; Chinese protest, July 4, 1967, New China News
Agency, July 4, 1967.

60. Chinese note, July 25, 1967, New China News Agency,
July 26, 1967. Later, Peking proposed to send an investigation and
relief mission to Burma. Again Rangoon refused permission. New
China News Agency, September 1 and 6, 1967.

61. Chinese protest, July 5, 1967, New China News Agency,
July 5, 1967; Chinese protest, July 20, 1967, New China News
Agency, July 25, 1967.

62. Chinese note, July 3, 1967, New China News Agency, July
4, 1967; Chinese note, September 4, 1967, New China News Agency,
September 6, 1967; Chinese note, November 23, 1967, New China
News Agency, November 24, 1967.

63. Van Ness, op. cit., p. 226; "From Coexistence to Condemnation," op. cit., p. 3.

64. "China's Foreign Policy and International Position During
a Year of Cultural Revolution," Current Scene, December 1, 1967,
p. 8.

65. New China News Agency, July 4, July 25, and August 20,
1967; Jen-min jih-pao, July 10 (editorial) and July 25 (commentary),
1967.

66. Fitzgerald, op. cit., p. 171; New China News Agency,
November 24, 1967 and March 30, 1968.

67. For details, see J. A. Cohen and Shao-chuan Leng, "The
Sino-Indian Dispute Over the Internment and Detention of Chinese in
India," in Chinese Practice of International Law: Some Case Studies,
ed. J. A. Cohen (Cambridge, Mass.: Harvard University Press,
1972), pp. 273-79.

68. For instance, Chinese Foreign Ministry's note, November
24, 1962, in Indian Ministry of External Affairs, ed., White Paper
(New Delhi) 8 (1962): 99.

69. Chinese Foreign Ministry's note, December 18, 1962, ibid. , p. 105.

70. See Chou Keng-sheng, "The Persecution of Chinese Nationals and Infringement of the Right of China to Protect Chinese Nationals Are Serious Internationally Illegal Acts," Jen-min jih-pao, January 22, 1963.

71. For the PRC's position, see its note to India, December 18, 1962, in White Paper, p. 107. Chinese legal arguments in this respect appear to be less persuasive than over other issues. For a legal analysis of Chinese claims, see Cohen and Leng, op. cit. , pp. 294-308, 318-19.

72. White Paper 10, pp. 64, 65.

73. Lok Sabha Debates, 3rd Ser./5th Sess. 14 (1963): 368.

74. Chung-kung nien-pao, 1973 [Yearbook on Chinese Communism, 1973] (Taipei: Institute for the Study of Chinese Communist Problems, 1973), pt. 3, p. 31.

75. New China News Agency, September 29, 1972.

76. For the relevant part of the constitution, see Peking Review, January 24, 1975, p. 15. For an analysis of the 1975 constitution, see Chün-tu Hsüeh, "The New Constitution," Problems of Communism (Washington), May-June 1975, pp. 11-19.

77. For the text of the joint communique, see Peking Review, June 7, 1974, p. 8.

78. South China Morning Post (Hong Kong), June 7, 1975.

79. Peking Review, June 13, 1975, p. 8.

80. Ibid. , July 4, 1975, p. 9.

81. Ming pao (Hong Kong), June 5, 1975.

10

DEFENSE OF DIPLOMATIC FUNCTIONS AND IDEALS DURING THE CULTURAL REVOLUTION: THE NEPAL CASE

Roger L. Dial

In our compulsion to see international relations in terms of states as actors or individual leaders as actors, we often forget that most states maintain foreign affairs bureaucracies. What is more, in a strict empirical sense it is these bureaucratic organizations rather than "the state" or "the leader" that act out most international relationships. The normal functions of a diplomatic bureaucracy (that is, the foreign office and related organizations) are not easy to summarize; nonetheless, we must try to do so here as a foundation for considering bureaucratic behavior in a specific "abormal" time.

It may be said that the first task of a foreign affairs bureaucracy is to put the international relations of a state on a firm, realistic basis. First and foremost, foreign offices (in particular their embassy appendages) are information gatherers. At optimum efficiency, they take the guesswork or idiosyncratic intuition out of foreign policy formulation.* Secondly, foreign affairs bureaucracies facilitate the compromise of interests among states, that is, the negotiation process.† Third, and somewhat more broadly speaking, they "develop" relations between states by cultivating more and

---

*Elsewhere, applying Weberian notions of the potency of the "rational bureaucratic form," I have argued that this information gathering function, in part, has given the Chinese foreign relations bureaucracy a strong hand in the actual formulation of Chinese foreign policy.[1]

†It may also be said that foreign affairs bureaucracies facilitate the compromise of interests between states by developing strategies for controlling the foreign policy interests and demands of their domestic constituents.[2]

richer exchanges at a variety of levels.* Fourth, and largely as a
product of their "developmental" function, a foreign affairs bureaucracy seeks to maintain some level of basic stability in relations between states.

A key to stability, it would appear, is to be found in the multi-
dimensionality of relations between states. That is to say, states
that interact at a variety of levels (for example, government-to-
government, people-to-people, and perhaps party-to-party) and have
a relationship in a variety of functional areas (trade, political affiliation, foreign aid, cultural exchanges, military exchange, and so on)
tend to have a more stable and continuous overall relationship. Even
serious tensions or failures at one level or in one functional area are
generally offset by the broader scheme of positive interactions.
Suitable examples of this stability dynamic may be found in the cases
of Anglo-American relations or Canadian-American relations.

Diplomatic bureaucracies, then, cultivate and manage stable
multidimensional relations between states. Within the overall pa-
rameters of such stability they may pursue the interests of their
governments to the best effect. It is also the case that diplomatic
bureaucracies develop an organizational stake in the various mech-
anisms of multidimensional interaction in the same way that organizational stakes are developed in other functional organizational
areas.[3] Similarly, it can be argued that, generally speaking, diplomatic organizations develop an ethical perspective on their functions.
Few diplomats or professional international relators would argue
that instability is the preferred state of relations between states.
From the truly professional diplomatic perspective, military crises
or wars are pathological situations in international relations, and
are typically beyond the functional orientation or competence of foreign affairs bureaucracies. Normalcy, or multidimensional stability, then, is the ideal pattern of life for a foreign affairs bureaucracy; such a pattern is worth building and worth protecting.

Between 1956 and 1966, the Chinese foreign relations bureaucracy had put Sino-Nepalese relations on such a footing. Sino-
Nepalese interactions were multidimensional, including political
exchanges, both officially and unofficially, and exchanges in trade,
aid, culture, education, transportation, and so on. What is more,
these exchanges took place simultaneously at multiple levels: government-to-government, people-to-people, and party-to-party. It was

---

*There are, of course, situations in which State A maintains a
"correct," but nothing more, relationship with State B. Though this
is an interesting situation from an organization theory perspective,
it will not be our focus here.

the Chinese foreign relations bureaucracy that cultivated, imple-
mented, and, to some extent, coordinated these complex sets of
interstate relations. What is more, the sheer complexity or multi-
dimensionality of interaction did account, in large measure, for the
overall stability and continuity in Sino-Nepalese relations. Failures
or tensions (and there were several) at one level or in one functional
area were always offset by the broader scheme of positive interaction. From the perspective of the Chinese foreign relations bureaucracy, Nepal was a success story. [4]

However, normalcy is not always maintained. International
relations also have their periods of crises. The Cultural Revolution
in China is one type of crisis situation. Though perhaps not as common as international crises rising out of interstate conflict of interest, the Cultural Revolution, as a source of interstate crisis, is not
unparalleled in other times and other places. Domestic upheavals do
very often radically affect foreign affairs. Our question here, then,
is how does a diplomatic bureaucracy behave in such a situation?
How does such an organization relate the ideal of functional diplomatic stability abroad to a stressful and antagonistic domestic environment?

One level of empirical analysis is to focus on the behavioral
response of a single diplomat in a stress situation. In the case of
the Cultural Revolution, C. P. Fitzgerald has written:

> Chinese diplomats abroad were placed in a very
> difficult situation by the Cultural Revolution. They
> learned that at home people like themselves were
> under attack, denunciation, and sometimes physi-
> cal assault. Even to ride in an official car had
> provoked Red Guard rage and violence. In foreign,
> above all Western, capitals, the Chinese staff,
> although having few contacts among their col-
> leagues or the general population, still certainly
> lived like diplomats. They dressed in foreign
> clothes, rode in cars, dwelt in good houses.
> They mixed to some extent with "bourgeois"
> people, even if only in the course of duty. All
> this was highly dangerous. At any moment some
> zealous employee might (and some did) denounce
> his ambassador as a revisionist, a bourgeois, a
> secret supporter of Liu Shao-ch'i. It became es-
> sential to make some clear and public demonstra-
> tion of the purity of their Maoist thinking, and
> the most obvious way to get this message across,
> by means of the world press, was a brawl with

the London police, the representatives of the bourgeois imperialist regime. A few broken heads and
bruised limbs were a small price to pay for demonstrating true revolutionary zeal and complete adherence to the Cultural Revolution.[5]

Fitzgerald's analysis essentially rests on implicit notions of
the personal or individual psychological response to stress. That is,
in a critical and turbulent environment, the individual under threat
acts to defend himself--specifically, in this case, by espousing the
line of his attackers. This strikes me as a highly reasonable form
of analysis and one that might also be usefully applied to earlier
periods in the history of China's external affairs. It does, however,
deserve to be built upon, both conceptually and empirically. For instance, although Fitzgerald implies that the Chinese diplomats came
to adhere to the line of their assailants, this was not necessarily the
case. We are left with an interesting research question: If the Chinese diplomat defends himself by adopting the fiery rhetoric of his
potential assailants, why (and how) does he not generally in fact do
as his assailants would have him do with respect to actual foreign
affairs business, that is, reduce foreign relations to a single dimension of revolutionary action? This strange behavior/rhetoric contradiction has aptly been sloganized by China's Red Guard as "waving
the red flag while opposing the red flag."

To get at this contradiction in diplomatic behavior, let us move
the focus from Fitzgerald's individual diplomat to a focus on the diplomatic organization. What follows is not meant to be a fully developed organization "theory" analysis; it is at best only an eclectic expansion of Fitzgerald's perspective by borrowing in a very limited
fashion from organization theory. The two concepts we shall apply
are those of staff functions and line functions. Staff and line functionaries, of course, fulfill a multitude of tasks within any organization. We usually concern ourselves with line officials (the "bosses")
when our interests are policy making, recruitment, command communications, and so on. On the other hand, staff functions are generally considered those of functional specialization, expert problem
solving, information seeking, and so on.

For our purposes here, we need only consider one line role--
that of organizational defense. It is the task of the line officer, at
any level, to ensure that his staff functionaries can devote their en-
ergies to their assigned information-seeking and problem-solving
areas without fear or interference from the outside. If staff members need to be disciplined, then it is conducive to organizational
stability for the line official to do so, not some outside authority.
If authorities external to the organization (that is, its constituents)

are dissatisfied with organizational performance, then it is expected
that the line officials of that organization will assume the responsibility, and that the staff-level actors will not be thrown in disarray.
Such disarray would limit the organization's effectiveness. In short,
"bosses" (line officers) can come and go, but a high degree of continuity is essential for efficient staff functioning. The Cultural Revolution situation is one that defies this well-understood logic of organizational change and effectiveness. Here, one constituent-
environment (the Maoists) of the Chinese foreign relations bureaucracy sought to remove the "natural" line defense functionaries of
the organization at all levels and personally reorient the staff functionaries. Let us look at these developments in the context of Chinese diplomatic behavior in Nepal.

PHASE I: A COORDINATED BUREAUCRATIC
STRATEGY OF DEFENSE

It was no mere accident that the original guidelines for the Cultural Revolution proscribed any Red Guard penetration of economic
and governmental organs essential to the state.[6] While the Party
organization was to be reformed, dysfunctional spillovers into the
mainstay organs of state were to be minimized. Obviously, since
most of the top-ranking line actors in China's economic and governmental enterprises were also ranking Party authorities, there would
be some disruptions as these people were attacked, removed, or reformed. By the fall of 1966, those intent upon having a thorough-
going purge of "capitalist roaders" in the Party came to realize that
the accused individuals were literally taking refuge in their statist-
government functions, and that the battleground must shift if the sus-
pects were to be brought to account. In November 1966, the shift
came home to the Chinese foreign relations bureaucracy as Foreign
Minister Ch'en Yi came under Red Guard attack for his ideological
backsliding tendencies.

The attack on Ch'en Yi was not primarily one on the Chinese
foreign relations bureaucracy or the job it was doing, but rather on
the general bureaucratic tendencies of the foreign minister and his
immediate coterie.[7] Only later was it to be asserted that these tendencies had consequences for actual Chinese foreign policy. At the
outset, Ch'en resorted to a defense tactic by mobilizing hand-picked
work teams to criticize and repress the Red Guards within his
bureaucratic system.[8] Consequently, he was brought to public account by the end of 1966.

Beginning in December, a new defense ploy was adopted. As
the Red Guard investigations of Ch'en Yi proceeded, Chinese officials

serving abroad began a piecemeal return. In some missions the
secondary line officials (counselors and so on) rather than the ambassadors returned. This was the case in Nepal where Ambassador
Yang Kung-shu was a particularly vital component of the embassy.
In January 1967, 14 members of the Chinese diplomatic staff in Nepal
returned to China. [9] At the same time, Ch'en Yi began his "confession."

The confession, and presumably those given by lesser officials
who had been on the "caviar circuit," was, in retrospect, a sham.
For Ch'en Yi, the individual, and other line functionaries, it was, as
Fitzgerald put it, "a small price to pay for demonstrating true revolutionary zeal." It was an equally small price to pay for the defense
of a bureaucracy that had brought stability to China's foreign relations. Victory, however, was not complete, for a new antibureau-
cratic instrument had been established during the hiatus in effective
line defense of the organization. [10]

The Revolutionary Rebel Liaison Station had been created to
monitor and inspect the business of the Ministry of Foreign Affairs.
It was, in our theoretical terms, a control agency of an external
group planted within the Ministry of Foreign Affairs, and was, therefore, a means of bypassing the responsibility of the top line official,
Ch'en Yi. New defense repertoires were in order lest the staff work
of the foreign relations bureaucracy be upset.

It would appear that at the Foreign Ministry in Peking, Ch'en
and a select group of department heads moved fast to restore their
control. Their confessions had been well received, and their "revolutionary credentials" were in apparent good order. The trouble-
makers within the foreign affairs organs were removed, old hands
restored, and "responsible" people put in the Liaison Station. All
of these moves, the latter one in particular, were characterized by
Ch'en's rather arrogant manner. In fact, by virtue of a February 3,
1967, order issued in the name of the Central Committee, the Liaison
Station in the Ministry of Foreign Affairs was to have been abolished. [11]
While at first a potential threat to Ch'en, this organ had been taken
over by him and made a part of his organization defense system. He
continued to ignore the dissolution order. Red Guards would later
cite this as evidence that he ran the bureaucracy as an "independent
kingdom."

Meanwhile, another aspect of the Chinese foreign relations
bureaucracy defense repertoire centered on missions abroad. While
many Chinese officials were returning home, sufficient "responsible"
(line) diplomats remained at their posts abroad. The maintenance of
stable foreign relations required that this be the case, and this was
precisely what the organization leaders sought to preserve. To head
off a general recall of officials abroad, those who remained at their

posts were obliged (called upon?) to establish their revolutionary
credentials under the somewhat more difficult circumstances of foreign service. Thus, for example, we find Ambassador Yang on January 29 giving a speech in Kathmandu's National Theatre Hall, violently assailing U.S. imperialists, Soviet revisionists, and reactionaries among the top leaders of the Chinese Communist Party. [12]
The substance and tenor of the speech seemed irrelevant to Nepalis,
but, of course, the speech was not essentially for Nepali benefit.
From the Nepali perspective, such rhetoric was essentially regarded
as curious, not threatening. And, as such, this device--violent
rhetorical attack on safe shibboleths while pursuing one's diplomatic
duties without substantive change--saw repeated use throughout the
Cultural Revolutionary period.

    Back in Peking, other vital bureaucratic functions came under
attack and required defense. It is now well known that the hardest-
hit organs of state during the Cultural Revolution were those dealing
in propaganda functions. [13] In the foreign affairs bureaucracy, the
propaganda organs were similarly vulnerable, and the line officials
in those organs were among the first to come under attack, for example, Lo Chun, director of the Foreign Language Press. During
the Cultural Revolution, the Foreign Language Press and its leading
organs, such as the Peking Review, were to serve as the convenient
recording place for the "true revolutionary zeal" of China's diplomatic establishment. One might suppose, of course, that if the objective was to maintain stable relations, then expressing revolutionary zeal in print was preferable to doing so in actual foreign service.
However, as an organizational defense repertoire, even this had some
unfortunate repercussions in Nepal, where Chinese publications are
widely distributed.

    The January 27, 1967, issue of Peking Review carried a col-
umn entitled "International Fighters in the Service of the World's
Peoples: Afro-Asian Peoples Praise Chinese Experts Educated by
Mao Tse-tung's Thought." The title more or less tells the story.
The objective was to establish that Chinese cadre serving abroad
were not living bourgeois lives, but rather were serving the masses.
In this initial piece there was no claim that the many hundreds of
Chinese experts abroad were making revolution in the strict sense,
that is, agitation, organization, and subversion. Rather, it was the
proletarian virtues of hard work, plain living, equal wages with in-
digenous technicians, and heroic individual acts that were emphasized. The article was essentially factual and testimonial, rather
than polemical. It concluded with a statement of praise by three
"friends" from Mali, Tanzania, and Nepal. Reportedly, the Nepali
friend said: "The Chinese people are our dear friends whom we can
trust. We love New China dearly, we dearly love Chairman Mao."[14]

On the same day in Nepal, Ambassador Yang Kung-shu donated Rs. 50,000 to the Nepal Medical Association.[15] The one-line indiscretion in Peking Review drew no press comment from Nepal. In January 1967, Chinese deeds, not words, better symbolized the relationship from the Nepali perspective. In China, however, the carefully conceived words of January 27 were insufficient proof of the diplomatic establishment's support for revolution and the thought of Mao.*

The February 10 issue of Peking Review institutionalized a regular weekly feature entitled "The World's People Love Chairman Mao."† What had been the one-line conclusion to the January 27 article was to become the whole substance of this new weekly column. The Foreign Language Press line officials, such as Lo Chun, were under repeated attack throughout the spring. Under the circumstances, one might have expected the propaganda escalation that came with this new column. That these organs were under extraordinary surveillance became evident in April when Red Guard attacks were resumed on Ch'en Yi. The foreign minister's defense of Lo Chun was later heavily criticized.[16]

On two occasions during February and March, Nepal was dragged into the Cultural Revolutionary game being pursued in Peking Review. The first appearance depicted some Nepalis saluting a photographic display of Mao in Kathmandu. The caption asserted, "Nepalese friends acclaim Chairman Mao as the red sun in the hearts of the world's people."[17] The second appearance came in the form of a poem, supposedly written by a Nepalese journalist:

"In This Fight, Teacher, I Assure You . . ."
by a Nepalese Journalist

After Marx and Lenin, Friend!
Mao Tse-tung, new teacher of mankind, has appeared!
He is not only leader of China. To us
He is also leader of all the oppressed.
Revolution never dies nor does the history of peoples.
Mao Tse-tung's brilliant teachings on revolution,
On the history of peoples, will live for ever
And continue to vitalize the revolution.

---

*There were, no doubt, other reasons for the escalation of revolutionary rhetoric after the January 27 issue, including the desire in certain quarters to shore up the internal Maoist struggle by creating the impression that the events inside China were merely part of a general international revolutionary upsurge.

†The column title was later changed to "Mao Tse-tung's Thought Lights Up the Whole World."

As followers of Marx and Lenin
We equally take pride in calling and claiming
   ourselves to be
True followers of Mao Tse-tung as well,
By action and not by word or name.
We pledge you, our teacher Mao Tse-tung,
That we will fight U.S. imperialism to the end!
The exploited peasants and youth of Nepal
Have an ardent love and admiration for you!
All revolutionaries are with China's new revolution
In this fight, Teacher, I assure you![18]

While the Nepali press reaction was not uniform (the government-backed news services completely ignored the issue), it was
treated in some quarters. The Motherland editorialized: "This
type of publicity does more harm than good to Nepal-China friendship, which is being strengthened through mutual cooperation."[19]
Nepal Samachar's nationalistic reaction was, "friends of Nepal
should understand that for the Nepalis it is His Majesty who stands
head and shoulder above any other person."[20] Naya Sandesh (Weekly)
asserted, "Mao Tse-tung is not the leader of Nepal, nor can he ever
become so. This journalist, who wants to please Mao Tse-tung, is
a traitor and deserves severe punishment . . . it is regrettable that
a nation which is friendly to Nepal should have publicized the product
of such an unbalanced brain and thus adopted an irresponsible policy
towards Nepal."[21] However, no serious damage had been done to
Sino-Nepalese relations; for the time being, the editorials remained
embedded in a larger array of positive reports on Chinese aid projects, cultural agreements, and trade. Nonetheless, this type of organizational defense for the Chinese foreign relations bureaucracy
had definitely begun to taint China's public image in Nepal.

    During the first week of April, the Red Guards renewed their
attack on the foreign relations bureaucracy and its leading line officials, including the foreign minister, several vice ministers, and
department heads. Although in February, Ch'en Yi had taken a lead
in verbal attacks on the Soviet Union,[22] and had paid long praise to
Mao in a number of official diplomatic functions (including a reception at the Nepal embassy honoring the Kingdom's National Day),[23]
his overall behavior was one of restoring the old order in the ministry and related organs. A new Revolutionary Liaison Station was established by the leftists to monitor the performance of "diplomatic
workers." On April 19, Ch'en was relieved of his foreign ministerial
functions and placed at the full disposal of his assailants.[24]

    Chou En-lai assumed the ultimate responsibility for external
relations, but the actual output of the ministry itself reflected the

power struggle between the new Liaison Station and the beleaguered line officials at the departmental level. Organizational defenses were collapsing fast, and the bureaucratic center was being penetrated by leftist agitation right to its core "staff" functions. On May 13, the ministry was, in fact, invaded physically by Red Guards; files were opened, staff assaulted, and extensive documentary evidence against professionalism and revisionism in China's diplomatic establishment gathered.[25] Even Chou En-lai, protector of the essential state bureaucracies in general and the foreign affairs system in particular, was incapable of defying the overwhelming left trend of these months.*

Thus, during May, June, July, and early August the situation in China's foreign affairs system was reduced to a situation of "every man for himself." The normal processes of organization defense exercised by line officials had collapsed completely, and China's foreign affairs personnel, from the minister to the lowest file clerk, were obliged to demonstrate their revolutionary faith through all manner of unfamiliar and unprofessional ritual.

PHASE II: "EVERY EMBASSY FOR ITSELF"

In the missions abroad, the situation was less dire. However, the remoteness, which was ironically an important line of defense, also engendered suspicion and confusion. Although the work of several hundred Chinese officials and technicians in Nepal was proceeding according to plan on various projects, some of these foreign relators took on extracurricular activities proselytizing Mao's wisdom among Nepali colleagues and nearby peasants. There is no evidence that such activity was coordinated; and, if it was, one might suppose the coordinators to have been the remaining line officials of the Chinese embassy seeking to "wave the red flag to oppose the red flag." Orders from Peking were apparently contradictory and confused, and the Chinese in Nepal, line and staff alike, no doubt sought to build into their performance records whatever ideological insurance

---

*Following the sacking of the Ministry of Foreign Affairs, Chou was able to win support from colleagues within the Central Cultural Revolutionary Group for a general order that Ch'en Yi, Ch'iao Kuan-hua, and Chi P'eng-fei could not be removed from office (although they were functionally already out) without sanction from the top, and that three months only would be allowed for criticism and reform of these individuals. At the end of that period they would be restored to normal duties.[26]

they could (short of destroying the multidimensional stability of Sino-Nepalese relations) in the event that the left succeeded in reorganizing completely China's external affairs bureaucracy.

Furthermore, the level of such revolutionary extracurricular activities in Nepal during this four- to five-month period cannot be said to have been excessively high. It was, to be sure, a theme played on in the Nepali press for several weeks, and some papers urged His Majesty's government to stop visiting Chinese technicians from engaging in propagandistic activity at their project sites. However, with one exception, there were no full-scale public incidents. The exception came in late April when a bridge over the Sunkosi River collapsed, killing several Nepali peasants. Reportedly, they were returning from propaganda films being shown by the Chinese staff on the nearby hydroelectric project. The government-backed press, Gorkhapatra, reported the event, but simply referred to the activity as a film exhibit.[27] The same issue of the paper also carried a lengthy report on the progress of the Sunkosi development project. However, while the government sought to overlook the incident, several other papers did not. The showing of propaganda films was asserted to be subversive, and His Majesty's government was again urged to restrict such activities on the part of "certain" foreign technicians.[28]

The main focus of attention in Sino-Nepali relations in May 1967 was the inauguration of the Kodari Highway (linking Tibet and central Nepal). This was clearly an occasion that required a high-ranking Chinese representative. However, the peculiar stage of the Cultural Revolution complicated such matters of protocol. It was announced that Fang I, the chairman of China's aid bureaucracy (Commission for Economic Relations with Foreign Countries) would preside along with King Mahendra.[29] However, on May 8, Fang came under Red Guard attack, and a replacement for the mission was found in Lin Hai-yun, acting minister of foreign trade. Only in retrospect is it clear that Lin, along with a few scientists and military people, was exempt from Red Guard harassment throughout the Cultural Revolution. At the same time, Fang I, almost alone among the top half-dozen line officials in the Chinese foreign relations bureaucracy, had not come under criticism until the heightened crisis of May 1967.* Thus, it is not surprising that even a seemingly "protected" line official such as Lin took precautions to salt his public performances in Nepal with diatribes for reactionaries, imperialists, and revisionists at home and abroad.[30] Lin was

---

*Fang I, incidentally, was to maintain his alternate membership in the Ninth Central Committee announced in April 1969.

perhaps the foremost ranking foreign trade negotiator in the Chinese foreign relations bureaucracy. He was by no means an ideologue and had in the past been very closely identified with the most "professional" approach to international trade--business with any nation, if they have something to offer, regardless of politics.[31] However, his demonstrable Maoism was well conceived in terms of the safe shibboleths used earlier by Ambassador Yang, and thus inoffensive to the Nepalese.

In Peking, the Kodari inauguration ceremony was presented in a more ideological light. To the dissatisfaction of some Nepalis, the editors of Peking Review reported: "Many Nepalese people said that it was Chairman Mao who had sent the experts to help Nepal build the highway. They shouted: 'The great leader, Chairman Mao, is the red sun which shines most brightly in the hearts of the people of the whole world.'"[32]

The desire of Chinese diplomats in Nepal to satisfy their personal and organizational defense requirements without upsetting the stable patterns of interstate relationship became very apparent during the so-called Gaucher affair. On June 18, Ambassador Yang Kung-shu led a group of 300 Chinese diplomats and technicians to Kathmandu's Gaucher Airport to greet a party of Chinese diplomats who had been expelled from New Delhi and were to stop over in Nepal.[33] These "red diplomatic fighters," like colleagues in London, Burma, and Indonesia, had seen physical combat at their overseas post and were viewed by the Maoists at home as symbols of the true revolutionary spirit (their self-perception may have been better characterized by C. P. Fitzgerald).

For the official Chinese community in Nepal, it was, of course, a prime opportunity to demonstrate their own revolutionary spirit. Whether or not the ambassador was ordered (by some faction in the ministry in Peking) to make a show of support for these "soldiers in Chairman Mao's diplomatic army" is unknown and probably unimportant. A better mechanism could hardly have been found for the defense needs of the local Chinese diplomatic community.

Where the Gaucher affair had its advantage as an organizational defense repertoire was in its relationship to the Nepali community. There was the potential for maximum control (the airport is outside the city) and minimum spillover into Nepalese affairs. That the demonstration was well planned by Chinese line officials in Nepal is evident in the number of Chinese participants. Numerous aid technicians on projects throughout Nepal were brought into Kathmandu to participate. The simple logistics of such a maneuver would require at least several days advance organizing. By comparison, there were only a dozen Nepalis present, led by Purna

Bahadur, chairman of the Sino-Nepali Friendship Committee.* Apparently even the whole membership of the Friendship Association was not notified or mobilized for the demonstration. Furthermore, the local Maoists were purposely kept in the dark, lest they make an appearance and complicate matters for local Chinese officials. It seems apparent that Yang's objective was to have a discretely Chinese demonstration of support for the returning "heroes" of the Delhi mission, which would be well reported in China, but would have no spillover effects in the Nepali community. However, complications arose.

As approximately 300 Chinese chanted Maoist slogans and waved their red books, the plane from Delhi arrived. To the very apparent surprise of Ambassador Yang, the heroes of Delhi were not aboard.[35] After demonstrating his concern by leading a thorough search of the aircraft, Yang dismissed the crowd. An additional complication had arisen when the plane was required to make a prior emergency stop in Patna, keeping the demonstrators at Gaucher airport several extra hours. Local publicity increased proportionately. The immediate effect of the whole fiasco was to supply considerable ammunition to the local pro-Indian press.[36] The government-run press ignored the incident and His Majesty's government made no comment.

A week later, the scene was remade, and this time the expelled officials from Delhi arrived on schedule. Because many of the Chinese technicians had returned to their projects, the crowd was somewhat reduced (approximately 200).[37] The publicity of the previous week also had the effect of mobilizing 30 or so of Nepal's more militant elements.[38] The crowd reportedly chanted, "Farewell to red diplomats tortured by aggressive Indians" and "Down with all anti-Chinese reactionaries," but was orderly and dispersed without further ado.[39] Again some of the local press condemned China's verbal attack on India from Nepali soil, and the government was urged (criticized) to take measures against such misuse of diplomatic privilege.[40] Again His Majesty's government and the government press network expressed no public comment. Later, as we shall see, the deputy chairman of the Government Council discussed the incident before the National Panchayat.

What had potentially been an uncomplicated organizational defense operation in fact escalated into a threat to the stability of Sino-Nepalese relations. The maneuvers of the Chinese ambassador and

*Also in the group was Bhuwan Lal Pradhan, a former minister of His Majesty's government. The small Nepali contingent was most likely selected for its respectability.[34]

his staff, though discreet in intention, were taken as a hostile indiscretion by segments of the Nepali community and surely by certain other embassies in Kathmandu. Both the American and Indian missions registered complaints with His Majesty's government about Chinese printed and verbal assaults on their countries. On June 27, His Majesty's government was obliged to circulate a general "request" to the missions in Kathmandu that all parties refrain from pursuing third-party disputes and polemics while in diplomatic residence in Nepal. At the same time, a potpourri of hostile Nepali forces began to mobilize to confront the Chinese diplomatic groups in Nepal. The allegiances of these forces remain unclear and were probably mixed--genuine, albeit extreme, Nepali nationalists, pro-Indian, pro-Soviet Communists, and so on.

On July 1, at a "fun fair" to celebrate His Majesty's birthday, an anti-Chinese demonstration broke out in front of the Chinese "propaganda stall" (alternatively reported: "literature display"). Nepali Maoists came to the defense of the display, apparently spontaneously.[41] Although Nepalese police broke up the disturbance, the "nationalist" youth formed a "chanting procession" (alternately: "mob"), returned to the city, burned a Chinese vehicle, and sacked the Nepal-China Friendship Association Bookstore in Kathmandu.[42] The following day (July 2), Ambassador Yang met with Foreign Secretary J. N. Singh, though, according to a Foreign Ministry spokesman, no Chinese protest was submitted.[43] It would appear that the Chinese ambassador merely wanted to make clear that the Chinese mission was not responsible for the acts of Nepali Maoists, and that he wished to make nothing of the unfortunate anti-Chinese demonstration. The personal cordiality existing between the Chinese ambassador and Nepalese officials would be evident at several junctures in the ensuing three weeks and particularly in Chairman (Deputy Prime Minister) Bisht's report to the National Panchayat on July 13.

At this point we must again recall the situation at the Ministry of Foreign Affairs in Peking. The regular line officials of the bureaucracy were absent, and authority, though confused, was essentially divided between genuine ardent Maoists and those obliged to pretend to be ardent Maoists. At the highest level it has also been established that Wang Li, a member of the Cultural Revolutionary Group, and Yao Teng-shan, repatrioted "hero" of China's diplomatic melee in Indonesia, were moving rapidly forward with a plan to completely oust Ch'en Yi from the foreign ministership and probably Chou En-lai from his beleaguered position. In August, Yao was, in fact, to seize the foreign ministership for a two-week period. The coup would prove to be abortive, and Wang, as well as Yao, would be purged in the fall as Chou En-lai and Ch'en Yi came back to authority with a new moderate phase of the Cultural Revolution. However, in July, the anti-Chinese demonstrations in Nepal came to the Maoists in the Foreign Ministry as a blessing in their attempt to brand Ch'en with having followed the revisionist Liu-Teng (Liu Shao-ch'i Teng Hsiao-p'ing) line in foreign policy.

On July 5, Ambassador Yang received instructions from Peking. Confusion was such in the ministry that the exact author of the protest is unknown, and was quite possibly just as unknown to Yang at the time. The ambassador dutifully delivered the official protest, which, among other things, charged the Nepali government with "conniving" with anti-Chinese forces. There was no response from His Majesty's government. In fact, His Majesty's government was never to make a public response to the July 5 Chinese note (in contrast to Burmese and Indian responses to similar bombasts from China's Ministry of Foreign Affairs).

If His Majesty's government and the Chinese mission in Kathmandu sought to sweep the crisis under the rug, elements in Peking who wished to reduce Sino-Nepalese relations to a single revolutionary dimension persisted in exacerbating conditions. On July 9, the New China News Agency launched a most provocative attack on the Nepal government. The article was also carried in the Peking Review and is worth quoting in its entirety:

> Protest Against Nepalese Government
> Connivance at Anti-China Outrage
>
> On the evening of July 1, a group of Nepalese hooli-
> gans, instigated and directed by U.S. imperialism,
> Soviet revisionism and the Indian reactionaries,
> and with the connivance of the Nepalese Govern-
> ment, carried out anti-China activities in front of
> the Chinese photo exhibition hall in Kathmandu.
> They made several attempts to break into the ex-
> hibition hall, clamouring hysterically for removal
> of the portrait of the Chinese people's great leader,
> Chairman Mao, and of the Chinese national flag.
> They shouted anti-China slogans and viciously in-
> sulted Chairman Mao, the red sun that shines most
> brightly in the hearts of the Chinese people.
> Nepalese progressive students, who cherish
> boundless love for Chairman Mao, the great teach-
> er of the world revolutionary people, and treasure
> the friendship between the Nepalese and Chinese
> peoples, rushed to the exhibition hall to defend
> Chairman Mao's portrait. They shouted: "We
> will defend Chairman Mao with our blood!" "We

will always be loyal to Chairman Mao!" "We
pledge to fight to the end against the U.S. and
Indian reactionaries!"

The Second Secretary of the Indian Embassy
in Nepal, Singh, who took part in plotting the
anti-China outrage, came out into the open and
beat the Nepalese who defended the friendship between the Nepalese and Chinese peoples, when he
saw that the scheme was not fully realized.

The hooligans also hurled stones at the cars
of the Chinese Embassy, the Kathmandu branch of
the Hsinhua News Agency and Chinese experts,
and wounded one Chinese diplomat.

It was reported that U.S. "peace corps" and
military men were backing the anti-China hooligans from behind the scenes. The U.S. Embassy
sent personnel to Nepalese universities to spread
rumours against China and incite Nepalese students to oppose China. The Soviet Embassy was
also extremely busy those days. The TASS correspondent in Nepal openly incited Nepalese students
and reporters to oppose China.

The Nepalese Government approved and supported this anti-China outrage. In the past six
months, the reactionary Nepalese press has con-
tinually carried articles slandering China. Reactionary forces in Nepal forbade Nepalese students
to wear badges with a profile of Chairman Mao or
carry Quotations From Chairman Mao Tse-tung.
At the time of the outrage, the Chinese side repeatedly demanded that the Nepalese Government
stop it. However, this demand was ignored.
When the hooligans were committing the outrage,
the Nepalese Commissioner in Bagmati was right
on the spot.

On instructions from the Chinese Government,
Chinese Ambassador in Nepal, Yang Kung-shu,
lodged a serious protest with the Nepalese Government on July 5 against this anti-China outrage.
The Ambassador stressed that the great socialist
China was not to be bullied. In conducting anti-
China activities, imperialism, revisionism and
all reactionaries would break their own skulls.
Those who follow them in their anti-China campaign would suffer the consequences of their own
actions. [44]

Both the New China News Agency and <u>Peking Review</u> releases were, of course, available in Kathmandu, and His Majesty's government was compelled to issue a strong statement in response, if for no other reason than to satisfy Nepali public rage. The following day (July 10) Ambassador Yang was summoned to the Foreign Ministry by J. N. Singh and presented with a strong Nepalese protest against the "wild charges" leveled against His Majesty's government in the New China News Agency release. [45]

On July 13, Deputy Prime Minister Bisht spoke of the crisis before the National Panchayat. His statement is particularly interesting in that it distinctly separates Chinese activity at Gaucher Airport (June 18 and 24) and at the Fun Fair (July 1), that is, the actions of the resident Chinese diplomatic community from the attacks being launched on His Majesty's government in the Peking-based Chinese press. Referring to the first two incidents, he maintained "that investigations into reports published in connection with the Gaucher incidents . . . had established that nothing had happened that might have affected relations with other friendly nations and that the employees of the Chinese Embassy had done nothing objectionable. Some excitement had been displayed there, but, thanks to proper arrangements made by His Majesty's Government,* success was achieved in preventing any incident from happening there on that day." Bisht also discussed the "unpleasant and unbecoming" (Nepali) incidents that occurred at the Chinese stall at the Fun Fair on July 1. He then turned to the New China News Agency publication, declaring, "His Majesty's Government regrets such propaganda. It had in no way connived at these happenings. His Majesty's Government expressed a strong protest [July 10] to the Government of the PRC against such false and baseless propaganda. . . ."[46]

Conditions in the Ministry of Foreign Affairs were such that a full ten days were required to respond to the Nepali protest, which had been forwarded to Peking on July 10. On July 21, the Chinese ambassador was instructed to "categorically reject Nepal's protest and lodge the most serious protest with the Nepalese government against insulting the Chinese people and the deliberate sabotage of Sino-Nepalese friendship."[47]

---

*One wonders what these "arrangements" were, since His Majesty's government had been conspicuous by its absence during and after the Gaucher incident. Possibly Bisht is making an oblique reference to arrangements between His Majesty's government and the Chinese ambassador prior to the demonstrations regarding ground rules of behavior and the ambassador's rationale for having the display.

Within hours of delivering the message of his government, Ambassador Yang Kung-shu checked into the Kathmandu's Bir Hospital with a "suspected appendicitis."[48] His diplomatic position could hardly have been less tenable. Every communique from his home ministry drove a deeper wedge into the stable relationship between China and Nepal, which his professionalism obliged him to maintain if at all possible. His own reports to Peking, which presumably recorded the concern and conciliatory attitude of His Majesty's government, had been without apparent effect. The strength or permanence of the leftist group in the ministry (and at the ministry's keyboard) could only be guessed at, but the consequences of a total Red Guard seizure of power could only spell disaster for a professional diplomat of Yang's stature. *

His appendicitis took Yang away from the embassy communications room where at any minute a cable might appear ordering him into some further provocative act. Without the ambassador's presence, the Councillor, Li Chung-ho, and lesser officials might feign lack of authority and confusion over the lines of responsibility and thus stall implementation of any putschist command. No line official will find this particular organization defense repertoire in the formal definition of his role.

The conciliatory attitude of the Nepal government was mentioned above. It would appear that His Majesty's government in consultation with the Chinese embassy had taken steps to alleviate any Nepali fault in the emergent dispute prior to the inflammatory Peking statement of July 21. On July 17, Foreign Secretary Singh disclosed that "he would meet with the press every fortnight in the future. If any clarification of foreign policy matters was required, press representatives could contact the Foreign Ministry personally before publishing any news on Nepal's foreign relations."[50] The purpose of this new policy was to suppress any inflammatory reporting in the Nepal press, which would serve the provocative intentions of the Red Guards then occupying the Chinese Ministry of Foreign Affairs. It would be fair to assume that Yang had communicated Singh's concilia-

---

*Yang's diplomatic service runs back to 1949. He might well be regarded as China's leading Himalayan area specialist, having participated in the recognition negotiations with Nepal, the negotiations with India on the border dispute, and served on the China-Pakistan Boundary Commission. Yang served in a number of foreign affairs capacities on the Preparatory Committee for a Tibetan Autonomous Region and was at one time deputy head of the First Asian Department (non-Communist Asian states) of the Ministry of Foreign Affairs.[49]

tory actions to Peking. This knowledge was, of course, ignored completely in the July 21 note drafted in Peking. Also ignored was the fact that on July 20 His Majesty's government had actually banned one paper, Samiksha, and arrested the editors of three others in the "national interest."*

China was scarcely mentioned, and certainly nothing derogatory appeared in the Nepal press for many weeks to come. On July 23, as Ambassador Yang was still in Bir Hospital, a spokesman for the Nepali Foreign Ministry stated that His Majesty's government had not confiscated any Chinese literature, which was (still) being allowed to be sold freely in the market.[52] Four days later, the Chinese press would again lambaste the government of Nepal for "restricting the sale of Chinese publications, confiscating copies of Quotations from Chairman Mao Tse-tung . . . and intimidating bookshops dealing in Chinese publication."[53]

Thus the situation by mid-July was one in which the tensions in Sino-Nepalese relations, partly brought on by the extraordinary organizational defense needs of Chinese officials in residence in the kingdom, had been corrected by responsible Nepalese and Chinese authorities at the local level. However, these amicable measures were having no apparent effect on the pronouncements of the ministry in Peking. For all practical purposes, effective relations between the state hierarchies of Nepal and China were cut off due to a short-circuiting in the Chinese Ministry of Foreign Affairs. Ambassador Yang's return to Peking on July 26, after five days of seclusion at Bir Hospital, may have been an attempt to break through the communication barriers being put up by the leftist group in the Foreign Ministry.

It is worth noting in this regard that Yang had enjoyed a long professional association with Foreign Minister Ch'en Yi in both external affairs and on the Preparatory Committee for the Tibetan Autonomous Region. If it was the case that Yang sought to communicate directly with Premier Chou En-lai or other senior government officials about the situation in Nepal and the attitude of His Majesty's

---

*Virtually every paper in Nepal, regardless of political ties, vehemently protested the government's action against Samiksha, Nepal Times, Swatantra Samachar, and Dainik Nepal. These four papers long had taken the lead in urging His Majesty's government to repress what they called Chinese "subversion." Their journalistic methods were often somewhat extraordinary. It would appear that His Majesty's government's action on July 20 was directly stimulated by reports in these papers about Naxalite-Maoist agitation in Kathmandu.[51]

government, it was not to be the only such case of the hamstrung ministry being bypassed during the summer of 1967.[54] At the same time, it is equally possible that Yang was recalled by the radical elements in the Ministry of Foreign Affairs, and in such an event his association with Ch'en could hardly have been an advantage to him.

CRISIS ABATEMENT AND AFTERMATH

In the final analysis, the precise mixture of causes (including Yang's possible role) of the abatement in Chinese hostilities toward Nepal will remain unclear. On August 7, Wang Li and Yao Teng-shan moved decisively in their plan to seize the Chinese foreign relations bureaucracy. The more moderate elements of the Peking leadership moved with equal rapidity in bringing to a conclusion the criticism-reform of Ch'en Yi. On August 22, the British Chancery in Peking was burned, widely felt, at the instigation of Yao Teng-shan. This Red Guard excess led quickly to a shift of direction, formalized in the September 1 directive prohibiting any further revolutionary violence. Wang and Yao were removed; Ch'en and coterie resumed direct responsibility for the functions of the foreign affairs bureaucracy.[55] The hiatus of a dysfunctional foreign relations bureaucracy had not lasted long enough to interrupt the stable pattern of interaction between China and Nepal (in contrast to Sino-Burmese relations). Alongside the Cultural Revolutionary actions of Chinese in Nepal and in Peking, Chinese aid technicians continued their work, trade exchanges were pursued, and cultural exchanges continued. *

It is suggested that the Chinese Cultural Revolutionary activity in Nepal was essentially geared to the organizational defense needs of the operating bureaucracy (in Kathmandu and Peking), and that the appropriate and cautious response of His Majesty's government indicates that it was either independently very insightful or was apprised of the need for these measures. The proponents, both Chinese and Nepali, of a multirationale, multilevel kind of relationship had ridden out a storm inspired by those who would have had a foreign policy based on revolutionary rather than stability principles, and would have reduced the level and rationale of interaction with Nepal accordingly. However, if the Nepal government understood the strange Chinese struggle, the Nepali public became apprehensive. Thus,

---

*For example, throughout much of the heated May-June period, a Chinese art troupe of some 40 members toured and performed in Nepal.[56]

even in having sustained the storm, the managers of the interaction, Nepali and Chinese alike, were obliged to launch a public relations campaign in the aftermath of the turbulence to restore public confidence. Nepal, while a monarchy, is not a totally undemocratic state, and wide-scale public antagonism toward China could have long-range effects on both the Nepalese and Chinese governments' designs for stability.

In the first week of October, the Nepal-China Friendship Association sponsored a week-long film festival to celebrate the eighteenth anniversary of the Chinese revolution. The festival was opened by the vice chairman of the Nepali National Panchayat and attended by a host of Nepali officials.[57] The Chinese charge d'affaires, Li Chung-ho, was also particularly evident in the festivities. He asserted that "such cultural exchanges would help China and Nepal to know each other more intimately and promote mutual friendship and unity."[58] The Chinese charge d'affaires would, in fact, be much in evidence throughout the fall with this kind of message.[59]

By the spring of 1968, the Chinese public relations offensive had taken on a clear direction. Nepali journalists and editors were singled out as essential for repairing the Chinese image in Nepal. In May, a large party of Nepali pressmen was taken on an extensive tour of Chinese aid projects in Nepal, while Prime Minister Bisht and another group of journalists toured China as guests of Ch'en Yi.[60] Naya Samaj succinctly wrote, "By taking a party of journalists on a tour of the Kathmandu-Pokhara highway in the context of Prime Minister Bisht's visit to China, the Embassy of the PRC has definitely demonstrated a timely and diplomatic behavior."[61] At year's end, a delegation of editorial officials from His Majesty's government's Department of Information, Gorkhapatra, and the National News Agency were invited to tour China.[62] By the fall of 1968, Nepali public apprehension toward China had been greatly ameliorated.

POSTSCRIPT

The case focused on in this research illustrates some interesting theoretical as well as empirical questions in the study of international politics. On the whole, we know very little about the effect of organizational dynamics on foreign policy behavior. It is convenient to think of the foreign office and professional foreign relators as "tools" or implementors of policies made by the "real leaders" of the state. Yet the diplomatic-organizational variable very likely has much more saliency and strength than is indicated by that assumption. To what extent are diplomatic organizations transnational bodies with perspectives, interests, and ethics only partially congruent with those of their constituent societies?[63] How does a domestically inspired crisis, exemplified here by the Cultural Revolution, affect the perspective and behavior of such organizations? These are important questions in an era when peaceful coexistence, as a model of interstate relations, is an apparent necessity. Does one arrive at such a state of interaction from a joint declaration by protagonist heads of states, or does, perhaps, peaceful coexistence approximate the organizational ideal of multidimensional stability, arrived at through unfettered diplomatic bureaucratic development?

NOTES

1. See "An Organization-Decisionmaking Approach to Chinese Foreign Policy: Toward an Explanation of Revisionism," in Advancing and Contending Approaches to the Study of Chinese Foreign Policy, ed. Roger L. Dial (Halifax, Canada: Centre for Foreign Policy Studies, 1974).

2. Cf. Denis Stairs, "Publics and Policy Makers: The Domestic Environment of the Foreign Policy Community," International Journal, Winter 1971-72.

3. "Stake" can be conceived at both the organizational and individual actor levels. See, respectively, James March and Herbert Simon, Organizations (New York: Wiley, 1967), Chap. 7; and Goodwin Watson, "Resistance to Change," in The Planning of Change, ed. Warren Bennis, Kenneth Benne, and Robert Chin (New York: Holt, Rinehart and Winston, 1961).

4. For an elaboration of Sino-Nepalese relations prior to the Cultural Revolution and the stability dynamics involved in that relationship, see R. L. Dial, "Flexibility in Chinese Foreign Relations: Nepal, a Case Study" (M.A. thesis, University of California, Berkeley, 1967), p. 249; Leo Rose, Nepal: Strategy for Survival (Berkeley: University of California Press, 1971); Leo Rose and Roger Dial, "Can a Ministate Find True Happiness in a World Dominated by Protagonist Powers: The Nepal Case," Annals of the American Academy of Political and Social Science, November 1969.

5. C. P. Fitzgerald, "A Revolutionary Hiatus," in China: After the Cultural Revolution (New York, 1970), pp. 157-58.

6. See CCP Central Committee's Decision on the Great Proletarian Cultural Revolution, August 8, 1966.

7. "Ch'en Yi's Self Criticism," Chinese Law and Government, Spring 1968.

8. Ibid.

9. Naya Sandesh Weekly, January 20, 1967.

10. For further details on the Liaison Station, see Melvin Gurtov, "The Foreign Ministry and Foreign Affairs During the Cultural Revolution," China Quarterly, October-December 1969.

11. Ibid., p. 77.

12. Nepali, January 30, 1967.

13. Cf. Donald Klein, "The Council and the Cultural Revolution," China Quarterly, July-September 1968.

14. Peking Review, no. 5, January 27, 1967, p. 23.

15. Gorkhapatra, January 28, 1967.

16. Wai-shih hung-chi [Foreign Affairs Red Flag], May 8, 1967.

17. Peking Review, no. 9, February 24, 1967, p. 17.

18. Peking Review, no. 11, March 10, 1967, p. 28.

19. Motherland, March 30, 1967.

20. Nepal Samachar, April 2, 1967.

21. Naya Sardesh (Weekly), April 7, 1967.

22. Cf. "Comrade Ch'en Yi's Speech: At the Rally of Revolutionary Rebels of Peking Indignantly Condemning the Soviet Revisionists' Fascist Atrocities," Peking Review, no. 8, February 17, 1967, pp. 11-12.

23. Peking Review, no. 9, February 24, 1967, p. 27.

24. For further details, see Gurtov, op. cit., pp. 77-78.

25. Asahi Shimbun (Tokyo), June 1, 1967.

26. For further details, see Gurtov, op. cit., pp. 78-80.

27. Gorkhapatra, April 26, 1967.

28. Cf. Nepal Times, April 27, 1967; and Swatantra Samachar, April 28, 1967.

29. Gorkhapatra, May 10, 1967.

30. Gorkhapatra, May 27, 1967.

31. Cf. Lin Hai-yun, "China's Growing Foreign Trade, Peking Review, January 22, 1965.

32. Nepal Times, June 16, 1967; and Peking Review, June 2, 1967.

33. Nepal Times, June 18, 1967.

34. For further details, see Nepal Times, June 18, 1967.

35. Ibid.

36. Cf. editorials by Swatantra Samachar, June 19, 1967; Nepal Times, June 21, 1967; Samaya, June 20, 1967; and Nepal Samachar, June 23, 1967.

37. Nepal Times, June 25, 1967.

38. Motherland, June 26, 1967.

39. Ibid.

40. Nepal Samachar, June 30, 1967.

41. Nepal Times, July 2, 1967.

42. Nepal Samachar, July 2, 1967.

43. Nepal Times, July 3, 1967.

44. Peking Review, no. 29, July 14, 1967.

45. Gorkhapatra, July 10, 1967; and Nepal Times, July 10, 1967.

46. Gorkhapatra, July 14, 1967.

47. Note referred to in Peking Review, July 28, 1967, p. 29.

48. Gorkhapatra, July 22, 1967; and Motherland, July 22, 1967; Yang's ailment was never verified at any subsequent point.

49. For further details on Yang's career, see Who's Who (Hong Kong: Union Research Institute, 1970).

50. Gorkhapatra, July 17, 1967.

51. See Gorkhapatra, July 29, 1967.

52. Motherland, July 24, 1967.

53. "Nepalese Government Must Stop Anti-China Activities," Peking Review, July 28, 1967, p. 29.

54. Cf. Melvin Gurtov, "China's Policies in Southeast Asia: Three Studies," Studies in Comparative Communism, July-October 1970, p. 37.

55. Ibid., p. 90.

56. Gorkhapatra, May 19, 1967, and later issues.

57. Gorkhapatra, October 9, 1967.

58. Gorkhapatra, October 14, 1967.

59. Cf. Gorkhapatra, September 28, 1967.

60. Nepal Sandesh Weekly, April 5, 1968.

61. Naya Samaj, May 20, 1968.

62. Samaya, November 12, 1968.

63. Cf. Horst Mendershausen, "The Diplomat as a National and Trans-National Agent: Dilemmas and Opportunities" (Paper delivered at the 65th Annual Meeting of the American Political Science Association, New York, 1969).

ABOUT THE EDITOR AND THE CONTRIBUTORS

CHÜN-TU HSÜEH (LL.B., Chaoyang University College of Law, China; M.A., Ph.D., Columbia University), professor of government and politics at the University of Maryland, is currently chairman of the Washington and Southeast Regional Seminar on China and chairman of the Executive Committee of the Asian Political Scientists Group in the USA. He is formerly visiting professor and acting director of the Research Unit for Chinese and East Asian Politics at the Free University of Berlin. He has taught at Columbia University and the University of Hong Kong.

A member of the editorial board of Ethnicity and other journals, Dr. Hsüeh is the author of Huang Hsing and the Chinese Revolution (Stanford, Calif.: Stanford University Press, 1961; reprinted 1968); Sino-American Rapprochement: Retrospect and Prospects (Washington, D.C.: American Enterprise Institute for Public Policy Research; and Stanford, Calif.: Hoover Institution, Stanford University, 1977), editor and contributor, Revolutionary Leaders of Modern China (Oxford University Press, 1971; reprinted 1973), and Les dirigeants de la Chine revolutionnaire (Paris: Calmann-Levy, 1973).

DAVIS B. BOBROW (Ph.D., Massachusetts Institute of Technology), professor of government and politics at the University of Maryland, has taught at the University of Minnesota, Princeton University, and the School of Advanced International Studies of The Johns Hopkins University. He is currently a member of the Steering Group on Chinese Foreign Policy and International Relations of the Joint Committee on Contemporary China. Author of International Relations: New Approaches (New York: Free Press, 1972) and editor of several books on applied foreign policy analysis, Dr. Bobrow recently completed a study for the U.S. Department of State on "The Feasibility of Establishing an Information Center on China."

KING C. CHEN (Ph.D., Pennsylvania State University), professor of political science at Rutgers University, was a senior fellow at the Research Institute on Communist Affairs of Columbia University for 1972-73. He is the author of Vietnam and China (Princeton, N.J.: Princeton University Press, 1969) and editor of Foreign Policy of China (1972).

ROGER L. DIAL (Ph.D., University of California, Berkeley), associate professor of political science at Dalhousie University, Canada, is the author of Studies on Chinese External Affairs: An Instructional Bibliography (Halifax: Dalhousie University Press, 1973) and editor of Advancing and Contending Approaches to the Study of Chinese Foreign Policy (Halifax: Centre for Foreign Policy Studies, 1974).

A. M. HALPERN (Ph.D., University of Chicago), adjunct professor of international affairs at The George Washington University, was formerly with the RAND Corporation, Council on Foreign Relations, and the Center for International Affairs at Harvard University. He has taught at the University of California (Berkeley) and the School of Advanced International Studies of The Johns Hopkins University. He is the editor of Policies Toward China (New York: McGraw-Hill, 1966), and he has written extensively on China and Japan.

SHAO-CHUAN LENG (Ph.D., University of Pennsylvania) is Doherty Foundation professor of government and foreign affairs and chairman of the Asian Studies Committee at the University of Virginia. Among his publications are Japan and Communist China (New York: Institute of Pacific Relations, 1959; Westport, Conn.: Greenwood Press, 1973) and Justice in Communist China (Dobbs Ferry, N.Y.: Oceana, 1967). He is the co-author of Sun Yat-sen and Communism (New York: Praeger, 1961), and Law in Chinese Foreign Policy (Dobbs Ferry, N.Y.: Oceana, 1972).

STEVEN I. LEVINE (Ph.D., Harvard University), formerly assistant professor of government at Columbia University, is now research associate at the East Asian Institute of Columbia University. He is the translator (from Russian) of Two Years in Revolutionary China, 1925-1927 (East Asian Research Center, Harvard University, 1971) and associate editor of and contributor to The Indochina Story (New York: Bantam, 1970).

ROBERT C. NORTH (Ph.D., Stanford University), formerly president of the International Studies Association, is professor of political science at Stanford University. He is the author of several books, including The Foreign Relations of China (Encino, Calif.: Dickenson, 1969), Chinese Communism (New York: McGraw-Hill, 1966), and Moscow and Chinese Communists (Stanford, Calif.: Stanford University Press, 1953), and co-author of Nations in Conflict (San Francisco: W. H. Freeman, 1975).

YITZHAK SHICHOR (Ph.D., University of London) is the executive director of the Harry S. Truman Research Institute of the Hebrew University of Jerusalem.

ROBERT L. WORDEN (Ph.D., Georgetown University) is China research analyst at the Library of Congress and lecturer in history at Georgetown University.

*CHINA AND SOUTHEAST ASIA: Peking's Relations
with Revolutionary Movements
                    Jay Taylor

CHINA'S AFRICAN POLICY: A Study of Tanzania
                    George T. Yu

*CHINA AND JAPAN--EMERGING GLOBAL POWERS
                    Peter G. Mueller and
                    Douglas A. Ross

*SINO-AMERICAN DETENTE AND ITS POLICY
IMPLICATIONS
                    edited by Gene T. Hsiao

FACTIONAL AND COALITION POLITICS IN CHINA:
The Rebuilding of the Chinese Communist Party
                    Y. C. Chang

*Also available in paperback as a PSS Student Edition